Praise for *Rainbow Bo*

"Francis Tiso has written an astonishing work of broad and deep scholarship that blends a personal spiritual journey, erudition, and on-the-ground interviews with witnesses of the rainbow body to reveal a conversation that began long ago in Central Asia about postmortem transformations of the body in a variety of religious traditions. He has delved deeply into esoteric texts and carefully reviewed recent scholarship to present a detailed history and explanation of practices leading to the attainment of the rainbow body as well as the doctrine of the resurrection in Christianity. General readers and scholars alike will find much of interest in [this book]."

—SERINITY YOUNG, PhD, professor, Queens College, research associate, American Museum of Natural History, author of *Body & Spirit: Tibetan Medical Paintings*

"The right medicine for people who forgot how they used to wonder about the afterlife. Stories about this and other boundary crossings are found here and told well. Many will learn to welcome the author's discomforting approach to normalizing the paranormal, and his bold yet entertainable historical claims linking Tibetan Dzogchen with Central Asian Christianity."

—DAN MARTIN, Hebrew University of Jerusalem

"I have read with great pleasure Tiso's magnificent work and have truly appreciated his reading and interpretation of the Chinese text, Zhixuan anle jing (*The Book of Profound Peace and Joy*). Here, finally, I am seeing a theological study of the text, which makes me very happy. I greatly appreciate your contextualization of this text in its grounding in the theology and spirituality of the Syriac Church of the East. I would like to thank Tiso very much for having pioneered this fascinating and difficult work of interpretation."

—MATTEO NICOLINI-ZANI, monk of Bose

RAINBOW BODY
AND
RESURRECTION

October 30, 2016

for Paul —

Keep in mind :
- it's not as difficult as it seems
- it's nearby
- in the universe
  where we are.

Love, Francis

Portrait of Khenpo A Chö

RAINBOW BODY
AND
RESURRECTION

Spiritual Attainment,
the Dissolution of the Material Body,
and the Case of Khenpo A Chö

FRANCIS V. TISO

North Atlantic Books
Berkeley, California

Published by   Cover photo of kLu Khang mural used by
North Atlantic Books   permission of David Germano
Berkeley, California   Cover design by Nicole Hayward
Printed in the United States of America   Book design by Susan Quasha

About the cover: This photo is of a portion of a mural at kLu Khang (Serpent Deity Temple), also known as the Dalai Lama's secret temple, probably built in the 1680s, in Lhasa, Tibet.

Rainbow Body and Resurrection: Spiritual Attainment, the Dissolution of the Material Body, and the Case of Khenpo A Chö is sponsored and published by the Society for the Study of Native Arts and Sciences (dba North Atlantic Books), an educational nonprofit based in Berkeley, California, that collaborates with partners to develop cross-cultural perspectives, nurture holistic views of art, science, the humanities, and healing, and seed personal and global transformation by publishing work on the relationship of body, spirit, and nature.

North Atlantic Books' publications are available through most bookstores. For further information, visit our website at www.northatlanticbooks.com or call 800-733-3000.

Library of Congress Cataloging-in-Publication Data
Tiso, Francis, author.
  Rainbow body and resurrection : spiritual attainment, the dissolution of the material body, and the case of Khenpo A Cho / Francis V. Tiso.
     pages cm
  Summary: "Francis V. Tiso, a noted authority on the rainbow body, explores this manifestation of spiritual realization in a wide-ranging and deeply informed study of the transformation of the material body into a body of light. The result is an illuminating consideration of previously unimagined relationships between spiritual practices and beliefs in Central Asia"—Provided by publisher.
  ISBN 978-1-58394-795-1 (paperback)"—ISBN 978-1-58394-796-8 (ebook)
  1. Rdzogs-chen. 2. Resurrection. 3. Mkhan-po-a-chos, 1918-1998. 4. Spirituality"—Asia, Central"—History. I. Title.
  BQ7662.2.T58 2016
  294.3'423—dc23

                                    2015013194

1 2 3 4 5 6 7 8 9 UNITED 20 19 18 17 16
Printed on recycled paper

Then the Day of the Lord, like a thief, will come, and the heavens will disappear with a great explosion; the elements will be consumed by the heat and dissolve. The world with all its actions will be destroyed.

—II Peter 3:10

Inside Khenpo A Chö's hermitage: his personal shrine.

CONTENTS

INTRODUCTION

The Rainbow Body: Finding a Method

In Italian we have a slightly cynical expression used to inquire about some-one we haven't heard from in a while: *"Che fin ha fatto?"* Literally this means: "What end did he come to?" As if to ask, did he die and did his death vindicate his hopes? Or did it rather confirm our doubts? Did someone make good, or was he a flop? We might translate it: "Whatever became of so and so?" In the case of Christ, we could imagine the folks of Nazareth asking such a question and after being told about the crucifixion, responding: "We told you so!"

The cynicism of the village lives on in many of our verbal expressions and even in the methods by which we think we are establishing "scientific truth." Historian John Lukacs observes that science is, after all, a product of scientists and is therefore a cultural product or even *mirabile dictu*, a "fashion of the times."[1] Einstein, for example, refused to accept the Heisenberg uncertainty (or indeterminacy) principle. "He remained a convinced determinist during the rest of his life, fiddling uselessly with unsuccessful experiments and for-mulations hoping to disprove indeterminacy in Princeton, with no effect to his enduring reputation."[2] Physicists in the 1920s, while making remarkable contributions to science and civilization as a whole, spent a good deal of time and energy on what can only be called beliefs, i.e., they were "people who believed or disbelieved this or that, because they wished to believe this and disbelieve that,"[3] which is as much as to say that their science was condi-tioned by their cultural and even political commitments. Erwin Schrödinger "as early as 1932 said, in a lecture to the Prussian Academy of Sciences that, yes, Science can be (and often is) A Fashion of the Times, a consequence of The Temper of the Age."[4] This means that sometimes what seems to be a search for a "scientific" explanation is in reality an attempt to provide a verbal explanation for phenomena that in fact cannot be explained. Moreover, the explanations offered amount to analogies that accord with the mentality of the literate public at any given point in history. This is the real meaning of "paradigm shifts" in the history of science.

In 1913, the French physicist and historian of science, Pierre Duhem, wrote: "The study of the method of physics is powerless to disclose to the physicist the reason leading him to construct a physical theory."[5] The scientist is as dependent on accepted and acceptable ideas within the general climate of opinion of his or her times as anyone else; unfortunately, science is embedded in larger tendencies of thought and their power. As a consequence, science is really not automatically self-correcting and can indeed be led astray. One of the ways by which science, i.e., scientists, can be led astray is when a particular analogy becomes predominant to the extent that theorists forget the reasons they were motivated to construct a new paradigm. Often these reasons are cultural and even *ad hominem*, i.e., based on the personalities of the individuals who formulated the paradigms.

What can be said of science most certainly can be said of religion, as we shall see in our research on the rainbow body! In his workshops on neurophenomenology, philosopher Michel Bitbol is making use of mindfulness procedures to enhance self-awareness among scientists[6]. Thus, researchers may become more conscious of why they do what they do, and how certain subjective motivations could distort their interpretations of the data they gather. Recent writing in cultural anthropology gives evidence that in intercultural research, the same risks of distortions are present, and the same level of critical attention needs to be directed towards motivations and subjective biases.[7] This means becoming more aware of the interaction between the "emic" perspective, which is the perspective of an inside group and the views maintained by a particular culture, and the "etic" perspective, which is that of an outside observer attempting to gain a degree of understanding of the emic point of view.[8] In addressing the rainbow body phenomenon, one is constantly challenged to go back and forth between emic and etic perspectives. However, many writers on this subject do not distinguish clearly enough between these two perspectives, and I must confess the distinctions have not been easy for me either. In particular, in view of the fact that this research began with a request from my spiritual teacher, Brother David Steindl-Rast, to find out if there might be a connection between the rainbow body phenomenon in Tibet and the resurrection of Jesus, the boundaries between insider and outsider have been imprecise for the entire period of research. The relationship between two believers, master and disciple, is prevalently emic. However, the research is to some extent committed to an etic discipline that allows us to communicate our views with others who may not believe as we (Brother David and I) do. I hope by the end of this volume, the reader will understand more fully why the boundaries are vague, and why this research has been, and can be, extremely fruitful if we remain mindful throughout. Suffice it to say that, when it comes to paranormal phenomena, what we really have are two emic communities of discourse: believers within a religious tradition and skeptical scientists working within their cultural milieu. Both groups think their view of reality is the "really real" one, and that the other side's view is, to put it kindly, imprecise.

This is why I think that the project of examining possible connections between the resurrection and the rainbow body moves us from an investigation of certain claims made by religious people into a thought experiment involving ourselves. We have to imagine ourselves as characters in a work of fiction; the characters are being changed by the effect on their own minds of the act of doing research on this fascinating, and devastating, material. One of the changes is certainly a sense of being distanced from the ordinary views that prevail among both religious and nonreligious persons in our culture. We are like characters on stage, visible through tinted gauze only when a beam of light falls on us; the rest of the time, all the action is taking place among "stage-front characters" whose story line has very little to do with what we are doing backstage in the dark. This strange perception of what we are doing came to me as I was reflecting on the comment of a Japanese monk, ordained in the Burmese *sangha*: "You wouldn't be asking these questions if you did not already know the answers."[9] On the one hand, this comment could be understood as referring to grace, or perhaps to that which the Tibetans call *tendel*, meaning sacred connections established in a former lifetime. As a result of grace or *tendel*, some people have the ability to perceive certain things that are hidden to others, and are given occasions in which to exercise that ability.

On the other hand, the comment left the researchers wondering about where our intuitions may have been sharp, and where they may have been misled by subjective wish-fulfillment impulses.

The challenge of doing research on the rainbow body is made more difficult by our own innate dream-like fantasy that would like us to be rainbow bodies. At times we dream of flight as swift and easy as thought itself. Fully aware of this fantasy, Buddhist scriptures recounted the myth of human origins: In the Pali Canon, the *Aggañña Sutta* tells us, not without a hint of irony, that we were at the beginning of this cosmic cycle primordial beings "mind-made, feeding on delight, self-luminous, moving through space, glorious."[10] All the discouraging news of death, decay, failure, anonymity, ordinariness, hell, and damnation are just a sort of conditioning context that keeps us tied down to embodiment, to materialism, to fear. The Sutta's critique is aimed at a particularly pessimistic culture: that of the village mindset of Vedic India, a culture fused of religious and skeptical elements that the Buddha is said to have subverted in his own search for enlightenment. This culture, as assailed in the Buddhist scriptures, is perceived as keeping human beings "ill informed" with hopes and fears about life, based upon inadequate definitions of what a good or a bad life might be. Like my own Italian neighbors, the voices of this culture gleefully ask, the question, "*Che fin ha fatto?*" so as to admire those they wish to admire, no matter how foolish and degraded those people might be, and to admonish those who dare to think differently. It is the end that vindicates: how one dies and how one is remembered at death allows people to voice mockery and gloating, or admiration and adulation. The more this habit persists, the more power we give to death because we sharpen the point of fear and the edge of expectation. Think of the glories of a pyramid and try to imagine the vast ceremonies that would have attended the death and embalming of a pharaoh, no matter how cruel, stupid, ugly, or feeble he might have been. Then think of crucifixion. For twenty centuries we priests have been waving the crucifix at the world and still hardly anyone gets the point: There are no bad ends! The pyramid with its pomp and circumstance is not easily waved away. Death is the last enemy of spiritual freedom and it dies hard. The *Book of Apocalypse* (20:14; cf. I Corinthians 15:54-55) in fact makes death the last to die, but die it must.

If the rainbow body is the death of death, then the way it is discussed must also be free from any tone of vindication of one system or another, of one end or another. Otherwise, the rainbow body phenomenon runs the same danger as the Christian doctrine of the resurrection, which at times has been presented not as an affirmation of transcendence but as a message compelling sectarian conversion.

For this reason, we need to look beyond the particular sectarian features of the rainbow body as presented in the Bonpo and Nyingma schools of Tibetan tantrism. Some of the recent literature, and in particular the popular blogs on the subject, indicate that the phenomenon is being misused as a sectarian proselytizing device. Here, we need to ask ourselves if an encounter with a phenomenon that compels our thoughtful response, in other words a *life-changing experience*, is cheapened if it is reduced to a reason for putting oneself into a particular category or group. The old legal principle seems strangely apt: "That which touches all, ought to be approved by all." If the resurrection is only the resurrection of Jesus, it remains a claim that one may or may not believe, without particular implications for one's own life. If that resurrection implies that everyone will sooner or later rise from the dead, then one must either remain a skeptic, or else, "you [everyone!] must change your life" as Rilke wrote in his exquisite poem on "An Archaic Torso of Apollo." The same universal implication can only be avoided in the case of Khenpo A Chö by a willful act of indifference. Both the rainbow body and the resurrection are claims that make statements about human possibilities attainable by all human subjects under certain conditions. What has been imagined to have taken place in one person may be imagined as happening to anyone, independently of the subjective faith or point of view of any particular person. The deeper impulse of the religious imagination, in other words, stretches out beyond mere denominational recruitment to make universal claims about the nature of the human person, and those claims are what demand a change in our lives.

Thus, the Christian doctrine of the resurrection is not restricted to Jesus's resurrection; rather, St. Paul tells us, "If the dead are not raised, it follows that Christ was not raised." (I Corinthians 15:16) The resurrection of the redeemer is repeated spiritually in the life of the redeemed and unequivocally at the end of history with the resurrection of the bodies of all human beings. In fact, the universality of the resurrection and the emergence of the "new heavens and new earth" (Apocalypse 21:1) would seem to require not only the resurrection of humans but also of all beings that have ever lived, since all have a place in the unfolding of the process of creation. Recent thought on the topic of eternal life, among the "ecotheologians" such as Thomas Berry, is increasingly clear that humanity at the final resurrection will not be recognizably human in the absence of those species that have contributed to the emergence of the human species itself. Being human is essentially to be in relationship to a surrounding web of relationships. Eternal life, if it is to be the "resurrection of the body" in the full sense of the word, is inseparable from that web of relationships, transfigured by the gift of grace. The "newness" of the heavenly Jerusalem would have to lie in its inconceivably vast presentation of the completeness of all things simultaneously, free of the trammels of temporal evolution and the limits of perception with which we live from day to day. What "has been" in temporal sequence, becomes manifest all at once, in the eternal now of the fullness of life. Thus, the blueprint of all creation in the Logos, "In the beginning was the Word/Logos," (John 1:1) reaches fulfillment in the simultaneity of the universal resurrection, now enlivened completely by the *Ruah*, the Divine Spirit that completes the work of creation and redemption by making all things holy and new. It is this new creation that is worthy to be offered to the *Abba* (Romans 8:5) beyond all names and forms, the divine silence from whom the Word has come forth, whose name is to be sanctified, the "supreme source" who pours forth the life of all beings. At any rate, this is a possible viewpoint within the circumference of Christian faith in a personal, triune God.

In classical Buddhist thought, this notion of an infinitely transcendent creator God whose ineffable act of creation entails coming forth and returning in fulfillment is formally denied.[11] The universe has no external cause and is a chain of interactions with no point of departure, no beginning. In fact, in spite of many admirable efforts to relate Buddhism to ecological theories, classical Buddhism seems to view the six realms (demons, ghosts, animals, humans, titans, and gods) of existence to be largely the manifestation of negative karma, the product of ignorance, desire, and rage; the wheel-of-existence icons typically seen in the entryway to Buddhist temples visually depict this idea.

One of the greatest weaknesses of both classical Buddhist philosophy and of nondualist theistic presentations in Indian religions is that there is apparently no grand design, at least none accessible to the ordinary human mind. Other than the occasional theistic depiction of divine lila (transcendental divine play), there is no clear articulation of why there is something rather than nothing at all, or why things return to nothing and then re-emerge after the grand silence of universal pralaya (periodic cosmic dissolution). In spite of the widespread Indian practice of rituals of offering and receiving, with all that those rites suggest of the nature of the cosmos, there is no ritual of universal oblation comparable to the Christian Eucharist—no ritual in which the entire cosmic process can be summed up and directed towards a transcendent and definitive future. This reluctance to embrace a liturgical analogy for the cosmic process has always puzzled me. After all, in so many other aspects Indian religions have shown enormous creativity in making mythical and poetic analogies on every conceivable level of religious thought and action.

As David Germano points out in his magisterial study of the dzogchen (Tibetan transliteration: *rdzogs pa chen po*, the "great perfection") approach,[12] it seems that at some point in the evolution of tantric Buddhism, an attempt was made to express a grand design beyond the workings of karma. "The range of [dzogchen scriptural] texts is nothing short of stunning, and constitute a radical revolution in the history of Buddhist thought that assumes everything that preceded it as a basis, and yet is primarily concerned to go beyond such lower order systems in its exploration of the final nature of the Universe itself, and how that nature bears upon our present state of existential despair, the possibility of spiritual liberation, and the nature of the Awakened One (i.e., a Buddha)."[13]

In other words, at some point some great contemplative genius understood that the dynamic nature of the relationships among all the phenomena of consciousness and manifestation indicates that the human presence has a purpose. In effect, that purpose is inseparable from the capacity of certain gifted human beings not only to break through spontaneously and occasionally to the original nature of the mind itself but to abide permanently in that state of primordial awareness. Not only that: The entire structure of mind, consciousness, and the manifestation of phenomena is "designed" to bring about the emergence of this primordial awareness. The universe explores itself in and through such awakened beings.[14] The title of Lipman and Peterson's book,[15] based on the teachings of Namkhai Norbu Rinpoche, seems to summarize the whole point: "you are the eyes of the world," an insight not very far from the understanding of German idealism that man is the universe become conscious of itself. If the human provides the consciousness and the "eyes," the universe nevertheless provides the indispensable matrix, and thus there is no duality between phenomena and consciousness. This means that those systems of asceticism that alienate the contemplative practitioner from the universe of phenomena are at best training exercises for a much grander degree of realization in which alienation completely gives way to highly energetic interaction. The cessation of the vibrations of the mind[16] postulated in the Yoga Sutras of Patanjali seems here to pass through a kind of cosmic singularity to become the sum total of the energies of the cosmos, present to the contemplative in every cell of his or her embodiment. Instead of dying in segregation from the universe of phenomena, the contemplative in the dzogchen system seems in effect to become one with all phenomena to the point of claiming the attainment of the dissolution of the material body into its energetic components. This dissolution, which we will be calling the rainbow body—in a somewhat imprecise manner that will be clarified later on in this book—is understood as a particularly dramatic sign of a degree of spiritual attainment that goes far beyond the particulars of the phenomenon.

In order to move beyond theories and claims, however, it is necessary to establish the criteria of research. I will speak at greater length of this in subsequent chapters, but it is clear that the researcher is in a particularly precarious position. Any study of postmortem paranormal phenomena will be limited by the fact that such research cannot be repeated in the laboratory under the obligatory conditions for scientific verification or falsification. What is more, in order to gather the basic data on the phenomenon, the researcher must to some extent enter into the world of contemplative practitioners in the relevant traditions. As a participant observer, the researcher is placed in the "emic" context of those who believe in the phenomenon and regulate their lives and their cultural expressions accordingly. At the same time, the researcher is answerable to a skeptical outsider voice, the "etic" approach of classical science, into whose categories the results of research must be translated in order to communicate from one culture to another. In my work, it has become clear that the emic and the etic perspectives cannot hold their respective grounds if one perspective is considered more valid than the other. Etic interpretations are as biased as emic ones. In fact, it is possible to depict the scientific or materialistic worldview as a kind of emic experience, as a cultural product with its own peculiar history and its own rigorous, but at times limiting, philosophical justifications. In anthropological research, the tribe of the scientists meets the tribe of traditional human groupings in different parts of the world. Human knowledge is enhanced when the encounter is perceived as a mutually beneficial exchange of cognitively meaningful communications. When one emic view is reduced to another (particularly when the emic is subsumed within a dominant etic interpretation), experience indicates that human knowing is distorted and even obstructed, sometimes with lethal consequences.[17] Without being overly reductive, might we not think of the cultural destruction of Tibet itself as an outward, and violent, manifestation of the idea that one worldview is absolutely correct and others are more or less wrong? And if we study the history of scientific thought and the notion of "reason" in Western Europe, can we be immune to the fact that these notions were the product of policies involving the destruction of monastic institutions? For all their flaws, these institutions were pursuing the cultivation of cognitive spiritualities that in some way disturbed the way "reason" was being constructed by a dominant minority of European thinkers at the time. Is this not exactly what has happened in Tibet over the past sixty-five years? The same policies worked their will in China, in Russia, in Eastern Europe, and even to some extent in Latin America. The United States, by implementing tolerance and respect for all religions in its constitutional and cultural system, seems so far to have avoided the worst consequences of secularism. At least for the moment in the U.S., one can found a monastery without the fear of it being expropriated[18] by a hostile bureaucracy later on. Let us return, however, to the topic at hand.

The rainbow body is a seductive topic, and even more seductive is the temptation to compare the rainbow body with the resurrection. In a sense, both claims amount to being the ultimate non-bad ending. They are both the ultimate confirmation of a person's having been on the right track all along: a confirmation that's better than a promotion, better than canonization, better than being recognized as the reincarnation of the previous abbot. Both claims can also be considered miracles, as Matthew Kapstein points out.[19] When I arrived at Mindrolling Monastery in Clement Town in 2001, it was Lodi Gyari, H. H. the Dalai Lama's representative to the U.S. government, who pointed out to the abbot that my research on this miracle was standard practice in the Catholic procedure for canonizing a saint.

Now consider the precarious position of those researchers who might try to bring a miracle into the realm of scientific fact. Someone will show up with a video camera and tripod and capture the moment of the body's dissolution on digital tape; he or she will feed it into the internet and everyone on earth with see that someone did not come to a bad end. Death in general, and someone's death in particular, becomes infinitely more interesting than we had previously thought.

When it comes to the topic of death, one must remain mindful and attentive. Is the science we hope to employ really a search for truth, or is it a subtle trick whose aim is self-vindication? Wouldn't it be better to celebrate the fact of mortality and leave it at that? Wouldn't it be more dignified? Sustaining the discourse on mindfulness, what happens is that death or threat of danger presents the mind with an invasion of its ego-territory. The response to the invasion is mental self-defense, sometimes leading to physical action, whether fight, flight, or verbal self-vindication. The events surrounding the manifestation of rainbow body by the Bonpo monk Rakshi Topden in 2001 suggest that we are indeed on risky ground: The monk's nephew tried to get journalists involved, tried to measure the corpse with a tape measure, tried to get attention. The Chinese authorities were alerted, the nephew was arrested, and the monk's body was cremated in secret. In spite of these sad events, Loppon Tenzin Namdak, head of the Bonpo order, assured us that very year that the rainbow body is a reality; it is not just a metaphor, not just a hagiographical decoration.[20] Some bodies do disappear soon after death, manifesting remarkable signs. Loppon is, if anything, something of a rationalist. The monastery he founded not far from Swayambhu, on the next hill north of Urgyen Tulku's Nagi Gompa, is rigorously committed to dialectical studies, debate, philosophy, and scholarship. But it is interesting to hear Loppon speak of the rainbow body and related matters with certitude and clarity, from experience.

The same kind of frankness was apparent in the interview and dialogues we had in 2003 with several masters of the Tamil Siddha tradition in South India. Yet in spite of all these expressions of assurance, do we have here an indication of certitude, or only the possibility of something more likely to be a hagiographical symbol? Not all the Tibetan traditions are convinced that the rainbow body literally occurs, although there is some idea that attainment of buddhahood in the embodied state is an authentic sign of what tantricism is meant to disclose. At the same time, the radical subjectivism that attends Buddhist realization leaves a great deal of open space in which the fate of the ordinary individual, the practitioner of the tantric body of light, and the dzogchen yogin's rainbow body can be seen as various ways in which primordial reality manifests itself to a set of faith communities. In order to open up the field of research to more than one emic perspective, let us take a look at the traditions of southern India regarding spiritual attainment.

The Tamil Siddha tradition is a branch of Shaivite Hinduism that is typically practiced among marginalized, non-caste based, non-Brahman yogis and medical practitioners. It is not a religion in the sense of having its own priesthood and scriptures at the service of a clearly defined community. Although there are certainly temples served by Brahman pujaris (ritual specialists) connected to Tamil Siddha tradition, their existence is more a matter of classic Hinduism acknowledging the validity of the attainment of these siddhas than a defining institutional base for the movement.

The reason that the Tamil Siddhas interest us is that their approach to spiritual attainment[21] is firmly grounded in the material body. Like the set of spiritual traditions loosely called "tantra," the Tamil Siddha tradition recognizes the *jiva* (life principle or soul, which it calls the *uior*), the subtle body of classic Patanjali yoga, and the material body, but this tripartite division does not constitute a hierarchy of value, much less is it a system for "saving the soul" at the expense of the body. The body is directly involved in the process of attaining *siddhi* (spiritual objective attained by a yogin). Since siddhi is attained by means of *tapas* (austerities and penances), the body has to be in excellent condition so as to be able to endure the *tapas* required to attain realization. For this reason, yogic practices, diet, and medical procedures are used to strengthen the body and prolong life. The process of prolonging life, called *kayakalpa*, uses medicinal substances including poisons such as mercury, cinnabar (mercury ore, red vermilion), arsenic, alum, and related ores and salts. These are the same materials used in alchemy in various parts of the world and, in particular, in China as part of the similar Daoist quest for bodily immortality. David Gordon White, in his acclaimed book, *The Alchemical Body*, has investigated the connection between China and South India, and has summarized the procedures that we also encountered in our fieldwork in Tamil Nadu.[22]

What has all this to do with the rainbow body? It seems that the Tamil Siddha tradition has its own accounts of the body of masters disappearing after death. The most famous recent case—that of Swami Ramalinga whose body dissolved into light in March, 1874—is attested to in police reports of the time. Ramalinga's religious movement, which continues to the present day, insists on the literal disappearance of the body. The ongoing presence of Ramalinga in the work of his succession of disciples—as well as wherever the poor are fed, compassion exercised, and oppression opposed. Swami Ramalinga's devotion focused on the famous image of Shiva Nataraj, the Lord of the Dance, in the awesome temple of Chidambaram in the countryside of Tamil Nadu. He also made use of much from the collection of Shaiva poetry, the *Tirumantiram* by Tirumular[23] in the eighth century CE. Tirumular is for all intents and purposes the source of the spiritual reform movement that Ramalinga (also known respectfully as Vallalar) set in motion in the nineteenth century. Ramalinga established a still extant religious order that carries out his work and example. In addition, Sri Aurobindo continued the Ramalinga/Tirumular tradition in his own way, remaining faithful to the yogic, scientific, and social reform aspects of Ramalinga's program.

Some examples of the poetry of Tirumular help us understand why bodily transformation through contemplative practice cannot be restricted to solely one tradition. In the first example, the poet describes the pervasion of the smallest particles (here translated as "atoms") of his physical body by the divine substance, such that a kind of transubstantiation takes place. As a result of this change of substance—and the intervention of Shiva Nataraja of Chidambaram—the various yogic attainments manifest themselves:

> I was truly and completely changed
> Into the very substance of the Almighty
> Who pervaded every atom of my body;
> The mighty and benignant siddhis
> Came under my control.
> All these are, of course, the gifts of the Lord,
> The Universal Dancer.

The transformation is described allusively as alchemical in character, closely resembling descriptions of Chinese inner alchemical processes:

> He showered on me a form shining
> Like gold, a heart unblemished,
> A full and divine knowledge.

The poems frequently express imagery of light, not as a metaphor but as an actual experience of the yogin who has performed the meditation practices. In effect, he or she brings down the energy of the sun into the heart chakra by the grace of Shiva, and that energy spontaneously pervades the entire body of the yogin:

> You are the love that enlightens
> The soul and its knowledge;
> You are the Effulgent Lustre
> That abides even in a small atom;[24]

> You fill with the ambrosia of your Grace
> Every pore of their bones, their flesh, their five senses,
> And the sense organs, their breaths, the Five Elements,
> That constitute the human body, the soul, and its active love

That has helped to gain the divine knowledge to know you.

You are the Divine River that springs within them,

Becomes brimful, and overflows with Grace and Bliss.

Swami Ramalinga took up these ancient teachings as part and parcel of his controversial anti-caste social reform movement, which he conceived of as inseparable from mystical transformation. Hagiographical accounts of Swami Ramalinga find their inspiration in Shaivite, Tamil Siddha, and even Christian sources of inspiration. Even in his student days at Madras, it was said of him that he left no footprints on the sand and had no shadow.[25] Thus we have a classic mystical saint who also articulates a program of social transformation typical of the late nineteenth century.

Ramalinga's esoteric teachings revolve around the notion of three bodies in the human embodied state:

·⟡· *Shuddha deha*: the "pure body," the attainment of which produces a glow and golden color

·⟡· *Pranava deha*: the body of primordial sound (i.e., the sacred syllable "OM")

·⟡· *Jnana deha*: the "gnosis" body, the existential experience of total mercy and divine grace[26]

Ramalinga's practices involve opening the third eye and the fontanel; the fontanel, which is the aperture at the top of the skull, is also important in Tibetan *'pho wa* practices (practices involving techniques for expelling the consciousness principle from the top of the skull). As in Tibetan dzogchen, the red sun at sunrise is contemplated with open eyes. A mantra favored by Ramalinga, the *jyothi* (light) mantra, (emphasizing the grace and compassion of the Dancing Shiva) is repeated continuously for six months. Having attained the signs of completion, the practitioner can contemplate the "white" sun of midday. At this point, light begins to develop a direct relationship with the body of the yogin. Entering the eyes, sunlight travels through the subtle channels of the yogic body, permeating the cells. Our Tamil Siddhi informants told us, "This is a secret; when you think of it, it will be there." In fact, a crucial feature of dzogchen practice is also to work with these subtle channels connected to the eyes.

In Ramalinga's system, the inner sun in the space of consciousness is called "the true thing." This space is an inner space, which would seem to have resonances with the subtle body theory that was known to the medieval mahasiddhas—both Buddhist and Shaivite—and was transmitted to the Tibetans as part of Vajrayana Buddhism. However, as we will see in our description of dzogchen practices later in this book, the true thing might also refer to the true nature of mind, which the guru introduces to the disciple at the very beginning of their working relationship. The true nature of the mind is already the first point in the *Cuckoo of Awareness,* instruction attributed to the early dzogchen translator Vairotsana and found among the Dunhuang manuscripts.[27] This true nature is visualized as the letter "Long-A" in the Tibetan system, with the letter floating in an indigo void and surrounded by a sphere of rainbow light. In the Ramalinga system, as in the most typical dzogchen teachings, these practices are not supposed to entail visualizations that have to be elaborated or constructed in the mind. The visualization occurs as the practitioner allows a process to unfold and take over on levels inaccessible to the conscious mind—levels that elaborate ideas, images, or concepts. This depth of consciousness is why the Tamil Siddha tradition understands this process to be a divine process, inaugurated by the touch of the guru's grace. In dzogchen, which is a nontheistic system, guru yoga provides the crucial connection that enables the process to unfold. Guru yoga in the dzogchen system basically entails blending the mind ever more deeply with the liberative intentions of the spiritual preceptor. This process continues in daily life with blending the mind with whatever occurs as a manifestation of the guru's liberative intent towards all sentient beings, in harmony with the classic articulations of the bodhisattva vow.

Ramalinga suggests some stages of practice, again typical of the gradual approach:

- ⋄ Vegetarianism to facilitate working with the bodily elements
- ⋄ Reduction of the number of breath cycles
- ⋄ Observation of the stages of increasing subtlety in the three "bodies" (*deha*)

Beyond these stages comes the stage of the light body (Tamil: *oleo tambe*) and experience of union with Shiva. In actual practice, the student begins with the mind, since it is the easiest to work with, then the *uior* (*jiva*), and then finally the material body, perhaps because actual physical transformation of the material body is the hardest to produce.

Ramalinga is said to have appeared by bilocation to Colonel Olcott and Madame Blavatsky. Since his disappearance in 1874, he is reported to have appeared to many people in the form of a luminous hologram; there are also many reports of Ramalinga locutions. Tulasiram, a Pondicherry author and practitioner who has written voluminously on Ramalinga, reports on a woman devotee who in 2001 was awakened from sleep by a slap from Ramalinga and was put into a state of meditative absorption. Tulasiram claims to have seen a luminous apparition of Ramalinga in his private apartment in 1982.[28]

Members of Ramalinga's order observe that the Tamil Siddhas do eventually die, in spite of their assiduous practice of *kayakalpa*. Ramalinga's way was supposed to lead to a transcendence of death and to bodily immortality. He advocated for a transformation of the entire body-mind complex at the atomic level, on the level of the pure elements, in a way that also resonates with Tibetan tantric systems description of the coarse elements and their subtle substratum (space, air, water, fire, and earth). The light body arises from the *vishuddha bhutas*. These purified *bhutas* or elements are drawn upwards and outwards from the aperture of Brahma. In effect Ramalinga is describing a bodily alchemy of distillation made possible by the energy of solar light that has been brought down into the cells. Although it sounds like he is describing a visualization practice, what is important is the use of the eyes as an entryway into the subtle channels that bring the light energy into the cells and down to the molecular and atomic levels of the body. The eyes and channels provide a vital interface between the material body and the subtle body. These practices are very similar to the methods of *tregchod* and *thodgal* in Tibetan dzogchen,[29] both Bonpo and Buddhist, as we verified in our February 2001 interviews with Loppon Tenzin Namdak. Once brought inside the body, the light brings about the transformation *of itself*: the practitioner does not manipulate it with the conscious mind; it just happens spontaneously. Ramalinga is particularly interesting not only for having revived the yogic teachings of Tirumular but also for his more modern understanding of the atomic nature of material phenomena. We need to recall that, for ancient Indian and Tibetan science, an atom was thought of as an infinitesimal metaphysical construct (as in Vasubandhu's *Abhidharmakosha*, from the late fourth century). Only a person with a scientific background such as Ramalinga (he had studied at Madras University in the 1850s) might have had a rudimentary exposure to the science of electricity and to some of the earliest proposals for a modern theory of atoms, at least as relevant to chemical processes. Here we are fifty years before the experiments that revolutionized atomic theory at the start of the twentieth century. At Madras, the young Ramalinga may have also studied pre-Socratic philosophers such as Empedocles and Heraclitus, and learned of their ideas of atoms, elements, and the flux of material phenomena.[30]

Looking at the Tamil Siddha traditions provides a way of opening up a conversation about bodily transformation in a variety of religious traditions. The resurrection of the body is already present in late Judaism,[31] in earliest Christianity, and in Islam. A notion of a reconstituted body was present even earlier in Iranian religion where it is found in Zoroastrianism.[32] We might think of yoga as an embodied spirituality, but the work of classic hatha yoga is meant to prepare the body-mind complex for mental exercises that in the end require the absence of embodiment. However, in the Tamil Siddha traditions[33] we do have a clear description of the material body subsumed into the liberating process of illumination, as expressed in the poetry of Tirumular. A similar process seems to be part of the Daoist alchemy of immortality, and several observers have noted that both systems work with mercury and other mineral agents for bodily transformation.[34]

Even Hindu and Buddhist tantras are certainly focused on the body, unlike the Buddhism of the earliest sutras, which seems in some passages to be overly intent on working with the mind. In the tantras, the body is seen as a vehicle, a deity palace, a mandala, and the practitioner's body is engaged in ritual activities of various kinds. Even the notion of "transgression" requires a relationship to embodiment, since that which is defiling in orthodox Hinduism amounts to the substances of the body, the status of one's caste, and contact with the dead. Each of these defiling categories becomes the occasion for acquiring magical power and for pursuing the path of enlightenment beyond those conceptualizations that bind the imagination to notions such as impurity.

The true focus of the Buddhist tantras, however, is on transforming the subtle body rather than "being present to" the material body. In the Buddhist tantras, the material body is the matrix within which the subtle body of the tantric deity is visualized and stabilized as a mental construct in the "stage of generation." This stabilized construct makes possible the higher yogas of the transformation of consciousness, the "stage of completion." As the dzogchen master Namkhai Norbu makes abundantly clear, this is not the approach of dzogchen.[35] Only in Tibetan dzogchen, both Buddhist and Bonpo, do we find the body "as it is" in union with mental factors—from the primordial dawning of awareness to the end of conceptualization when, returning to the primordial natural state, the body dissolves into a rainbow body, the 'ja' lus, which is completely open to all possibilities and therefore capable of benefiting sentient beings without limit. This is not to say that the subtle body is not part of the dzogchen path but simply to say that material, mental, and subtle bodies are the locus of the salvific process and are not mere vehicles. In my opinion, the extraordinary visions[36] of *thodgal* are in some way an intuition of the biochemical structure of the cells, very much in harmony with the spread of solar light described in the Tamil Siddha practices. This is the closest we get to a working hypothesis on how a set of yogic practices brings about bodily transformation as radical as that claimed in the rainbow body.

A number of writers have suggested that there is a connection between the notion of a rainbow body and the Manichean teachings on liberating particles of light through spiritual practice. In fact, as Jason BeDuhn has demonstrated in *The Manichean Body*, the liturgical rites of the Manicheans involved a sacred meal by means of which the auditors made efficacious offerings to the elect, who then consumed the offerings as food so as to liberate the particles of light trapped therein.[37] Even in this system, it is not the human body that is transformed into a being of light. Rather the body is employed here as a kind of distillation device for the return of light particles to the realm of divine light. If we are to search for Manichean influences in dzogchen notions of luminosity, it will have to be from the periphery of Manichean belief, rather than from its central liturgical self-expressions.[38] Far more credible are the proposed connections between Daoist immortality and alchemical practice. However, with the exception of terms such as *wu-wei* (non-action) and the idea of bodily immortality as a soteriological goal, the methods of *early* dzogchen and those of standard *early* medieval Chinese Daoism seem worlds apart when one actually sits down and reads the texts.[39] Later on, there is more evidence for convergence of and even borrowing between these two traditions as can be seen in a comparatively recent Daoist work, *The Secret of the Golden Flower*.[40]

For these reasons, and others that will emerge in the chapters that follow, I am inclined to favor—at least as a working hypothesis—that the Christian doctrine of the resurrection merits consideration as a primary source for the notion of the rainbow body as it develops in the dzogchen milieu of imperial Tibet. This is not to say it is the *only* source, but it does seem to be crucial for the entire development, which is by no means complete in the period before,[41] the so-called second diffusion of Buddhism in Tibet (taken to be after 1000, and concluding perhaps with the final contacts between Tibetans and Indian Buddhist panditas in the 1500s). Not only is the bodily resurrection a distinct and emphatically Christian doctrine, it is sustained by claims made by Christian mystics of the Syriac tradition about light mysticism and its effects on the human body-mind complex. These claims are not found in other central Asian mystical traditions, but are attested to by an extensive body of literature datable to the period of the first diffusion of Buddhism in Tibet. At the same time, with due respect for the work of a number of other researchers in the field of dzogchen studies, there is little doubt that Manicheans, yogis, Daoists, Ch'an (and other) Buddhists, Zoroastrians, shamanic peoples, and Muslims played a part in this remarkable spiritual conversation along the great Silk Road.[42]

Before proceeding with the study of the earliest layers of archeology attesting to this conversation, I am going to offer a presentation of our fieldwork on the life and death of Khenpo A Chö, a monk of the Kandzé Gompa in eastern Tibet (formerly Khams, now western Sichuan Province in the People's Republic of China). At times it will seem as though we have a long chimney-pipe cylinder in our hands. We will start by looking inside from the more recent end, and then we will look again through the far end, because what we have in the eye-witness accounts of Khenpo A Chö is the culmination of a long and deeply rooted experience of faith and devotion in Tibetan culture. It makes sense to encounter the phenomena that are closer to us in time at the start of our investigation so that our exposition of the historical developments related to what we have seen can contribute to a meaningful interpretation of the fieldwork data. In order to preserve the immediacy of the events and interviews described, the fieldwork reports are given in temporal order and taken almost verbatim from our research notebooks. I have added some comments by way of clarification in this written version. After giving what is essentially the raw data of our research, I offer the reader a contemporary account of dzogchen practice and attainment from within the Nyingma school, again adding some explanatory comments of my own in order to keep this material in conversation with other mystical traditions relevant to transformation and embodiment. This chapter is followed by historical research on the origins of dzogchen as a distinctly Tibetan system of spirituality. I then move into new territory, by juxtaposing Tibetan spirituality with the teachings of the Syro-Oriental Church, including its unique appropriation of the teachings of Evagrius of Pontus and related mystical teachers from the fourth and fifth centuries in the Eastern Roman Empire (Byzantine Empire). Finally, I attempt to support a model for interreligious exchange in Central Asia, China, and Tibet from the eighth to the eleventh century. This model is based on two important literary sources: the *Book on the Realization of Profound Peace and Joy* by a Syro-Oriental Christian of the eighth century, preserved among the Dunhuang manuscripts, and the earliest known version of the life of Garab Dorje, the human "originator" of the dzogchen teachings, datable to the eleventh century.

For the purposes of this study, it will be necessary to overcome a great mass of historical forgetfulness, both in Tibetan and in Western scholarship. The period of the first diffusion has recently become a topic of intense interest among Tibetologists, and thanks to a number of recent works, the period is beginning to seem somewhat less murky.[43] For the discussion of Christian presence in Central Asia and China, a handful of recent works[44] have begun to displace the centuries of neglect and misunderstanding, but these works have not attracted the attention of the Tibetological community because heretofore no one has been able to document Christian presence in early Tibet, except via a few ambiguous inscriptions and Dunhuang fragments.

We are at a point in the history of humanity in which all religions, all systems of contemplative training and practice, are under extremely critical scrutiny. Not only are some marginal lineages in danger of extinction but also some of the more historically significant contemplative systems are on the verge of near-collapse. The Syro-Oriental "Assyrian" Church of the East, which only reconciled with the Catholic Church in 1994 with a common statement on Christological belief,[45] now faces extinction in Syria and Iraq. The destruction of Tibetan culture continues with new forms of tragedy and ferocity, more than sixty years after the Chinese Communist invasion. Catholic monastic institutions in Western Europe and the Americas are declining after centuries of diastole and systole under a variety of anti-religious regimes. Eastern Orthodoxy in Russia and Eastern Europe is enjoying a period of flourishing under not always reliable government support. The Copts continue to struggle for survival in Egypt, with some remarkable achievements in maintaining and increasing the presence of Christian monasticism in their homeland. Journalist William Darymple describes the plight of Christians in the Middle East in his classic account, *From the Holy Mountain.*[46]

It has been my personal task to restore and reinforce some small instances of the institutional presence of Catholic Christianity in Europe and America, with special attention given to ecumenical and interreligious dialogue. Whenever it seems necessary to struggle for the basic survival of a religious tradition, I have discovered, there is less compelling impetus for the cultivation of the more mystical or contemplative approach within that tradition. For this reason, in the spirit of those teachers of the past who managed to hand on their wisdom in spite of unfavorable times and hostile circumstances, it is necessary to write a book of this kind.

—PRESBYTER FRANCIS V. TISO
January 28, 2015, Memorial of St. Thomas Aquinas,
Priest and Doctor of the Church
Hermitage of Colle Croce, Isernia, Italy

I

❦

The Life and Death of Khenpo A Chö:
Research on Paranormal Postmortem
Phenomena in Tibet

It was therefore necessary for the appearance of sky-like realities
to be purified by such means, but the sky-like realities themselves
had to be purified by means of sacrifices even more sublime.
—HEBREWS 9:23-24

The body is the vehicle for spiritual practice, even when it is experienced as a weight, an obstacle, a fortress vulnerable to temptation, a fragile temporary dwelling that is subject to old age, sickness, and death. Traditions of spiritual practice have reshaped the body in order to make it a more fitting vehicle for the sacred. These interventions from the outside work to exploit the body's symbolic capabilities through circumcision, tattooing, hair modifications, piercing, coloring, flagellation, incision, fasting, adopting fixed bodily postures, dance (with concomitant bodily development and decoration), costuming, and nudity.

However, some instances of bodily modification seem not to be the result of an external intervention. Rather they arise either spontaneously or in connection with ascetic practices. These occurrences would seem to indicate that some spiritual practices, either directly or indirectly, produce bodily modifications on a very deep level: stigmata, spontaneous healing of diseases, incorruption of the body after death, symbolic objects formed of human tissue in the bones or organs (found after death, as in the case of St. Veronica Giuliani or in the cremation of highly realized Tibetan lamas), longevity or "immortality," bilocation, levitation, resurrection, spontaneous combustion, the body of light, and the rainbow body.

Our research is directed toward the manifestation of the rainbow body after death and is based on the case of Khenpo A Chö, a Gelugpa monk of Khams (eastern Tibet) who died in 1998. I am defining the rainbow body in generic terms: the shrinkage and disappearance of a human body within a short time after death accompanied by paranormal phenomena such as unusual emanations of light and altered atmospheric conditions in the locality of the deceased. My spiritual teacher for many years, Brother David Steindl-Rast, O.S.B., had heard about the death of this Khenpo from a friend in Switzerland and was intrigued by the reports of paranormal phenomena, including the manifestation of the disappearance of the corpse within a week of death.

Father Francis Tiso, Doctor Tenpa Shitsegang, Venerable Vanja Palmers

In part, Brother David's interest was specifically directed toward an eventual comparison of the rainbow body phenomenon with the bodily resurrection of Jesus, which is of course one of the central faith-convictions of Christianity. Since the days of late-nineteenth-century European biblical scholarship directed along secular lines, the resurrection for the most part has been consigned to the category of those miracles that comprise a symbolic account of the faith experience. This approach, associated with the humanistic tradition of textual hermeneutics (the historical-critical method), asserts that miracles did not happen literally. Rather, paranormal phenomena are retold from the point of view of the disciples of Jesus as an explanation for their continued belief in him after his death on the cross and the reason for their courageous persistence in spreading his message in the face of violent opposition. The historical-critical approach, however, does not seem to answer all our questions. Brother David had been in touch with some of the scientists who were able to study the Shroud of Turin, and he came away convinced that this relic is not a fraud made some time during the Middle Ages. When he tried to raise the question of the shroud as an archeological source in conversation with his historical-critical biblical scholar colleagues, he ran into a total lack of interest. It was as if discussion of the shroud represented of the opposite style of discourse from that of modern literary critics of ancient texts. Worse yet, the scientific aspects of shroud research turned out to be almost incomprehensible to the biblical scholars. Just as archaic tribal societies have their insider ways of articulating reality, so too, literary scholars have an insider language that cannot be violated, and the same is true for scientists. Each community of discourse seems to live in its own emic worldviews. At the interdisciplinary boundaries, communication becomes very difficult and at times almost impossible. Brother David entrusted me with the task of engaging with this risky terrain of research, knowing that I had studied Tibetan Buddhism, had done anthropological fieldwork in the Himalayas, and have a strong background in biblical studies and theology. Moreover, we have been working together on our respective spiritual journeys, including interreligious dialogue, for over forty years.

Working with the fairly recent instance Khenpo A Chö has an obvious advantage in that we can talk to living eyewitnesses. Another advantage is that written accounts were produced within months of the events described. For these reasons, we are able to overcome some of the criticisms of the New Testament accounts of the resurrection of Jesus that were written down at the earliest about twenty years after the event. At the same time, given that the rainbow body has been a topic of interest in Tibetan culture for more than a thousand years, we are confronted with a well-established community of discourse that requires careful interpretation.

As a point of departure this chapter takes us into the biography of Khenpo A Chö, which introduces key elements of this particular instance of the rainbow body. The following excerpt is taken from a translation of biographies from Tibetan sources close to the Khenpo. The text moves us directly into the inner world of the Khenpo and his disciples. It is followed by an account of his death and the postmortem preternatural phenomena that are the topic of this research.

A Brief Biography of Khenpo A Chö

> *The Song of the Queen of Spring Sung from Afar: Unique Ornament of the Land of the Rose Apple Tree, Adorning the Nyingma Vajrayana: The Condensed Biography of the Precious Abbot A Chö, Whose Body Dissolved into Atoms without Remainder on the Seventh Day of the Seventh Lunar Month of the Year of the Earth-Tiger of the Seventeenth Rabjung in Nyarong County of Khams* (1998).[47]

In Ase Lumorap, located in the upper part of Nyak Adzirong in Kham in the Dome Region of Tibet, his [A Chö's] father and mother requested a prediction from Gyelwa Changchup, an accomplished yogin who had accumulated merit. He said, "If you set up an image of Lord Tsongkhapa, a supreme son will be born to you, one who will hold, sustain, and spread the doctrine of the Buddha." They did as they were told, in the Year of the Earth-Tiger (1918) of the sixteenth *rabjung*, on the auspicious date of the first part of the month of Vesakh (the fourth lunar month); when the sun appeared on the peak of the mountain, this son was born.

Meditating on the Tibetan letter Long-A.

He [A Chö] began to exert himself in reading and writing from the age of seven. In order to address several adverse circumstances that appeared in that period of his life, he sought protection from Dorje Dudul of Tshophu, who predicted: "Son, if you study well, there will be extensive benefit for the Doctrine and for living beings!" He was given the name Choying Rangdrol, and was already treated as a holy person.

He took his Refuge Vows from Lama Ozer Dorje, thus entering the gateway of the Doctrine. From the junior abbot, he received the precepts of the Lama Entirely-Good (Samantabhadra), which turn the mind away from cyclic existence.

He received the vows of a novice monk from Jampel Dewe Nyima, taking the name Ngawang Khyentsei Nangwa. By the age of thirteen, he had completed the traditional intensive study of the ritual traditions of monastic life such as offering ceremonies and the like. At the age of fourteen, as a student in the monastic college of Lurap Monastery, everyone praised him because of his good behavior, perseverance, and lucid intelligence.

In this period of his life, he received as many empowerments and teachings as he could from lamas who had authoritative lineages of transmission. In this way, he received the instructions on the creation and completion Stages of tantric practice, along with supplementary instructions from the termas such as the *Dudjom Tersar* and the *Longchen Nying Thig* cycles.

At the age of sixteen he learned the *Treasury of Virtuous Qualities* with the commentaries on the creation stage such as the *Ears of Union* and the *Practices of the Sons of the Enlightened Ones*. He undertook retreats in the mountains in solitude in order to attain the meaning of these teachings.

At the age of eighteen, he completed the study of the *Guhyagarbha Tantra*, the *Hundred Mind Training Exercises of the Kadampas*, the *Vinaya*, and *Madhyamika*, by studying day and night.

When he was twenty, he took the vows of full monastic ordination from his uncle Tenzin Rinpoche, who acted as abbot and master, in an assembly of ten other fully ordained monks, including junior abbots and other masters.

Then, because of his own intentions and dispositions arising from his birth and training, he followed the advice of the two junior abbots and went to Lhasa to study at the monastic college of Sera. There he learned the *Five*

Treatises of Maitreya from Dargon Ge Jampa Khedrup, Gyapon Chodze and other tutors whom he relied on for instruction.

He also went to Mindrolling Monastery where he carefully studied all the relevant sutras and tantras in accordance with the intentions and activities of authorized lamas in the lineage of transmission. He absorbed all these teachings and generated wisdom through hearing. Through mind training, he removed misconceptions. By practicing meditation, he tamed his mindstream.

Urged to ordain by Ge Jamling, he repeated the vows of a fully ordained monk before Jampa Rinpoche, who was considered to be a manifestation of Maitreya.

At the age of twenty-six, having become seriously ill with a fever, he requested the empowerment of Vajrakilaya from Dudjom Yeshe Dorje in order to eliminate obstacles.[48] The latter gave him the complete cycle of liberating and ripening empowerments of the *Heavenly Iron Blade of Vajrakilaya,* as expounded in the profound *terma* he had discovered. Dudjom Rinpoche gave him the text, material provisions, and other requisites, saying: "Perform the practices of a retreat, completing one hundred thousand recitations of the mantra. Adverse conditions will be dispelled, and maturation of the practice will be enhanced." Accordingly, he went to Khardo and recited the mantras one hundred thousand times. The obstacles were calmed without leaving a trace.

He showed great respect towards Dudjom Rinpoche, whom he envisioned as an actual manifestation of the Buddha and as his guru in many lifetimes. With limitless faith he offered the Rinpoche his body, speech, and mind. He viewed anything he said as spiritual instructions, and anything he did as Dharma. By practicing with such faith and devotion, Dudjom Rinpoche became for him the Dharmakaya of equanimity. He received the direct extraordinary practical instructions on primordial purity from Dudjom Rinpoche, including the secret dzogchen (*mahasanti*) practices of "cutting-through (*trekchod*) awareness of the basis and spontaneity," and the "leap-over (*thodgal*) of the path." These practices are capable of liberating a person of the highest abilities in one lifetime. In accordance with the lineage of this guru, who was a holder of the oral transmission of these teachings, the Khenpo developed his understanding, experience, and realization, sustaining the continuity of primordial natural awareness through relentless practice.

From the holy gurus of the Sakya, Nyingma, Geluk, and Kagyu schools, he also received teachings leading to spiritual maturity and liberation, without sectarian preferences. He performed the retreat practices for accomplishing the attainments of all the deities of the three tantric roots (guru, deities, and dakinis), and studied the scriptural traditions though they are oceanic in extent.

One day in that period of his life, Dudjom Rinpoche said, "Tomorrow I am to give the empowerment of Vajrakilaya. Therefore, you, A Chö, should come." When the Khenpo came to the empowerment, Dudjom Rinpoche intentionally placed him on a throne among many great personages, disciples of the various traditions, and began the root empowerment with him. He conferred the empowerment that leads to maturity and to liberation in Vajrakilaya, making the Khenpo a dharma lineage holder of the *Vajrakilaya Tantra*. This empowerment fulfilled a prophecy of Vajrakilaya: "I passed down to you the word of my Vajrakilaya tradition, thus returning the Dharma to its owner." At that time, Dudjom Rinpoche gave him an authentic ritual iron dagger (*kila*) to attach to his waist, as is done in this tradition. From that time on, he made retreats to perfect the accomplishments of the *yidam* Vajrakilaya so that signs of accomplishment appeared. His mind became one with the mind of the Fourteenth Victor (His Holiness the Dalai Lama, as a lineage holder of Vajrakilaya).

Then, returning to his hometown, he brought along only the text of the *Great Treatise on the Stages of the Path* (by Je Tsong Khapa) and a bowl used in monastic ritual gatherings. For this reason, his relatives and friends mocked him, saying, "You spent so much time studying in Lhasa, but have accumulated possessions not even worth the value of a *karnga* (a type of small Tibetan coin). You are a useless beggar from Domé!" But the saint [A Chö] said, "Being content with whatever comes to me, I am happy with whatever is done. If the mind is directed towards the Dharma, everything is easy, even dying. If our consciousness is realized as unborn, one is no longer subject to death." In accord with these words, he remained always free from worldly deeds, abiding in the noble mind stream of contentment.

Then he was made abbot of the monastic college of Lurap[49] Monastery, where he taught the sacred texts, provided resources for the monks, and so forth. Some people there were infected with erroneous views, and they criticized him by saying: "His is mostly Sarma teaching [i.e., Sakya, Kagyu, and above all Gelug]. Therefore this Nyingma monastery is going to be converted to Gelug." He himself traveled to more than sixty monasteries in upper and lower Nyak, and to monasteries of different traditions in Hor, Drak, and so forth, to turn the wheel of the Dharma, imparting the teachings on maturity and liberation according to the individual aspirations of teachers and disciples. Everything that was offered to him was used to commission images for each monastery and to support retreat practice.

In 1959 when he was forty-one years old, there were great changes in Tibet because of the Chinese invasion. This saint experienced various difficulties: in spite of the situation, he took upon himself poverty and defeat, in order to provide benefits to the people. He did all he could to offer food, clothing, and money to the people of his region. In secret, he constantly exerted himself in order to purify obscurations and accumulate virtues. At different times, he completed 2.5 million full prostrations and several hundred fasting periods. He composed various commentaries for the future benefit of the Dharma, for living beings, and disciples. During a Vajrakilaya retreat, he was inspired by his connections to the prophetic word of this deity and composed an extensive commentary on the Vajrakilaya practice. These and other texts comprise the five volumes of his collected works.

At that time when it was not even permitted to say the word "religion," he would hide at night and move about during the day; in this way he made it to Nyak Tome, Kardrak, Dzakhok, and other places where the faithful had invited him to secretly spread the Dharma for the benefit of others. He taught the *Stages of the Path and Mind Training* along with the preliminary practices for the *Longchen Nying Thig (The Heart Drops of Longchenpa)* and other practices. He also conferred novice and full monastic ordination. In all that he did, he worked vigorously and exclusively for the sake of the Dharma and for sentient beings.

In 1976 during the Year of the Fire Dragon when some freedom of religion was permitted, it became possible to undertake the rekindling of the embers of the Dharma. He gathered his writings together, traveling to those monasteries that had remained faithful both near and far; and gave extensive teachings on maturity and liberation in the Dharma, without distinctions based on sect or school. He used any possessions he received exclusively for virtuous purposes: to restore ruined monasteries, cast statues, publish the scriptures, build stupas, provide sacred rituals, and make offerings.

At the age of sixty-four, he returned to Lhasa to see the statue of the Jowo in order to make the traditional thousand offerings. He made offerings of money and tea to all the monks of Sera, Drepung, Ganden, and other monasteries near Lhasa. Returning to his own region of Doto/Domé, he conferred both novice and full monastic ordination on approximately two thousand people. He visited the present manifestation of Padmasambhava, Sera Yangtrul Rinpoche, receiving from him various profound teachings and becoming his son disciple. Since he had been informed by Ge Jampa Khedrup that he would encounter obstacles to his health, he recited 1.4 million mantras during a White Tara retreat, made a hundred thousand fire offerings, recited a thousand long *dharanis* of Vijaya, and did other practices to promote a long life. Clear signs appeared that the obstacles had been pacified and the Lord of Death appeased.

In the cave in which Berotsana (Vairotsana) [50] had practiced, and in other places as well, he made retreats in which he practiced the rites of various tantric deities such as the *Solitary Hero Vajrabhairava*, the *Noble Lady Vajrayogini, Vajrakilaya, Hayagriva, Yamaraja, Manjushri, Vajrasattva, Avalokiteshvara*, and others. For thirty years, he constantly recited the one hundred thousand mantras of Avalokiteshvara. [51]

In 1992 at the age of seventy four, he began to mainly devote himself to retreat practices. Since the highest deity of living beings in general and of Tibetans in particular is Avalokiteshvara, the lord of boundless compassion towards the vulnerable beings who dwell in cyclic existence in this degenerate age, he recited more than 400 million of the mani-mantra (*Om mani padme hum*) within the ritual context of the practice of creation and completion in the tantra of Avalokiteshvara. Over and over, he recited and promoted the recitation of the *Long Life Prayer of the Protector of the Snow Ranges*, and the *Heart Prayer of the Enlightened Activities Pervading Space*, related to His Holiness the Dalai Lama and Avalokiteshvara.

Once when his attendant, Lama Norta, went to take care of some practical matters, the outer door of the hermitage was closed from the outside.

Since the saint himself had realized that all external appearances as well as this internal body and mind are the clear appearance of voidness—similar to a reflection of the moon in a pond of water—he obtained stability in the meaning of space-like primordial awareness. He trained himself in the exhaustion of appearances into Dharmata, giving rise to his body itself becoming like a reflection of the moon in water. Thus, he was able to pass through walls and fences without obstructions and was seen making circumambulations [outside the hermitage].

In 1997 when he was eighty, on the eight day of the fifth lunar month in the Year of the Fire-Bull, the Supreme Tulku Orgyen Drimé came to visit him to hold a joyful spiritual discussion. When A Chö placed his hands together, a photo was taken that shows the lama, himself, and an empty form like the image of a reflection of the moon in water. While Khenpo A Chö stayed inside his inner room in the hermitage, and Tulku Orgyen Drimé was seated in the outer room with his back to the closed door to the inner room, another photo was taken showing the Khenpo in the outer room. The image of the Khenpo as a fully ordained monk dressed in the ceremonial robe and upper cloak, wearing the crown ornament of the five buddha families and holding the ritual damaru in his right hand is shown in the photo. His face and hands are clearly seen, and his rosary is seen above the Tulku's head. Thus, as with the light of the moon reflected in a pool of water, the body of the Khenpo in the union of appearances and voidness transcended the duality of external and internal, the appearance mingled with the bodily presence, shining like a reflection in a mirror.

I also heard it said that at the same period that saint A Chö asked his attendant Lobsang Nyendrak, "What do you think? Am I the reincarnation of a buddha or bodhisattva, or an ordinary person?" The attendant answered, "Your wonderful activity shows that you are the reincarnation of a buddha or bodhisattva." The Khenpo said, "How can it be? All this is the result of the practices of a beginner who has just entered the path. So isn't that a great wonder?" It is clear that he considered himself a person who gradually entered and progressed on the path.

To bring the biography to its culmination with the manifestation of the body of light and complete dissolution of the physical body, we present an excerpt from the biography of Khenpo A Chö that we received from the nuns who were his disciples. Their gompa is found across the river from Kanzé:

How Khenpo A Chö Attained Rainbow Body

[The life of] this lord from birth till when he was seventy-five is clear from what was explained before.

For six years, from the age of seventy until he attained the rainbow body, every day and night, he continuously practiced the yoga of different *yidams,*[52] [planting] important roots of happiness (*bde ba*) in the Doctrine and for migrating beings [in samsara] without partiality. Apart from this, he came to the end of his life exerting himself exclusively in retreats on the six syllables through [the practice] of *yidam* Avalokiteshvara....

On the tenth day of the sixth Tibetan month a letter from His Holiness the Dalai Lama arrived from India through the courtesy of the teacher Wangchuk Puntsok. The letter said:

> To Khenpo Achung [*sic*] from Nyagrong.
>
> I'm happy that you are staying in good health without losing courage, bringing benefit to others. Here [I am] also in good health and keep acting for the benefit of the Dharma and sentient beings. In the future as well let your intention of trying to help all beings pacify their accumulated evils and enjoy the happiness of their accumulated virtues remaining unshakable.
>
> From Shakya[muni] bhikshu Tenzin Gyatso, 23 of 4th Tibetan month, 1998.

Along with that [letter] His Holiness sent images of great compassionate Avalokiteshvara and the lady-owner of desire realm [Shridevi, Pelden Lhamo], along with signs of his own hand-prints. [Khenpo] was especially pleased and for long time was making profound and extensive prayers.

During that period, it was raining for long time, [but people] didn't think it to be an omen of the teacher [A Chö] passing away. Instead, they took it as a sign of the arrival of Tulku Jigmé. For this reason, they prostrated and offered many prayers.

Soon after that a flat, long five-colored rainbow penetrated the expanse of the sky above [Khenpo's] hut. First it was witnessed by five people—mother Nordron (Nor sgron) with her sons. Then gradually it was witnessed by many people, and they became apprehensive, taking it as a sign that the teacher [A Chö] would not live [long]. Nevertheless, in their minds they [tried] not to look at it [in such a way], and rather continued to think of it as a sign of the imminent arrival of Tulku Jigmé. Mother Nordron, prostrating, prayed: "Let Buddha's doctrine spread! Let there be happiness for all sentient beings! Let the abode of the Tulku remain firm! Let the doctrine of Trulshik father and son/s spread!" I've written down these words of prayer as I actually heard them from her mouth.

At that time bad signs such as dream omens appeared to many of the son-disciples [of A Chö] from upper and lower Shulring. Besides that, the attendant Lopsang Nyendrak saw His Holiness the Dalai Lama in a dream saying, "Tashi Delek" quickly, before leaving the teacher's room in the western direction. Then [Lobzang Nyendrak] asked [him], "Please, stay just a little bit," but not listening, the teacher went away. Due to that, everybody was unhappy and became apprehensive.

[Once] in the morning [Khenpo] called his heart son Lobzang Nyendrak, took his hand with both hands and said, "Although [one might] think that there is nothing for you to meditate upon, who has more than you to meditate upon? Contemplate on essential points of bodhichitta and the view of emptiness." With these words both father and son shed tears and prayed as deeply as they could.

At that time all the old and young people in the entourage of the [Khenpo] came into his presence, confessed [all] misdeeds including even stepping on [monastic] clothes [etc., and they promised to] restrain themselves [from them in future]. For the sake of reincarnation they made prayers of *Caring in All Lives*. Khenpo responded to them with great pleasure, and also without hurry he gave instructions on what is to be done in the future.

The next day, seventh of the seventh Tibetan month, he ate just a little bit, but didn't show even the slightest signs of bodily sickness or fatigue. At noon time he lay on his right side, turned his head to the north and face to the west, and thus, in the posture of sleeping lion, holding his rosary in his hand and reciting the six-syllable [mantra of Avalokiteshvara] from his mouth, he displayed at that moment the dissolution of his mind in the sphere of reality (i.e., he died).

Immediately after that all the appearances of bodily aging such as wrinkles, shriveling, etc., instantly disappeared. His face became youthful—smooth and pinkish. [Everybody from] the inner circle [of the Khenpo] unanimously says that [it was a pity they were] in sadness and haste—otherwise, had they taken a photograph, it would have been amazing.

Even before this the Lord naturally had a fragrant smell of morality, and I myself also detected this fragrance from the first time I met him. [After his death] it grew stronger, so that [it filled] not only the inside of the room, but also outside of the house, all the people making prostrations and circumambulations detected it without even trying.

Above his house five [colored] rainbows appeared for many days. Sometimes they pervaded the whole expanse of the sky, as was directly witnessed by all the monks and lay people of Lurap. There were also many people from upper and lower Horkhok who at the same time saw [the rainbows]. My niece Tserin Chotso, father and sons, [my own] father Tsega and others saw the whole sky in the east pervaded by rainbows. While I stayed in retreat in solitude, in the intervals between meditative sessions during two days, I saw how the rainbows appeared twice in the sky above the holy place of Tsanda. The next day I heard the bad news [about Khenpo's death] from his nephew Sonam Gyaltsen who was sent on purpose. The day after that I also saw [the rainbows].

Also, in the afternoon of that very [day] when [khenpo] was liberated in the body of light (*'od sku*), just before dark, the light similar to that of sun rays was shining for long time from the east, and it was seen by all of us.

Then his old and young attendants took the main responsibility [for the funeral services], and together with them the relatives, servants and close disciples of the Lord made extensive funeral ceremonies and prayers. During that time, each day the body was observed under the cloth, becoming smaller and smaller until finally, on the day after one week had passed, there was manifested the stainless rainbow body, the vajra body. This accords with the prophesy by Sera Yantrul Rinpoche, holy lama of this Lord, who said that this will happen to a couple of his most important disciples. From his *Nejang:* "There will appear a couple [of people whose] stains of illusory body will be extinguished and who will be liberated in stainless body of light. They will attain rainbow body—the body of great transference (*'pho ba chen po'i sku*)." "The rainbow body of great transference"[53] is considered to be the liberation into the body of light without leaving even hair and nails.[54]

[This concludes the literary biographical source.]

Khenpo A Chö's room, showing where his body reposed for seven days after death in 1998.

Research in Eastern Tibet: Field Notes

The following are notes from my fieldwork notebook covering our trip to western Sichuan Province (formerly the eastern Tibetan region of Khams) in 2000. They tend to confirm the accounts in the biographies excerpted above. It is also my intent to allow the reader to accompany our research expedition by providing a glimpse of the experience in the form of a travel diary and describing the sequence of events as we gathered information. Moreover, the participant-observer quality to these notes shows the researchers entering the sphere of life and faith of the circle of the Khenpo's disciples.

The research team gathered in Chengdu, the capital of Sichuan Province of the People's Republic of China in early July. Some of us had just come from research in Dolpo, at 4,200 meters, in northern Nepal. After making some fateful decisions about our travel arrangements, including choosing a less-than-reliable driver and vehicle, we headed west through the towns of Luding (famous bridge and site of a mythic battle between Communists and Nationalists in 1935), Kangding (site of the warehouses where Chinese block tea used to be traded for Tibetan silver), and finally to Kandzé. Beyond Kandzé is the former royal capital and printing house of Dergé, which we were unable to visit. After the first cycle of travel, another group set out with me from Chengdu; we then returned to Kandzé and explored Litang and other sites in what used to be called the Sino-Tibetan borderlands.

> July 17, 2000. A visit to the Gelugpa monastery, Kandzé Gompa in the town of Kanzé in West Sichuan.

This is the monastery with which Khenpo A Chö was officially affiliated. Douglas Duckworth, John Morgan, and I went up to the Gompa to attempt to interview the three Gelugpa rinpoches associated with this monastery. These three were identified as spiritual friends of the late Khenpo A Chö by our research consultant in Switzerland, Mr. Tshitsegang.

The monastery, which is shaped somewhat like a double amphitheater, was located on the elevated ground above the town. It is a very impressive structure whose main buildings have recently been reconstructed. As is typical of these large monasteries, the main buildings are surrounded by smaller houses that are occupied by the majority of the monastic community. Some monks also live in a complex of small private rooms within the main buildings.

We approached through narrow streets of Kandzé, which ascended to the left of the monastery, without any clear idea of how to find the main entrance to the building complex. We eventually came to a small entryway where we were welcomed by a young Khampa layman, Tashi Jamso, who fortunately spoke fluent Lhasa dialect. He immediately agreed to take us around the monastery and introduce us to monks who knew the late Khenpo. As we were to learn later, Tashi comes from a highly respected family in the village just outside Kanzé where there is an *Ani Gompa*, which means a community of nuns. This community is still very devoted to the Khenpo, who was their guru. With Tashi's help, we were introduced to Gelong Ba song who, without hesitation, gave us the precious text of the hagiography (*rnam thar*) of Khenpo A Chö as written by Gelong Sonam Puntsog before the death of the Khenpo. Among other things, the text tells us that the Khenpo's main teacher when he studied in Lhasa was Trijang Rinpoche, who also taught the Thirteenth Dalai Lama. The final chapter of the biography, which describes the death and manifestation of the rainbow body, is kept by the community of nuns across the river. We were informed that the author of the biography is now in jail for political agitation, apparently for writing an essay advocating Tibetan independence. Gelong Ba song and another monk listed the following known eyewitnesses and close disciples of the Khenpo:

- Lama Pu Yak (also pronounced Piyok), a cousin of the Khenpo, present at the time of his death.
- Lama Lobzang Nyendrak, a close disciple.
- Lama Norta (mentioned later), a relative and close disciple of the Khenpo.
- Two novice monks, whom we later interviewed in India.

Lama A Khyug (pronounced *Chyuk*), a Nyingma master who is the head of a monastery near Peyul, was not present at the time of death: he was consulted by the disciples about the details of procedures at the time of the death. He is now about seventy years old and was a close dharma friend of the late

Khenpo. When the Khenpo died at the age of eighty-one, Lama Norta and Lama Nyendrak were uncertain about what to do with the body of their master. Lama A Khyug told them to leave it for seven days because there would be signs, which they did. It is understood by the expressions "seven days" and "signs" that a manifestation of the rainbow body might occur. No one observed the body directly for seven days. In the course of the week, people began to arrive at the Khenpo's hermitage to pay their respects. After seven days, the body had disappeared. The monks tell us that the Khenpo "completed the intention of his spiritual practices" (*dgongs pa rdzogs*), which is the formal affirmation that he had attained enlightenment. This took place in 1998 during the seventh lunar month (August–September).

Khenpo A Chö's hermitage at Lumaga Village, eastern Tibet.

We were informed that the Khenpo's hermitage is located in the region of Nyarong, south of Kanzé; the name of the locality is Lo ma ga (i.e., Khampa dialect for kLu ma gompa, which means "monastery of the lady Naga"). There is a small hut there on the side of the mountain where the Khenpo had lived for about nine years. I showed Tashi, Gelong Ba song, and the attendant the photos in an article written in Dharamsala about the Khenpo, and they were able to recognize a dharma friend named Lama Tulku rDo Lo who lives at the Nyingma gompa at Nyarong Da gye, whom unfortunately we were unable to interview. He too has written an account of the life and death of the Khenpo.

After our visit to the main monastery in Kandzé, Tashi Jamso took us to the residence of Gertag Rinpoche, a married Gelugpa lama who has a home in the lower part of Kandzé in a complex of single-story buildings that house the other two incarnate lamas of the gompa with their families and assistants. Gertag Rinpoche was not feeling well, but he graciously received us. He told us that his previous incarnation had studied in Lhasa with Khenpo A Chö and that they were Dharma friends, both having studied under Trijang Rinpoche. His own hereditary monastery is Beru Gompa, fifteen kilometers west of Kandzé. This was formerly a great center of the Bonpo tradition. He suggested that we locate and interview Pemo Lhaga, a student of the Khenpo's who is now in India, but we were subsequently unable to interview him.

Gertag Rinpoche of Khandzé Gompa, Father Francis Tiso, and Tashi, lay Tibetan guide.

Gertag Rinpoche then described an episode that occurred one year before the Khenpo's death. Significantly, none of the biographies mention this episode, which reflects the close personal relationship between the Khenpo and the superiors of Gertag Rinpoche's own Gelugpa monastery.

From time to time, the Khenpo would visit the Rinpoche for the purpose of divination (*mo*). Because of their dharma connection and because of the Rinpoche's name (*sKye brTag*, which literally means "the result of a divination"),[55] the Khenpo wanted to have an idea of the time of his impending death. In 1997, he came for a session of divination. The result of this ritual was that the Khenpo should have a thangka of the Tushita heaven (*dga' ldan yid dga' chos 'dzin*) painted as a sign of what was to happen. Khenpo was to pass away and go to the Tushita heaven, manifesting the rainbow body on earth. We asked where the thangka is now. The Rinpoche did not know, but he suggested that it might be in Nyarong. He was reluctant to discuss further particulars of the rainbow body manifestation. It is also significant that the Tibetan form of the name of the Tushita heaven is that of the great abbey of Galden founded by Je Tsongkhapa, near Lhasa and the location of the head lama of the Gelugpa Order. In a subtle way, the Rinpoche was confirming the Gelugpa affiliation of the Khenpo, both in the experience of divination and also in the fact of recounting this episode—and none other—in our interview. It is also of some interest that none of the biographies mention the divination, although specific long-life rituals are reported to have been performed. Perhaps it was omitted because this practice implies that the Khenpo was in some sense an ordinary monk with a burden of karmic traces yet remaining to purify.

I went on to ask about how the Rinpoche felt when he realized during the divination that Khenpo A Chö was going to die. He replied that the disciples had already been doing long-life pujas for the Khenpo, so he was not too surprised that the Khenpo had come to the end of his life. After the *mo*, the students continued to pray for his long life, even knowing that he would die soon. Khenpo was very happy to die and go to the Tushita heaven, because he knew that he would thereby acquire the good karma to eliminate all defilements. It is significant that this intimate conversation between two spiritual friends refers to the "elimination of defilements." This contrasts with

the biographical account, which implies that the Khenpo had already elimi-
nated all defilements long before the final year of his life. During the *mo*, the
Khenpo told the Rinpoche to say "whatever came into his mind." So, instead
of doing the usual procedure,[56] he spontaneously told the Khenpo to commission the thangka. I asked if the Khenpo will come back from Tushita as
a tulku. Were there any indications of this kind? The reply was that it is not
clear at this time. His Holiness the Dalai Lama has informed the community
that there is no need to look for his incarnation; the Khenpo will benefit beings in ways that will eventually be made known.

The Rinpoche told us that he does not know of other manifestations of the
rainbow body in recent times, which accords with the reticence of his order
with regard to these phenomena.

As for any mysterious signs left behind, the Rinpoche said he hadn't seen
any, but the disciples of the Khenpo told him that on the place on which the
body lay, there was a full cup of water that became empty after one or two
days. This rather banal observation was not mentioned by any other informants. It seems to have been an evasive reply.

On the afternoon of the same day, accompanied by Tashi Jamso, our team
visited the Ani Gompa across the river from Kandzé to meet with the chaplain, Lama Puyok. He was an enthusiastic "promoter of the cause" of Khenpo
A Chö, by which I mean that he seemed eager to encourage devotion to
this lama, who was very dear to him. Thanks to his kindness, we were able
to acquire the final chapter of Sonam Puntsog's biography of the Khenpo
from the nuns. This text, which we have presented above, covers the time of
his death and the rainbow body manifestation. We also had a very moving
meeting with the nuns, who had received many teachings and initiations
from the late Khenpo. While looking over the text of the final chapter in the
presence of the nuns and of Lama Puyok, I saw the words "*dad-gus*," which
mean "faith and devotion." The expression is meant to sum up the intentions
of the author in writing the biography. I pointed delicately to these words and
explained how important they are. The nuns began to weep heartfelt tears of
devotion, one after another, until all of them had wet faces, including the
members of our research team.

Community of nun disciples of Khenpo A Chö near Khandzé in eastern Tibet.

After this conversation, we made plans to leave on the following day for the monastery of Lama A Khyug, Dharma friend of the Khenpo, with Lama Puyok and three of the nuns.

That evening, we visited Lama Kangsar Samgyel, a Gelugpa master, who told us that Tulku rDo Lo had also written a short *rnam thar* (hagiography) of Khenpo A Chö. He said that he never received teachings from the Khenpo, but that Lama rDo lo and Lama Puyok knew the Khenpo better than he and would be able to provide us with more information and detail. He emphasized that the Khenpo was a great scholar of the Gelugpa tradition and spent his whole life in retreat. His teacher was Trijang Rinpoche. He told us he knows nothing of other manifestations of the rainbow body, confirming our impression that the Gelugpa lamas are unwilling to discuss matters outside the competence of their own tradition. In the biography of Khenpo A Chö, we have seen that he had received teachings from both Gelugpa and Nyingmapa masters from his childhood, without any apparent controversy except with regard to his monastic ordination. (He seems to have first been ordained a Nyingma monk, and then later re-ordained as a Gelugpa.)

> July 18, 2000. At Ya chas Gompa, Chung T'ai
> village on the road to Pelyul (Baiyu).

To find this remote place, one passes by the small Nyingma Gompa, Trogay (Tromgey), associated with the lineage of Chagdud Tulku, who has founded a center in Northern California that is well known to me. There is a sharp turnoff toward Pelyul on the right after the gompa. I follow the roads with a highly detailed map in Chinese that I had purchased in Chengdu. I was attempting to memorize the Chinese characters for the various towns that we passed on our journey.

The road trip in the rented land cruiser was difficult not only because of the rough road conditions but also because of the continual bickering between the Chinese driver and Lama Pu yak. In spite of the fact that we were accompanied by a prominent lama and three nuns, the driver was convinced that we will be set upon by Khampa bandits. The ongoing battle between tea (China) and chang (Tibetan beer) interfered continually with our travel and research. In fact, finally we had to cut short the number of days in this phase of our work because this situation got out of hand.

In any case, we were able to interview Lama A Khyug, the Dharma brother of Khenpo A Chö at the large and very primitive monastic community of Ya Chas Gompa, near Chung T'ai city, farther west on the road to Balyul, near the border between the Tibet Autonomous Region and the province of Sichuan. This lama was a relative of Lama Puyok, who was serving as guide and helper to our translator, Douglas Duckworth. The monastic community was said to consist of a thousand monks and a thousand nuns, all of whom were studying under Lama A Khyug's guidance. The two communities were gathered like two huge flocks on either side of the lama's residence. The setting was in a surreal environment of high steppe grasslands, with hardly a tree in sight. Rolling hills were all around us and in the extreme distance we could make out snow-capped mountains.

After considerable confusion as the fascinated young monks gathered to observe the newly arrived foreigners, we were admitted in the presence of the lama. Without a great deal of ceremony, Lama A Khyug informed us that he has all the teachings on the rainbow body and has realized them himself.

Lama A Khyug told us that Khenpo A Chö, his Dharma friend, attained the rainbow body because he obtained the teachings from a legitimate, realized guru and had practiced those teachings until they became an integral part of his own experience. To attain the rainbow body, one had to obtain the teachings and practice assiduously. He and his teacher were together for fifty-four years. One needed to practice for at least sixty years for results to occur. Students built up their practice over a long period of time. The lama did not allow us to tape this interview.

I could not help but notice that the lama had a spectacular collection of fine bronze yidam statues and over twenty very old *drilbu*s (ritual hand bells), which stood out in startling contrast to the extremely rudimentary surroundings. At a certain point in our interview, he showed us two photographs of himself taken in the dark that were supposed to show his ability to manifest the subtle body of light. I was able to examine these photos quite closely in the fading daylight because we were obliged to leave the lama's room to allow a group of visitors to offer *khataks* and make offerings. One photo was of the lama's body in faintly luminous silhouette in meditation position. The other photo, which was more intense than the first, showed three bodily outlines in light, with streaks of light coming forth from each of the outline-bodies, one slightly superimposed on the other. Unfortunately, it was twilight and I was unable get the camera to focus on these photographs in order to reproduce the images. These photos, if authentic, would have been our only nonverbal evidence for the paranormal phenomenon of a body being able to radiate light.

Later in the evening, we had another meeting with Lama A Khyug in order to clarify what he wished to say about the rainbow body. During this interview, he became more confrontational, almost like a *smyon-pa* yogin (mad yogin, crazy wisdom master). He asked us, "Are you willing to stay here forever? Do you have faith that in front of you is a lama who has attained the rainbow body?" I was in fact profoundly moved by a statement that he repeated several times, "You do not see the rainbow body with the bodily eyes, but with the eyes of the heart (*sems*)." He said this while gesticulating emphatically and continued insisting that "the view"[57] is in our mind and cannot be learned from books. "Only from practice, and from seeing the lama as Buddha, can the view be brought into our own experience. It is not helpful just to talk; one has to practice. So I advise you: receive teachings from a lama on the correct view. Then practice. When you have realized the view, then and then alone can you benefit others. Only then can you really bring benefit to people."

As he spoke, Lama A Khyug frequently emphasized the contrast between bodily eyes (*mig*) and the eyes of the heart (*sems*). He also referred to his own mala that he held in his hand, saying, "You can recite many malas of mantras, but it is inner realization that matters." The message seemed quite clear to me: neither philosophical study nor pedestrian forms of religious practice are sufficient. To realize the rainbow body requires a more advanced form of spirituality that must become an intimate part of the life of the yogin.

Although what he said made a great deal of sense within the Vajrayana tradition and beyond, it seemed at times that he was replying not to our actual questions but to our use of the Lhasa dialect to ask those questions, as if that dialect were for him a symbol of mere philosophizing, unsupported by meditation experience. The wrathful pose of the lama was somewhat disconcerting to Lama Puyok, who is a jovial and open-hearted monk. I was able to follow most of Lama A Khyug's rough Khampa dialect, because his message was actually quite simple and insistent. He would frequently point to his heart when he used the word *sems*, for heart-mind, and he gesticulated with his mala of 108 beads to emphasize the need for inner realization.

That he meant a mystical experience was necessary as a sign of realization became clearer as he shared a personal anecdote. Once he went to Kandzé Gompa where he met a lama of that monastery. He looked at him and saw the image of Chenresì (Avalokiteshvara) on his forehead—an image invisible to most people but one that was visible to Lama A Khyug. He recognized that this was a good lama and he had faith in him. This seemed to be Lama A Khyug's way of expressing a certain kind of ecumenical spirit: by recognizing a Gelugpa lama as having some degree of realization, enough to give rise to his own response of faith. He challenged us to find something on his own face, in order to test our ability to understand his intentions. I looked closely and noticed a certain similarity between his appearance and presence and that of Archbishop Ettore Di Filippo, the bishop who ordained me to the priesthood. Lama A Khyug was pleased with this reply, which harmonized with the attitude of guru-yoga. While conversing with us, he blessed other visitors standing outside his window with a small banner affixed to a wooden pole that he held in his hand.

Douglas Duckworth's excellent Lhasa pronunciation seemed to suggest to the Lama the tone of a Gelugpa philosophy professor. He emphasized the risks of getting too deeply imbued with scholastic philosophy and, perhaps, with the Lhasa attitude. It would have been interesting to hear a conversation between him and the Khenpo about their years of study in the early part of their lives.

Having understood that I am some kind of Christian lama, he asked me if the rainbow body is a phenomenon in Christianity. I gave an interpretation of the resurrection, but he seemed quite unimpressed. He also dodged further questions about his friend, Khenpo A Chö, and returned to emphasizing the contrast between sights perceptible to the eyes (*mig*) and that which is accessible only to the heart-mind (*sems*). His evasiveness left me feeling a degree of ambiguity that was only partly removed by what happened a number of days after this interview. Was he telling us that the rainbow body is reducible to a mental phenomenon or that it amounts to a verbal expression of reverence for a holy person? It seems difficult to believe that a person who has two luminous photographs of himself, claiming to be able to manifest the rainbow body would not have faith in the literal paranormal phenomenon.[58]

Lama A Khyug reciting the Gesar Epic at a festival near his Yaché Gompa in eastern Tibet, July, 2000.

July 19, 2000. Ya chas Gompa on a day of
festival.

I had hoped that we could interview Lama A Khyug again this morning,
but he was unavailable because the monastery is celebrating a huge festival.
There was an encampment of the local Khampa population in the field to
the northwest of the village. Several thousand people set up colorful tents for
the occasion and the field was teeming with horses, yaks, and people in traditional dress. This morning there would be a danced recitation of the *Gesar
Epic*. Gesar is said to have come from this part of Tibet, so it was particularly
impressive to be here at this time. This afternoon, there is to be a danced re-
cital of the life of Milarepa, which we will unfortunately have to miss because
of the twittering of our driver, "Mr. Tea." Lama A Khyug , the singer of these
tales, was seated above the parade ground in a small booth festooned with
khataks (silk scarves). All the monks and nuns were present around the parade
ground in the first ranks of the spectators. The large numbers of Khampas
gathered with their horses and yaks, gave one the impression that nothing
has changed here since the days of the Silk Road. Like Marco Polo during his
journeys at the end of the thirteenth century, we of the research team are the
only non-Tibetans present. The performance is completely free of the usual
for-the-tourists corruptions promoted in many parts of Asia. It is all pure
Khampa, pure Tibetan, and completely pervaded by a sense of awe among
people who are here to practice the Dharma in the form of a festival.

Part of the epic was danced dramatically, with the dancers wearing elaborate regal costumes. Gods and goddesses, heroes, and queens paraded before
the crowds as Lama A Khyug chanted the ancient melodies over a makeshift
public address system. We were invited into the actors' tents where young
monks were putting on elaborate makeup and adjusting their complicated
costumes. A charming young novice monk, not more than fourteen years
old, was dressed as the old crone, a clown figure who serves as a counterpoint
to the solemnity of the drama. His mask had matted gray hair and a huge
hooked nose. While we photographed the actors, he played around—never
out of character—as a true clown. While posing for a shot with a few of the
actors, I asked Douglas Duckworth, who was focusing the camera, "Am I

in the picture?" The boy-clown piped up spontaneously: "*Ma yin, ma yin,*" punning on "am I in," and intuitively replying to the question, since "*ma yin*" means "he is not." Of course the boy knew no English, but he didn't seem to be deterred from punning by something as slight as a language barrier.

The monks were having a fine time at this festival, but our presence became something of a distraction; everyone wanted to look through our cameras and binoculars, as if this were the first time in their lives that they had ever seen such things. (In all likelihood, it was.) The fact that such events are still taking place in modern Tibet suggests the resilience of Tibetan culture, especially in remote areas. It also alerts us to the firm boundaries of insider discourse in this kind of cultural world. This environment is rarely penetrated by the outside world, and the exchange of information, even with the availability of the internet in some of the larger towns such as Litang, must be highly filtered.

In the course of the day, we researchers attempted to interpret the real meaning of the wrathful, mad yogin posturing of Lama A Khyug. Perhaps he doesn't like to waste time with people who are unlikely to become his disciples, as is true of Chatral Rinpoche in Pharping, near Kathmandu. Since at the time of the research trip I had no official church assignment, I would have been quite willing to go into retreat under the direction of an authentic lama, but here the government might not look kindly on a foreigner with an expired visa. We are required to lodge only with government inns; in fact, last night's sojourn in the monastery, though logistically the only possible solution, was strictly speaking illegal. Somehow I feel we might have made some progress had we gone to see the lama early this morning, perhaps even before sunrise.

We had to return to Kandzé before the Milarepa performance because of a supposed lack of gasoline in Chung T'ai. A buildup of heavy rainclouds contributed to the anxiety as we retraced the extremely difficult road back. Along the way, we stopped at a police station to find four trucks blocking the road. One of them had just been held up by five armed bandits who got away with the gasoline money. Oddly, instead of leaving the area immediately, the truck drivers were dallying and commiserating. The land cruiser finally managed to squeak past the trucks on this one-lane highway; it seems we missed the excitement by minutes.

On July 20, 2000. At Khenpo A Chö's hermitage, Lo ma ga (kLu ma Gompa) village,
Nyarong County.

After another harrowing drive along the same road from Kandzé to Baiyul
(Peyul), only a short distance from the police station/caravansary where we
had encountered the robbed truck, we turned off the highway onto what
must have been a fine sanded road used by logging trucks up until a few years
ago. I tried to identify this road on the detailed maps of western Sichuan and
it seems that it would have to be the now impassible road from Litang to
Kandzé. After a few kilometers into the backcountry, the land cruiser could
go no farther because the river that runs alongside the road had encroached
upon the embankment and eaten away great chunks of the highway. We then
most happily proceeded without Mr. Tea, in the felicitous company of Lama
Chang (i.e., Lama Puyok), after promising to meet up again with Mr. Tea at
about 6:00 p.m. at the same spot. After a short walk of about twenty minutes
we were met—as if by magic or telepathy—by two teenaged novice monks
and two of the nuns that we had left at this turnoff the day before on our
way back from Ya chas Gompa. They insisted on carrying our backpacks,
running on ahead to gather a large quantity of fragrant flowers for the altars
of the hermitage. Significantly, all the flowers were either red or yellow, as if
to reflect the harmony between the red and the yellow traditions of Tibetan
Buddhism, which characterized the life of the Khenpo! Along the way, we saw
evidence of the imprudent clear-cutting that has caused ecological damage
throughout the region. No dwellings were in sight, but we came upon a lama
and his wife drying valerian roots by spreading them out on the roadway.
We stopped briefly for an idyllic lunch, far away from the intrusions of cell
phones and computers. Continuing along the ever more washed-out road,
we encountered an old man with a horse who kindly offered to carry some of
the baggage. After about a three-hour trek, we crossed a river on a relatively
recently constructed bridge, from which we entered the immediate vicinity of
the Khenpo's hermitage. A small stupa appeared on the left. Further down in
the valley, the village of Lo ma ga (kLu ma gompa) with its modest monastery
was now visible. The village was a charming place, and the approaching valley

one of the most beautiful landscapes in this part of the world, in spite of the severe deforestation in the region.

Our team of researchers in eastern Tibet, on the trail to Lumaga village.

We could see the hermitage, which is a small cabin built entirely of unpainted wood, above the stupa on the mountain slope. It was set apart from the meadow adorned with the flowers of midsummer by a straggling stockade meant to protect the vegetable garden positioned in front of the rickety porch. We ascended the slope and soon, inspired by the spiritual feeling of the place, we removed our shoes and begin to make prostrations along with the novices and the nuns. Fortunately, John Morgan and I were already acclimatized to the altitude because we had arrived fresh from doing research in Dolpo. We must have been at about 3,700 meters. Completing our climb, we found ourselves surrounded by a group of disciples and relatives of the Khenpo who had been awaiting our arrival. Lama Norta invited us in to join in venerating this place of the life, practice, and death of the holy Khenpo. Masses of fresh flowers placed in vases were situated in every possible empty space inside the hermitage. We were so happy to have arrived that we spontaneously offered prostrations, mantras, supplications, and tears of devotion and joy. Thanks to the explanations of Lama Puyok, Lama Norta agreed to the interview process: then we all settled down to tea.

Douglas Duckworth and I interviewed Lama Norta on the manifestation of the rainbow body by Khenpo A Chö. Lama Norta, nephew of the Khenpo was an eyewitness of the death process. The interview was conducted in the hermitage of the Khenpo, where these paranormal events had taken place in the summer of 1998. We were assisted by Lama Puyok, chaplain of the Ani Gompa outside Kandzé, one of the main towns of this part of Sichuan. Lama Puyok who was a close disciple of the Khenpo, assisted in clarifying aspects of Lama Norta's Khampa dialect during the interview.

Francis Tiso and Douglas Duckworth interview Lama Norta with the help of Lama Piyok inside Khenpo A Chö's hermitage.

Our First Interviews

Lama Norta explained that his uncle was a very humble man. He did not brag about the teachings he had received or the lamas under whom he had studied. He spoke often of the importance of cultivating compassion, both in meditation and in practice. Those who knew him recognized his high level of spiritual realization. Khenpo A Chö would lock himself inside the hermitage for periods of strict retreat. However, Lama Norta told us that he had seen Khenpo A Chö *outside* the hermitage, circumambulating it during one of these strict retreats, an episode recounted—in interviews conducted a few years after ours—by a Nyingmapa Khenpo. The Khenpo gave few initiations but would work intensively with select disciples, many of whom were from the Nyarong region. He was also very supportive of the nuns whom we met near Kandzé and favored them with many special teachings, which may explain their extraordinary joy, devotion, and energy.

Lama Norta told us that two young nephews of the Khenpo, Chung Cherow and Pakpa (Purba) Dorje, were present at the time of the Khenpo's death. Lobzang Nyendrak was also present, but he was now in retreat, two day's journey from the village. There were also two young monks, Sonam Gyaltsen and Rinchen Tsering, who were in India studying at Mindrolling Gompa in Clement Town. Because of our time constraints, we focused on interviewing Lama Norta.

Lama Piyok and Lama Norta during an interview, July 2000.

Lama Norta recounted some of the extraordinary things that occurred two years previously, at the time of the death of his beloved teacher. Lama Puyok interrupted quite often to clarify the conversation. As we had read in the biography that we obtained in Kandzé, at the time of the Khenpo's death the five colors of the rainbow manifested in the sky. Moreover, on several occasions, the air was pervaded by music, which was heard by monks and lay people. There were many witnesses to this from Khor Khot and the upper and lower regions of Khor Khot. His niece Tsering Tshitsho and her father and other relatives saw in the eastern direction that the sky was pervaded completely by rainbow colors.

The author of the biography, who was in retreat at the time, saw rainbow colors in the sky for two days in the direction of the road to the retreat place. And on the next day, Gyu Ja Sherab Gyaltsen heard the news of the lama's death, and he too saw some signs, which we presume to have been rainbows. Moreover, the light of the sun, which was like copper, appeared like a body of light for a long time at the time of liberation (death) in the eastern direction. All the persons from the inner circle of disciples witnessed this. During days following the Khenpo's death, his attendants and servants, young and old, performed daily circumambulations of the cabin, offering supplications and prayers. Day after day, the Khenpo's body became smaller and smaller. After seven days, there was nothing left. He had manifested the uncontaminated *vajra body*. His own lama had prophesied that this would occur. This manifestation could be considered the uncontaminated rainbow body of great transformation, liberation into the body of light, without leaving hair or nails. Both the Khenpo and his teacher, before they had met, already directly knew the outcome of his entire life. Lama Norta quotes from the guidebook to the region of Ne Tang, which states: "not far from this place there will be a glorious incarnation of wisdom; this embodied one will be endowed with experience and realization and all the fortunate disciples will meet him at that time by the power of their aspirations." It is also said that he was an incarnation of the great siddha, Ye she Yung Nan, one of the twenty-five disciples of Padmasambhava. This incarnation was referred to by his "self-liberated name," given him by his holy teacher when he was young studying electricity. This was prophesied by the previous Tulku Dollung, the name illustrating the name of the Dharmadhatu. Lama Norta told us that the other prophecies are easy to understand without needing to elaborate on them.

Researchers welcomed within the stockade at the hermitage of Khenpo A Chö.

In this interview we immediately note that the notion of fulfillment of prophecies is at least as important as the paranormal phenomena being described. Within the world of discourse of our Tibetan informants, prophesy is a key feature of hagiographical accounts,[59] in marked contrast to the way Buddhism is described by Western scholars. There is the "real" Buddhism of traditional communities in the highlands of Southeast Asia and Tibet, and there is an academic description of Buddhism that seems to be missing some of traditional Buddhism's characteristic DNA. The problem impinges on our research because it requires us to interpret the data with greater sympathy for the insiders' view. At the same time, sensitivity to the insider view also cautions us against adopting a literally descriptive approach to the whole range of phenomena that are presented as expressions of faith and devotion. Just as Lama A Khyug warned: what is seen may, in fact, not be what is known.

Having reviewed the main points of the biography of the Khenpo, we proceeded during the rest of the interview with the set of questions that I had written out and had translated into Tibetan.

Q. What was the date and time of the passing away of Khenpo A Chö?

A. It was two years ago, almost exactly at this time of the year. The seventh day of the seventh Tibetan month.

Q. Did his passing away take place here in this house?

A. He was lying on the bed (the meditation box) with his right hand under his cheek; he was not sick, he was lying there reciting the mantra *om mani padme hung*. His breath was very weak. They were discussing that this would be the time when he would be passing away.

Q. So did he die at that moment?

A. There were six people present. Lama Norta with his two nephews, Lama Nyendrak, Sonam Gyaltsen, and Rinchen Tsering—the latter two are now studying in India.

Q. Are they monks?

A. Yes, they are the monks.

(They are the monks we later interviewed in Clement Town, India.)

Q. After his death, what happened to the body right away and in the days that followed?

A. After his breath stopped, his body remained there, and his face become pinkish, like an eight year old child's flesh; the wrinkles disappeared. They did not take pictures, but if they had taken pictures it would have been amazing. At that time, they were so sad that he passed away. For this reason, they did not think to take pictures, it did not occur to them.

Q. After that, did they notice any changes in the body? Did it get wrinkled again? Did it shrink? Were there any signs of decay? What happened in the next day or two?

A. They asked Lama A Khyug of Ya chas Gompa what to do with the body; he said to wrap the body in a yellow robe, it is the robe all Gelug monks have, a symbol of Shakyamuni. He said not to tell anyone that he had died because there might be obstacles if there were disciples and great lamas present. According to the Lama, there are some good people, but there are some bad people round about, and they might spread the word in a way that would create problems, or they might even try to steal objects that belonged to the Khenpo. Day by day, observing the yellow robe that covered the body, they noticed that the bones of his arms and legs diminished in size. Lama A Khyug at Ya chas gompa said to leave the body alone for seven days.

Q. Were there any other phenomena besides the shrinking that they noticed?

A. They were very saddened by the death of the lama so they did not wander around looking for signs, but there were many people in the monastery below this mountain, old monks and nuns, who saw many rainbows over this hermitage, and they wondered to themselves, why are there so many rainbows over the hermitage? Also people from where Lama Puyok is from, near Kandzé, could see the rainbows. Another monk, Sonam Gyaltsen, while walking outside, heard an amazing song coming out of the hermitage. He entered the hut and heard the voice coming from the sky above. At the time, he thought that it would have been good to have been able to make a recording of that music, but he did not have a tape recorder.

Q. How long did it take for the body to dissolve completely?

A. Seven days. Lama A Khyug at the Ya Chas monastery told them not to look below the robe for seven days. They followed these instructions. After seven days Lama Norta, Sonam Gyaltsen, Rinchen Tsering, and Lobzang Nyendrak looked under the robe and found nothing. There was no body to be found.[60] (So it might have taken less than seven days.)

Q. Where was the body all this time? Was it here in this room where we are having the interview?

A. No, it was in the bedroom full of shrine objects, not in the room where we were taping the interview. Even from outside the hut there was an amazing fragrance emitted by the corpse, an amazing perfume. Lama Norta says he himself experienced this perfume, as did many of the older people who were outside, circumambulating the hermitage.

Q. Does Lama Norta know of any other manifestations of rainbow body that have taken place in recent times?

A. There was one monk from Nyarong, Pema Dudul, who attained rainbow body, this was a long time ago, but he heard about it. This was about 150 years ago.

Q. Did he ever hear of some holy person who attained rainbow body and who left an imprint or impression at that time on cloth or on stone or some other kind of imprint when they attained it?

A. No, he has never heard of such a thing.

Q. On the yellow cloth, there was no mark of any kind?

A. No, there was no mark.

Q. Do they still have the robe?

A. It is in the possession of Lobzang Nyendrak.

Q. Anything else that they would like to say about this beautiful experience?

A. He does not have anything else to say about the way the rainbow body was manifested. When the Khenpo was young, he studied the *Five Main Treatises* [of Maitreya-Asanga] at Sera Monastery in Lhasa and memorized them all. Whatever questions you would ask him, he would know the answers. He was always giving teachings that would benefit people. Even when he was dealing with someone that was quite busy or rude, he could give appropriate teachings that would make their minds workable. He was a truly unique teacher.

Q. Has anyone had a visionary experience, a visit from Khenpo A Chö since his passing away?

A. Yes, certainly. Lama Puyok has had a vision of Khenpo A Chö. He had a lot of disciples and many of them have had this experience. He has appeared in dreams.

Q. And Lama Norta?

A. He says yes, he has had such an experience. Also, Lobzang Nyendrak was in retreat at one time. This happened to him when he was not sleeping. At that time he had the experience of Khenpo A Chö tugging on his shirt sleeve and telling him, "Practice well, meditate well. Be attentive."

Q. I commented that once I was saying Mass, and at the time of reciting the Our Father, my mind opened and I had a visionary experience of a monk who was one of the founders of Brother David's monastery, in happiness and surrounded by light. So I know what they are talking about and I have a lot of respect for their willingness to speak to us. So I am very humbled by your willingness to tell us these things.

A. Lama Norta resumed speaking. Once a nun had a dream of a high cliff. She was falling off the cliff and the moment she thought of the Khenpo, he came to rescue her.

As we left the hermitage compound, we exchanged gifts and greetings with the various disciples and felt ourselves surrounded by a great sphere of peace and luminosity, as if we had truly connected with the essential reality of the rainbow body, which is not so much the manifestation of one man's spiritual attainment as it is a state of authentic liberation from all that weighs us down. This message became more and more vivid in the days to come, during which we would be dealing with ever more depressing misadventures. One of these was a road washout that made it impossible to travel to Nyarong Gompa to interview Lama rDo lo and Lama Nyendrak. We also had further difficulties with our driver, Mr. Tea, so we regretfully decided to conclude our research trip after eight days. However, upon our return to Kandzé, while having a light supper with a Tibetan family, we were treated to a magnificent display: a huge, perfect half-circle rainbow over the entire city of Kandzé. The sign seemed to be a kind of reassuring confirmation that whatever we had done was in some way worthwhile.

Later that summer, I was back in Kandzé, on August sixth, the day of the Feast of the Transfiguration, and I most intensely wanted to celebrate the Eucharist. After all, it is the day when the church celebrates the pre-resurrection manifestation of a kind of light body in Jesus Christ. The day grew later without an opportunity to celebrate the Mass. My companions, one of whom is a Catholic priest, seemed indifferent, and I felt extremely bad about this. By August eighth this feeling had grown into a real sense of total detachment—not a pleasant kind of detachment, but a sense of alienation from all rituals, ceremonies, prayers, verbalizations, rinpoches, priests, lamas, and so on. I felt that we are all victims of circumstance and linguistic convention and that the whole game of research and religion in general is really quite futile. I felt that I had no access to truth in the ultimate sense, but at least I should make an effort to end inauthentic behaviors in my own life. Over the next few days and weeks, this viewpoint matured into a constant state of awareness that seemed to blend my mind, my perceptions of things, and the things perceived into a single pure act. The blending seemed more real than the distinctions among mind, sense data, and the otherness of any object. I nurtured this awareness with readings from the *Avadhuta Gita*, a radical nondualist text rooted in the Upanishadic tradition. I felt my alienation and repugnance softening into a persistent nondual view, abiding in that sense of blending, with ready access to the "natural state of contemplation" about which I had learned from the dzogchen master, Namkhai Norbu Rinpoche, which can also be found in Milarepa's teachings on contemplation. This state of awareness was open to me at any time I cared to examine it. I did not have to force or fabricate anything to enter into or to meditate within that state, and I found no difficulty in dealing with daily activities as well. They were effortless. This lasted to the end of September. After about six weeks, things apparently returned to normal, but I continued to have access to that natural state, which sometimes has a very ordinary quality, but which often leaps out at me as if reality had a unique, if unromantic, vividness. I feel that this mindstate is a gift from the mad yogin of Ya chas Gompa, who has passed away in recent years, apparently manifesting the rainbow body in a restricted form, as he promised. His words and his insistence on heart-mind (*sems*) over physical seeing (*mig*) crashed in on me and stayed with me; perhaps that change of heart (*sems*) is more valuable than what might be recorded by a video camera.

The following winter, in February 2001, I was able to go to India in order to interview the two young monks who had been eyewitnesses to the phenomena surrounding the death of Khenpo A Chö. These two young monks, very modest in demeanor as is appropriate to their vocation, confirmed the raw data gathered in Tibet. In the course of the translation process, however, a few things have been lost. For one thing, they definitely confirmed that Khenpo A Chö had been a disciple of the great dzogchen master H. H. Dudjom Rinpoche, one of the most important Nyingma lamas of modern times. Moreover, the tone of monk Rinchen Tsering at times seems to convey a lack of enthusiasm. One might have expected that a person who had seen such a remarkable occurrence would have been taken up, even three years later, with a vigorous conviction that he had undergone a life changing experience. However, that kind of enthusiasm is almost entirely lacking. In this interview, the young monk's behavior was in total contrast with Lama Puyok in Kandzé. Even his companion, monk Sonam Gyaltsen, was modest and low-key in style. Their affect may simply reflect the humility appropriate to their status as monks in formation. At the same time, since their testimony corroborates the materials in the previous interviews and the written accounts, I wondered if they had simply decided to respond in a rote, identical fashion to my questions in the two separate interviews. We also have no way of knowing if they had been coached by someone at Mindrolling. Keep in mind, however, that Tibetan monks are used to memorizing extensive liturgical and philosophical texts, and the nearly identical character of their responses to my questions could have been the result of intentional preparation on their part. Usually an oral account of an event, or the retelling of an epic poem by a "singer of tales" involves the use of varied poetic themes, elements of creative embellishment, interpretations on the basis of personal insights, and the like. We find little of the oral tradition in these interviews. In fact, both monks resist any attempt to elicit an account of their personal experiences before or after the death of the Khenpo. Could this be a kind of evasion, somewhat like that which we found with the Gelugpa rinpoches at Kandzé?

> February 11, 2001, At Mindrolling Gompa:
> Interview with monk Rinchen Tsering by
> Francis Tiso; the translator was Lobsang, a
> teacher at Dekhyil Ling in Dehra Dun, on
> Sahastradhara Road.

The interviews had been arranged on February nine. On that day, I had gone to meet with the abbot of this historic Nyingma Gompa, Ven. D. G. Khochhen Tulku. After some difficulties with communication in the monastery office, one of the two monks, Sonam Gyaltsen, turned up. He seemed the classic village simple soul, totally monastic, completely humble. He graciously endured our attention, and then we headed over to the Abbot's office. I was greeted by the huge hand of someone used to glad-handing, a beefy Tibetan with a somewhat British affect. It turned out to be Lodi Gyaltsen Gyari, the official representative of the government in exile of H. H. the Dalai Lama to the United States, who just happened to be there at the right time. He explained my project to the abbot while poor Sonam-la was standing on the cold floor in bare feet. The rest of us were all seated on comfortable chairs and tea was provided. It turned out that Lodi Gyaltsen Gyari is none other than the former king of Nyarong, a classmate of our Swiss-Tibetan friend Mr. Tenpa Shitsegang, and he was fully informed both about the case of Khenpo A Chö, and of Catholic Christianity. He made an effort to explain (in Tibetan) to the Abbot what the Catholic Church believes about saints, miracles, and causes of canonization. Also present was a young dignitary, Tulku Penor, whose previous incarnation we would hear about in the interview with Rinchen Tsering. Thanks to the support and kindness of the *rgyal po* (king), the Abbot gave his approval for the interview, which would take place on the following Sunday at 2:00 p.m.

At Mindrolling Gompa, Northern India: Abbot Ven. D. G. Khochhen Tulku, Ven. Tulku Penor, Hon. Lodi Gyaltsen Gyari (formerly H. H. the Dalai Lama's Representative to the U.S. Government).

It turns out that there is a close historical connection between Mindrolling (in central Tibet) and kLu ma Gompa in Nyarong, which explains why the two disciples were now studying here at Mindrolling-in-exile.

On the day of the interviews, I concelebrated the daily Mass at St. Mary's Parish Church in Clement Town. Afterwards, I went back to Dehra Dun by cab. I then proceeded by the same cab along the Sahasradhara Road where the Sakyapa place is and, a little further on, the Drikung Kagyu Monastery. I picked up Lobsang, the translator who hails from the region around Tabo monastery (northern

India, in a region of Tibetan language and culture famous for the translations done in the tenth century by Rin chen bzang po). He turned out to be a reasonably skillful translator who understood my accent, both English and Tibetan, and could deliver my questions to the young monks in their Khampa dialect.

Both of these monks, whom we had heard about during our interviews in kLu ma gompa, impressed me with their intelligence and reasonable character. Sonam Gyaltsen (who is now serving as the Abbot's attendant) is a bit dreamy and detached, but on the day of the interview it was also evident that he is quite penetrating and precise. Rinchen Tsering has the same sideburns as the old Khenpo, and has a more assertive, almost athletic, personality, and is more eager to engage in back-and-forth discussions.

We had no difficulty interviewing each of them separately in a relatively quiet room overlooking the new construction to the back of the Mindrolling Temple. I presented each of them, on Friday, with a burgundy colored shawl, and today with an offering of rupees and khataks.

Interviews at Mindrolling Gompa, Dehra Dun, India

The first interview was with Rinchen Tsering on the life, death, and manifestation of rainbow body of Khenpo A Chö:

At Mindrolling Gompa, Clement Town, India: Interview with Lobsang (translator) and eyewitness monk Rinchen Tsering.

Q. When exactly did he pass away?

A. He does not know the exact date. The month was July.

Q. Was it the month of July, or was it the seventh Tibetan month, which would have been August?

A. He thinks maybe it would have been August.

Q. Where did his passing away take place?

A. Nyarong, Lho mo gompa, Lho mo ga village. There is a meditation place set up by a rock. He passed away inside that place.

(We knew where this is, since we visited it in August of 2000; this question was just to verify the facts.)

Q. How did he die? What was the cause of his death?

A. The Tibetan date was the sixth (of the month); it was noticed that the lama felt very weak and sleepy at that time. He was praying the mani (*om mani padme hum*) prayer a lot. The lama took a very deep breath. He stayed very quiet and the disciples left the room. After that, he passed away.

Q. Who was present at the time of his death?

A. There were four persons, three of whom were nephews of the Khenpo and the other was Lobsang Nyentak, a very old student of the Khenpo. He had studied twenty-three years under Khenpo A Chö. Lobzang Nyentak has stayed in Tibet. Tsultrim Gyamtso (Sonam Gyamtso?) was also there.

Q. Weren't there two little boys there as well?

A. Yes, Purba Dorje, the son of the Khenpo's younger sister, and Chung Cherow.

Q. After the Khenpo's death, what happened to his body?

A. At that time, they saw that the Khenpo's body was getting whiter and whiter. It started to get very shiny. There was a very sweet smell. Outside [the hermitage] there was a very fine rain and they saw rainbows in the sky. Tsultim Gyamtso was doing puja at that time and the two of them set things up and placed the body in a box [this would be the wooden bed that Khenpo used also as his place of puja and meditation] and covered it with a yellow cloth.

Q. Who went to see Lama A Chö at Ya Chas Gompa [to let him know that the Khenpo had passed away and] to ask him what to do? One of them went to see him at that time.

A. Well, they were all in the same place and the Khenpo was praying and the others were doing other practices.

(They misunderstood the question because the two names are the same, even though I had identified the other master pretty clearly.)

Q. You see there is Khenpo A Chö and there is this other monk named Lama A Khyug at Ya Chas Gompa and I understand from the other people [I interviewed] that when the Khenpo died, one of the four disciples went to talk to Lama A Chö to ask for instructions because the two of them were good friends. They had the same name, so it is a little confusing.

A. He [Rinchen tsering] went to see Lama A Chö. So, at that time he went also to see Sonam Puntsog, who was also a teacher, and he went to Lama A Chö.

Q. Is Sonam Puntsog the one who wrote the *rnam thar* (the hagiography)?

A. Yes, he is. I have this text. He is in prison now.

Q. All right. So now we can get all the facts straight. Was there any evidence of shriveling up or decay?

A. The body was shriveling. It was becoming smaller and smaller. On the spot, it disappeared.

Q. Was there any evidence of decay? Was there a bad odor, did flies come, anything like that?

A. At that time, no flies, nothing came near the dead body.

Q. Any phenomena around the body? Please be very detailed.... Did any birds come, etc.?

A. He doesn't know a great deal. As he said before, the body looked very white, and [outside of the hermitage] there was a [fine] rain, and in the sky they saw rainbows, and there was a very good smell. They also heard sounds, melodies. Someone was singing outside, near the temple. When they went out, they felt the sound was coming to meet them; if they remained inside, they felt the sound inside [the hermitage]. It was as if someone were playing a tape recorder somewhere nearby.

Q. And was it a song with words that they heard and could understand?

A. They did not hear any words, they only heard melodies, sounds.

Q. What were your own experiences in that period of one week after Khenpo died?

A. At that time they felt very sad from the bottom of their hearts; they felt nothing else, just very sad.

Q. How long did the process of dissolution take?

A. The body of the Khenpo was in the box for seven days; because on the eighth day, it was the fifteenth day of the lunar month, a very important day on the Tibetan calendar. On that day they looked in the box and there was nothing there; so the body had disappeared in the course of seven days.

Q. Do you know of any similar events that have occurred in recent times? (The case mentioned in Tibetan was one that took place in Nyarong about a hundred years ago.)

A. Yes, according to the *rnam thar* it was about a hundred years ago.

They have heard about Tenpa Yungtso and Tashi Gyamtso. When Lama Tashi Gyamtso died, he manifested rainbow body, too.

Q. How long ago did he live?

A. He doesn't know how long ago it was. We would have to look carefully in the *rnam thar.*

Q. After the seven days had passed, were there any traces of the body?

A. When the Khenpo died, they removed all his clothing (monastic habit) when they covered him with the yellow cloth. In the course of seven days, as the body got smaller and smaller, they left it alone. Then on the eighth day the time had come to open up the cloth and do what needed to be done, to give the remains to [be eaten by] the animals. But nothing was left under the yellow cloth.

Q. No hair, no nails?

A. They saw nothing.

Q. What happened to the yellow cloth with which the body was covered? Where is the yellow cloth now?

A. At the present time, the yellow cloth is in the temple, the monastery. At the monastery they are planning to build a new temple and when they do they want to keep the cloth inside that temple [as a relic].

Q. Were there any signs or impressions of Khenpo's body on the cloth?

A. Nothing was there on the yellow cloth.

Q. Did you see his body at any time before it was covered? Did you see the body at any time after it was covered?

A. He saw the body.

Q. Yes, before it was covered. Did he see it at any time after it was covered?

A. It was always covered.

Q. Now, have you had any experiences of the Khenpo since his death, such as visions or dreams?

A. He says that he has not had any dreams of this kind.

Q. Have you ever heard of someone who manifested the rainbow body who left an imprint on rock, on cloth, or something like that?

A. Yes, he has heard.

Q. That they left an impression? Like whom?

A. In Kanzé, when Lama Pema died, all this happened.

Q. He left some kind of an impression?

A. When he died there were rainbows. He says is now getting many ideas about when the lama was dying. If you want to see about Tulku Pema (Penor?), when he died, his body shriveled up very small and at the present time you can see his body which is this big (indicating about ten inches). [This young man cannot be the tulku of Penor Rinpoche, former head of the Nyingma Order. He is too old.]

Q. They preserved his body?

A. Our Penor Tulku is the young man who was here [with the Abbot and with Mr. Gyari] the other day; is he the incarnation of the one who you are now describing?

A. Yes, he is the reincarnation of that lama.

Q. That's good, that's very important. What do you understand to be the Buddhist meaning of the manifestation by Khenpo A Chö of the rainbow body?

A. The meaning of the manifestation is that these men studied Buddhism very deeply and this is the reason. That is the cause.

Q. When somebody does something like this it shows they have attained a high state of realization. So this is a very obvious Buddhist question: if someone has made the Bodhisattva vow, how would the manifestation of the rainbow body show us something about [their faithfulness to] the Bodhisattva vow? Compassion, realization of wisdom, bodhichitta, and so forth? How does this show us these things?

A. He doesn't know exactly how to reply, but he feels that if they studied what Buddhism teaches, that would be the reason.

Q. It isn't an easy question, I know, but what is the connection between the Buddhist teachings and this wonderful experience? Maybe we have to think about that for our whole lives? What were the practices that the Khenpo followed in his hermitage? What was he doing? Dzogchen, *yidam, ngon dro, bodhichitta*?

A. After he had studied for twenty years in the Nyingma monastery he went to Sera, to the Gelugpa gompa in Lhasa. There he has studied with the help of Sherab Gyalpo and Khyentse.

Q. What did he practice, what were his favorite practices?

A. His favorite thing was not to do debate, his preference was to stay in meditation.

Q. There are many types of meditation. There is *samatha, vipasyana*, mind training, there are many *yidams*, what were his preferences?

A. He did many different kinds of meditation, one month one kind, another month another kind. This went on for eighteen years continuously.

Q. If you read, for example, the retreat manual of Jamgon Kongrul, you can see a three-year retreat in which many practices are to be done sequentially. Maybe this was what he was doing.

A. Rinpoche has already announced that Khenpo A Chö is one of the famous lamas of Tibet and the main point is that this has been acknowledged.[61]

Q. OK. What was Khenpo A Chö's relationship with the Lama of Ya chas Gompa, Lama A Khyug?

A. The main thing is that they are relatives and both have a great deal of understanding and they are good friends.

Q. What are the key teachings of Khenpo A Chö? What are the things we should remember about his life?

A, He doesn't have many ideas about this. Lobsang Puntsog knows much about this.

Q. Well, what did he get out of studying with Khenpo A Chö? What teaching really helped him a lot?

(tape ends)

We also learned that the original writings of Khenpo A Chö are now kept by Lobzang Nyendak at Kanzen Zong, Zakhok Shang, Drakchok Monastery. This place is about a three-hour walk from Zakhok Shang, in eastern Tibet (now Sichuan). The two young monks left Tibet about three weeks after the rainbow body manifestation to seek further studies at Mindrolling Gompa in India. The main themes of Khenpo's life were peacefulness and *ahimsa* to all sentient beings.

The second interview was with monk Sonam Gyamtso, a young disciple and eyewitness of the death of the late Khenpo A Chö. Interview conducted by Francis Tiso; translator was Lobsang of the Sakyapa Gompa and Tibetan Colony on Sahasradhara Road, Dehra Dun. Date: Feb. 11, 2001

I began by explaining that I went to kLu ma Gompa in Nyarong last summer and was able to visit with Lama Puyok, Lama Norta, and the two nephews of Khenpo A Chö. The young monks had already seen the questions in written form, and now they would be able to answer them orally. I told them that the translator, Lobsang, would help me with the English version which will appear on the same tape as our conversation in Tibetan.

At Mindrolling Gompa, Clement Town, India: Interview with Lobsang (translator) and eyewitness monk, Sonam Gyamtso.

Q. Regarding Khenpo A Chö, when exactly did he pass away?

A. The seventh day of July, 1998 (i.e., the seventh Tibetan month).

Q. And where did his passing away take place?

A. Near to the kLu ma Ga Gompa.

Q. How did he die? What was the cause of death?

A. Due to old age; at that time there was no evidence of trouble at all, no suffering [from disease], just old age.

Q. Who was present at the time of his death?

A. At that time there were four persons. Three were his students; one was his nephew.

Q. Just one nephew?

A. Well, more exactly three were his nephews and one was his disciple.

Q. And Lama Norta?

A. He is the nephew, and Khu Shu and the other one were nephews, and Lobsang Nyiendrak was a disciple. (Note that he fails to mention himself and Rinchen Tsering! So what he means is that there were six people present, as we will see below.)

Q. After the Khenpo's death, what happened to his body?

A. After the death, for seven days, according to the Tibetan tradition, the body was covered and kept in the room. After the seven days, in accordance with Tibetan tradition, the body should be uncovered and removed from the box. But at that time, nothing was there in the box.

Q. You mean in the bed? (The Khenpo did his meditation and slept in a box in his shrine-room; this is normal practice among hermits in Tibet.)

A. Yes, we were obliged to find the body, but the body was gone.

So after seven days...

Q. Now this is another question that occurs to me. When the Khenpo died, did he stay in meditation position (i.e., in so-called *thugdam*, when the region around the heart remains warm after death), or was he lying flat?

A.When he died, he was not meditating.

Q. Was there any evidence of shriveling up or decay?

A. He said there was no bad odor. The dead body decreased, it got smaller and smaller.

Q. So there was no bad odor, no flies, no insects coming near the body?

A. No, nothing. Everything was clean at that time.

Q. We are just establishing facts, and his personal testimony to these facts. And now, were there any phenomena around the body? Please be very detailed and precise.

A. At that time, no one was there except these four persons. They smelled a very good odor at that time, and the environment was very exciting. They saw rainbows. There was a fine rain, not a heavy rain. In this rain, one's body did not get wet. After three or four days, they heard a very melodious song. When they looked outside, they saw nothing at all. They enjoyed it very much.

Q. What was it like? Were there musical instruments?

A. Both of them heard something like a voice that was singing, at other times it sounded as if there was someone playing a guitar.

Q. What were *your* experiences in the time after his death?

A. So at that time, they felt very sad, all of them, because such a famous lama had died. They prayed; their Lama was a very old man, and so he died, but they prayed at time that his reincarnation would come very soon. They prayed a great deal at that time.

Q. Did he perhaps have any dreams in that period of time, that week, those seven days after the death?

A. No special dreams, but a month [before] the death, Khenpo celebrated a *den shuk*, what we call a *den shuk*.

Q. Was this the one-month ceremony for after death?

A. This is the *den shuk* ceremony. For example, His Holiness or some other famous lamas put on their ceremonial hat and go outside the temple. Khenpo A Chö did a *den shuk* ceremony with the princesses.

Q. The princesses?

A. The *Khadroma* (*dakinis*).

Q. Oh, the *Khadroma*.

A. In Khandey Temple, on the day of the *dakinis*. Khenpo A Chö took *den shuk* with the *Khadroma* (*dakinis*).

Q. How did ... did this happen in a dream ... who saw this?

A. It was in front of all the lamas. It was with a group of lamas.

Q. One month after...

A. One month before he died.

Ah, one month before the death! OK, good.

Q. How long did the process of dissolution take, how long did it take?

A. It took only one week.

Q Yes, he said that already. Just to be precise. Some people said it took less.

A. Exactly seven days. On the eighth day they opened the box and Khenpo's body had disappeared.

Q. Good, that was reported by Rinchen Tsering. Do you know of any similar events that have taken place in recent times?

A. He has no idea of this.

Q. After the seven days had passed, were there any traces of the body?

A. No. Only two or three hairs on the cushion. Nothing else.

Q. No *ring sel* [solid relic droplets], anything like that?

A. No, nothing.

Q. What happened to the yellow cloth with which the body was covered? Were there any signs on the cloth?

A. There were no traces, nothing, on the yellow cloth. The cloth was very clean.

Q. Did you see his body at any time after his death?

A. No.

Q. Because it was covered?

A. Yes, and because we two lamas are younger than the other nephew [Lama Norta], and he might have some idea regarding the body, but not us.

Q. What experiences did you have personally in the week after the death, or more recently?

A. He had no experiences about the death of the Khenpo.

Q. Not even some time after the death?

A. The main thing that he felt is that he was happy that the Khenpo died without any suffering. That was the main reason why he was happy at the time.

Q. Have you ever heard of a rainbow body manifestation that left a mark on cloth, rock, or some other material, in the past?

A. In Nyarong, there was the case of Pema Dudul. When he died, he also manifested this experience.

Q. Did he leave any mark on cloth or stone?

A. At that time there was a lot of rain in the air; when he passed away, nails and some hair were left.

Q. What do you understand to be the Buddhist meaning of the passing of Khenpo A Chö?

A. The Tibetans believe that if there are rainbows in the sky on the day of death of a person it is a very important sign of accomplishment.

Q. What practices did the Khenpo follow when he was living in the hermitage? What was the relationship between his Nyingma and Gelugpa training and practices?

A. He had a relationship between both Nyingma and Gelug traditions because he studied his basic knowledge from a Nyingma gompa, and after a number of years, he studied with the Gelug in Lhasa.

Q. And so he studied both. Now what practices did he actually do while he was in the hermitage? What texts did he follow, what practices was he doing for all those years that he was in the hermitage?

A. When he studied with the Gelug, he studied the *Five Treatises*, when he was in Lhasa.

With the Nyingma he studied Lung ma and then with the Gelug he studied the Five Treatises and *lho jhong*.

Q. Did he also study dzogchen?

A. After he completed his Gelug studies, he studied dzogchen with Tenzhup Rinpoche.

Q. Where did Tenzhup Rinpoche live?

A. He has no idea.

Q. We met Lama A Khyug of Ya Chas Gompa, and we understand that he was a dharma friend of Khenpo A Chö. What was their relationship and do you know Lama Khyug?

A. They are relatives, cousins.

Q. Does he know this Lama?

A. He knows him.

Q. They told us in Nyarong that it was Lama A Khyug who told them to cover the body with the cloth and all those instructions. Now, what were the key teachings of Khenpo A Chö, anything important we should remember about his life?

A. Khenpo has written many books, small books. He has written very important *pechas* and those *pechas* have been handed over to Lobzang Nyendrak. He is at the present time in Tibet. It is important that the Khenpo has written a number of books and he has written a very good book that was handed over to Lobzang Nyendrak. At that time Lobzang was living with these old monks, and one of these monks was a nephew, who is living in Tibet. He has copies of the books; so if you want copies of that *pecha,* you can contact Lobzang Nyendrak or that nephew.

Q. We should write down those names and we can try to write a letter, or maybe ask Lama Piyok from Kandzé to help us locate the texts. What do the people in Nyarong say about Khenpo A Chö?

A. They say he was a very good Lama. The people of Nyarong spoke very sad words at that time, and they used to pray. All the religious people would come to the monastery to gather earth [as relics].

Q. Now that we have finished all the questions, would he like to say anything else to make things clear?

A. He doesn't have any special words for you. To know more about Khenpo A Chö, you will have to go to Tibet and talk to Lobzang Nyendrak; Sonam Gyamtso will write you a letter of introduction.

Q. We went last summer, and we met some people, but we can also go again to Tibet and interview some more people.

A. So, if you want to go to Tibet, he will give you some persons' names and he will write you some letters of introduction.

Interview with a Bonpo Master

After the interviews with the two young monks, I traveled to Kathmandu to meet with Loppon Tenzin Namdak, a Bonpo Rinpoche, at Triten Norbutse Bon Monastery. These are the notes from that conversation on February 17, 2001. In fact, we met on more than one occasion thanks to the kindness of several Western disciples of the Rinpoche.

Bonpo Abbot at Swayambhu, Kathmandu, Nepal: Ven. Loppon Tenzin Namdak.

Rinpoche spoke excellent English, having spent time in the Catholic monastery of Cauldey, which is located on an island in the British Channel. His style is that of a skilled lecturer, familiar with his subject. He told us this:

> The rainbow body *is* the realization attained through dzogchen. The Bonpo system has three paths: sutra, the path of renunciation; tantra, the path of transformation; dzogchen, the path of

liberation (*dol-lam*). Buddhahood is attained by purifying defilements, transforming impulses and emotions into wisdom, and self-liberation by which one leaves thoughts alone without following them. The true rainbow body is realized only through dzogchen, recognizing that everything comes from the basic nature of things. There were twenty-five masters of Bon in Tibet before the arrival of the Buddhist teachings from India, and each of these in succession attained the rainbow body. In the eighth century, the master was Tapihritsa, who transmitted the written text, *Zhang Zhung sNyan rgyud.*[62] Recent manifestations of the rainbow body include Sha dzar Rinpoche in 1934 and Ra dza Dawa Tragpa, his disciple. In 1987, Tso po Rinpoche attained the *jalus* in Khams at Teng Che in the Chamdo region, where there is a gompa at Ri Tse Drug (Six-Peak Mountain). There are two kinds of *jalus*: complete (*chen po*) or shrinkage of the body (*chung po*). *Chung po* is sometimes caused by an interruption, as when the body is touched by someone. *Chung po* can also be the result of a different technique of practice, which does not necessarily mean a lesser attainment. In dzogchen, attainment has nothing to do with thoughts. The nature of thought is arising and disappearing. Thoughts do not go anywhere! So the nature of thoughts is not a thing. At the time of death, after three days there is unconsciousness. A practitioner of dzogchen can handle this, but normal people think of nothing and are unconscious. They then are susceptible to believing that the lights and colors that appear are real, when such phenomena present themselves to consciousness in the after death state. Soon we are back in our normal fabricated reality. As we practice dzogchen, things become subtler and even solid things return to the source and appear as light. The same kind of thing occurs during the experience of dark retreat. You see lights, forms. The dark retreat gets us *thodgal* vision, which perceives that all things are a projection of mind itself; then one stabilizes this vision of things. You come to discover how *sems* arises from primordial awareness (*rigpa*). There is nothing beyond *rigpa*. Keep in mind that the motivation is, at the basis, compassion. Within the fact of practice itself is compassion. Without realization, our help for others is only temporary, mere palliatives. The realization of the true nature of mind enables one to benefit others with permanent benefits. Thus we can see that the perfection of giving is attained in the perfect non-attachment that arises in the realization of the natural state (*gnas lugs*), the stabile realization of which leads to action, not because of attachment or preference but in relation to the perceptions of others. The phenomena associated with the manifestation of the rainbow body include observing a rainbow light enveloping the body, both outside the room and inside; there are various shaped rainbows—straight, small and round, and so forth; a fine rain may fall, which is a sign of the proximity of the nagas, who are a symbol of welcome even for the living; there may be snowflakes (*me tog 'char*, which literally means a rain of flowers); the great realized masters' attainment of rainbow body (*'ja' lus*) includes sounds and harmless earthquakes; they can appear to others in dreams, but this is not considered too important. The body of light (*'od lus,*) is attained through tantric practice such as the six yogas; the *'ja' lus* is different—it depends on the instructions given in practice (and in fact, can be the same as the *'od lus*).

Rinpoche very kindly allowed us to photocopy a large number of texts from the Bonpo dzogchen teaching tradition, including a manual on the practice of dark retreat.[63] It is during dark retreats that the Bonpo masters work with the transformative energetic visions called *thodgal*, which bear fruit in the attainment of the rainbow body.

While we were interviewing Rinpoche, word came from Tibet that a Bonpo yogi named Rakshi Togden had died and was manifesting paranormal phenomena similar to those associated with the rainbow body. The rainbow body does not arise for those spiritual masters who are manifestations of action in the Buddhist sense of the term. The yogins who have manifested the rainbow body seem to have been, in most cases, people deeply committed to the contemplative path who chose not to perform

charitable services on a grand scale—to found organizations, to pen grandi-
ose literary self-promotions, and the like. The rainbow body flees from such
circumstances, and that is why the story of the yogi reveals the risk of what
we are doing in this research.

This ninety-two-year-old Bonpo monk of the Luphug Gompa passed away
in Bachen, Nagchu, in eastern Tibet on January 3, 2001, about forty-five
days before our interview with Loppon Tenzin Namdak in Kathmandu. This
monk had already predicted the date of his own death. He had been doing
spiritual practices from childhood. The body manifested signs of the rainbow
body including special sounds, a particular kind of snowfall, birds sitting qui-
etly while facing towards his room, circular and straight rainbows in the sky,
and white light in the sky. In fact, these phenomena were continuing on the
day of our interview, February 17, 2001.

Later we learned that the monk's nephew decided to publicize the event
and actually took a tape measure to determine the progressive shrinkage of
the corpse. He then made the two-day journey by car to Lhasa to tell the story
to some journalists. When he got back to the monastery, the shrinkage had
stopped. To make matters worse, the publicity naturally attracted the attention of the authorities who arrested the nephew and harassed other people
as well. Finally, in desperation, the nephew secretly cremated the remains.
Now there is no mention of relics, and the whole matter is something of an
embarrassment. At the same time, given the negative consequences, one can
still make a case for the reality of the paranormal phenomenon in this case.
Had there been no paranormal manifestations, the nephew would not have
tried to publicize the event.

As I look out on a world growing more ugly and violent, I might be inclined to say that at least spirituality should be a way towards beauty and
peace, but it in fact seems not to be that at all. Beauty and peace are available,
for a while, by means of wealth skillfully employed. Soon enough, however, the advantages of wealth come to an end. And to acquire wealth, one is
obliged to surrender to the ways of this world, which are always morally ambiguous. The religious institutions of the world today are either under assault
or are involved with corruption and violence. It is hard to find a cottage in the
country to which one might go to be quiet and nonviolent without provoking

a storm of controversy among secular authorities and religious bureaucrats. There is still the alternative to be of direct service to people in need, which is to plunge directly into ugliness and violence out of love: a form of aggressive renunciation. Perhaps in the final analysis, contemplative spirituality is like a gem crystal, embedded all-but-inextricably in the matrix of the common stone of a given time, place, and culture. It cannot be extricated from the matrix, so it rises and falls with its cultural context. Under such circumstances, we come to doubt the value of this research on the rainbow body for anyone who is committed to living in a densely populated area, even apart from the ever-menacing grimace of materialism and modernity. The rainbow body is about being a renunciant, being beyond the reach of anything utilitarian, beyond anything that could be exploited. The ways of this world—culture, conflict, forms and shapes of things—are a dream, an illusion, a product of the deluded mind. The contemplative path is for those who understand that every concept and every practice, however holy and enshrined in tradition, risks becoming a trap. According to the great traditions of yogic practice, attainment of the results requires evading the traps; this is learned with the guidance of a master with whom the student lives in an out-of-the way place.

Might this key principle itself be an illusory concept? Sometimes I feel that practice can consist of flash upon flash of insight, lived and offered up under any and all circumstances. The environment itself, pregnant with illusions, becomes the guru. This approach is found in some Tibetan traditions such as mahamudra and dzogchen. It is also the Christian way of the cross.

Observations on the Natural and Paranormal Aspects of Death and Dying

When a person dies in my parish here in rural Southern Italy, the body is not embalmed. Burial, by law, must take place the day after death. Most deaths still take place at home, although the dying are frequently brought to the provincial hospital in an ambulance. After death, the body is washed and dressed by funerary personnel, after which it is placed in the casket or laid out on a hospital mortuary slab in open-sided visiting rooms. A person may pass away at 5:00 a.m. on a Monday and be buried at 5:00 a.m. on the following

Tuesday, thirty-six hours later. In the summer months, the body will show signs of decay during that period of time. The mouth especially begins to deteriorate and putrid gases emanate from the bodily orifices. We know that in the past it was not uncommon to postpone burial for two or three days, in which case the deterioration would have been even more pronounced. In the summer, a portable air conditioning unit is used to slow down the decay process, but this seems to have little practical effect.

Therefore, when we interview persons who were present at the death of a frail, elderly person in the summer months in eastern Tibet and are told that the body did not deteriorate or decompose for seven days, we know that we are dealing either with a remarkable phenomenon out of the normal course of nature, or else the witnesses are making something up, perhaps in collaboration with one another, perhaps following the dictates of a cultural tradition. Let us critically examine the facts from our research in order to frame some kind of a response to the claims advanced about Khenpo A Chö.

All the eyewitnesses reported a week-long process of shrinkage, visible beneath the yellow cloak that covered the body of the Khenpo. They affirm that, shortly after death, the flesh of the Lama turned white or pink, resembling that of a young child. They also attested that on the eighth day there was nothing left under the cloak, and no evidence of decay, stains or bad odors. They further attested to rainbow patterns in the sky, but at the same time they spoke of a fine drizzle. Anyone with experience of weather in the mountains knows that drizzle, haze, and light rain are often associated with rainbows. Rainbows are produced when sunlight passes through air that is saturated with moisture or light rainfall, so it is not surprising that rainbows and a delicate rainfall might occur at the same time. The body gave off a pleasant odor or perfume. We know that elderly persons who have been observing a vegetarian diet and rigorous spiritual discipline (physical chastity, meditation and prayer, light manual labor) will emanate a delicate odor after death.

It is possible that a person who has been particularly abstemious with regard to fluids might die in a moment in which the balance of salts in the body was particularly high, contributing to several days of resistance to decay. When people make salted meat, for example, the process requires a careful balance between salt applied to the exterior of the meat so as to prevent mold from growing on the outside, while encouraging the evaporation of fluids from the tissue below the surface. An expert in preserving meat with salt knows how to keep the evaporation going just to the right point, without hardening the meat. When the natural salts in the cells of the tissue being preserved balance out the concentration of the salt added on the surface of the meat, decay will not occur. In this way, salamis and prosciutto remain tender and not overly salty. It is possible to preserve a corpse, particularly that of an abstemious, slender person in this way for several days even without incision and removal of the internal organs, as can be seen in the case of the mummy of an eight-year-old child in the Museo Palazzo Massimo in Rome. This child's body was entirely preserved without removal of the organs, using myrrh and herbs as a preservative. The Egyptians, however, did remove the brain and internal organs to prepare their mummies, since the soft tissue of these organs decays rapidly.

Even today, the bodies of high Tibetan lamas are preserved by packing the body in a box with salt and camphor, sometimes for as long as six weeks. Only after this period is the body cremated. The mixture is changed periodically when it becomes soaked with bodily fluids. Some cases of the shrinkage of the body might be explained by the use of this procedure. In some cases we have had reports of the shrinkage not only of flesh but also of bone.[64] Moreover, it is the normal practice in eastern Tibet to dispose of the body of the deceased a short time after death. Usually, after an appropriate astrological calculation has been performed, the body can be dismembered and fed to the vultures, or else thrown into a river where the flesh will be consumed by fish and crustaceans. To return the body as quickly as possible to the component elements seems to be a widespread concern of Tibetan funerary customs, attested in Khams[65] by Marion H. Duncan as well as in Mustang by Charles Ramble.[66] I was able to observe the same kinds of practices in Dolpo (northern Nepal) and at Drikung Til in central Tibet. However, none of our informants spoke of the use of salt, camphor, or other embalming procedures in the case of Khenpo A Chö, nor was there any hint of hastening the dismemberment of the body. On the contrary, once they saw the change in his facial color after death, they immediately assumed that a paranormal sequence of phenomena might begin to manifest. At this point, they consulted a Nyingma master, Lama A Khyug, about how to proceed.[67]

Another phenomenon that is harder to explain is the mysterious sound that was heard, a melody without words, both inside the hermitage and outside it at the same time. Surely these villagers and monks are aware of the sounds of winds during storms and in a variety of weather patterns in the mountains. What they describe was not the screeching of wind, but a beautiful melody.

One would think that being present for the mysterious disappearance of the body of a revered person would be a life-changing experience. Both Lama Norta and Lama Puyok demonstrate the kind of enthusiasm that we might expect to accompany such a life-changing event. Our team interviewed them almost exactly two years after the events described, and there is no doubt about the vividness of their memories. It is most unfortunate that washed out roads prevented our visit to Lobzang Nyendrak in Nyarong. He was the closest disciple of the Khenpo and would have been able to discuss in greater depth the kinds of practices that the Khenpo had embraced over the years. In the case of the two young monks in India, interviewed in February 2001, we were struck by their lack of enthusiasm and the vagueness of their replies. In part, this could be because we had to work through a translator who spoke English poorly. However, under the highly controlled conditions of these interviews, I was in a much better position to speak Tibetan during the interviews and to listen to the spoken Tibetan of the interviewees than I had been in the Khenpo's hermitage. Listening carefully to the responses, I am struck by the lack of energy and interest that the two young monks, especially Rinchen Tsering, display. Aside from the basic information about the death of the Khenpo and the various phenomena that occurred for seven days, they are unable to give us the slightest glimpse into the man himself, his life, his practices, his spiritual relationships, his teachings, and so forth. Our encounters with the community of nuns, who were clearly full of faith and devotion after having received many teachings over the years from this saintly monk, communicated much more eloquently something of the Khenpo's charismatic character. They had been receiving his teachings over a long period of time, and the fruits of spiritual maturity were evident in their way of being themselves.

Even the rinpoches at Kandzé Gompa gave very reserved responses with regard to the rainbow body, but they provided quite in-depth responses regarding what was obviously a long-term and very warm relationship between the

Khenpo and Gertag Rinpoche. This sense of warmth is almost wholly absent from the interviews at Mindrolling, leading me to wonder if the monks are in some way discreetly playing a formal role.

In an interview, it is clear that the interviewer's tone and wording of the questions may influence the reponses he or she receives. In the case of Lama A Khyug, the precise and somewhat philosophical Lhasa dialect of our translator seems to have alienated the lama to some degree, giving rise to his comments about the team being only interested in philosophy, or that we were "rich Westerners." Granted, perhaps the lama was enacting the role of a mad yogin. In the case of the young monks, were they performing the role of humble monks, not wanting to say anything that might attract attention to themselves, or worse, that might get someone in trouble with the authorities? It is possible. Nevertheless, every occasion to speak with warm faith and devotion was skillfully evaded.

Another possibility might be that the young monks in fact did not see any of the reported phenomena, and were only cooperating *pro forma* for some reason. Something seemed overly planned and overly convergent in their respective responses to the questions. Only Sonam Gyaltsen revealed anything of his personal opinions and observations; the testimony of Rinchen Tsering is apathetic and flat. When I listen to the tapes, I detect the same absence of affect in his voice. A great deal of conversation was recorded on tape but not translated into the English transcript, so perhaps a future researcher more fluent in eastern Tibetan dialects may detect significant nuances in these untranslated sections. Another possibility is that the two monks did, in fact, observe a set of strange phenomena, but are intentionally following a hagiographical script in their retelling of these events. As a result, anything that does not fit the script—the official narrative perhaps shaped by other saints' lives or by Lamas Norta and Puyok—is not communicated. In some cases, my questions fell outside the script, and so the interviewees were baffled and unable to respond. For this reason, it would have been useful to have had more than one translator and to have done a series of interviews, with questions prepared from a variety of points of view.

In his book on healing among the Bonpo of Nepal, Robert Desjarlais[68] points out the relationship between poetry, illness, suffering, and healing.

Desjarlais illustrates how participant-observer methods require greater sensitivity and more refined intuition on the part of the researcher. Moreover, research done in this way in fact endows the anthropologist with sensitivity and intuitive insight, taking research into a higher cognitive mode and encouraging deeper understanding of the human. When these skills have been acquired, science can be said to have transcended the study of medical conditions, genealogy, geography, agriculture, family structure, material conditions, and economics. It is possible that a more poetic mode of exchange would have produced more credible results with the eyewitnesses to the Khenpo's death. This is one important example of the tension between a scientific approach to the reality of a paranormal phenomenon and a cultural or poetic approach to the same phenomenon, and it is one of the reasons I set this work aside for more than a decade. Regrettably, in the absence of follow-up grant support, it was impossible to design more incisive interview methods in subsequent research periods. However, in our interviews with Loppon Tenzin Namdak in 2001 and again in 2003, we were able to meet with a guide who is fluent in English and who trusted key members of our research team. He is also familiar with Western ways of thinking, both religious[69] and academic. His unique blend of critical thinking and strong convictions about the literal veracity of the rainbow body phenomenon give us the courage to present this research in spite of its flaws. Something significant happened in the summer of 1998 in eastern Tibet. Thanks to Loppon's incisive testimony, we know that this was not an isolated incident, and it bears further investigation.

Another interesting confirmation from within the tradition came to light in my recent trip in September 2014 to Nepal. Two monks from the Nyingma monastery in which the shrine stupa of Dudjom Rinpoche is venerated helped me locate an account of the death of Khenpo A Chö by Khenpo Tsultrim Lodro. Apparently, this young Nyingma lama, following the practices of Western researchers, interviewed some of the eyewitnesses that I had interviewed in kLu ma Gompa, and confirmed the accounts of the paranormal phenomena that had occurred after the death of Khenpo A Chö. He published this report in 2006. However, a careful reading of his account[70] reveals a strong insider approach, told from the perspective of Buddhist convictions in this tradition. Nevertheless, it seems that Khenpo Tsultrim Lodro learned something about sensitivity and intuition, and wanted to move his own research beyond mere chronological facts and also beyond emic religious claims.

When the story is told from an experience of faith, that faith alters the perception of observed phenomena—as does skepticism. In fact, a preternatural death like that of Khenpo A Chö reveals what we truly are—but only to a faith-conditioned receptive consciousness. This kind of consciousness is a strongly felt cultural reality, something that defines the faith of people who live in a very closed society with its own highly nuanced way of telling the stories of holy persons. In 2002, I interviewed Chinese Buddhist master, Zi Sheng Wang, in Oakland, California, on this question. Master Zi Sheng Wang is a dzogchen teacher who brought his disciples to kLu ma Gompa to venerate the Khenpo's memory, but the group was unable to cross over the flooded river.

He emphasized the traditional view that a person is drawn to these very high teachings because of previous karmic connections involving the study of key sacred texts, belonging to a blessed lineage of guru transmission, and heart-to-heart bestowal of the sacred teachings that took place perhaps many times in previous incarnations. This master told us that lamas are now making pilgrimage to the site of Khenpo A Chö's attainment so as to accelerate their own attainment of the rainbow body. In contrast to some Buddhist teachers who have objected to our style of research, this master told us that, by doing careful research we not only were enhancing our own eventual attainment of the rainbow body but we were also encouraging others to commit themselves more fervently to the relevant practices. He also pointed out that, by introducing research methods such as interviews, we were stimulating the masters in the dzogchen tradition to rethink their methods of teaching and to reformulate their answers to urgent questions.

The categories used by Nyingma scholars that we will examine in chapter two are profound intellectual constructs, a language for expressing respect and faith for the person who has gone beyond mental constructs. Within the sphere of tradition, it makes perfect sense. When we try to communicate these experiences to the general public, when the whole matter "goes global," it acquires a kind of literalist, almost fundamentalist, meaning that is not appropriate. Sorting this out will require a more demanding body of research into the entire history of the dzogchen approach.

II

Later Developments in Dzogchen History

I saw the sky opened wide, and a white horse, its rider is called trustworthy and true: he is the one who judges and struggles justly. His eyes are like a flame of fire, and on his head are many crest jewels on which are written a name which no one knows but he.

— APOCALYPSE 19:11-12

Having begun our investigation with an account of the life of Khenpo A Chö and the eyewitness reports of his death, we will now examine the kind of dzogchen practice that made up such an important part of the Khenpo's life. Keeping in mind that he was apparently a highly favored disciple of the great Nyingma teacher Dudjom Rinpoche we need to examine the key features of relatively recent Nyingma appropriations of the dzogchen traditions of practice that would have been transmitted to the Khenpo. Basically, we are about to describe the integration of dzogchen into Vajrayana Buddhism, a process that was probably already under way in the time of the first diffusion of Buddhism in Tibet in the eighth and ninth centuries.[71] Later, in the course of the second diffusion of Buddhism in Tibet, this integration became increasingly urgent, to the extent that David Germano can refer to it almost as a corruption of "pristine dzogchen" by the addition of "funerary Buddhism."[72] However, it is at the height of this period, in the time of Longchenpa (1308–1368), that dzogchen attains its philosophical high-water mark, brilliantly presented in Germano's 1992 dissertation.

In the centuries after Longchenpa, dzogchen developed its own cultural milieu within the Nyingma order, particularly under the influence of the

88

tertons, those masters who are believed to have discovered previously hidden teachings (*terma*) that usually orbit around the dzogchen approach to spiritual practice. These apocryphal teachings, vigorously defended and rigorously critiqued depending on sectarian affiliations among the Tibetan schools, were particularly effective in sustaining native Tibetan traditions and symbolism at key moments in the history of the Land of the Snows. As a result of the persuasive power of the *tertons* as thaumaturges and revealers of sacred texts associated above all with Padmasambhava and his circle, this apocryphal literature contributed to the formation of the Bhutanese state.[73] The "treasure" tradition also contributed to the spiritual practices of the great Fifth Dalai Lama and to those of the Sixth Dalai Lama (as witnessed in the kLu Khang wall paintings that honor Pema Lingpa, one of the great *tertons,* and an ancestor of the Sixth Dalai Lama[74]). Jigmé Lingpa, a major terton of the 1700s who identified himself with Longchenpa, contributed greatly to the flourishing nineteenth- and twentieth-century devotion to that fourteenth-century master's approach to dzogchen.[75] What we have in the teachings of Dudjom Rinpoche and his circle of disciples is an assimilation of patterns that have been received by the tradition over the past two hundred and fifty years.[76] They are therefore extremely relevant for any research on recent manifestations of the rainbow body, such as that of Khenpo A Chö, because it is this more historically recent dzogchen that he practiced and taught. However, as we will see in subsequent chapters, this kind of dzogchen has undergone dramatic evolution[77] in comparison to the earliest expressions of a nontransformational awakening to the "natural state" of buddhahood known to us.

The Basis of Appearances, Path, and Result and the Basis of Appearances of Samsara and Nirvana

The attainment of the rainbow body *('ja' lus)* as understood by the Nyingma tradition of Tibetan Buddhism is always connected to the practice of the great perfection (*rdzogs pa chen po,* or dzogchen[78]). The Nyingma tradition describes a set of nine vehicles,[79] the highest of which is that of the great perfection, considered the swiftest of the tantric methods for attaining supreme realization, identified with buddhahood. We recall this notion of a "swift path" from the life of Milarepa (1050–1136, ca.). Once the youthful sorcerer was able to perceive that his deeds of black magic would lead to a long future rebirth in a hell-realm, the next step was to find a master who could guide him to liberation in his present lifetime—"in one lifetime."[80] By following the swift path, he would be able to evade his karmic bondage to the dark entities he had been invoking in the practice of destructive magic. He therefore had to seek out a highly realized master. In the thirteenth-century biography by rGyal Thang pa, we find the following account of Milarepa's experience with dzogchen:

> The Lord Mila Happy Report destroyed many people by his magic and destroyed fields with hail, thus causing great misery and harm to beings. Immeasurable grief and penitence grew within him. He went before Lama g.yu ston Khro rgyal, saying: "On my own, I asked you, my Guru, for the two teachings on hail and sorcery, in which I have succeeded. By relying on that power, I have heaped up an immense negative karma by having caused the death of sentient beings. At dawn this morning, immeasurable grief arose in me. Now I offer a confession of all my sins. Please, holy lama, consider granting me a Doctrine that gives rise to buddhahood in one body, in one lifetime." He supplicated in this way. The lama replied: "Very well! I have many teachings by which you can become a buddha in one life, in one body, but I cannot be your Guru. In upper Nyang there resides a holy, perfected Lama named 'Bre ston Lha dGa'. Go there to request the holy Doctrine." Both he and the Bonpo sorcerer furnished Mila with many provisions for Dharma practice. He went to Upper Nyang and met Lama 'Bre ston Lha dGa', telling him all that he had previously done. The lama said: "My son, you are a very great sinner. Practicing the method of dzogchen under my guidance in the morning, you can realize buddhahood that morning; learning it in the evening, you can become a buddha that evening. Overcoming all sin, you can become a buddha in one body, in one lifetime; I will teach you this holy Dharma practice." Mila was truly delighted with this proposal. He listened to the Teaching and tried to put it into practice. But the

power descending through Lha dGa''s Lineage had no effect. He therefore supplicated the lama again, who said: "How many sins have you heaped up?" Mila replied: "I have sinned by using magic power, creating hail storms, and a great deal more." He retold the story of his life in detail. The lama replied: "I had no idea that you had so great a burden of negative actions. How can I be your spiritual guide?" And he, too, shed many tears. "Now, my son, the lama who is going to be your spiritual guide is a direct disciple of the great Saint Naropa, named Marpa the Translator, who dwells in Lho Brag. Go to him and ask for the Teachings. He is capable of being your spiritual guide."[81]

Thus, Milarepa left behind this "swiftest" vehicle in order to undertake the arduous training of the *anuttara yoga tantras* under the severe tutelage of Marpa. It is interesting that Lha dGa' does not require Milarepa to practice lengthy preliminaries before giving him dzogchen teachings. It seems that as late as the eleventh century, preliminaries were not part of the structure of the path of dzogchen, although there is some evidence that the "extraordinary" preliminary practices (one hundred thousand refuge prayers and prostrations with the Bodhisattva Vow; one hundred thousand Vajrasattva mantras and visualizations; one hundred thousand mandala offerings; one hundred thousand Guru Yoga Prayers) were already part of the path of anuttara yoga tantra. In order to understand the path that was closed to Milarepa, we need to investigate further the overall structure of the great perfection worldview and spiritual path.

Traditional teachings in the Vajrayana approach to Buddhism offer a three-fold description of the way toward the realization of buddhahood: the anthropological (human body-mind complex) basis of the path, the detailed description of spiritual practice, and the result of that particular set of practices. Milarepa himself applies this threefold description to the path of mahamudra attainment.[82] Basically, the Mahayana view of phenomena is that all of them are without any enduring metaphysical substrate. This is often translated from the Sanskrit word, *nihsvabhava*, as "lacking self-nature" and corresponds to the Buddhist teachings on *shunyata*, or "emptiness" (or voidness, or better yet, openness). It basically means that, by means of an intuitive grasp of all phenomena, mental or physical, attained by long hours of meditation practice, a yogin is able to see through all appearances. The yogin perceives that everything is impermanent, mutable, and interconnected. There are no irreducible units of thought or of matter that have a permanent essence or nucleus; everything is in flux, and conventional reality reproduces itself, from microsecond to microsecond, out of the residues of previously arisen phenomena. In this way, one can describe bondage as the result of our habits of drawing erroneous conclusions from what we perceive, and constructing more or less elaborate explanations for everything on the basis of those conclusions. All subjective experience—including visions and other mystical states, along with attachments to material objects—fall under the radical criticism of this approach. Liberation therefore consists in developing a deeper, inherent level of awareness that, gradually or suddenly, recognizes the radical openness of being in all its forms. That awareness is nurtured by the various skillful means of Buddhist contemplative practice.

The inherent capacity of human persons to attain such a level of awareness is called "buddha nature" or the embryo of buddhahood *(tathagatagarbha).* This is the true basis of the spiritual path: buddhahood is therefore not something to be acquired, far less, constructed. It is already there, from microsecond to microsecond. It *is* that radical openness of being, inseparable from the deepest level of awareness. A fully enlightened person is one who, as a result of disciplined practice, abides continually in the state of awareness *(rigpa)* of that openness. As a result of being in that state, such a person embodies heroic and extraordinary compassion toward all sentient beings. A fully enlightened being—in other words, a buddha or awakened one—is not confined to a state of pure static consciousness. Rather, a buddha abides nowhere and confers compassionate presence everywhere. From this perspective, it is possible to speak of the basis of the path, the practices that constitute the path, and the results of the path practices within an authentically Buddhist worldview. It is also very important to keep in mind as we go along that an authentic Buddhist worldview might be elusive to our usual ways of thinking and that we can easily err in trying to understand the rainbow body from a point of departure that is different from that of Mahayana Buddhism. For this reason, we are also going to have to explain the methodology of our research on this difficult topic, in which we are attempting to bridge the Buddhist and scientific worldviews. Later, we will look at the ways in which several contemplative worldviews were interacting in the fertile historical period in which the dzogchen teachings emerged in Central Asia.

One quite convenient and simplified way of describing the great perfection approach would be to posit an uncreated, primordial basis that we might understand as the origin from which all aspects of the universe arise. This uncreated basis, being itself essentially immaterial, is capable of creating spiritual, mental, and material phenomena. In this view, energies emerge from the primordial basis that become "light" of various colors associated with the five classical elements (space, wind, fluidity, heat, and solidity). In the course of cosmic evolution, these five lights gradually become gross matter: the visible universe. When a yogin attains the rainbow body, the process of evolution is reversed: gross matter dissolves into its own subtle nature of light and the light returns into the primordial basis of all phenomena. In effect, this view corresponds to the notion of a transcendent creator God, capable of engendering the full spectrum of phenomena—spiritual, mental, and material—as understood primarily in Hindu theology (*citta-acitta-Brahma*) and, in a somewhat different way, by Muslims, Jews, and Christians (in which God is believed to be absolutely independent in his own being, believed to be eternal, and all creation believed to be utterly dependent on God for both its origin and its continuance). It is therefore very important not to confuse a doctrine of creation of this kind with the Buddhist perspective. If the Buddhist dzogchen authors write descriptions of lights, energies, particles, elements, and so forth, it is important to recognize that these descriptions don't refer to material things. Instead, they represent a variety of subjective visions that arise from the *basis* of consciousness, of which they are merely a display. Moreover, the basis is individual and corresponds to the conscious individual; it is *not* a supreme one for all sentient beings! Even when the texts speak of the dissolution of the primordial mind into an "ultimate sphere" at the time of attaining Buddhahood, it simply means that appearances come to an end, and the mind is left in its natural state. The notion that the individual mind is going to dissolve into a metaphysical absolute is simply not the view of Mahayana and Vajrayana Buddhism. Keeping this caveat in mind, we can describe the basis and its appearances from the perspective of the great perfection approach as it developed after the eleventh century.

In the first place, we need to make a distinction between our ordinary mind with its appearances and the subtle mind referred to as "awareness" or *rig pa*. This distinction only really makes sense to those who have begun to train the mind by means of one or another form of meditation practice, and yet it is fundamental to all the contemplative systems we will be examining in this book. Moreover, in the view of dzogchen (as harmonized with Mahayana Buddhism), awareness can also develop into the mind of enlightenment or *bodhicitta*. Bodhicitta can mean several things: the orientation of the mind towards enlightenment, the awakening of the desire to save all sentient beings, the awakening of erotic desire in the controlled context of yogic/tantric sexual practices (*karma mudra*). Taken together, "awareness" and "the mind of enlightenment" are understood to be the basis within the human person for spiritual development. Ordinary consciousness is not the basis, however, and there should be no confusion about the distinction between ordinary mind and awareness.

An important figure in any presentation of an integral dzogchen system within Tibetan Buddhism is Long chen pa (kLong Chen Rab 'Byams Pa, 1308–1363). It is Longchenpa whose mastery of Buddhist philosophy and dzogchen practice made possible the future development of dzogchen, beyond its possibly non-Buddhist origins, down to the present day. In referring to Longchenpa, therefore, we need to be aware that his life's work was precisely to integrate dzogchen within the larger mandala of Tibetan Vajrayana. For this reason, we will use his approach and that of later dzogchen masters cautiously, keeping in mind that they are operating with a specific philosophical agenda. We can see quite clearly in the following excerpt that Longchenpa is heavily invested in the integration of the dzogchen view with that of classic Buddhism, particularly the system of the two great philosopher brothers, Asanga (circa 300–370) and Vasubandhu (circa 320–410).

In his auto-commentary on *The Precious Treasury of the Mode of Being* (*gnas lugs mdzod*), Longchenpa explains the meaning of "the mind of enlightenment" and "awareness" in relation to mind in general and the appearances to the perceiving mind of cyclic existence (*samsara*) and liberation (*nirvana*).

Mind (*sems*) and the mind of enlightenment are not the same. Mind consists of the temporary stains that result from contact with the three spheres (past, present, and future), the eight consciousnesses (the five senses plus the three aspects of the consciousness principle), along with the other three mental factors (the remaining *skandhas*: notions and impulses). The mind of enlightenment is awareness understood to be self-arisen primordial wisdom (*rang byung ye shes*), free from the characteristics and the qualities of phenomena. It is the dimension (*dbyings*) of all cyclic existence and liberation. The world of appearances arises from the play (*rol pa*) or potentiality (*rtsal*) of this very mind of enlightenment. In this way, the mind of enlightenment is the name of a result given to a cause. Thus, that which appears as cyclic existence and as liberation is to be known as the potentiality of awareness (*rig pa'i rtsal*). Awareness itself, which is not to be posited as either cyclic existence or liberation, is known as the unobstructed basis of appearance (*'char gzhi ma 'gags pa*). Thus objective appearances (*yul snang*) are understood as the luminous appearances of that which does not exist (*med pa gsal snang*), posited as neither being mind nor as different from mind. These are pure from the beginning, grounded in voidness without a basis and in luminosity. At the moment of liberation both potentiality and play, being baseless, disappear by themselves, as happens when one awakens from a dream. One should know that both phenomena and their characteristics completely disappear when buddhahood is attained, even though one continues to abide in the unchanging dharmakaya of self-awareness (*rang rig chos sku 'gyur med*).

Longchenpa goes on to complain that no one else in his time was able to make these distinctions. Apparently, there was considerable confusion about the ontological relationship between that which appears before the mind's awareness, and the mind in itself. One can easily see that, for someone who has never attained any degree of stability in meditation practice, it is rather difficult to distinguish between the normal flux of mental events and a deeper level of consciousness. Moreover, if we are told that things are "pure from the beginning" and "there is nothing to transform or correct," someone might indeed conclude that the ordinary flux of mental events is identical with the mind of enlightenment. For this reason, even master Lha dGa''s excessive optimism about Milarepa's practice of dzogchen back in the eleventh century is perfectly understandable. But for the same reason, we can see why Longchenpa's correctives were urgently needed.

The mind that operates dualistically and the various appearances of phenomena that are perceived are both rooted in basic ignorance. If there were no ignorance to posit the absolute reality of the basis of phenomena and their appearance, no dualism or impure appearances would arise. Dualism and impure appearances are temporary; the Pali Canon [*Anguttara Nikaya* 1.8–10] had already called them "adventitious defilements" that are layered upon the basic luminosity of the mind; their disappearance is required to attain the final liberation of buddhahood. However, we are to understand that the primordial mind of the basis (*ye shes*)—the mind of enlightenment—is the origin of both pure and impure visions, including our individual mind and that which appears as the material world. These visions are merely luminous appearances of something that does not actually exist. The primordial mind undergoes no changes at all, whether one is trapped in cyclic existence, or liberated in nirvana. Milarepa says exactly the same thing with regard to mahamudra, and in fact recent Tibetan masters of the *ri-mé* (nonsectarian) movement assert the compatibility of the views of dzogchen and of mahamudra.[83]

The basis of great primordial purity (*gzhi ka dag chen po*) has three aspects: its essence (*ngo bo*), its nature (*rang bzhin*), and compassion (*thugs rje*). They are considered to be one in being and inseparable. Each aspect presents different descriptions of the same reality, given so that reality might be more fully understood. Traditionally the metaphor of fire is used to explain this: fire is hot, it is capable of burning, it is capable of consuming burnable substances. But each characteristic describes the same thing, fire.

How Appearances Arise from the Basis of Phenomena

Similarly, we need to distinguish between descriptions of the primordial basis (*gzhi*) prior to the arising of appearances (*gzhi snang*) and upon the arising of appearances. Although the basis does not change, the description changes according to the modality and moment of manifestation.

Prior to the arising of appearances, the basis in essence is primordial purity (*ka dag*). This is the continuity of the ontologically open (*stong pa*) primordial mind. This openness is described metaphorically (in fact, in terms of tantric visualization) as the mode of abiding of the youthful vase body (*gzhon nu bum pa'i sku*). It is luminous (*gsal ba*) in nature, having the appearance of the five lights that are without discontinuity and do not, at this level, have distinctive colors. The basis possesses all-pervading (*kun khyab*) compassion, and for this reason is the basis for the arising of all the apparent qualities associated with buddhahood.

However, it is also the basis for all appearances, pure and impure. One becomes a Buddha when all the types of ordinary mind-based appearances disappear like clouds in the sky. When innate ignorance obscures these appearances (*lhan cig skyes pa'i ma rig pa*), the perceiver holds that the objective appearances are ontologically separate from the basis. This is the cause of subject-object dualism, from which the dreamlike appearances of cyclic existence emerge. Clearly, this suggests that we are talking primarily about the experience of mental phenomena during meditation. The same principle applies to the material body, as we shall see in the case of the rainbow body. In any case, the appearances of both cyclic existence and of liberation come exclusively from the basis. Thus the basis is *in relation to all phenomena* by means of the arising of appearances but is not itself, ontologically speaking, the same thing as those phenomena.

Instead, the basis is described as both primordial purity and spontaneity. From the point of view of the fundamental openness of being (emptiness), it is primordially pure because it is free from any signs or characteristics. It is spontaneous because, from the perspective of appearances, its luminosity is ceaseless; it is a self-renewing energetic process of manifestation. In fact, this quality also corresponds to buddha nature, or *Sugatagarbha/Tathagatagarbha*. Being primordially pure in essence, it never really falls into cyclic existence. However, cyclic existence manifests from the inherent playfulness (*rol pa*) and potentiality (*rtsal*) of the ceaseless spontaneity of the basis. Primordial purity, like the luminous qualities of a crystal, shines forth when it meets with conditions such as sunlight. Otherwise, its reflective qualities do not manifest. And in fact, to penetrate this aspect of the basis, dzogchen yogins meditate on crystals.[84] Prior to the arising of appearances, the basis is also called the youthful vase body and is described as having the qualities of openness (voidness), luminosity, and compassion within, but these qualities do not manifest outside the vase; it is "withdrawn but not obscure" (*thim la ma rmugs pa*).

The image of the vase, too, seems to correspond to the condition of embodied existence, a condition that presents the human form with the opportunity for the development of yogic practice and the eventual attainment of enlightenment. The human birth is precious and the human body, with its particular configuration of energy fluxes, channels, and droplets is capable of the breakthrough that allows Buddha nature to manifest itself. I am taking the notion of a basis (*gzhi*) to be, for this reason, an anthropological category because it describes the human person as the means in and by which enlightenment manifests. This, too, is in harmony with the earliest Buddhist teachings that place the breakthrough to enlightenment in the fourth *jhana* (state of contemplative absorption) and not in the "higher" and subtler states that go beyond the bioenergetic structure of a human being.[85]

The vase image suggests enclosure and hiddenness; until one has undertaken spiritual practice, the value of embodiment is obscured, but still present. Thus the basis is in essence primordial purity (*ka dag*) and its nature is the spontaneity capable of manifestation (*lhun grub*). This purity is defined as the absence of signs, characteristics, concepts, and limitations; in fact, this purity cannot be deeply penetrated by such features. Instead, all defilements are superficial. The basis is also described as the primordial mind of self-awareness (*so so rang rig pa'i ye shes*), which is ontologically open (*stong pa*). Its spontaneity consists of both its own luminosity and its potential to give rise to appearances.

All of these are the features of the basis from "within," that is to say from within the sphere of radical openness. From the perspective of the outside when appearances arise, we have to adjust our thinking accordingly. It is important to keep in mind that on the level of the basis itself, any kind of arising cannot be described because by definition the basis is free from the appearance of that which does not exist. It is therefore free from any outwardly "shining" manifestations. For this reason, our description of "arising" comes from the perspective that perceives the appearances of the basis, which is necessarily outside the perspective of the primordial openness of being.

The basis, as we have said above, has three aspects: it is open in essence (*ngo bo stong pa*), it is luminous in nature (*rang bzhin gsal ba*), and its compassion is all pervading (*thugs rje kun khyab*). On the level of the youthful vase body (i.e., when the manifestations of the basis do not arise), the aspects correspond to the threefold Buddhist categories of body, speech, and mind. Thus, the essence corresponds to the body (*sku*), nature to speech (*gsung*), and compassion to awareness/Mind (*rig pa*). Also present in the youthful vase body are the essence of the five fluxes of energy (the five winds)—of which the life energy (Sanskrit, *prana*; Tibetan, *srog lung*) is composed—and the inwardly shining five lights (*'od gsal lnga nang gsal*). The life energy breaks the shell of the youthful vase body and the glow (*gdangs*) of its spontaneity arises as outward luminosity or visibility (*phyir gsal*). An aspect of this visibility is the glow of compassionate awareness, which appears as conceptuality (*dpyod byed*), which in this system is burdened with considerable ambiguity. Conceptuality amounts to unawareness in relation to awareness (*rig pa la ltos pa'i ma rig pa*). Upon the production of appearances, this state is called the mode of abiding of spontaneity of the basis (*gzhi lhun grub kyi gnas lugs*). What really happens is that the basis did not change in itself, but it appears to have changed due to the subtle shift (*gyos pa*) that occurs in its potentiality (*rtsal*). This shift consists of an increase in the "glow" of the awareness aspect of the basis (*rig cha'i gdangs mched pa*). The steps in the process of the arising of appearances from the basis are the following:

·࿔· The state of the basis prior to the arising of appearances.

·࿔· The state in which appearances arise but are not yet perceived as different from the basis.

·࿔· The state in which appearances are conceived as separate from the basis, which is the state in which one becomes caught in illusion.

The second step, in which appearances arise but are not yet perceived as having separate existence, is particularly important for our topic. This step, called "the precious conch of spontaneous accomplishment" (*lam lhun grub rin po che'i sbubs*), serves as the origin both of all appearances of cyclic existence and of liberation (even of the two buddha-dimensions or bodies with form: *sambhogakaya* and *nirmanakaya*). It is also the origin of all the visions of the dzogchen path, including the four visions (*snang ba bzhi*) of the leap-over (*thodgal*) practices that bear fruition in the attainment of the rainbow body. It is an example of the difficulty of teaching about a path that leads beyond words, concepts, and appearances. The teachings inevitably involve one in words, concepts, or symbols of some kind. Milarepa's oral teachings drive home this point on a number of occasions.[86] He emphasizes the distinction between conceptual teachings or practices that lead beyond themselves toward the attainment of enlightenment, and conceptualizations that create obstacles to that attainment.

One can easily fall into illusion and cyclic existence by misreading this particular point about the arising of appearances from the basis. At the same time, only by means of authentic appearances can the compassion of a buddha be made manifest in a variety of forms so as to liberate sentient beings from cyclic existence. The difference here is that while visions on the path and individual aspects of the appearances of cyclic existence are produced by the confused minds of individuals on their own, visions of the *sambhogakaya* and *nirmanakaya* buddha forms are produced by the compassion of the buddhas interacting with the karmic profile of various individuals. One should also keep in mind that the collective karmic profile of communities of individuals contributes to creating the commonly recognized features of cyclic existence. Similarly, if we have a manifestation of a liberative appearance, it means that the karmic profile of many individuals has been touched by an authentic manifestation of compassion. Our understanding of this compassionate aspect of paranormal manifestations should help us understand what occurs when bodily dissolution is the result of spiritual practice. Within all appearances of phenomena, there is a gossamer field of higher knowledge. Thus the ordinary appearance of interdependence among causes and conditions contains within it an opening toward universal compassion.

How Ignorance Emerges and Takes Over Consciousness

Now the breaking open of the youthful vase body and its outward luminosity are not caused by ignorance. These appearances occur because the structure of the basis, particularly spontaneity and compassion, allow them to happen.

The first moment of ignorance occurs only after the "breaking" of the youthful vase body. The dzogchen masters note that the yogi, unaware of having made mistakes in meditation, nevertheless encounters mistaken concepts that arise out of potentiality. The natural state shines forth without obstacles from the unchanging base of reality, and even ignorance arises from compassion exercised without precision. The eighteenth-century dzogchen master, Jigmé Lingpa, writes in his *Chariot of Omniscience*:

> Since the essence is primordial purity, no cyclic existence is experienced in the basis. However, in relation to potentiality and spontaneity, play arises in all ways possible. Thus, from the perspective of the essence that is primordial purity, no delusions that might produce different categories of sentient beings is possible in the basis itself. Even so, such appearances arise from the aspect of spontaneity in the potentiality and in the playfulness of the nature of the basis.[87]

Here we come to one of the great difficulties in Buddhist thought: how to distinguish arising or "appearing" from the notion of creation and, logically, of a creator. The Buddhist theorists insist that the basis is not the *cause* of delusion. The basis does *not cause or create anything*, since it is free from the category of action known as causality.[88] In fact, once we are at the level of cause and effect, we are already in the realm of mistaken appearances. Rather, the basis allows phenomena to occur in the same way that space allows the clouds to gather there, without any causal commitment at all. The sky does not "create" clouds. As stated previously, all forms of dualistic appearance are already the "appearance of that which does not exist," and being nonexistent, such appearances cannot be the result of causality within the basis. The basis is free from causality, and appearances manifest without having inherent existence.[89]

Then what is ignorance? If ignorance is an aspect of the basis, then the basis itself is ignorant. If it is not an aspect of the basis, how does it come to be? The reply is that, although the primordially pure entity of the basis is free from any errors and can never be considered ignorant, its outwardly manifested glows arise unceasingly (*gdangs 'gag med du 'char ba*). Thus, ordinary minds with their appearances arise from the spontaneous nature of the basis. When these appearances are not recognized as self-manifestations of the basis and instead are seen as having separate (subject-object) existence, delusion occurs. However, if they are recognized as self-manifestations of the basis, the error of attributing separate existence to them does not occur, and liberation happens.

Ignorance continues to develop, however, even though there is no ignorance in the basis. Ignorance of three types is said to occur when appearances arise from the basis. The five root life energies (*rtsa ba srog rlung lnga*) arise from the basis and from these five we have the outward appearance of the five lights, five wisdoms, the body-speech-mind complex, qualities, and activities, and so forth. Each of these may give rise to a dualistic response, or an occasion for liberation.

The Path of the Great Perfection Approach and Its Visions

The goal of earliest Buddhist practice was to attain liberation from the sufferings of infracosmic cyclic existence, known in Sanskrit as *samsara*. In the Mahayana Buddhist path, this attainment of liberation is coupled intimately with the attainment of complete buddhahood, which not only frees the individual from the bondage of cyclic existence but also assists other beings to attain the same goal. In the process of integrating dzogchen with Mahayana Buddhism (in its Vajrayana form), it was necessary to assert that dzogchen attains the same goals as early Buddhism and Mahayana Buddhism. These goals are attained by uprooting the principal cause of unenlightened existence, which is ignorance. In order to achieve buddhahood, even the subtlest forms of ignorance must be uprooted from the mind stream of the yogin. As we have said above, uprooting this level of ignorance cannot be done by means of spiritual practice undertaken in an ordinary state of mind. The ordinary state of the mind is already caught in a dualistic, subject-object perspective that reifies every phenomenon that the mind perceives. If one practices with an ordinary view of reality and in an ordinary state of consciousness, one will not attain liberation in any form. For this reason, dzogchen does not limit itself to asking the question, "What kind of an antidote can one find to dualistic thinking?" since this is already the question of Mahayana theorists from Nagarjuna to Asanga and their commentators. Dzogchen goes after increasingly subtle forms of ignorance by exploring and eventually liberating the visions and states of mind that arise from the roots of such subtle levels of ignorance. We can see the same concerns expressed in the classic work of Vajrayana theory, *Tilopa's Oral Instructions to Naropa on the Banks of the Ganges*, which I published with Fabrizio Torricelli in 1991.[90] A very careful presentation of these states of ignorance and their antidotes from a dzogchen perspective may be found in Keith Dowman's *Flight of the Garuda*.[91]

Dzogchen theory seeks to exceed the penetrating analysis of the mind that we already find in Madhyamaka and Yogacara Buddhist theories. Already, these systems demonstrated that there are no permanent natural phenomena, no "uncuttables" (Greek: *a-tomos*: that which cannot be further divided into parts): all phenomena are composite, interdependent, and impermanent on the most radical ontological level. Dzogchen goes on to say that the best states of mind that are accessible to the ordinary mind, such as states of clarity and heightened awareness, are themselves rooted in subtle forms of ignorance. Only what we have been calling the basis and its visions arising prior to ignorance or dualistic thinking are free from ignorance. Therefore, the antidote for all forms of ignorance, including the subtlest, must be primordial mind awareness, in other words the mind of enlightenment, which the contemporary dzogchen master Namkhai Norbu rightly calls "the contemplative state." It is this state of awareness to which the disciple is introduced by the master. All the practices of the dzogchen path are based on this insight regarding both the primordial mind and those appearances that arise from this level of mind. We need to be aware that the latter appearances are seen as prior to the arising of ignorance, i.e., the erroneous interpretation of the phenomena that appear.

The Two Key Practices:
Cutting-Through (Threg Chod) and Leap-Over (Thodgal)

There are two main divisions of the practices associated with full-fledged dzogchen: "cutting-through" (*khregs chod*, pronounced *trekchö*) and "leap-over" (*thod rgal*, pronounced *t[h]ogal*). Cutting-through deals principally with cultivating the basic state of the primordial mind, in other words pure awareness (*rig pa*). Leap-over works with cultivating various appearances or visions that arise from the primordial mind. Cutting-through concentrates on the essence of primordial purity, whereas leap-over focuses on the nature of what we have called spontaneity, since the visionary phenomena arise due to that quality of primordial mind.

The yogin must first acquire facility in realizing the primordial mind through the practice of cutting-through; only then can one practice the leap-over disciplines. Failure to realize the primordial mind leaves one in the unenviable position of working merely with the appearances that arise out of the ordinary state of the mind. The yogin wants to work with appearances before they become reified and conceptualized in order to achieve the remarkable goal of the "self liberation" (*rang grol*) of all thoughts from moment to moment.

For the yogin in retreat, understanding the distinction between these two practices, and the working relationship between them, is extremely important in terms of understanding the phenomena that occur at the time of death. At death, different kinds of bodily dissolution can occur, depending on the yogin's primary practices over the course of a lifetime. As Jigmé Lingpa says in his work, *The Chariot of Omniscience*: "There are two ways: reliance on the side of openness, primordial purity, awareness, attains freedom from conceptualization and one completes (*zad par byed pa*) the nature of openness [emptiness]. With reliance on the side of appearance, i.e., spontaneity, the material body (*rdos bcas*) is purified into clear light ('*od gsal*) and one completes the nature of appearance."[92] This principle is well known in all yogic systems. The one who practices, the yogin, is called a "*sadhaka*," one who has committed to a certain path. The practice is called a "*sadhana*," i.e., that which produces a result if followed assiduously to completion. That which is attained is called "*siddhi*," or realization of the results of practice. Siddhi can take the form of ordinary siddhis, or miraculous powers, and the supreme siddhi, i.e., complete enlightenment. One who attains siddhi is called a siddha or even a mahasiddha, a great accomplished yogin. If a yogin does not complete the practices, it is believed that he or she will need to take another body in order to continue the practices to completion. Some of the death phenomena that are reported of yogins may indicate the degree to which that particular yogin has achieved the completion of the sadhana to which he or she has been committed.

With regard to the paths of leap-over and cutting-through, it is understood that the former is quicker than the latter in obtaining results. One of the critical concerns of a Buddhist path revolves around the distinction between meditative equipoise (*mnyam bzhag*) and post-meditation attainments (*rjes thob*). For example, in traditional Mahayana practice—following the Buddhist sutras—during meditative equipoise one meditates on openness (emptiness) as the ultimate truth, as an antidote to the defilements of ignorance, afflictions, desires, and so forth. During the periods between meditation sessions, the yogin is to view all phenomena as illusory and the mind is poised to see things this way thanks to the kind of realization attained while meditating on openness. In his or her actions at this time, the yogin follows the counsels of the sutras on the level of conventional truth (*samvrittisatya*), such as the cultivation of compassion, generosity, patience, and the other virtues (*paramitas*). These practices are performed in a somewhat dualistic frame of mind and serve as a preparation for the next meditation session. Step by step, one accumulates the attainments of wisdom, or the realization of openness, and of merit, based on one's virtuous actions and thoughts between meditation sessions. Very gradually, the yogin attains enlightenment as a buddha, perhaps after many lifetimes of practice.

The sutra system, however, does not explain in sufficient depth three essential points: how to deal with the appearances that arise in post-meditation experience, how to transform such appearances, and how to perceive them as a display of the primordial mind. For this reason, Vajrayana and dzogchen practitioners consider the sutra-based path to be excessively long and refer to the "three countless aeons" that are needed to attain complete buddhahood in this kind of sadhana. Moreover, the negative states of mind—such as hatred, lust, and so forth—are seen as objects to be abandoned. Positive thoughts such as compassion, purity, patience, generosity, and so forth are considered to be the antidotes to negative thoughts. For this reason, the traditional Buddhist sadhanas based on the sutras are called "the path of abandonment" (*spong lam*).

The tantric, or Vajrayana, systems other than dzogchen explain how to *transform* ordinary appearances into divine appearances in the form of the mandalas and heavenly abodes of enlightened deities, buddhas, and bodhisattvas.

In the beginning, the yogin undertakes these kinds of transformations employing the ordinary, dualistic mind that in a certain sense "pretends" to be enlightened. Of course, one should at least have a degree of control over the mind through the practice of *shamatha* meditation. Moreover, most tantric systems make use of a rigorous series of preliminary practices[93] to train the mind to undertake the full-fledged sadhana in a proper state of awareness. Tantric systems overcome the problem of dualistic thinking by showing the yogin how to utilize and transform all states of mind, including negative ones, into various manifestations of primordial wisdom. For this reason, the Vajrayana path is generally called the path of transformation (*sgyur lam*). For attaining the supreme siddhi of buddhahood, the Vajrayana is a quicker path than the strictly sutra-based path of the Mahayana because it makes use of a wider set of skillful means within the view of ontological openness that it shares with the Mahayana. One can attain buddhahood "in one body, in one lifetime" by practicing the highest category, the so-called *anuttara yoga tantras* (i.e., highest yoga tantras), as we have seen in the life of Milarepa.

The uniqueness of the dzogchen sadhana is that, from the very beginning of the yogin's practice of the path, the practice involves entering into the primordial state and perceiving all appearances as the display of that state. One inaugurates one's sadhana by receiving initiation from a dzogchen master who is capable of introducing one into the state of primordial mind and in that moment conferring the "empowerment of the potentiality of awareness" (*rig pa'i rtsal dbang*). This key introduction can be quite spontaneous, brief and direct, without any ritual accoutrements. The experience is not something to hold on to; rather, it prepares the disciple for all that will come later in the spiritual journey.

Since one applies that awareness to all subsequent moments of perception, there is no need to abandon or transform appearances. By the very fact of sustaining the state of primordial mind, appearances are liberated of their own accord. For this reason, the path of dzogchen is called the path of self-liberation (*rang drol lam*), and it is for this reason that it is considered to be an even more rapid path to complete enlightenment than the highest yoga tantras. As we have seen, however, in the life of Milarepa, not everyone is suited to this rapid path!

Within dzogchen, the path of leap-over is considered to be more rapid than that of cutting-through. This is because, although one realizes primordial purity and sees all appearances are without foundation (*gzhi bral*), or (for those of lesser capacity) as illusory (*sgyu ma lta bu*), in cutting-through one does not learn the skillful means by which the "five lights," i.e., the appearances of the dimensions of awareness ('*od lnga dbyings rig gi snang ba*) arise as objects of perception. Cutting-through is effective in self-liberating ordinary perceptions, but the pure appearances of the primordial state do not manifest in cutting-through practice. Only in leap-over do the five lights arise. From the very beginning of the practice of leap-over, one can quickly leave behind the ordinary appearances of external matter and so forth, since they are replaced (not transformed or abandoned) here by the spontaneous arising of pure appearances from the basis. In fact, in this practice, the pure appearances of the basis "consume" impure appearances and act as their antidote, and thus one does not slip into dualistic thinking. Phenomena are never reified or conceptualized.

Furthermore, if the practice of cutting-through is used exclusively, meditating only on the primordial nature of the mind—often making use of short, sharp sounds or gestures—one is not free from the danger of sliding into the notion that the nature of awareness is merely unobservable, sheer openness (*stong pa ltar med pa*). The practices of leap-over in a certain sense protect the yogin from this erroneous approach to openness: conceptuality ceases, but the inner glow of the ultimate nature (*chos nyid kyi nang mdangs*) does not cease manifestation. In the field of perception, there are manifestations of so-called vajra chains[94] and spheres that may contain the appearances of the buddha bodies (buddhakayas) in various forms. In this way, the clear light continuously arises and the glow of primordial nature appears. Therefore, it is said that in the practice of leap-over, awareness ripens as the body (*rig pa sku ru smin pa*) and the three bodies of a buddha are perfected as appearances of the path in itself (*sku gsum lam snang du rdzogs pa*).

The Four Visions and the Four Lamps

There are four visions (*snang ba bzhi*) that arise due to the practice of leap-over based on what are called "four lamps" (*sgron ma bzhi*). These four result in the attainment of the body of light, which is, as we shall see, one of the types of the rainbow body. The four lamps are considered the basis for the four visions of leap-over practice. Even before describing them, the reader should be aware that the authors are describing inner experiences that have the appearance of luminosity!

- ⟡ "The Water Lamp of an Expanding Lasso" (*rgyang zhags chu'i sgron ma*) is described as the door through which the glow of awareness (*rig pa*) manifests in the form of external objects. A subtle channel of light (*'od rtsa*) extends from the region of the navel to the heart and from there up to the brain, where it divides into three channels. One reaches the front of the skull, from the forehead to the crown, and the other two end at the midpoint of the eyes. The endpoints of these channels gather the appearances of the primordial mind (*ye shes kyi snang ba*) such as luminosity, consciousness droplets, dimensional bodies, etc. related to the aspect of nirvana. The actual material organs, the eyes, which are their instrumental supportive matrix, gather in mistaken appearances (*'khrul snang*) related to bondage to samsara. The two channels of light and the corresponding physical eyes are called the water lamp of an expanding lasso. Like a rope or lasso, these channels can bind mistaken appearances into openness, if their nature is realized by the yogin-observer. However, if their nature is not realized, the channels can bind them to gross appearances (*rags pa'i snang ba*), producing the effects of conceptualization and dualistic thinking. Ideally, the true lamp of an expanding lasso is that which gathers up the appearances of primordial mind.

- ⟡ "The Lamp of the Pure Dimension" (*dag pa dbyings kyi sgron ma*), which can also be termed the "Lamp of the Dimension of Awareness" (*rig pa dbyings kyi sgron ma*): This is the externally manifested glow of the basis of manifestation from the perspective of its inner dimension (*nang dbyings*). It is oriented toward the aspect of openness within the basis.

It acts or appears as a kind of "fence" (*rwa ba*) or boundary for the appearances of awareness as vajra chains (*rdo rje lu gu rgyud*) and related visions. It is perceived as a five-colored luminescence, similar to multi-colored silk.

‧✧‧ "The Lamp of the Open Droplet" (*thig le stong pa'i sgron ma*): This lamp supports the yogin's exertions in observing aspects of manifestation. It is oriented toward the aspect of appearance, as distinct from openness. It consists of appearances of the three bodies that abide inseparable, one from the other, in the ultimate dimension. It manifests as the objects of direct sensory perception within the practice of leap-over, where it is seen as pure round droplets surrounded by rims of the five elemental colors.

‧✧‧ "The Lamp of Self-Arisen Wisdom" (*shes rab rang dbyung gi sgron ma*): This lamp is the essence of awareness and the instrument by which the other lamps are perceived. Its essence is clear, pure and without object. Its sharp and swift cognitive wisdom relates to the feature of potentiality in the basis. Its glow is the vision of vajra chains similar to floating golden threads. Its base is the lamp of the pure dimension.

These lamps are most effectively seen in retreat, especially dark retreats, in which it becomes possible to clarify their exact meaning based on meditative experience. The subtle aspects of all four lamps are already present in the basis prior to the arising of appearances. If one meditates regularly on the lamps during one's lifetime (in other words, if one practices the relevant sadhanas), they can also arise after death, during the intermediate state (*bardo*). The lamps manifest as follows: The expanding lasso appears as connected "ropes" of light rays (see kLu Khang paintings); the pure dimension appears as the five lights; the open droplet appears as buddha bodies surrounded by rims of light of the five colors; self-arisen wisdom appears as awareness.

With regard to attaining the body of light, it is potentially possible within the realization of the practices that give rise to the four lamps. Jigmé Lingpa, in his *Chariot of Omniscience*, observes: "The unobstructed essence of the body of light (*'od lus zang thal mnyam pa'i dgongs pa*) abides as the nature of great spontaneity within the basis. It abides, as it were, in its own place. This is due to the regular practice of situating the resultant glow of awareness (*'bras bu'i rig gdangs*) (as a vajra chain) into a sphere that appears from its 'abode' in the primordial purity of the basis." If one did not grasp the subtle distinctions that this tradition ascribes to the "within" of the basis, such a statement would be incomprehensible. Once one has understood that the author is writing about a sadhana, a regular practice of meditation, that gives access to the phenomena that are described by these distinctions, there is some hope of making sense of all this! Fortunately, we have the paintings in the kLu Khang in Lhasa, some of which were published by Ian Baker and Thomas Laird, others of which were photographed by a team jointly sponsored by David Germano and myself, which enable us to go beyond the text in order to appreciate the extraordinary character of the practices that dzogchen yogins undertake to complete in one lifetime or less.

Beyond the four lamps, there are "four visions" that develop one at a time. They are discerned as signs and measure of the yogin's progress towards final liberation.

- ☼ "The Direct Manifestation of Dharmata" (*chos nyid mngon sum*): At this level, direct visions of the ultimate nature of reality begin to manifest themselves. These visions are discerned to be authentic when three or more conjoined droplets arise in the awareness of the yogin.

- ☼ "Increase of Experiential Appearance" (*nyams snang gong 'phel*): On this level, the classic appearances of spiritual attainment, already known to the Chandogya Upanishad, begin to appear without obstructions, both externally and internally. These are the appearances of fireflies, clouds, smoke, mirage, the moon, the stars, a butter lamp, and the sun. These appearances are not stabile: they undergo flux. Wheels, stupas, arrows, ritual implements, and deity seed-syllables shine forth without any particular order. Day and night, they expand into the space around the retreat cabin of the yogin. Authenticity and completion are discerned by the appearance of a head or tiny body of Vajrasattva without consort within a droplet of light.

- ☼ "Perfection of Awareness" (*rig pa tshad phebs*): One's ordinary perceptions of the elements of earth, water, fire, and wind are purified of themselves. The space around the yogin is filled with the mandalas of the five buddha families (ratna, vajra, padma, buddha, and karma) with the principal figures in union with consorts. There are three aspects to the completeness of this phase of practice:

1. Perfection of external appearance: The yogin can dominate appearances (*dbang bsgyur*) and can move objects to which he directs his mind; the yogin is unobstructed by the four elements and can move through gross matter, as did Milarepa when he passed through a mountain, trailing Raschungpa behind him.

2. Perfection of internal body: All visual perceptions are spheres of the Buddhas of the five families. Light rays from their hearts emerge and blend with the heart of the yogin, conferring the empowerment of Great Rays of Light (*'od zer chen po'i dbang*). The yogini perceives herself as sitting on a large lotus made of light; her hands shine with light; in the pores of the skin, limitless spheres of Buddhas and infinite sentient beings are seen (as in the *Avatamsaka Sutra*). Inside the body, she sees the mandalas of the peaceful and wrathful deities (as in the teachings on the intermediate state between death and rebirth). These mandalas fill the space around the place of meditation as the pure appearances of the basis arise.

3. Perfection of secret awareness: Clairvoyance, visions of infinite buddha realms, various categories of meditative absorption, and so forth arise at this stage.

· ◌ · "Exhaustion into dharmata" (*chos nyid zad pa*): In the metaphorical language of the dzogchen yogins, the third level, perfection of awareness, is compared to the new moon, which becomes full on the fifteenth day of the lunar month. Exhaustion into dharmata, the ultimate nature of all phenomena, is comparable to the moon that disappears on the the thirtieth day of the lunar month. The external appearances of the four elements—along with the material moon, sun, and so forth—disappear without leaving a trace. Bodies dissolve into droplets, which in their turn dissolve into the inner sphere or dimension (*nang dbyings*), i.e., back into the youthful vase body. Just as the moon does not increase or decrease during its various phases, so too awareness does not increase or decrease. Its glow, however, dissolves into the basis, in the manner of the shine on a crystal withdrawing into itself. At this stage, there is only the ultimate nature (*chos nyid*) without any appearance, which is here called exhaustion (*zad pa*) and emptying (*stong pa*). Here the distinctions between cyclic existence and nirvana are erased along with other conceptualizations. The elements dissolve of themselves and the yogin attains the highest form of the rainbow body, that of the "body of great transference." In this way, with the burning out of external, experiential appearances, with the exhaustion of internal phenomena of the illusory body, and with the elimination of innermost mental conceptualizations, buddhahood is attained.

The Results of Dzogchen Practice

Those who practice the sadhanas of the great perfection system (i.e., dzogchen/atiyoga) may attain liberation in various ways. In accord with the traditional typologies of realization, one speaks of three degrees of ability: lower, middle, and highest capacity for liberation. Practitioners of lower capacities achieve buddhahood in the intermediate state after death when impure visions that would normally have preceded the next rebirth begin to arise. Practitioners of middle capacities achieve liberation in the intermediate state of dharmata or reality (*chos nyid bar do*), which is the state immediately after death in which pure visions of the basis arise. Practitioners of the highest capacities achieve liberation in this very lifetime. Those who become a buddha in this very lifetime may choose either to dissolve or not dissolve the material body, depending on their abilities and intentions with regard to compassionate action on behalf of other beings.

The term "rainbow body" may often be used as a generic term to describe the death of a yogin in which no visible corpse, perhaps with the exception of hair and nails, is left behind. A person (a practitioner of the sadhana) dies, but a body is not found. Moreover, people in the vicinity of the death of such a yogin may see rainbows in the sky and other light phenomena, both before and after the death occurs. For these reasons, one says that the yogin has attained the rainbow body. In the light of the practices we have described above, what is the nature of the attainment of the rainbow body?

Differences in the Results That Arise from Cutting-Through and Leap-Over

The tradition claims that there are various types (at least four) of rainbow body, which correspond to different styles of previous practice. Great perfection texts discuss the differences in typology, corresponding to the sadhanas of cutting-through and leap-over.

A significant author of the seventeenth century, Tsokdruk Rangdrol, in his *Key Simultaneously Opening Hundreds of Doors of Samadhi*, composed a *"Song of Spontaneity of the Leap Over of Great Perfection's Clear Light"* (*'od gsal rdzogs pa chen po'i lhun grub thod rgal gyi glu dbyangs ting 'dzin sgo 'phar brgya phrag gcig car 'byed pa'i ldeu mig ces bya ba*) that states:

> At the time of the exhaustion into dharmata, two achievements manifest: one who achieved control over both birth and entering [the womb in a future rebirth] attains buddhahood in a moment if so desired. If, however, one wishes to bring benefits to beings caught in cyclic existence, one is free to remain until cyclic existence is left empty. A yogin who achieved control over rebirth manifests in the body of great transference and brings immeasurable benefit to beings in cyclic existence.

This manifestation arises as follows:

> When all appearances become gradually exhausted, one may direct the mind towards the five fingers of one's hand, gleaming clearly in the light; returning from that appearance, the yogin sees the world with inhabitants like a reflection of the moon on the surface of water. The body, similar to a reflection in a mirror, appears in itself as the illusory body of primordial wisdom (*ye shes sgyu ma'i sku*). Such a yogin attains the vajra-like body (*rdo rje lta bu'i sku*), unobstructed internally and externally (*phyi nang zang thal*) and

not subject to harm by the four material elements. It is the yogin who perceives this body in this way; others, since their eyes are still impure, see this body as it was previously, and not as unobstructed internally and externally. Such a phenomenon is reported for Mutri Tsenpo (*mu khri btsan po*), whose hand reached through the body of Padmasambhava to touch the seat on which the vajra body of Guru Rinpoche was positioned. Such a being sends forth inconceivable numbers of manifestations and brings immeasurable benefit to beings migrating from lifetime to lifetime among the six categories of infracosmic rebirth.

He continues:

A yogin who has achieved control over entering the womb who wishes to bring extensive benefits to others, attains the great power of liberating three thousand beings simultaneously by focusing on them in the state of awareness. This may take place at the time in which such a person enters the primordial dimension of primordial purity (*ka dag gdod ma'i dbyings*). Even the microorganisms of the material body disappear into light. Reaching the internal dimension of primordial purity (*ka dag nang dbyings*), body and primordial mind exist inseparably, even though the solid matter has become invisible in the manner of fog dissolving into the sunny sky. Such a being is able to take rebirth many times in order to bring benefit to beings in the six categories of rebirth whose number is equal in number to the atoms. These are features of the leap-over of spontaneity, in which one shines like light (*'od du gsal*) upon disintegration (*dengs*) into atoms, attaining one's personal control (*rang dbang thob*) over birth-category and entering the womb. However, in cutting-through the body can be broken down into atoms and mind, down to the state of dharmata (*chos nyid*), so that there is liberation in the ground of primordial purity.

Longchenpa describes the same process as follows:

> Since one moves into the open state of self-purification (*rang sangs*), one first purifies the tendency to grasp at the subtle and gross elements and there is an increase of the open and luminous primordial wisdom. After that, the atoms of subtle and gross elements disappear individually (*so sor dengs*), matter (*rdos pa*) is cleared away like the disappearance of fog, and awareness encounters the state of exhaustion (*zad pa*), i.e., the primordial purity of dharmakaya. This is the point described as "seizing upon one's own ground" (*rang sa zin*).

Longchenpa goes on to explain a little more precisely the difference between realization by means of cutting-through and realization by means of leap-over. Cutting-through entails exhausting the elements through penetrating primordial purity. Leap-over exhausts the elements by penetrating the dimension of spontaneity of the basis. The two realizations resemble each other in their attainment of the purification of matter, externally and internally. In cutting-through, the atoms disappear and one is liberated in primordial purity, in an instant, but no body of light appears. In leap-over, the body of light appears as an aspect of the attainment of the great transference (*'pho ba chen po*). The difference in attainment is signaled by whether or not there is the body of light, but there is no difference in the mode of liberation in the primordial purity of the basis. Jigmé Lingpa also confirms this insight, explaining that by cutting-through, the elements are purified down to the level of atoms, but by leap-over one brings about the ripening of the vajra body of great transference by which enormous benefit is conferred on beings in cyclic existence. Jamgon Kongtrul the Great, the nineteenth-century notable who preserved and promoted many lineages in eastern Tibet that were in danger of extinction, commented on Jigmé Lingpa's observations as follows:

> By purifying that which appears as the [four] great elements into the great primordial wisdom of clear light, all mistaken appearances and grasping tendencies are self-liberated, externally and

internally. In this way, without abandoning anything, one brings
the three Buddha dimensions to completion as the appearance of
the path, and actualizes the path…. In the practice of leap-over,
one brings about the ripening of the impurity of the elements
(*snyigs ma*); this appears as the primordial mind of union (*zung
'jug gi ye shes*), free from birth, death, aging and decline. Since
this is the Vajra Body of Great Transference, great benefit accrues
to other beings until cyclic existence is emptied, as in the case of
Master Padmasambhava.[95]

Thus, the final result of both practices is the state of buddhahood. The
resultant difference is in the mere disappearance of the atoms, or if the atoms
themselves are purified into primordial clear light so that the body of light is
attained and one achieves the great transference.

Four Types of Bodily Dissolution Recognized in Dzogchen

On the basis of these two overall distinctions, the tradition distinguishes four
types of bodily dissolution, in an effort to be more precise about the results
of the two relevant sadhanas. Jamgon Kongtrul the Great catalogued the four
types as follows:[96]

·◊· "The Way of Death Like the *Dakinis*": Yogins whose capacities, fortune
and endeavor are perfected to the utmost capacity reach the primordial basis of liberation (*gdod ma'i grol gzhi*) in this very life. As the sign
of this attainment, the atoms of their bodies are purified (*rdul phran
dwangs pa*). They leave this life without any remaining traces of the
body. The tradition refers to this as being like the death of a dakini;
nobody sees her corpse. It is taken as a sign of having attained buddhahood without passing through the intermediate state.

·◊· "The Way of Death Like Knowledge-Holders" (Tibetan: *rigdzins*; Sanskrit: *vidhyadharas*): A yogin of supreme accomplishments disappears
accompanied by mystic sounds amidst a mass of light in the sky in such
a way that many people can see it. This is done for the sake of setting

others on the path of the Dharma. This is comparable to the progress of knowledge-holding yogins who go from stage to stage of the spiritual path accompanied by sounds and lights. However, they still have their bodily components and others can see them. This is considered to be the sign consisting of "inconceivable manifestations on inconceivable continents" so as to bring benefit to sentient beings.

◦ "The Way of Self-Exhaustion Like Fire": A yogin who has perfected the sadhana dies in the way that a fire dies out once it has completely consumed the firewood. The elements and conditions for the further arising of defilements and afflictions become nonexistent for such a yogin. This is taken as a sign of the afflictions being liberated in their own ground (*rang sar grol*).

◦ "The Way of Death Like Space": The yogin's body, comparable to a terra cotta pot made of atoms, breaks in the ground of primordial purity (*ka dag sa*) and the awareness mixes with the primordial dimension. It is called the way of death comparable to space in the way that space is that which lies in the interstices between atoms of bodily appearance (*lus snang*). Since primordial purity, the disclosure of which is realization, abides in the clear light in the heart within the body, when the pot-like body "breaks," external space and the internal space of the pot mingle so that the two volumes of space cannot be distinguished. Here, the atoms of the body disappear and the yogin becomes a Buddha without distinguishing between the bodily aggregation and the awareness that abides inside the body. This is taken as the sign of unobstructed liberation (*zang thal du grol ba*) in the ground of primordial purity.

These four categories disclose the distinctions between the results of cutting-through and leap-over. The way of death of *dakinis* and the way of death like space are related to the perfect attainment of the secret path of cutting-through. The way of death like knowledge-holders and the way of self-exhaustion like fire are related to the perfection of the secret path of leap-over. The body breaks down to atoms and the mind goes down to dharmata in cutting-through, becoming liberated in the ground of primordial purity. In leap-over, when the body is breaking down into atoms, it further clears into light (*'od du gsal*), at which point one attains control over birth and entrance into a future rebirth. In this way, the body of great transference arises in order to benefit beings migrating through cyclic existence.

These teachings find expression in the biographical tradition of various realized masters. In fact, it would seem that the descriptions in the theoretical works take into account the biographical narratives (*rnam thar*) of these saints, especially at the time of their death. For example, Jigmé Lingpa states: "… Regarding those who pass away with five signs: lights, sounds, [buddha] bodies, relics (*gdung*) and earthquakes, it is said that they have attained buddhahood." We saw something of this in the accounts of the death and dissolution of the master Khenpo A Chö, who passed away in eastern Tibet in 1998. Other examples are cited in various biographical works. The earliest large-scale biography of Milarepa recounts the miraculous manifestations in the sky at the time of his passing in similar terms.[97]

In keeping with the intentional harmonization of dzogchen realization with Mahayana Buddhist doctrine, we see that some yogins may wish to perform extraordinary service to the Dharma and sentient beings. The ground of the exhaustion of the elements of embodiment may be attained, but it is still possible not to exhaust the karmic energy fluxes (winds) completely. The winds remain as various kinds of relics (*gdung; ring bsrel*) that can benefit sentient beings. Jamgon Kongtrul the Great stated: "If it is beneficial for others, they also leave that which was dissolved (*dengs pa*) into atoms, having blessed it as relics."[98] From a strictly Buddhist *Abhidharma* point of view, what dissolves here is not gross matter, but only its appearance. From the *Abhidharma* doctrinal perspective, when we are alive, our body is held in continuity by our own mental continuum (*rang rgyud kyis zin pa*), whereas other external phenomena are not held by our mental continuum. The external appearances are considered as the common perceptual field held by different individuals because of previous karmic experiences they have shared. In the dzogchen practitioner, the predominance of the mental continuum of the yogin over the perceptions associated with the common perceptual field of others allows for the appearance of a material body to dissolve. It is as if the very sacredness of the body of the yogin has an impact on the observers such that the observers no longer perceive in accordance with their karmic propensities but with the enlightened perception of the yogin! The power of the yogin's realization in relation to the mental continua of observers prevails over the power of the corpse in relation to the common perceptual field. Thus, if he performs great perfection practices that bring about the simultaneous dissolution of mind and body, not only the mind becomes "invisible" but also the body. In this way, we might say that everything that was directly related to the person of the yogin now disappears. For this reason, occasionally hair and nails may be left behind when the body disappears, since these features remain in the field of common perception. Clearly, this insight illuminates the traditional teaching that a guru is indispensable for tantric realization. In other words, one needs to connect with an authentic master whose very presence evokes the necessary changes of perception—of being and of presence.

The Rainbow Body

First of all, we need to understand what the body of light is. Please note that the disappearance of the body at the time of death of a practitioner of cutting-through sadhanas is strictly speaking neither the rainbow body nor the physical body, it is the absence of the body. This absence, or disappearance, is sometimes loosely termed the rainbow body.

It is the teaching of Mahayana Buddhism, including the Buddhist tantras, that the final result of practice is the state of buddhahood, in which all possible negative qualities are extinguished and the full omniscience of all phenomena of the three times is obtained. As soon as one becomes a Buddha, disclosing the body of reality (*dharmakaya*), one can emanate personal manifestations without number to the various realms of the universe so as to liberate sentient beings. These emanations are all called *rupakaya*, the body of form, whether *sambhogakaya* (accessible only to beings advanced on the path) or *nirmanakaya* (accessible to ordinary individuals, *pṛthagjana*). Buddhahood can in fact manifest in any form: as a subtle body of light, gross physical body, human, animal, demon, titan, deity, bridge, raft, flower, etc.[99]

What, then, is so special about the attainment of the body of light? There are six features that seem to distinguish it:

1. Attainment of the body of light is uniquely the result of the great perfection leap-over sadhana, which is considered to be the most profound Buddhist practice.
2. The body of light is the most efficient means for benefiting sentient beings when other means are unsuccessful.
3. The body of light demonstrates the uniqueness and efficacy of the leap-over sadhanas, in which psychological and physical transformations take place simultaneously.
4. Not being caused by artificial techniques, the manifestation of the body of light is the spontaneous display of the primordial ultimate nature of our being.
5. In the manifestation of the body of light, the personal body is not discarded, but transformed.
6. The body of light can be seen only by buddha (mind).[100]

Once we have understood these features of the body of light, we can understand how the disclosure of this attainment resolves a number of problems in the classic presentations of buddhahood. For example, if the buddhas have so many transcendent qualities and can emanate *nirmanakayas* (appearance bodies) in the entire universe, why are there still unenlightened beings cycling through samsara? Whereas all buddhas are equal in their omniscience, freedom from negativities, and in compassion and so forth, they are not equal in benefiting this or that particular person. Prior to their final enlightenment, in the accumulation of merit, they built certain links with individuals, groups, places, times, and so forth, just as ordinary individuals develop karmic relationships with buddhas and bodhisattvas in the course of their spiritual development. For this reason, certain persons will be more rapidly or efficiently benefited by one buddha rather than by another. In Tibet, the unique impact of Padmasambhava's mission is attributed to his attainment of the body of great transference, the supreme manifestation of the rainbow body. By his charismatic abilities, Padmasambhava was able to pacify demonic forces and political opponents within Tibet in ways that other great masters were not able to do, as a result of his mastery of the sadhanas bearing fruition in the body of great transference.

In the traditions that accept the doctrine of reincarnation, it is understood that our pleasant or repulsive physical appearance can indicate how good or bad we were in a previous incarnation. Our current mental condition may also indicate the prevalence of inclinations that can create the situation of our next rebirth. The Buddhist canonical literature describes various abilities, clairvoyance, and magical powers, as mental and physical signs of the transformation that occurs as one makes spiritual progress. Only in the practice of leap-over are the signs of attainment manifested as mental, verbal, and physical changes that are inseparable from the increase of one's degree of spiritual realization, until finally the whole physical body transforms into the body of light.

An important distinction between great perfection practice and the stages of creation and completion in the Vajrayana systems is that great perfection utilizes the ultimate state of awareness on the path *as* the path. One does not visualize the body as a deity form, nor does one work with the visualizations of channels, energy fluxes and consciousness droplets as in the six yogas of Naropa and other practices derived from the Buddhist tantras. The illusory body (*sgyu lus*) is achieved in the Six Yogas by binding the channels and fluxes of energy so as to make the channels flexible and dissolving grosser energies so that the subtle energies will manifest. According to the critical view of dzogchen, this approach will not produce the vajra body (*rdo rje'i sku*), or body of light. According to dzogchen, the latter is attained through the dissolution of the appearances of outer and inner elements into the primordial ultimate dimension.

Another feature of the body of light is that at the time of attaining buddhahood, having completed the four visions of leap-over practice, one does not discard the body, leaving behind a corpse. Nor does the body dissolve into atoms, as in the resultant phase of cutting-through. What happens is that coarse matter is transformed into the subtle nature of light, or more precisely (since this is not really a transformation of matter), it is a question of the transformation of the vision that seems to transform matter in our sensory perception. Since the body remains connected to the subtle mind or awareness (*rig pa*), and not severed as in ordinary death or in the dissolution of the atoms, the body of light is able to bring about benefit to innumerable beings.

This doctrine very closely resembles what is described for the resurrection body of Jesus Christ: the resurrected body is not severed from the divine and human consciousness of Christ. Moreover, the resurrected body continues to be present in the sacramental rituals of the church, particularly in the Eucharist, in order to bring about salvation without limits of time, space or ordinary perception. It is interesting that, according to the research in primary sources presented above, there is a question of the relativity of perception and there is also a possibility for leaving behind relics. In the Christian experience of the resurrection, the category of "faith" (Greek: *pistis*) describes the relativity of perception, as is clear from the earliest Christian texts that survive (the authentic letters of Paul[101]). At the same time, the category of anamnetic memory (that is, memory that brings about presence, and not just memory of a past event) is operative in the Eucharist and other sacraments that make present the risen Christ. The mysterious relics of the shroud, the Eucharistic elements, and the various visionary experiences also coincide with what has been said above about relics for the benefit of sentient beings. Some of the Eucharistic miracles are quite extraordinary, defying the normal decay processes associated with flesh and blood (Lanciano, and more recently in Argentina[102]). It is also significant that the blood relics of the Shroud of Turin and other physical relics (the Holy Face in Manupella, Abruzzo, Italy, and the Sudarium [wiping cloth] in Orviedo, Spain) as well as the Eucharistic relics all have characteristics in common, such as the relatively rare AB blood type. These phenomena suggest that the resurrection of Jesus had, and continues to have, features in common with the Tibetan rainbow body/body of light phenomenon.

In our next chapter, we will explore a kind of Christian spiritual practice, historically antecedent to Tibetan dzogchen, in order to coordinate our study of both the rainbow body and the resurrection. This moves our essay forward towards a consideration of the origins of the great perfection.

III

❧

The Spirituality of the Syriac Church of the East, From Egypt to China: History of the Evagrian Trajectory in the Syriac Churches and the Doctrine of the Resurrection in Early Christianity

What is yet to happen to our bodies should now take place in our hearts.

—St. Leo the Great, De Passione

This chapter on the resurrection is the most difficult of all precisely because of the emic/etic problem we discussed in the introduction. Although Christianity is considered the prevalent religious tradition in the English-speaking world, in terms of actual practice, it has become a complicated minority of competing religious denominations. Each denomination has its own history, theology, and self-definition, often in contrast to the other denominations. The author belongs to one of those Christian churches and is deeply sympathetic to a number of the other branches of the church. In this chapter, it will be necessary to enter into a conversation with readers who belong to religions other than Christianity, nonreligious persons, Christians of various theological persuasions, and persons trained in several scientific disciplines. Although this entire book faces the challenges of such a dialogue, the present chapter encounters those challenges in a particularly dense way. Christianity is nearly two thousand years old. In the English-speaking world, there are probably millions of publications about, for, and against Christianity. The extant literature on each verse in the Bible is so large that no one person could ever hope to master it entirely. In order to explore the meaning of the resurrection in dialogue with the rainbow body, it will be necessary to examine a handful of biblical verses, and to make adventurous forays into forms of historical Christianity that are not at all well known to most English-speaking people. It was the great multicultural theologian Raimondo Panikkar who advised us many years ago that "The impossible is the only thing worth attempting," and indeed what this chapter aims to accomplish is the impossible.

In order to enter this vast territory, it is necessary to make several long sets of connections. We need to begin with some familiar verses from the Bible, along with some obscure ones, in order to understand some very ancient ideas about ascension and resurrection. The resurrection of Jesus is connected to the resurrection of all persons; in order to clarify this relationship, we need to examine some ideas about life, death, and personhood in the earliest Christian centuries. To understand how those ideas informed actual spiritual practices, we will visit the Desert Fathers in fourth-century Egypt and their heirs in Byzantium and the Middle East. In Mesopotamia and Persia, we will encounter the Syriac-speaking Christians whose role in the history of civilization is still poorly understood in the West. Thanks to these Christians, however, over the course of the fifth century the mysticism of the Greek-speaking world entered the very heart of Central Asia with the emergence of a stabile Nestorian Church in the Middle East. Among these Christians, the Egyptian contemplative teachings acquired distinctive features from the sixth to the eighth century. These teachings connect with Central Asian, Chinese, and Tibetan Buddhism in surprising ways. No one has yet surveyed these connections in depth, and the unfamiliarity of the material may make the reader suspect that this author is engaging in special pleading for the Christian side. Most readers will probably find the kind of Christianity I am about to describe to be completely alien to their experience of Christian life and piety. However, since at this very moment we are observing with dismay the systematic destruction of this particular Syriac-speaking[103] Christian tradition in its homeland, it seems that a wider diffusion of these teachings is an urgent task for Christians of our times.

By demonstrating the kind of spiritual exchange that took place in the history of Central Asia, we may be able to contribute to the dialogue of shared spiritual experience in our own times. In this way, we can perhaps diminish the prejudice that is sweeping through many cultures, East and West, making the positive contributions of Christianity to culture and spirituality ever more difficult to nurture and communicate. I have found that not only Western university students, but also leading American Buddhist scholars are astonishingly lacking in awareness of the spiritual disciplines that have characterized all forms of Christianity from the earliest times. Some students have picked up a prejudice that Christianity is a religion of moralism and dogmatism without any grounding in life experience, meditation, or life enhancement. When it comes to mystical contemplation, it is as if the question no longer arises. These prejudices are now typical of the view of Christianity in all its forms among educated people, in both the East and West. A serious study of this crucial Asian trajectory might challenge thoughtful people to reexamine the basis for their views about Christianity. Committed Christians willing to openly encounter this history and its implications might even participate in a significant revival of contemplative Christianity in our own times. There have been already many tantalizing experiments along these lines over the past fifty years, few of which (Bose[104] is an example, and there are a handful of others) have flourished significantly.

The open-minded reader may consider being persuaded that a contemplative form of Christianity spread across Central Asia to encounter Buddhism and other religious traditions in the eighth century. However, the full implications of this encounter may challenge the religious convictions of both contemporary Christians and Buddhists and may become more explosive when we attempt to compare the resurrection and the rainbow body. Perhaps that is why we are here, turning these pages.

Traditional Christianity, both Eastern and Western, proclaims as a central article of faith that the resurrection of Jesus is a unique demonstration of his divinity and saving power. Catholic Christians speak of "the paschal mystery" of the death and resurrection of Jesus as the foundation of the entire complex of Christian belief and practice. The tradition also carefully distinguishes between the resurrection and the ascension of Jesus. The resurrection occurs on the third day after the crucifixion, and Jesus makes himself present in various mysterious but unmistakable ways to the disciples in the course of forty days.

At the end of the forty days, Jesus is taken up into the heavens. Catholic tradition asserts that the Virgin Mary, the mother of Jesus, was taken up body and soul at the time of her passing away; this dogma is called the Assumption of the Blessed Virgin Mary. Thus Mary's body anticipates the general resurrection that is to occur on the last day of human history.

However, both Jewish and Christian traditions acknowledge other forms of the transformation or translation of the incorrupt body: for example Enoch, Elijah, and, in apocryphal works, Moses. Moreover, Catholic tradition accepts the possibility that Jesus's resurrection body may appear to living human beings at various times in the course of church history. The conversion of St. Paul, reported three times in the New Testament, serves as an important witness to this belief. A classic but not unique example in more recent times is that of St. Margaret Mary Alacoque (1647–1690) in the seventeenth century. Her visionary experiences were enshrined in Catholic piety as the devotion to the Sacred Heart. Similarly, the visions of Christ experienced by St. Faustina Kowalska (1905–1938) in the 1930s are the basis for the ever more popular devotion to the Divine Mercy.

It is also Christian belief, rooted in the biblical witness, that the bodies of deceased human beings will resurrect at the end of the world when Christ returns in glory. It is not thought to be possible for human beings to resurrect before the Last Day,[105] although some neo-Protestant groups believe in something called the rapture in which living human beings are taken up by Christ into the heavens before the end of the world[106]. In the New Testament, there are episodes of resurrection, including several miraculous resuscitations of the dead performed by Jesus and the apostles. As reported in Matthew 27:52-53, a number of holy persons came forth from their tombs at the time of the resurrection of Jesus.

The resurrection of the dead as a necessary feature of life after death—including judgment, punishment, and reward—was known to early Zoroastrianism, pharisaic/rabbinic Judaism, most forms of Christianity, and Islam. In addition, such hagiographical legends as the *Seven Sleepers of Ephesus*[107] (cf. surah 17, Qur'an) illustrate how the idea of the resurrection in symbolic form is closely associated with saintliness. In medieval Christianity, in both the East and West, the veneration of relics was often expressed in terms that describe the sacred remains of holy persons as a kind of luminous resurrection body, anticipating the body that will be recovered at the end of the world by all, the good and the condemned alike.

Ancient and medieval Christianity insisted that the resurrected body be as nearly intact as possible. Even the specific body parts, the fleshly substance, of the living person must be reunited with the same soul in order to assert the integrity of the individual human person, good or bad. According to this line of belief, the dissolution of a human body would seem to undermine the integrity of the resurrection body of human beings. For this reason, until fairly recently, Christian churches forbade cremation.

From a Christian theological perspective, the claim that Christian or non-Christian contemplatives such as Khenpo A Chö might have attained the resurrection body before the end of the world is highly problematic. In the first place, the only recognized means for obtaining sanctity is belief in Christ and participation in the sacramental life of the church. The sacraments are the means by which God confers the grace of Christ on believers, preparing them for full participation in the divine life at the end of the world. The resurrection of the body occurs for all at the end of the world, but those who did not in some way lead a life of faith and charity will not "inherit the kingdom of God." Those who did otherwise are damned for all eternity as a just consequence of their evil actions or because of their resistance to the grace of salvation, which is always offered to every human being through the mercy of God. In his recent apostolic exhortation, *Evangelii Gaudium*, Pope Francis has indicated quite clearly that other religions can be the means by which non-Christians receive divine grace:

> Non-Christians, by God's gracious initiative, when they are faithful to their own consciences, can live "justified by the grace of God" and thus be "associated to the paschal mystery of Jesus Christ." But due to the sacramental dimension of sanctifying grace, God's working in them tends to produce signs and rites, sacred expressions which in turn bring others to a communitarian experience of journeying towards God. While these lack the meaning and efficacy of the sacraments instituted by Christ, they can be channels which the Holy Spirit raises up in order to liberate

non-Christians from atheistic immanentism or from purely individual religious experiences. The same Spirit everywhere brings
forth various forms of practical wisdom which help people to bear
suffering and to live in greater peace and harmony. As Christians,
we can also benefit from these treasures built up over many centuries, which can help us better to live our own beliefs.[108]

However, it should be clear that the Pope's comments, open and reassuring as they are, do not allow us to make strictly theological assertions about
the extraordinary charisms that are being claimed for Buddhist and Bonpo
attainers of the rainbow body. By "signs and rites" the Holy Father is directing
our attention to formal, visible aspects of other religions, and not to charismatic phenomena. However, by referring to sacramental grace operative in
other religions, Pope Francis leaves open the possibility that holiness might
become visible in transformed human persons in their psychosomatic integrity. This is because, by definition, a sacrament is a visible sign instituted by
Christ to confer grace on persons in their body-soul lived reality. It would be
a very great challenge, nonetheless, for Christian theology to acknowledge
the claims of dzogchen practitioners regarding paranormal phenomena that
in some ways resemble the resurrection. For this reason, it seems more helpful
to make use of the methods of cultural anthropology and history of religions
to articulate what is meant by the attainment of the rainbow body. This basic
research is a necessary prelude to a meaningful, long-term theological reflection on the claims we have been investigating.

At the same time, by investigating the one Christian tradition that had
documented and fruitful encounters with Buddhists in the early days of
dzogchen, we can advance the suggestion that at least some Buddhists were
changed by that encounter. Something happened between the 750s and
1100 to alter the doctrinal texture of tantric Buddhism in Tibet. The influence was subtle and combined with other important encounters, above
all with Indian Shaivite traditions, but it seems that the Christian themes
of eschatology and universal purpose, eschatology, and bodily resurrection
awakened new kinds of spiritual practice and philosophical reflection among
some Tibetan Buddhists.

Given the fact that the literal resurrection of the dead is not believed by many modern liberal Christians, it is at least of some pastoral value to reflect on the implications of the rainbow body for contemporary Buddhists and Christians. After all, the medieval problem of regaining the same fleshly substance at the resurrection of the dead seems strangely to be resolved by the way the rainbow body is understood in dzogchen. The actual body of the yogin is transformed into the "essence" of the elements, with no loss of identity at all, at least to the extent that the notions of person and identity are relevant in the nondualist Indo-Tibetan traditions. In my opinion, this is a good example of how a completely alien metaphysical tradition seems to support the Christian teaching more persuasively than the kind of Hellenistic philosophy that has traditionally been used in Christian theology. The intense concern with the "same" bodily parts arose because of debates over identity, substance, nature, and change in Aristotelian metaphysics. Just as in the earliest strata of biblical tradition, the spiritual life in Syro-Oriental Christianity and in tantric Buddhism engages the entire person in integrity. For these traditions, body-soul dualism is an articulation of philosophical distinctions that do not exclude the integrity of mystical experience and its unitary subject. The Syriac Christian traditions, although deeply imbued with the Hellenistic theology that gave them their identity, remained faithful to the old biblical anthropology. This preference for energetic embodiment both human and divine may be why this different Christianity was able to have the remarkable impact in Central and East Asia that we are going to claim for it. Instead of emphasizing the unchanging eternal substance of the divine as in Hellenistic theology, Syriac Christianity stood in awe of the dynamic presence of the triune God in the story of human salvation, both collective and individual. Syro-Oriental Christian mystics encountered Central Asian Buddhists at precisely the moment when Buddhists were integrating new, more dynamic theologies from the Shaivite yogins of India in the form of tantrism. It is out of this process of integration that dzogchen arose as a distinctive approach in Tibetan Buddhism. Our task is to find out more about both sides of this conversation in the period that interests us—a conversation that occurred long before the developments we have outlined in chapter two.

From a scientific, materialist viewpoint, any claims of postmortem survival, bodies resurrecting, or the rainbow/light body are at best literary expressions of the human need to come to terms psychologically with death through cultural and symbolic forms. These forms and their accompanying literature are not to be interpreted literally. Death is final; consciousness cannot be supported without a living biological (or, possibly, cybernetic) organism. Research on consciousness seems to be going anxiously in the direction of denying any nonmaterial basis for psychological phenomena of any kind. Even those with the most progressive leanings in the scientific community, who advocate the hypothesis of self-organization for the primordial structures of life on this planet, seem to be allied to this perspective: *no structure, no phenomenon*. Both traditional Christianity and tantric Buddhism oppose this reductionist perspective by insisting on nonmaterial features as part of their overarching view of reality, including postmortem survival. In order to understand traditional religious views on postmortem survival, it is impossible to restrict oneself to the ways in which science chooses to describe the object of its research. Entirely different methods of research have to be devised, some of which necessarily overstep the limitations of a merely materialistic worldview.

No one could formulate an experiment that would scientifically demonstrate the reality of the rainbow body or of the resurrection to the satisfaction of the scientific community. The phenomenon would have to remain outside the sphere of scientific discourse (in terms of the sociology of knowledge). Belief is suspect; therefore, the credibility not only of hagiographical texts but also of eyewitnesses is suspect. Science and literary criticism operate on the principle of a "hermeneutics of suspicion": texts are written, and testimony is given, on the basis of a need to defend, attack, or assert *a priori* beliefs, assumptions, axioms, etc. The *a priori* assumptions may be inferred at the investigator's own risk! An alternative methodology is called for, one that bridges the gap between emic and etic. For many of us, an even-handed approach borrowed from cultural anthropology begins to offer a solution; the observer is a participant observer, trained in the discipline of self-awareness. As research proceeds, the researcher develops an ever more rigorous analysis of his or her own motivations for doing research, and becomes more critical of personal biases in offering interpretations. As time goes on, motivations and biases may evolve in such a way as to shape the researcher into a capable communicator between the emic and the etic, between the culture under study, and the culture to which the researcher will return. As skilled anthropologists know, the researcher changes as a result of the experience of observation and participation. This change begins the process of moving with ordinary forms of reasoning in the direction of more profound typologies of cognition, such as those that are cultivated in monasteries, hermitages, and ashrams. Such a revised methodology will combine textual study, linguistics, geography, and history with the direct participatory investigation of human communities of discourse, in order to move beyond the materialistic impasse.

Biblical Texts Relevant to Resurrection and Ascension

Pre-Zoroastrian religion in Iran held to a notion of the restoration of a body to the virtuous dead immediately after death so that they might enjoy the delights of the heavenly world. Zoroaster's contribution seems to have been the idea that the resurrection of the body would have to wait until after the final battle between good and evil; it is from Zoroaster that Judaism, Christianity, and Islam receive their teachings on the resurrection of the dead on the Last Day. One might conjecture on the basis of text studies whether the ideas of immortality (and the practice of mummification) in ancient Egypt also shared in this vision of the afterlife as a place of enduring enjoyment requiring some form of embodiment. Ancient Chinese, Central Asian, and Tibetan royal burials included concubines, retainers, even horses and other necessary domestic animals, presumably because after death there would be another life in which these objects would be useful. According to Central Asian traditions, the companions of the ruler were to die with him and be buried in a large mound that symbolized the lord's authority as ruler of a portion of the cosmos. In ancient India, the *cakravartin*, the emperor of the four quarters, was expected to conquer neighboring kingdoms as a symbol of cosmic overlordship, embodied in the twelve-year-long horse sacrifice. The *cakravartin* ideal, which definitely shaped the notion of buddhahood, is not however accompanied by a notion of an embodied afterlife, nor have archeologists in India discovered collective mound burials.

Judaism after the exile in Babylon took on some of the religious ideas of Persia. The Persian Shah Cyrus favored the return of the Jewish exiles to their homeland and financed the rebuilding of the Temple in Jerusalem. This was a period of great importance for the Jews, for it was at this time that the Hebrew text of the Bible was extensively redacted. From the word *Persia*, South Asian languages derived the word *Parsees* to describe the Persian followers of Zoroaster's faith; it is not difficult to recognize the same root in the Aramaic word *Pharisee*. The Pharisees of the New Testament period were those rabbis who followed teachings that had affinities with Persian religion: resurrection of the dead, a last judgment, angelology, and even hope that a savior/messiah would be born of a virgin to lead the final battle between good and evil. This Pharisaic heritage survived to become rabbinic Judaism. The Qumran (Essene) community held similar doctrines in an even more emphatically eschatological form, as attested in the Dead Sea Scrolls. It is sometimes asserted that the Jews did not believe in the resurrection before this period, and a good deal of evidence would tend to confirm this fact. It is not all that clear, however, that there was no notion of an afterlife in Israelite religion prior to the Persian period (fifth century BCE), given such episodes as the act of necromancy by the witch of Endor in the time of King Saul. Some scholars will point out that the word "resurrection" is not found in the Hebrew Scriptures; it only appears in the Greek text of the Books of Maccabees. However, prophetic descriptions of resurrection are not lacking. For example, in Isaiah 26:19: "Your dead will come back to life, your corpses will rise again; Wake up and sing, you dwellers in the dust, for your dew will be a radiant dew." The subtlety of dew and radiance appears in other cultures as symbols of the subtle body. Another probably pre-Persian text is the famous "dry bones" vision of Ezekiel chapter 37. The bodily resurrection of the just was a consistent theme in the apocalyptic and eschatological texts of pre-Christian Judaism. Most scholars claim that bodily resurrection was an attempt to find a theological category with which to honor the memory of those Jews who were martyred under Hellenistic persecution. With ancient Israelite religion, the primary concern is always to live in accordance with the Torah in this life and to maintain the integrity of the people of the covenant. Thus, religious practice is always embodied and, for the most part, this-worldly, as can be clearly seen in the Law of Moses. The Torah cannot be lived in the postmortem state.

However, after centuries of religious and political challenges, even ancient Israel began to discover the value of honoring those who had been faithful. Thus we have the classic quotations, still in use in our Catholic liturgies for the dead, from the Book of Wisdom: "The souls of the just are in the hands of God; no torments will touch them. To the eyes of fools, it seemed that they died, that their end was a disaster, their departure from among us to be a ruin, but they are in peace. Even if it seems in the eyes of men that they suffered chastisement, their hope is filled with immortality." (Wisdom 3:1-4) In a verse applied to Christ himself, a determined reply to the cynical question "What was the outcome of his life?" we have: "The Just One, even if he were to die prematurely, will find rest ... true longevity is a life lived without stain." (Wisdom 4:7-9) In fact, the following verse uses the same expression used for Enoch in Genesis 5:24: "He was dear to God and loved by Him; since he lived among sinners, he was transported, he was rapt [taken elsewhere]." (Wisdom 4:10-11)

In the earliest layers of biblical narratives, there are obscure references to a kind of ascension not preceded by bodily death. Many of the later esoteric writings of the Jews turned to these traditions in devising narratives of the end times and visionary experiences of the heavens. An important example would be the books of Enoch, which were written between the second century BCE and the first century CE. The figure of Enoch appears in Genesis 5:23 as one who lived 365 years, a "full year of years," a much shorter life than that of his relatives, such as his father Jared who lived 962 years (Genesis 5:20) and his son the unforgettable Methuselah who lived 969 years (Genesis 5:27), the longest life claimed for a human being in the Bible. In Genesis 5:24 we read that "Enoch walked with God and then was no more, because God took him." The verse is terse and enigmatic, but has always been interpreted to mean that Enoch did not die in the usual way, but was in some way taken up by God as a special privilege related to his righteousness. The body of Enoch literature, largely written by sectarian Jews around the time of Jesus, employs the legends surrounding this mysterious figure to explore the esoteric secrets of creation and human destiny.[109]

In the story of Elijah (II Kings 2:1-12), the master prophet is accompanied by his disciple Elisha: "They went on talking as they walked and suddenly there appeared a chariot of fire and horses of fire, which separated them from one another and Elijah went up in the whirlwind to the sky" (verse 11). The episode is traditionally located in the place where Moses is said to have died and been secretly buried (Deuteronomy 34:5-6), or possibly ascended. The *Letter of Jude* in the New Testament, Josephus (*Antiquities* 4.325-26), St. Ambrose, Philo, Clement of Alexandria, Origen, and early rabbinic writings hint at the existence of an apocryphal account of the ascension of Moses.[110] For example, "Moses ascended in the cloud, was hidden by the cloud, and was sanctified by the cloud" (*Babylonian Talmud Yoma* 4a) and "When Moses was to ascend, a cloud descended and lay before him, and the cloud covered Moses and carried him up" (*Pesikta Rabbati* 20:4). These notions were important for Christians because of the account of the transfiguration of Jesus, in which both Moses and Elijah appear as representatives of the Law and the prophets. Their appearance raised questions for the disciples Peter, James, and John, regarding the identity of Jesus as "Son of Man" who would "rise from the dead." (Mark 9:2-13; Matthew 17:1-13 and Luke 9:28-36; see also: II Peter 1:17-18). It was understood that Moses had ascended as had Elijah, because he was recognizable in the form of his ascended human body. In the Book of Apocalypse (11:11-12), two mysterious prophetic witnesses to the truth of the Gospel are put to death and then rise again. The tradition understands these to be Moses and Elijah, the same ascended prophets present at the transfiguration (cf. Jude 1:9). Jesus's own ascension into the heavens is described in terms similar to those used for Elijah: "in the act of blessing he parted from them," (Luke 24:51) and for Moses, again written by Luke: "After he had said this, he was lifted up before their very eyes, and a cloud took him from their sight" (Acts 1:9).

The resurrection of Jesus was a turning point since it was being openly proclaimed that the miracle of Jesus's rising from the dead after his crucifixion was proof that he was "Lord (YHWH/*Adonai*) and Messiah (Christ, the anointed one of God)," as stated in the first verse of the First Letter to the Thessalonians, the earliest extant Pauline letter. This letter affirms the earliest Christian belief in the resurrection of Jesus, presented as inseparable from the postmortem destiny of those who believe in him: "As we believe that Jesus died and resurrected (Greek: *anestē*), so also those who have fallen asleep (died believing) in Jesus, will be led by God to be with him." (I Thessalonians 4:14) Although it has become commonplace to say that Paul in some way altered the original teachings of Jesus, one is struck by the authentic pre-Pauline tone of this expression of faith. Moreover, in chapter 5:2-4, we have a rare example of Paul quoting a saying of Jesus found in the Gospels of Matthew (24:43-44) and Luke (12:39-40). Most scholars would agree that I Thessalonians was written well before the year 50 or 51,[111] whereas Matthew and Luke are probably from the 70s or even 80s, two or more decades later than Paul. For this reason, one should be cautious about segregating the Pauline writings from the beliefs, practices, and Jesus-based teachings of the earliest Christian communities (30s to 50s). Paul is already, at this early phase of the history of Christianity, very much aware of handing on a living tradition of faith, as we can see in another key text about the resurrection (I Corinthians 15:3-7), the famous passage on the handing on (Greek: *paradosis*) of the earliest Christian beliefs: "First and foremost, I handed on to you the tradition I had received: that Christ died for our sins, in accordance with the scriptures; that he was buried; that he was raised to life on the third day, in accordance with the scriptures; and that he appeared to Cephas, and afterwards to the Twelve...." A few verses later, Paul connects belief in the resurrection of Jesus to the teaching on the resurrection of the dead: "Now if this is what we proclaim, that Christ was raised from the dead, how can some of you say there is no resurrection of the dead? If there is no resurrection, then Christ was not raised; and if Christ was not raised, then our gospel is null and void, and so too is your faith. For if the dead are not raised, it follows that Christ was not raised" (I Corinthians 15:12-16). Here it becomes clear that what matters to a thinker like Paul is not restricted to the terse tradition of faith of the earliest Christians. Paul's personal experience of the risen Christ impels him to explore deeper convictions with universal implications. There would be no need for a polemical tone if Paul had not seen in the criticism of the idea of a bodily resurrection an attack on the integrity of the entire gift of salvation. Paul experienced the risen Christ several years after the death and resurrection; he refers to this in Galatians 1:15-17. The episode is described in greater detail in Acts 22:1-16 and Acts 9:1-19, where it is clear that the risen Jesus is personally present and identifies himself with the community of believers in an intimate way: "Saul, Saul, why are you persecuting me?" This is another reason Paul, who is admittedly somewhat independent in his approach to the original disciples of Jesus (Galatians 1:16-19), never deviates from his strong convictions that the risen Jesus is embodied in the living Christian community (I Corinthians 12:27-31) and its sacraments (I Corinthians 11:16-29), especially the Eucharist. Thus, when Paul goes on to explain how the resurrection of the body is to take place, he is speaking on the basis of his intuitive grasp of church, Spirit, sacraments, and risen Christ. For this reason, he is a bit frustrated (I Corinthians 15:35-36): "But, you may ask, how the dead are raised? In what kind of body? What stupid questions!" He then asserts: (verse 44) "sown in a physical body, it is raised a spiritual body (*soma pneumatikos*)." It is this spiritual body that had to be explained by later theologians in terms that would reconcile all the Pauline teachings with various beliefs about body, soul, and immortality among Hellenistic thinkers.[112] What is important for our discussion is that this spiritual body is a *body*, it is the body of a *distinct person*, indeed of each and every person, and, in the case of a sanctified person, this body is *intimately united to the risen Christ*.

TABLE I. RESURRECTION IN SOME NEW TESTAMENT TEXTS

II Cor 12: 1-8: Paul's experience of heavenly ascent, revelations, similar to *merkavah* mysticism
John 5:24 "Whoever listens to my words and believes in the One who sent me *has* eternal life"—realized eschatology
John 5:28 "Do not be surprised at this, for the hour is coming when the dead will leave their graves at the sound of his voice."
John 5:29 "Those who did good will come forth to life; and those who did evil will come forth to judgment."
John 6:40 "It is my Father's will that whoever sees the Son and believes in him should have eternal life and that I should raise that person up on the last day."

Beginning with the Pauline letters, we are able to discern the origins of a Christian mystical tradition that continues to develop during the earliest centuries of the history of the church. The Letter to the Romans (chap. 8) gives us a kind of blueprint of the nature and character of the Christian's inner life, "in the Spirit" who not only moves the believer to pray and cry out, "Father!" (*Abba*) but also gives the Christian something quite unique in the history of religions: a dynamic, intimate participation in the life of God. By being united to Christ and sanctified by the Spirit, the Christian reorients his or her very existence toward the source of all Being, the "*Abba*" to whom Jesus directs his great prayer, the "Our Father." This new orientation is a reversal of all previous tendencies towards alienation and selfishness, which Paul calls "the flesh" (see Romans 8:8). Unfortunately, at times the later tradition failed to see the psychological and spiritual depths of this term, and imposed on the embodied human condition a kind of negative view that gave at least some people the impression that we should never have been embodied at all. Worse yet, asceticism was taught in *some* texts as a battle not so much against evil thoughts and tendencies but against the physical flesh of the human body itself. This is not what Paul meant at all, but unfortunately it is one of those mistaken interpretations that have made this great apostle the scapegoat for many unbalanced assertions by later writers. In the writings associated with Paul and his disciples, we can see more clearly how many mystical teachings flow from an authentic interpretation of the texts. For example, "[the Christian] is buried with him [Christ] in Baptism; you have been raised up with him in virtue of your faith in the power of God who re-awakened him from death" (Colossians 2:8). In this way, faith becomes a means by which resurrection takes root in the lived experience of the believer. On this basis a whole transcendent vision opens up: "If you have risen with Christ, seek the things that are above where Christ is seated at the right of God." (Colossians 3:1) Placing this verse alongside the moral teachings of the Pauline letters, we can see that the Christian is invited to live in a transcendent dimension simultaneously within the sphere of matter, space, and time. This is the entire basis for the Christian contemplative tradition, which is inconceivable without a personal, intuitive, and constantly renewed fidelity, not only to a set of predetermined beliefs but also to certain transformative practices.

The sixth chapter or the Gospel of John—probably given its final form in the last decade of the first century CE—is an extended discourse in which Jesus reiterates the doctrines that the Pharisees transmitted within Judaism. The Johannine Jesus connects these teachings with his own life in complex ways. "Anyone who does eat my flesh and drink my blood *has* eternal life and I shall raise that person up on the last day" (John 6:54). This, and related statements in this chapter, confirm the following:

TABLE II. ETERNAL LIFE IN THE GOSPEL OF JOHN

Eternal life (which, in the Gospel of John, means salvation-the kingdom of heaven) is given *now* to believers:
John 6:47 Everyone who believes *has* eternal life.
John 6:51 Anyone who eats this bread will live forever and the bread that I shall give is my flesh for the life of the world.
John 6:54 Anyone who does eat my flesh and drink my blood *has* eternal life and I shall raise that person up on the last day.
John 6: 56 Whoever eats my flesh and drinks my blood lives in me and I live in that person.

This is called "realized eschatology," meaning that the benefits of the end of time are already enjoyed through faith, which is certainly not reducible to the notion of accepting dogmatic formulas as merely a way of thinking. Rather, it is clear from the earliest theological writings and from the lives of the saints in the patristic period (approximately 200–700) that Christian faith is demandingly existential and experiential. In fact, it is linked to and empowered by the experience of transformation through faith and love engendered by heartfelt participation in the Eucharistic liturgy. In this way, appropriation of the benefits of the end time is accomplished through sacramental mysticism; receiving Christ's body and blood in the Eucharist is the way eternal life is given *now* to believers. At the same time, however, the earliest Christian writers acknowledge that there will be a bodily resurrection on the Last Day, just as Zoroaster taught in ancient Persia. In both letters to the Corinthians, datable to the early years of the 50s after Christ, as also in the Johannine writings, the bodily resurrection of believers is perceived as a reality inseparable from the resurrection of Jesus Christ, grounded in Eucharistic practice and moral self-discipline, and realized fully in the end times. The late first century Johannine texts reiterate the realized and mystical aspect, including the explicit sacramental component: "everyone who believes *has* eternal life." (John 6:47) Christian mysticism depends on both the Pauline sacramental vision and the Johannine insight about realized eschatology: the Christian lives in a timeless dimension while abiding in the temporal sphere, "in the world, but not of it." In the previous chapter, John 5:29, the ethical aspects of the resurrection are emphasized: "Those who did good will come forth to life and those who did evil will come forth to judgment," (John 5:29) exactly as we find in Jewish apocalyptic texts of the same Second Temple period.

Interpretations of the resurrection of Jesus evolved steadily in the Christian communities of the first to the fourth centuries: Whereas Paul (Corinthians 1:15) explains the nature of the spiritualized resurrection body, Matthew's account of Jesus's debate with the Sadducees shows his adherence to the Pharisaic understanding of the resurrection. However, in Matthew's gospel, Jesus also asserts that the resurrected live in a new dimension, radically different from the way of life enjoined in the Torah: "In the resurrection, no one has husband or wife, for they are to be like the angels in heaven" (Matthew 22:30). This phrase, too, was to have far-reaching consequences for Christian asceticism and mysticism.

Beginning in the late first century, non-canonical Christian texts proposed ascetic, gnostic, and docetic ideas emphasizing the nonmaterial aspects of resurrection, applying the notion to mystical experiences induced under ritual circumstances. Among mainstream Christians during the late first and second centuries, as a reaction against the gnostic docetic ("the body of Jesus was not material, it only 'appeared' to be a real human body") tendencies, there seems to have been a revival of corporeal literalism in writers such as the author of the pastoral epistles (I and II Timothy and Titus), in the Johannine epistles, in Irenaeus of Lyon, and in Tertullian. In the fourth century, this emphasis on "real human flesh" returns with Epiphanius of Salamis and Jerome. This sets the stage for a strongly embodied understanding of the Christian resurrection, in which the way of salvation is practiced as both ethical and sacramental.

The idea of the resurrection of the individual Christian, as distinguished from the resurrection of Jesus, underwent theological development in the earliest Christian centuries[113] because of an ever-deeper dialogue with Hellenistic philosophy. The articulation of realized and postponed eschatology indicate that there is a creative tension in the New Testament texts between the idea that Jesus alone has experienced the resurrection and that Christians will experience the resurrection, in part at Baptism and in the Eucharist, and fully on the Last Day. The "resurrection has already happened" refers to sacramental and mystical experiences, as shown in Colossians 2:8 and 3:1, and in *The Treatise on the Resurrection* in the Nag Hammadi codices, which may have been written as early as the mid-second century. Already in the mid-first century Paul taught that full participation in the risen life of Christ is still to be awaited: "We eagerly await the coming of our savior the Lord Jesus Christ. He will give a new form to this lowly body of ours and remake it according to the pattern of his glorified body, by his power to subject everything to himself" (Phil. 3:20b-21). Although the gnostic texts are frequently dismissed as being universally docetic, even there we find a more insightful appraisal of the spiritual body of Jesus and of the believer that definitely contributed to the later conversation on spirituality and embodiment that we will encounter in Central Asia. Both the Manicheans, who arose in Mesopotamia and Persia in the third century, and the Nestorians (more accurately, Syro-Oriental Christians) whose history we will recount below, were open to some gnostic ideas and had access to non-canonical Christian texts, including some of those found in Egypt at Nag Hammadi.[114]

The Shroud of Turin

Modern interest in the resurrection has been stimulated by two tendencies: liberal biblical scholarship that tries to deny that there was a literal resurrection of Jesus from the tomb and that the whole experience was the result of a spontaneous raising up of the hopes and vigor of the community gathered around the apostles.[115] On the other hand, the Holy Shroud of Turin has become a focus of study as *evidence* for the literal bodily resurrection of Jesus, perhaps in the form of an intensely energetic body of light capable of leaving an image on linen cloth. Most biblical scholars avoid discussing the Holy Shroud because of inherited Reformation-era prejudices against relics. However, this object is no ordinary relic. It is not a painting. It is a burial sheet, woven of herringbone-pattern linen cloth, faintly ivory in color, with traces of an image which—when viewed at a distance of about six feet—resembles the face and body of a man. The image shows the entire body, front and back, as if the body had been draped with a long strip of cloth folded at the crown of the head. Tradition claims the shroud to be the burial cloth of the historic Jesus of Nazareth. It is highly likely that the cloth is two thousand years old; the carbon fourteen dating (which gave results for around the year 1300) was deeply flawed by the fact that the cloth samples taken were from the edge, which has been handled for centuries every time it was displayed to the faithful. Study of the pollen samples embedded in the fabric demonstrate that the cloth has been in every country from Palestine to Mesopotamia to Asia Minor to France, the very route it would have had to traverse if it were the burial cloth of Jesus. The image on it was made by a burst of energy that, as yet, science is not able to explain; it is photographic in the literal sense of the word. The fact that science cannot at present explain how a dead body could leave an image of itself on cloth does not diminish the fact that scientific methods have clearly demonstrated that what we have on the shroud is like no other image ever produced by human beings. John Walsh, a noted Sindonologist, remarks: "The Shroud of Turin is either the most awesome and instructive relic of Christ in existence ... or it is one of the most ingenious, unbelievably clever products of the human mind and hand on record. It is one or the other—there is no middle ground."[116] Recent research has focused on theories of image formation. One hypothesis suggests that the body of Jesus dissolved into subatomic particles (for some as yet unexplained reason); the body dissolved while still enveloped by the shroud because the image had to have been formed on the linen fibers by the *same phenomenon* and *at the same time* as the bodily dissolution.

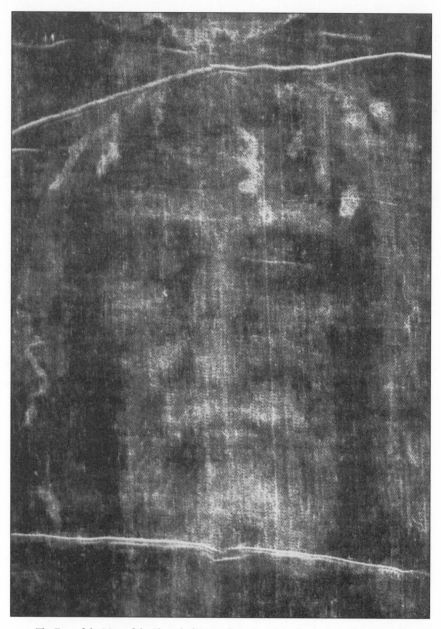

The Face of the Man of the Shroud of Turin, from the original negatives of Pio Secondo, Turin, Italy, 1898.

Our own research will take the implications of shroud research into consideration, proposing a connection between the kind of energy needed to make the image with the kinds of energetic displays that are seen in light body and rainbow body phenomena.

In the original shroud, the highlights of the features of the body are darker and the shaded portions are lighter, suggesting that the places on the cloth nearer the body were "burned" more deeply by the process by which the body itself transformed at the time of the resurrection. This is why, in the very first photos of the shroud taken in 1898, it was the sight of the negatives, not the positives, that was so striking to viewers. The dark portions appear light in the negative, and resemble a monochrome portrait of the front and back sides of a complete human body. No known work of art made before the invention of photographic negatives has ever shown the human body in that way, with that kind of shading. No paints, pigments, dyes, or coloring stains have been found on the shroud fibrils using x-ray fluorescence, ultraviolet light, infrared light, and microchemistry. Microchemical analysis has indicated that the image could not have been made by the decomposition of the spices, oils, or any biological chemicals known to be produced by the body in life or in death. The scientific consensus is that the image was produced by something that resulted in oxidation, dehydration, and conjugation of the polysaccharide structure of the microfibrils of the linen itself. Such changes can be duplicated in the laboratory by sulfuric acid and/or heat. In the historical periods attributable to the shroud, there would have been no known method for isolating the superficial microfibrils of the fabric to allow *only* those fibrils to be altered by chemical or physical treatment over such a large surface of linen cloth. There are no chemical or physical methods known that can account for the totality of the image, nor can any combination of physical, chemical, biological, or medical circumstances explain the image adequately.

Even more amazing is the fact, established by computer image enhancement and the VP-8 image analyzer, that the image on the shroud was not made on a flat surface: it is a projection of a three-dimensional body onto the cloth as if the cloth were actually wrapped around that body. This would tend to confirm that the image was made from some energy emitted by the very body it represents. At best, some Renaissance master of perspective might have been able to do this as a painting, but the shroud is on record long before the Renaissance. Besides, if the intention had been to make a fraudulent relic, it would not have been necessary to go to such lengths of artistry. The shroud image is that of a real human form of a scourged, crucified man. It is not the product of an artist. As an artist myself, I have long been impressed by the simple fact that this image has no style, no connection to any known period in the history of art. The bloodstains are real, and they test positive for hemoglobin and for serum albumin. The image also shows some blurred areas that may be explained by the movement of the body while the image was being formed. One recent theory proposes that these blurred areas can be explained by the cloth's falling through the dissolving body onto itself.

It is also worth noting that no instance of the rainbow body that we have yet encountered has ever left an image on cloth or any other material (Khenpo A Chö's yellow robe is now a relic venerated at the local temple in kLu ma Gompa). In the rainbow body phenomenon, although there are instances of hair and nails or a shrunken body left behind, no residues of bodily fluids remain. For these reasons, we are inclined to place the shroud alongside the evidence of the New Testament as an attestation of the fundamental significance of the resurrection of Jesus in Christian spirituality. The text of the New Testament and the shroud seem to complement each other down through the centuries. Various transformations in the artistic representation of Jesus suggest that this complementarity can be traced through the history of art and in numismatics.

This evidence allows us to understand why St. Leo the Great would explain that the resurrection takes place through faith and sacramental participation, in the hearts of believers. It also explains the periodic rediscoveries of this mysterious relic, attested in the writings of various Sindonologists such as Marinelli, Baima, and Frale.[117] Frale traces the Byzantine documentation with particular care such that we are able to affirm the translation of the relic from Edessa to Byzantium in 944 in order to protect it from the risk of destruction by the Muslims who had already conquered Edessa. Thus the shroud passes from the Syriac-Christian milieu to the Byzantine milieu (specifically: it was housed in a special chapel on the island of Pharos, from which it was removed by the Crusaders during the infamous sack of Constantinople in 1204.). The impact of this translation on Syriac Christianity must have seemed like a milestone in the long decline of Christianity in the lands of its origin and in the language of Christ. That there was impact is mostly attested in the Byzantine world by evidence of coinage in which many key features of the shroud image of Jesus's face are reproduced unmistakably, for which, see the iconographical and numismatic studies by Emanuela Marinelli, Pierluigi Baima Bollone, and Barbara Frale. These authors also mention the objections of the three Edessan Christian communities to the translation of the relic to the Byzantines. Since the coins inscribed with the shroud image circulated in the Muslim world and across Central Asia, it is more than likely that Syriac Christians across the Silk Route would have known something about the passing of the relic into Byzantine safekeeping. One explanation for the vigorous evangelization program of the Syro-Oriental Church in Central Asia (which in fact began much earlier, in the seventh century) might be that losses, such as those occasioned by the Muslim conquests in the Middle East, were being multiplied by the survival of rival Byzantine Christianity on the Bosporus. The Church of the East had no choice but to turn to the East, that is to the Silk Road, to spread its particular view of Christ—a view that gave greater emphasis to the distinction between his humanity and his divinity, while not neglecting the mystical theology that had been inherited from masters such as Evagius of Pontus, Peter of Damaskos, Isaac of Nineveh, Ephrem of Syria (Edessa), and the pseudo-Dionysius. The list of these giants of Christian spirituality could be considerably lengthened to take us to John of Dalyatha and his teaching on the formless light.

Light from Light: Light Mysticism in Early Christianity

One of the hardest connections to make is that between the New Testament assertions about the resurrection (of Jesus and the last-day resurrection of all people) and an actual contemplative process that involves the believer in some sort of systematic training that might give rise to a specific result. This is what the Nyingma and Bonpo are claiming for the phenomenon known as the rainbow body. There is evidence for bodily transformation connected to saintliness throughout the Christian centuries: resurrection, stigmata, postmortem apparitions, miracles, light phenomena, imperviousness to the elements, incorruption, etc. Still, many people who are only conversant with the New Testament complain that it seems to lack a path, meditation instructions, and skillful means, in apparent contrast to Hindu, Daoist, Jain, and Buddhist traditions. It is worth noting that the same lacunae exist also for the details of liturgical practice in the early Church, but there is little doubt (based on archeology and on the writings of early Apologists and Fathers) that ritual practice was already carefully regulated at an early period. Moreover, if we make a comparison between early Christian and early dzogchen texts, we will find that a distinctive strand of dzogchen tradition stoutly denied the notion of spiritual progress, opposed the articulation of a gradual path to enlightenment, neglected to mention the rainbow body, and had no explicit knowledge of the practices discussed in chapter two.[118]

Recent studies of early Christian manuscripts[119] indicate that the public reading of what we call the New Testament, even before an official canon was defined (the anti-Marcionite canon is datable to the late second century), was regulated in a most careful manner. Punctuation marks, pronunciation guides, key-word indications, paragraph marks, and corrections to accord with an exemplar are present in the second century CE, all very much in contrast to the practice of non-Christian Mediterranean manuscripts that survive from the same period.

Basing ourselves on a certain degree of optimism about the continuity of early Christian liturgical practice, we can also begin to construct connections between the time of Jesus and the apostles and the later ascetic and mystical traditions. We have excellent examples of the ascetic tradition in the Gospel of Thomas, parts of which are attributable to the first century. The work known as the Shepherd of Hermas (140s) also reflects this tradition of moral austerity. The third-century Treatise on the Resurrection and other Nag Hammadi codices are not only representative of heretical or gnostic Christianity; some of these works are from the mainstream of ecclesiastical practice, in direct continuity with such New Testament works as the Letter of James, the Letter of Jude, the Letters of Peter, and even the very early material called "Q" in Matthew and Luke. As for the mystical aspects, they are strongly present in Colossians, Ephesians, Hebrews, John, the Gospel of Truth, and the supposedly gnostic gospels and homilies (such as The Gospel of Truth, which is thought to be a work representing the authentic views of Valentinus). Colossians 2:8 states, "Buried with him in baptism, you have been raised up with him in virtue of your faith in the power of God who re-awakened him from death." And: "If you have risen with Christ, seek the things that are above...." (3:1), which is for many the charter verse for Christian mysticism.

The possibly Valentinian gnostic Treatise on the Resurrection from Nag Hammadi refers to a variety of ways or practices by which Christians may experience themselves as "risen already." "It is fitting for each one to practice in a number of ways, and he shall be released from this Element, that he may not fall into error but shall himself receive again what at first was." (Treatise on the Resurrection, 49:30). The text bears some attention, since it is likely that both Manicheans and at least some Syriac Christians knew of this text in a Syriac version available as late as the seventh or eighth century. As Armand Veilleux pointed out in 1986,[120] the purportedly gnostic works found at Nag Hammadi were lovingly bound in the bookbinding workshops of the otherwise rather conservative Pachomian monks. How can this be explained? Why would highly orthodox monks not only have preserved but even given deluxe bindings to the works of heretics? Veilleux proposes that these works were read in the community of discourse of the desert ascetic community, and not as speculative theology. Other scholars continue to assert that the treatises were indeed gnostic and reflect the presence of gnostic sectarians among the Pachomian monks. Pachomian orthodoxy is attested in writings, also translated by Veilleux, redacted in the period after the hiding of the Nag Hammadi esoteric library (the 360s). If indeed at least some of these works were valued for their ascetic content, then they may have been transmitted to the Syriac Churches along with other Hellenistic texts, including the most difficult works of Evagrius of Pontus.

Ascetic and mystical themes abound in the Treatise on the Resurrection:[121]

> The Savior swallowed up death ... for he put aside the world which is perishing. He transformed himself into an imperishable Aeon and raised himself up, having swallowed the visible by the invisible, and he gave us the way of our immortality. Then ... we

suffered with him, and we arose with him, and we went to heaven with him.

Now if we are manifest in this world wearing him, we are that one's beams, and we are embraced by him until our setting, that is to say, our death in this life. *We are drawn to heaven by him*, like beams by the sun, not being restrained by anything. This is the spiritual resurrection, which swallows up the psychic in the same way as the fleshly.

Strong is the system of the *Pleroma*, small is that which broke loose and became the world. But the All is what is encompassed.

We have received salvation from end to end!

The world is an illusion, not the resurrection. Everything is prone to change, but the resurrection does not change; it is the truth which stands firm. It is the revelation of what is, and the transformation of things, and a transition into newness.

Flee from the divisions and the fetters and already you have the resurrection.

Why not consider yourself as risen and already brought to this?

It is fitting for each one to practice in a number of ways and he shall be released from this Element that he may not fall into error but shall himself receive again what at first was....

However, there is hardly a phrase in the *Treatise* that could not be derived from the New Testament, especially the letters of St. Paul and the hints of "ascent to the throne" Jewish mysticism (*merkavah*) that crop up in the Gospels, II Corinthians 12, and the Book of Apocalypse. Not surprisingly, such ideas as being "drawn to heaven like beams by the sun" were treasured by the Pachomian monks of Egypt and probably transmitted to the circle of Abraham of Kashkar, the source of monastic observance in the Syro-Oriental Church. In the biographies of Milarepa, when he begins to manifest the siddha of levitation, he is criticized for merely "riding on a sunbeam."[122]And let us not forget that Milarepa's birth name was Thopaga, which means "good news," i.e., gospel. Strange resonances with Christianity may be found in the Nyingma world in which he grew up.

Some of these Christian texts may reflect the ascent-to-the-throne (*mer-kavah*) mysticism of sectarian Judaism of the time of Jesus. It is thought that such mystical experiences were cultivated by the Qumran community, which in many ways has been shown to be close to the worldview of earliest Christianity. St. Paul describes such an experience in II Cor. 12:1-8. Most of the Book of Revelation has the structure of such an experience. In the Gospel of John, Jesus's dialogue with Nicodemus seems to turn the pattern upside down: instead of the ancient practice of ascent to the throne of God, now it is the revelatory Son of Man who has come *down* from heaven to bring about spiritual rebirth. In any case, the practices involved intense concentration, prayer, and visualization practices. It is possible that some kind of out-of-body experience was taught to select disciples as well, as is hinted in II Corinthians 12.

Other early evidence for the types of spiritual practice known to the apostolic community can be found in Acts of the Apostles (chap. 6). The apostles are trying to run a sort of soup kitchen for the needy members of the community and are finding that it is occupying too much of their time: "It would not be fitting for us to neglect the word of God in order to assist in serving at tables (Latin: *ministrare mensis*)." They appoint deacons as assistants to the needy; "then we can devote ourselves to prayer and to the '*diaconia*' of the word" (Acts 6:2–4). *Diaconia* means service or ministry, but evidently the *diaconia* of serving tables is different from the *diaconia* of service to the word of God, with the latter being associated with prayer. The living tradition has always seen this passage as referring to the liturgical chanting of psalmody (which comes directly from temple and synagogue usage) and the slow, meditative reading of Scripture. Other evidence for an oral tradition of mystical prayer in the early church may be found in the terminology by which the Pauline letters refer to typologies of prayer; in the references to glossolalia and other mystical charisms; in the "secret" teachings of Jesus on the parables given privately to the disciples; the way of interpreting the Hebrew Scriptures (allegory;

typology; symbolism; prophetic words extracted in the manner of midrash, etc.); sacramental practices, including the link to a symbolic interpretation of the Passover *Haggadah* that lies at the heart of the Eucharistic tradition; in hymns such as those in Philippians, Ephesians, Colossians, II Timothy, and elsewhere; in Jesus's own prayer in solitude early in the morning; in discussions of prayer in relation to exorcism; in the fact that James, Peter, and John constitute an inner circle of initiates who are present at the transfiguration and at certain key miracles, such as the resuscitation of Jairus's daughter.

We are able to build a bridge, or identify a trajectory, from these texts of early mainstream, ascetic, and gnostic Christianity to the great teachers of the patristic era: to Clement, Origen, and Didymus the Blind in Alexandria, to the Cappadocians (Gregory of Nyssa, Basil the Great, Gregory of Nazianzenus), to Evagrius and the Desert Fathers's meditation on formless light, to John Cassian and the "prayer of fire," to the Origenistic monks of Palestine in the fifth century, to the Syriac Fathers including some who devise an entirely contemplative system based mainly on Evagrius, to Byzantine (and later Slavic) Palamite/Athonite mysticism (Maximos the Confessor, Peter of Damaskos, etc., in the *Philokalia*). I think we can attribute the synthesis of speculative theology in the Origenistic trajectory with a psychologically sophisticated system of contemplative training to Evagrius of Pontus. It is Evagrius who makes the training come to life, who devises the system of stages, the discernment of signs of spiritual progress, who recognizes the influence of demons and the value of dreams, whose *Kephalaia Gnostica* enables the advanced contemplative to acquire subtlety of insight along with balance, and who reintroduces the best of Valentinian insights within the Orthodox Christian creedal synthesis erected by his teacher St. Gregory Nazianzenus.

The history of the Syriac tradition, which appropriates so much from Evagrius and the Cappadocians, shows that we have a conduit to the Middle East, South Asia, and East Asia. Formless light meditation and descriptions of mystical states in which the divine light is seen interiorly were flourishing in Syria, Iraq, Iran, and the Gulf city-states of the fifth through the eighth centuries. It was from these communities that bishops were chosen for the "St. Thomas Christians" [123] of South India. The flourishing Syriac-Christian community (with its Aramaic linguistic roots in Antioch but with close ties to rational theology in the Greek tradition) spread along the Silk Route all the way to China and Tibet. Thus it is possible to imagine the pre-Buddhist civilization of Tibet (the Yar lung Valley civilization in the center-east and the semi-mythic Shang Shung civilization in the west) influenced by Syriac Christianity and Manichaeism coming along the Silk Route. Over time, one could imagine that the ideas and experiences of spirituality of these Middle Eastern religions might have encountered Vajrayana Buddhism and related tendencies. Could the human founder of dzogchen, Garab Dorje, have been a "cipher" for another Western master—perhaps Christ himself, or perhaps an unknown Syriac Christian master? The fact that the garbled eleventh-century biography of Garab Dorje identifies him as the son of a "nun who was also a queen" who was "embarrassed" by her virginal conception, and as one who rose from the dead as a "good zombie" who worked miracles, and who longed even as a child to see Vajradhara[124]—all suggests the kind of synthesis of Jesus stories with Vajrayana elements; this is something we also find in the way the Sufis appropriated Jesus as one of their own, at about the same time and in the same region. We also know that the Syro-Oriental Christians in China produced syncretic "Jesus Messiah Sutras" in imitation of Taoist and Buddhist scriptures at this time. Manicheans and Christians reshaped the life of Buddha Shakyamuni in the Barlaam and Ioasaph legend. The Garab Dorje figure is relevant only to the dzogchen lineages and is not universally appropriated by other Vajrayana systems; he is the source of those lineages in which the rainbow body is said to manifest, but his biography is traceable only to the beginning of the eleventh century. This seems to be the period in which the rainbow body comes to acquire importance for the dzogchen community of discourse that was beginning to coalesce as the Nyingma School in Tibet.

In Orthodox and Latin Christianity, meanwhile, the tradition continued through the mediation of the monastic communities. There, incorruption and phenomena of luminosity in Eastern and Western Christianity accompanied accounts of miracles of all kinds in the hagiographical literature. Examples include apparitions—sometimes at the time of death—of Jesus, Mary, and saints; mystical writers report detailed visionary experiences and extended verbal communications (locutions); private revelations that become universally acknowledged such as the Sacred Heart; the Eucharistic miracles such as Lanciano, Cascia, and Bolsena. Other paranormal phenomena are reported in the lives of literally thousands of mystics and saints: spontaneous healing; paranormal charisms such as precognition (prophecy); the stigmata as a manifestation of the risen body of Jesus; levitation and superhuman strength (St. Gerard Maiella had the ability to bend iron, rescue fishing boats in a storm, and levitate while carrying heavy objects); cures worked by saints acting on the living during dreams and visionary experiences; holy oils, manna, and myrrh exuding from icons, tombs, and bones; incorrupt saints' bodies manifesting perfumes; exorcism; and the like. I myself had an experience of the light body of Jesus, in the form of the shroud image, while meditating in a chapel in Italy in 1984. People with an exuberant visionary mystical life report light phenomena and the appearance of light bodies in the form of visions and in sacramental mysticism in which the consecrated Eucharistic host emanates light. Light-body visions not only confirm our intimations of postmortem survival but also suggest that the visionary himself or herself is already living on the level of the light body. In fact, before a person dies he or she already begins to show signs of attainment. Saint Padre Pio of Pietrelcina (died in 1968), in southern Italy, made use of the charism of bilocation to assist people in dire need far away from his southern Italian convent as a young priest even before he was marked with the stigmata. Our impressive Khampa yogin, Lama A Khyug of Ya Chas Gompa, assured us that he will manifest the rainbow body after death (he apparently did so, leaving a tiny shrunken body relic) and offered as proof two luminous photos of himself taken in meditation in the dark. Daoist alchemical practices, Tamil Siddha *rasayana* (alchemy) practices, Kabbalistic *merkavah* meditation, yogic subtle body practices, the six yogas of Naropa, and so forth all tend to confirm prior-to-death knowledge of attainment through verifiable signs.

In order to test the veracity of these experiences, it is necessary to cultivate contemplative experience under carefully regulated conditions. Although a sensitive reading of the mystical texts will disclose some remarkable experiences that could not have simply been psychotic delusions or mere metaphors, something more is expected of the reader than an ability to read a text. The present age reflects the degeneracy and destruction of contemplative institutions during the last five-hundred years around the world: an iron age of warfare against ancient spiritual traditions in almost every part of the world. These events are documented but not often cited in historical writings. Christian monasticism—and especially Eastern Christianity as a civilization—has been treated as badly by modernity as colonialism treated indigenous traditions.

There has been a devastating loss of training (of both trainers and places of training) for contemplative and mystical experience and the development of intuitive powers. Contemplative experience is a full-fledged art: an ability that must be developed as a calling. This ability was recognized as being innate in certain people. After a time of trial and initiation, the ability was subjected to a period of apprenticeship in the same way that other skills or crafts were taught. Once a person had attained mastery of the craft, he could be admitted to a guild of professionals. This pattern is found among shamans and even among the Hebrew prophets. It is very hard to obtain solid results on a part-time basis; it is impossible without a teacher. Perhaps even more indispensable than a teacher is the inner sense of a calling, a passion for this sort of life—the same kind of passion that a dancer, an athlete, or a painter has for his or her profession. All sorts of people may have cosmic-consciousness experiences, spontaneous peak experience, out-of-body experiences, near-death experiences, and so forth. These experiences suggest persuasively that we are not our bodies, but at the same time we come to know that our bodies are an irreducible part of the mystery of who we are and are becoming. It is possible to relate to the body as a nexus of energies that manifests transformation in conjunction with, and as a result of, spiritual development. It seems to me that the task before humanity today—along with ensuring peace, justice, security, health, and economic well-being for all—would be to develop programs of training that will enhance our natural capacity for spiritual development. From a contemplative point of view, to develop a world that is comfortable for the bodies of people without any attention at all to the soul is sheer folly. In fact, it is self-defeating because, even in the simplest terms, we know that if people focus on material comfort, without ethical or spiritual discipline, they quickly find reasons to be jealous and to squabble over those tiny differences that make someone else's grass seem greener. Material progress, unfortunately, does not enhance altruism but rather tends to produce arrogance and violence. The use of torture by great powers seems to be symptomatic of the frenzy to protect our "security" by means of state terrorism and Kafkaesque bureaucratic regulations. Isn't it time for humans to develop intuitive, mystical, and ethical capacities with the same rigor with which we train the body in athletics, the hand in artistry, and the rational mind in scholarship?

The Syro-Oriental Church on the Way to China

An important book by a monk of Bose, Matteo Nicolini-Zani, *The Luminous Way to the East*, gives us access to the history of Christianity in Central Asia.[125] The Christian and Manichean presence in that area could explain a great deal about the rise of new schools of spirituality in the seventh to tenth centuries. In this period we find ample evidence for the challenge of integrating notions of asceticism and embodiment. The exchange of ideas that characterized the now-lost civilizations of the Silk Road obliged the masters of various religions to revise their views and to imagine previously unknown ways to articulate the goals of spiritual life. Traditional Christian theology defended the bodily resurrection; Buddhists claimed a disembodied salvation as did those schools of yoga advocating "*kevalya*" (perfect isolation of the mind unencumbered by discursive thought). Christianity and Manichaeism were *par excellence* the religions of light mysticism, but so too were Mahayana Buddhists and Shaivite yogins, among others. The transition from earliest Christianity to mystical Christianity in the fourth and fifth centuries prepared the Syriac Churches for a remarkable encounter with religions unknown to earliest Christianity.[126]

Roots of Syriac Monastic Spirituality in Hellenistic Christianity

In order to assess the impact of Christian monastic spirituality in the cultural spheres of Central Asia, China, and Tibet, we must turn our attention to what may justly be called the Evagrian trajectory. This term attempts to summarize a set of principally monastic approaches to the Christian way of life, with a particularly strong emphasis on spiritual progress, austere moral self-examination, master-disciple relationships, intellectual speculation, and the prolonged, guided practice of meditation and contemplative prayer. These features are specifically directed to the attainment of a profound transformation of the monk into a transfigured *alter Christus* (an "other Christ," which is understood as an anointed Christian participating fully in the sacraments that sanctify the universal body of Christ). Other key features of the Evagrian system include a particular sensitivity to dream interpretation, combat with demonic illusions, and prolonged processes of spiritual discernment to determine the authenticity of the higher experiences of the mystical life. In its Egyptian setting, the pattern of life was basically that of a community of hermits who lived in solitude for most of the week in separate cells, following a set observance of psalmody, meditation on Scriptures, manual labor, and a very moderate diet. More advanced monks were given specific topics of meditation to ponder existentially during the week. These were to be discussed with the Abba or Amma (spiritual father or mother) at the end of the week in a spiritual conversation shared by all, or in certain cases, in private. The entire system presupposed the full commitment of monastic profession in the manner of the churches of the Christian East, especially in Syria and Egypt. These patterns of monastic observance of the Desert Fathers and Mothers of the fourth and fifth centuries impacted the monastic movement throughout the variety of Christian cultures flourishing at that time from Ireland to Palestine, from Ethiopia to Yemen, from North Africa to Mesopotamia, from Asia Minor to Persia—and eventually across Central Asia to China.

The roots of the Evagrian trajectory can be traced to the more mystical texts of the New Testament, such as the Johannine writings (Gospel of John chapters 1, 6, 14-17), the letters to the Ephesians and Colossians, certain passages in I Corinthians 15 and II Corinthians 12, and Romans 8. The mystical tradition also depends on the sayings traditions in the synoptic gospels and possibly in the *Gospel of Thomas*. In fact, the sayings tradition became a standard literary form for the Desert Fathers's tradition, the *apophthegmata*, handed down in numerous editions constituting the best-known memory of the desert/hermit experience in Christian literature.

Less well known, however, is the impact of the thought of the second- and third-century Alexandrian theologians, Clement and Origen, on the more learned among the desert hermits. With the arrival of Evagrius of Pontus in

Egypt in the 370s, the essential teachings of the Cappadocian Fathers (Basil the Great, Gregory of Nyssa, and Gregory Nazianzenus) come into the picture along with the Origenistic interests of the Latin scholars residing in Jerusalem: Rufinus and Melania the Elder. Evagrius[127] was a disciple of Nazianzenus at Constantinople, where he was a deacon with high administrative responsibilities while the First Council of Constantinople was in session. To escape a scandalous love liaison with a lady of the imperial court, Evagrius fled to Jerusalem, seeking monastic initiation from the wealthy Melania, a Spanish noblewoman who had created a dual (male-female) monastery on the Mount of Olives with Rufinus of Aquileia, a noted translator of the works of Origen into Latin. Melania is said to have sent Evagrius to the desert settlement of monks about forty kilometers south of Alexandria in Egypt, to place himself under the rigorous discipline of the great Coptic master, Macarius. In a few years, Evagrius himself came to be recognized by the more learned, Greek-speaking monks as a true spiritual master in the line of the great Origen. Evagrius seems to have assimilated the Origenistic teachings in a particularly unadulterated and strikingly bold manner. Not only did he accept Origen's cosmological vision of a world coming forth from pure contemplation as a result of distracted awareness,[128] but he also developed this insight into a truly contemplative path of training for monks. His *Chapters on Prayer* and the *Praktikos* set the stage for the mind training that would be expected of any monk living under a spiritual master. His short work, the *Gnostikos*, outlines the characteristics of a true spiritual master, so that the disciple would be able to discern whom to follow and whom to avoid.

In his almost unapproachable masterpiece, the *Kephalaia Gnostica*, Evagrius presented an existentially systematic work for the training of the monastic elite who would themselves eventually become spiritual guides for others. The *Kephalaia* consists of six major chapters divided into ninety paragraphs each. Oddly enough, these ninety paragraphs are called a "century," suggesting that a collection of one hundred monastic anecdotes or sayings was already a literary form by the end of the fourth century. The range of interests reflected in these paragraphs or "*kephalaia*" is extensive: cosmological speculations; mathematics; medicine; biblical meditations; theological insights; the psychology of the senses; dream interpretation; meditation experiences, all gathered in mixed bundles. It is as if we have a kind of Christian system of Zen koans, each of which would have been given as a meditation topic for the full week of solitary practice. At the end of the week, the disciple would return to the master to present the fruits of that meditation, thereby demonstrating the degree of his depth and realization. The topics were intentionally presented out of order so that the disciple would mature a contemplative vision across a range of topics, without becoming fixated on one topic for too long. The contents and method of the *Kephalaia Gnostica* are truly unique, and in a short time caused a great deal of controversy.

Evagrius died in 399, and only a few years later the Patriarch of Alexandria (instigated by the notorious heresy-hunter Epiphanius of Salamis) investigated the views of his disciples for heresy. Through the course of the fifth and sixth centuries, these views were the cause of dissention in the monasteries of Palestine, where the writings of Origen were profoundly appreciated. Evagrius gave the Origenistic writings a definite place in the monastic curriculum by making the views of Origen into the basis for a workable system of spiritual training. However, it seems that his bolder speculations, in part inherited from Hellenistic philosophy and possibly other sources, placed him outside the acceptable limits of Christian theology. Some of his ideas may be traceable to the Stoics, some to Valentinian Gnosticism, and some to Buddhist Abhidharma psychology.[129] In particular, he holds a remarkably nondualist view of the divine, "in which there can be no opposition" (*Kephalaia Gnostica* I: 1), a view that implies the entire created cosmos must in some sense be ontologically tethered to the divine. He holds that souls lost the warmth of their contemplative union within this vision without opposition, and so fell into the void. To rescue them, God as creator provided planets and bodies in proportion to the degree of the fall of each rational being, with demons falling the farthest, humans midway, and angels the least. The redeeming event of Christ turns the entire process around, as if at the turning point of a great parabola, enabling all beings to return to the infinite where once again there is no opposition in being and in adoration. Evidently, the system assumes that beings reincarnate many times along the way of their descent and ascent, and allows for the return of all beings, even the demons, to primordial unity. The system is outlined in part in the *Praktikos*, and more fully in the great letter "To Melania."

The *Kephalaia* allows the monk to discover this pattern existentially through contemplative practice, so that gradually in the course of years of training in his hermit's cell, he accumulates spiritual insight. It is also true that the system can be interpreted (Gabriel Bunge and Jeremy Driscoll)[130] in a purely orthodox sense, but it seems that in works such as the *Ad Monachos*, Evagrius is offering a body of teaching that would be disseminated freely among Christian monastics, whereas the *Kephalaia* is reserved for more advanced practitioners of a rigorous meditational system.[131] Evagrius was bold enough to assert that there are some Christian teachings that are to be kept for the few who would benefit from them, as in any strictly esoteric system.

What we need to keep in mind is that at the time of Evagrius, Buddhism was a highly scholastic monastic system, characterized by the teachings of Vasubandhu and Asanga. The Shaivism of Kashmir may have been entirely in the hands of a few yogins and unknown to the classical Hindu traditions of the Upanishads and the Bhagavad Gita. Vajrayana Buddhism did not exist as yet. Tibet was a remote territory where forms of shamanism prevailed. At least from a strictly historical perspective, it would be difficult to imagine a better source for a contemplative worldview than in the writings of Origen and Evagrius!

In any case, in view of the spread of the more esoteric teachings of Evagrius in some of the Palestinian monasteries, in the sixth century a furious controversy arose and came to the attention of the authorities in Byzantium under the Emperor Justinian. At a local synod, the emperor called for a condemnation of the views of Origen and Evagrius, and it seems that the Second Council of Constantinople (553) ratified the condemnation without promulgating it in the official acts of the Council. Nevertheless, later ecumenical councils repeated the formula of condemnation, leading to the destruction of many of the works of these writers in the original Greek. Often we only have quotations from the documents of condemnation, or citations from the works of other theologians, that enable us to understand the system, at least in part. Scholars such as Antoine Guillemot, Jeremy Driscoll, Columba Stewart, A. M. Casiday, and Alfonse Grillmeier have attempted to clarify the features of the Evagrian system of spirituality and to elucidate the historical context of its condemnation.

With the loss of the Greek originals in the Byzantine world, the ideas of Evagrius persisted only in works whose contents were above suspicion of heresy. For example, the *Praktikos* and the *Chapters on Prayer* survived under the name of St. Nilus since they contained nothing objectionable and were valuable for the training of novice monks. Other ideas from the trajectory were transmitted by St. John Cassian to the south of France and later to Ireland, from the great monastic center of Lérins. In the Greek-Slavonic anthology known as the *Philokalia*, we can see how the heirs of this tradition preserved its best features under such names as St. Isaac of Nineveh, St. Maximos the Confessor, St. Peter of Damaskos, and even under the very name of Evagrius.

For our purposes, fortunately the works of Evagrius were also transmitted to the non-Chalcedonian churches of the Christian East that used the Syriac language, i.e., Aramaic in the form used by Christians. Thus, the trajectory continued vigorously in parts of Syria, Mesopotamia, Persia, Armenia, and even South India. Syriac scholarship produced a wealth of translations from Greek originals, many of which were later (after the Muslim conquests of the seventh century) translated into Arabic. The *Kephalaia Gnostica* has been found among the works translated into Syriac. In fact, it was translated twice, once in a version quite faithful to the original controversial text, and once in a toned-down version so as to escape criticism for heresy, probably by Babai the Great in the late sixth century/early seventh century. Both versions can be found in a critical edition with French translation by Antoine Guillaumont in the *Patrologia Orientalis Volume XXVIII* (1958). English translations can now be found online.

Evagrius' writings have turned out to be a gold mine in research on monastic history and spirituality since the late nineteenth century, thanks to the discovery of many works previously unknown to Western European and Anglophone scholarship in Syriac, Arabic, Georgian, Armenian, Coptic, and other languages. The following is a survey of quotations from each chapter of Evagrius's *Kephalaia Gnostica* that indicate the direction of his spiritual discoveries and suggest some of the themes that will surface in later mystical writings of the Syriac Church of the East in Central Asia.

1. There is nothing in contradiction within the Primal Good because it is essentially good, and nothing could be contrary to that essence. (I, 1)

2. Contrariety is to be found in the characteristics, and characteristics are typical of embodiments; therefore, it is among created
   things that opposition is found. (I, 2)

3. Among beings possessing a rational nature, some possess spiritual contemplation and practice, others have practice and
   contemplation, and others have the shackle and the judgment.
   (I, 13)

4. If the human body is a part of this world and if "the form of this
   world is passing" (I Cor. 8:31), it is apparent that the form of the
   body is also passing. (I, 26)

5. The senses and the organs of sense are not the same thing, nor
   that which is perceived. The senses, in effect, are those powers
   with which we customarily perceive materials; the organs of sense are those members in which the senses reside; that which perceives is the living subject who possesses sense organs, and that
   which is perceived is that which falls under the purview of the
   senses. But it is not thus with the mind, because it is lacking one
   of these four (the material). (I, 36)

6. God is everywhere, and he is not some part thereof. He is
   everywhere because in all that which has been produced, he is by
   his "wisdom full of variety" (Ephesians 3:10); but he is not some
   part, because he is not an object among beings. (I, 43)

7. Among the angels, fire and mind predominate; among men,
   desire and earth; among demons, rage and air. The third group
   approaches the second by the nostrils, the first group approaches
   the second by the mouth. (I, 68)

8. The glory and light of the mind is knowledge; the glory and light
   of the soul is impassibility. (I, 81)

9. The mirror of the goodness, the power, and the wisdom of God
   are those things that at the beginning became something from
   nothing. (II, 1)

10. The spiritual body of rational natures is the contemplation of all
    beings; their true life is the knowledge of holy Unity. (II, 5)

11. The destruction of worlds, the dissolution of bodies, and the abolition of names accompany knowledge concerning the rational natures, whereas parity of knowledge remains according to the parity of substances. (II, 17)

12. The knowledge concerning the rational natures is prior to duality, and the cognitive nature is prior to all natures. (II, 19)

13. Just as fire has the power to consume the body of its fuel, so too will the mind have the power to consume the soul when it will be entirely blended with the Light of the Holy Trinity. (II, 29)

14. When the mind of the holy ones shall have received the contemplation of themselves, then too shall the nature of bodies be taken away from the midst of them, and at last vision will become spiritual. (II, 62)

15. If God has "done everything with wisdom," this means that there is nothing created by him that does not bear, each in a particular way, the sign of the luminaries. (II, 70)

16. If the knowledge of spiritual things is anterior to and primordial in relation to the knowledge of corporeal things, it is evident that their bodies are also lighter and more luminous than those latter things. (II, 72)

17. He who advances towards knowledge approaches himself to the excellent changing of the bodies, but he who advances towards ignorance moves himself towards a bad change. (II, 79)

18. Knowledge has begotten knowledge, and knowledge begets the knower in all times. (II, 81)

19. The movement of bodies: temporal. The transformation of incorporeal things: timeless. (II, 87)

20. The unity is that which now is only known of the Christ, he of whom knowledge is of the essence. (III, 3)

21. The minds of the heavenly powers are pure and full of knowledge, and their bodies are the luminaries that shine on those who come near to them. (III, 5)

22. The perfect mind is that one which can easily receive the essential knowledge. (III, 12)

23. It is understood that all worlds are composed of the four elements, but in particular each of them has a variety of proportions of the elements. (III, 23)

24. The image of God is not that which is capable of acquiring his wisdom, because in that case the corporeal nature would also be the image of God. Rather, it is that which has become capable of the Unity that is the image of God. (III, 32)

25. The world is the natural system that comprehends the different and varied bodies of the rational beings, so as to bring about knowledge of God. (III, 36)

26. The intelligible sun is the rational nature that contains in itself the primordial happy light. (III, 44)

27. Just as those who teach letters to children trace them on tablets, so also Christ, in teaching his wisdom to the rational beings, traced it on the corporeal nature. (III, 57)

28. Those who wish to see things that are written need light; the one who wants to learn the wisdom of beings needs spiritual love. (III, 58)

29. The corporeal nature and the incorporeal natures are knowable. Only the incorporeal nature is capable of knowing. God is knowing and knowable, but it is not in the manner of the incorporeal nature that he knows, nor is it in the manner of the corporeal nature (nor the incorporeal) that he is known. (III, 80)

30. Happy is the one who has arrived at unsurpassable knowledge. (III, 88)

31. That which is knowable is revealed to the knower, partly in the knower and partly in the non-knower. (IV, 5)

32. If all persons are a world of infants, someday they will break through to that adulthood which is appropriate to the just or to the wicked. (IV, 15)

33. "The firstborn among the dead" (Colossians 1:18) is he who has been raised from among the dead, and the first to have been clothed with a spiritual body. (IV, 24)

34. Christ appeared to men in various forms before his coming, and at his coming, he appeared to them in the truth of their bodies. (IV, 41)

35. The Sabbath is the rest of the rational soul, in which it is naturally made so as not to overstep the limits of nature. (IV, 44)

36. The demon of rage combats night and day against those who approach obscure topics wishing to write about them; he typically tries to blind their thoughts and to deprive them of spiritual contemplation. (IV, 47)

37. Interpretation is the explication of the commandments for the consolation of the simple. IV, 61)

38. The breastplate (of the High Priest) is to be understood as hidden knowledge of the mysteries of God. (IV, 66)

39. This body of the soul is the sign of the house, and the sense organs are the sign of the windows, through which the mind looks out and sees sensory things. (IV, 68)

40. He who is still subject to the passions and prays that his exit from the body occur quickly is like a man who is sick and who asks the carpenter to break up his bed quickly! (IV, 76)

41. Who will recount the grace of God? Who will scrutinize the Word of providence, and how Christ conducts the rational nature through varied worlds towards union with the Holy Unity? (IV, 89)

42. The knowledge of God has no need of a disputatious soul, but of a visionary's soul. Dialectic, in effect, can usually be found even by those souls who are not pure, but seeing is only for [souls] that are pure. (IV, 90)

43. Those who have cultivated their land during the six years of praktiké will nourish orphans and widows, not in the eighth year, but in the seventh. In the eighth year, in effect, there will no longer be orphans and widows! (V, 8)

44. Men fall from the angelic state in human behavior and from the latter they further lower themselves to the base condition of demons, but when they rise again, they pass through the degrees from which they have fallen. (V, 11)

45. The mind that has despoiled itself of the passions becomes entirely like light, because it is lit up by the contemplation of beings. (V, 15)

46. Life first gives life to the living, and afterwards to those who live, and to those who are dead, but at the end it will give life even to the dead. (V, 20)

47. The resurrection of the mind is the passage from ignorance to true knowledge (V, 25)

48. Just as seeing the light and speaking of the light are not the same thing for us, so also it is not the same to see God and to understand something about God. (V, 26)

49. Just as those who go to cities to see their beauty marvel at all the works they see there, so also the mind, as it approaches the understanding of beings, shall be filled with spiritual desire and shall never be separated from wonder. (V, 29) The "fishhook" (Job 40:25) is to be understood as the spiritual doctrine that makes the rational soul ascend from the depths of malice to the virtues. (V, 37)

50. A sky splendid to see and a spacious region have been imprinted in pure thought, wherein the understanding of beings is manifest to the worthy, and there the holy angels draw near. Irritation makes that imprinted vision to be seen obscurely, and it is completely destroyed by anger for as long as anger is inflamed. (V, 39)

51. If the "anger of dragons is due to wine," and since nazirites abstain from wine, the nazirites in this way have received the order to abstain from anger. (V, 44)

52. Alone among all the embodied, the Christ can be adored by us because he alone had in him God the Word. (V, 48)

53. Only the Holy Trinity is to be adored in itself, for by [the Trinity] at the beginning all the incorporeal and corporeal natures have become something from nothing. (V, 50)

54. The understanding of bodies requires a mind that is pure; understanding of incorporeal things needs a mind that is purer still; to know the Holy Trinity, a mind even purer than that! (V, 52)

55. The Holy Trinity is not a thing having component parts or qualities, or lack or excess; it is in effect a unique essence that in all is always equal to itself.

56. The mind admires while it perceives objects, and it is not troubled in contemplating them; rather, it runs as if it were heading toward family and friends.

57. The "city" (Matthew 5:14) is to be understood as the spiritual contemplation that contains spiritual natures. (V, 74)

58. The spiritual lock is the liberty of the rational nature, which, in its zeal, is not deflected by evil because of its love of the good. (V, 80)

59. When the mind shall have received essential knowledge, then it will also be called "God" because it, too, will be able to found various worlds. (V, 81)

60. The temple is to be understood as the pure mind that now has in it the "wisdom full of the varieties of God" (Ephesians 3:10); the temple of God is the one who is a seer of the Holy Unity, and the altar of God is contemplation of the Holy Trinity. (V, 84)

61. The first nature is for the One; the second is toward the One and the same [is] in the One. (V, 85)

62. The uncreated is the one who, because he is by means of his own essence, there is nothing that could be anterior to him. (VI, 5)

63. The Holy Trinity is not like a tetrad, a pentad, and a hexad; these numerical things are, in effect, forms without substance. But the Holy Trinity is essential knowledge. (VI, 10)

64. The numerical triad is constituted by the addition of units without substance; but the Blessed Trinity is not constituted by the addition of units; it is therefore not a numerical triad. (VI, 13)

65. Just as this very word teaches about the objects in this world, so also the word of the spiritual body will make known the objects of the world to come. (VI, 23)

66. The Father is the source of essential knowledge. (VI, 28)

67. The generation of Christ is the regeneration of our inner man, which the Christ, like a good builder, has founded on the principal rock of the edifice of his body in building it. (VI, 39)

68. The death of Christ is the mysterious work that takes those who have hoped in him in this life back to eternal life. (VI, 42)

69. Vivid temptations reveal to us the numerous passions that are hidden in our souls as they come forth from us; we need to "guard our heart with all vigilance," for fear that when the object for which we have a passion presents itself, we will be immediately dragged off by the demons and will do some one of those things that are abominable to God. (VI, 52)

70. It is not because the mind is incorporeal that it is the likeness of God, but because it is capable of the knowledge of the Holy Trinity. (VI, 73)

71. Equivalent to the body: he who is equal to it in quality. (VI, 78)

72. Equivalent to the rational nature: that which is equal in knowledge. (VI, 80)

73. The holy angels instruct certain people by the word; they lead others by means of dreams; they make others chaste by nocturnal terrors; and they make others return to virtue by blows. (VI, 86)

74. According to the word of Solomon, the mind is joined to the heart and the light that appears to the mind seems to arise in the physical head.[132] (VI, 87)

As these numerous quotations indicate, this fourth-century monastic father has already laid the foundation for school of contemplative practice order for the attainment of luminous bodily resurrection. The Syro-Oriental monastic tradition will take this trajectory much farther.

Nestorianism and Its Appropriation in the Syro-Oriental Church

In discussing the history of what is known today as the Assyrian Church of the East,[133] otherwise known as the Syro-Oriental Church, it is necessary to go into some detail about two crucial moments. The first is the conflict between two great Christian patriarchs of the early fifth century, Cyril of Alexandria and Nestorius of Constantinople. These two represent a long history of theological reflection centered in Alexandria in Egypt and Antioch in Syria. Alexandria—following the lead of Clement, Origen, Athanasius, Didymus the Blind, and the monastics of Nitria and Skete—tended to see a radical unity in the person of Christ, in which the human nature (Jesus of Nazareth) is taken up into the divine word of God to form one nature (*monophysis*), as if a piece of iron immersed in the flames of an oven were to become in effect, all flame. This kind of spirituality was reflected in anecdotes well known in the Desert Father's narratives, in which we find the goal of a monk to "become all aflame" in the Divine Spirit, and in which priests and bishops are seen by visionaries as "all aflame" while celebrating the Eucharistic liturgy. Alexandria also favored the allegorical interpretation of scripture and honored Mary as *Theotokos* (the God-Bearer), or as we say in the West, Mother of God (*Dei Genetrix*). Antioch, on the other hand, while also reading the works of Origen and of the Cappadocian Fathers that so strongly influenced Evagrius, tended to distinguish the two natures, human and divine, of Jesus Christ. The tendency in Antiochian theology was to emphasize the literal, historical Jesus of the Gospels, at times seeming not only to distinguish, but also to separate the two natures of Christ. For Antioch, Mary was Mother of Christ, but she was not appropriately titled Mother of God. A number of ecumenical[134] Church councils were held from the fourth to the eighth centuries to clarify these Christological issues. In retrospect, the debates of those centuries, which centered on the use of terminology in the Greek language, seem recondite to modern Christians. Since not all Christians even at that time made use of Greek, and since the philosophical positions on language were conditioned by the diversity of cultures in the Eastern Roman Empire, the debates had political ramifications that drove them with a great deal of passion. It is interesting that the positions of Nestorius could have been reconciled with the teachings of the Council of Chalcedon (451), even though they had been vigorously condemned in the Council of Ephesus in 439, but political issues and the attachment of the Eastern Christian Churches to certain controversial figures[135] made this reconciliation impossible. Only in recent decades has the Church of the East been reconciled with the Catholic Church, so that the tragic events transpiring in Iraq and Syria at the present moment are actually destroying a branch of the Catholic Church only recently grafted back onto the main trunk. Hopefully, the rich history of this branch of Christianity will contribute something to a rediscovery of a kind of Christian spirituality that is almost unknown in the West, particularly since the time of the sixteenth-century Reformation.

Nestorius became Patriarch of Constantinople in 428, at which time he discovered that the Christians of the capital of Byzantium were divided over whether to call Mary *Theotokos* or *Anthropotokos* (Mother of the Man). Nestorius tried a compromise with the term Mother of Christ, but was subjected to severe criticism by those who knew that Theotokos was already a time-sanctioned title of Mary going back to before the Council of Nicaea (324). Nestorius fell into the trap of criticizing this ancient title, earning himself not only a furor among the congregation in the capital, but also a full scale polemical war with the patriarch of Alexandria, Cyril. Even the Pope, Celestine I, was informed; and John Cassian, (a disciple of Evagrius of Pontus, who was now abbot of Saint-Victor of Marseille) was enlisted to defend the ancient title of Mary. With such an uproar, the only solution was to call an ecumenical council, this time at the city of Ephesus on the western coast of Asia Minor. Unfortunately for Nestorius, the majority of the bishops favored the title, Theotokos, and worse yet, Cyril proved himself to be an extremely tenacious, arm-twisting politician. In fact, the Pope chose Cyril as his personal representative to the Council. In spite of protests from Nestorius and his supporters, as well as of the representatives sent by the Emperor Theodosius II, Cyril's views won the day. The emperor even attempted to arrest both Cyril and Nestorius for breach of procedure during the course of the council, but to no avail. Nestorius, unfortunately, was deposed as patriarch of Constantinople, and returned to his monastery near Antioch. Later he was exiled to Petra (in modern Jordan) and then to the desert of Libya. Cyril returned to Alexandria, where he made good use of his control of grain shipments to gain support in Constantinople. He thus held on to his patriarchate.

At that point, one would have imagined that the objections of Nestorius should have been relegated to the dustbin of the history of ideas. However, the greatest theologian of the Syrian Church, Theodore of Mopsuestia, was also condemned with Nestorius. Theodore was not only a great theologian he also was head of one of the best theological schools in the Eastern Empire, at Edessa. Turmoil prevailed for several decades as various bishops tried to impose the views of the Byzantine Church on the theologians of the Syrian Church. One Bar-Sauma and his colleague Narses, supported by a number of Syrian bishops, moved the theological school outside the Byzantine Empire to Nisibis in the Persian Empire. "The School of Nisibis was in great demand; the organization was exemplary, the resources abundant, so that here generations of theologians and clerics could be trained who gave the Persian Church its best framework and helped it overcome the dangers of its isolated position on the border of the Universal Church."[136] With this kind of theological pre-eminence, the Church of the East began to develop on its own, using the Syriac (Aramaic) language to translate a broad spectrum of works from the Hellenistic tradition and establishing its own patriarchate at Seleucia-Ctesiphon on the Tigris River. A delicately crafted relationship with the Persian monarchy, which favored the Zoroastrian religion, enabled this Christian church to flourish to the point that it began to develop its own monastic, canonical, institutional, and cultural traditions. Great leaders such as Babai II (died in 502) and Aba Mar I (died in 552) governed in a time of peace with the Byzantines, which greatly enhanced their efforts to create a stabile church structure outside the Eastern Roman Empire.

With the outbreak of hostilities between Byzantium and Persia, however, in the first decade of the fateful seventh century, the Persians began to persecute the Nestorian Christians[137] out of fear that they might ally themselves with the Byzantines. This long war exhausted both empires, leaving them vulnerable to the Arab/Muslim incursions of the 630s and leading to the dismemberment of much of the Byzantine Empire and the complete destruction of the Persian Empire of the Sassanid dynasty.

Fortunately for the Church of the East, the principal abbot of the monasteries of northern Persia, Babai the Great, managed to gain control of the Church, allowing the election of a new patriarch Ishar Yahb in 628 at a crucial moment only a few years before the Muslim invasion. Ishar Yahb participated in negotiations for peace with the Byzantines and led the Church during the years of political disintegration that followed. Thanks to Babai the Great, the Syro-Oriental Church of the East had its own creed. Under the new patriarch, operating with considerable independence from the Persian monarchy, the church was able to hold synods, sustain theological studies, and create new institutions. As Jedin tells us, "the Nestorian Church was forced into a life of its own, which it kept closed against the entire West, hence against Europe and Asia Minor. For this reason the mighty missionary élan which especially characterized this Church ... pushed ever farther eastward ... as early as the sixth century Nestorian missionaries reached the western frontiers of India in Malabar ... and Sri Lanka."[138] Later, they reached China, Mongolia, and even Tibet. Along the way, the school of Nisibis had become a center of scholarship where many early Christian texts were collected, translated, and studied. Thus, an entire body of early Christian spirituality, both from the Antiochian theological tradition and from the Evagrian trajectory, came to influence the leadership of the Church of the East as its mission moved towards Central Asia and China.

The Church of the East: Monasticism, Theology, and the Mission to Central Asia

In a recent monograph,[139] Sabino Chialà has presented a study of one of the great monastic leaders of the Church of the East, Abraham of Kashkar (ca. 501–586), who is noted as the founder of the Great Monastery on Mount Izla, in what is now southeastern Turkey. Although a great deal could be said about this monastery, I will cite a number of aspects that are significant for our purposes in approaching the spiritual exchange that characterized life along the great Silk Road. Abraham studied at the great theological school of the Nestorian Church at Nisibis, bringing with him into monastic life the entire heritage of Antioch and Edessa. He also traveled to Egypt to observe and learn from the extant monastic communities there. His monastic "rule" seems to have been a kind of florilegium of biblical quotations and citations from the teachings of the Desert Fathers. In this way, he allowed his community considerable flexibility in organizing its way of life, which consisted basically of cells constructed in the vicinity of his own hermitage. Emphasis was therefore on the living master-disciple tradition, and not on canonical legislation. After his death, the community attempted to stay together under his disciples, but in the course of the early seventh century, in the time of Babai the Great, many of the monks dispersed and founded new monasteries under the direction of the disciples of Abraham. Thus the dispersion coincided with the consolidation of the Church of the East as an institution within the Persian kingdom, with a new orientation towards lands to the south and east. It was from this time of monastic controversy and flourishing that we can trace the roots of that theological creativity that will find full expression in the writings of the Chinese Syro-Oriental Christians in the eighth century. First, however, we must turn to the extraordinary spiritual teachings of the heirs of Abraham's and Babai's monastic achievements.

The Mystical Teachings of the Church of the East: The Formless Light and the Writings of John of Dalyatha

With the collapse of the Sassanid dynasty in Persia and the arrival of the Arab/Muslim conquerors, one would have expected the Church of the East to suffer depredation and contraction. Instead, in terms of monastic foundations, missionary work, and mystical teachings, the seventh century seems to have been a most extraordinary time of expansion. Under Babai the Great and his contemporaries, the Church of the East established monasteries and dioceses in the northern and northwestern parts of Mesopotamia, mainly along the entire Tigris River, into southeastern Persia and along the Persian Gulf. From these centers, new foundations were made in the great cities of eastern Persia: Herat, Nisabur, Merw, Zarang, Balkh, and Aprah. Already the church was in the territory of Bactriana and Gandhara, interfacing with flourishing Buddhist communities. From Merw, the church proceeded into Sogdiana, from which it began to spread along the Silk Road, making use of a flexible approach to the creation of new dioceses. In effect, there were missionary bishops who were able to accompany nomadic tribes across Central Asia without the need for a fixed diocesan see. Christian presence is attested archeologically in Bukhara, Samarkand, Talas, Urgut, Mizdaxkan (near Urganc in Khoresmia), Chotan, Pishkek, Tokmak, Saryg, Ak Beshim, Qaraxoto, and Dunhuang. By the 630s, the Christians had begun their entry into Tang dynasty China. Their leader was a certain Alouben, who arrived in the capital Xi'an in 635, where he was welcomed by the second Tang emperor, Taizong (627–649).[140] The history of the Church of the East—in Chinese, the religion of the light *jingjiao*—in China is recounted in the Xi'an Stele of 781. The author of this historical document, which contains both Chinese and Syriac inscriptions, was the monk Jingjing, a name meaning "purity" or "luminosity." The stele also explicitly states that there was a Christian monastery at Lingwe. Lingwe was the ancient name of the modern region of Ningxia in the northwest, not far from Gansu where Turfan and Dunhuang are located, where Christian artifacts and texts have been found.[141] Dunhuang is also the source of some of the oldest dzogchen texts and many valuable historical documents of the Tibetan empire during the eighth century.

It is only natural then for us to wonder if there might have been some kind of contact between Christians and Buddhists along the Silk Road and in China. There is, in fact, such evidence in the form of documents found at Dunhuang. In addition to the stele of Xi'an (found in 1623), which is inscribed in black schist, a number of texts written in Chinese on paper scrolls have been found. These include *The Hymn of Praise and Invocation of the Three Majesties of the Religion of the Light* (a form of the *Gloria), The Discourse on the One God,* "*The Book on Listening to the Messiah,*" "*The Book on the Realization of Deep Peace and Joy,*" and "*The Book of the Religion of the Light on the Disclosure of the Origin.*" Each of these works reflects much that we have said about the theology of the Schools of Edessa and Nisibis, and the Evagrian trajectory. As we shall see, they also contain references to the Daoist teachings, such as non-action (*wu-wei*), and to Buddhist notions of merit, bodhisattvas, compassion, emptiness, imperturbability (as in the Buddha Akshobya), *saddharma* (the good, or sound, teaching of Buddhism), relative and supreme reality, mindfulness, and many other technical terms typical of Mahayana Buddhism in China.

Was the Church of the East prepared for this encounter by the pluralistic theology of the School of Nisibis? Certainly the skillful theologians of the previous three centuries had accomplished something quite remarkable in translating Hellenistic knowledge into Syriac. They also managed to transmit this knowledge to the Arab conquerors in such a way as to stimulate a great era in Muslim philosophy.[142] They had also demonstrated extraordinary independence of thought and institutional skills, especially under unfavorable conditions. In my opinion, what truly prepared them for the encounter with Chinese thought at the very height of the Tang dynasty was their background of contemplative experience nurtured in the monasteries of the Middle East. Only the experience of monks who had meditated for many years in *cenobia* and hermitages in the hills of Kurdistan could have given rise to a body of knowledge that could be handed on to the missionary clergy, many of whom were monks who brought Christianity to China. Although much of the literary heritage of these Middle Eastern contemplatives does not survive, careful scholarship has brought to light a number of texts in Syriac, Armenian, and Arabic. At least one important text from this tradition was found in Turfan in a Sogdian translation, and we know of several works of Evagrius (such as his *Antirrheticus*, a work on antidotes to evil thoughts that arise during meditation), also in Sogdian. Sogdian traders, some of whom were Christians, were the key to the economic success and cultural impact of the Silk Road in the period from 600 to 800. Here for example is an excerpt of a text on hermit practice from the Syriac tradition, translated into Sogdian and discovered at Turfan:

> …What one needs is an understanding of conflicts (reached) by experience—that (experience) at which the wise and sensible have often been confounded and (which) comes to fools through action. Just as it is not possible that archery be taught amongst crowds and in the streets, but rather, (in a place apart) … in the same way they cannot reach anyone skilled in spiritual conflicts and how to race well towards the divine goal, and to learn skill in controlling the thoughts and the science of spiritual navigation on this terrible ocean, and to understand many stratagems, until

a man shall dwell in constant quietude and in retreat from everything by means of which the mind becomes *empty of or ceases from
constant prayer*—he who does not do thus shall fall.

The course of this quietude is in three periods. Labor is the
initial period, and to this first period belongs fear, and that grief
which results from the recollection of previous things. And to that
second period belong encouragement and the manifold consolation whereby the wise penitent approaches divine favors by virtue
of the purity which he receives from weeping and penitence....
when he shall complete this former period with manifold labours
by the help of Christ and shall begin to prepare for the second
period, the sign of his repentance will be turned to exultation,
although he does not wish it to be so because he fears that it is
perhaps an illusion. And the sign of this is that hope begins to
enter his spirit and by virtue of his repentance consolation begins
to increase little by little; then from time to time thoughts which
make him joyful stir within him, and he sees within himself that
he can easily cleanse the mind of wandering. These things come
about when he enters completely into this second period, when
his thought is changed into another which does not resemble the
former. Then those things which occur to his thoughts are not of
his nature and he begins to pay heed to the mystical words which
are hidden in the Psalms ... for sweetness begins to be mingled
with his service, both with his fasting, and with the words of his
worship and with the other labors of his way of life, and as soon
as he begins to pray his limbs become composed without his willing it and his thoughts begin to be collected, for they themselves
realize how to bring forth something which is above the struggle,
and he sees aright that the ship of his mind is going day by day in
growth towards improvement. These things, together with other
yet greater things, belong to this middle period, until by the Grace
of Christ a man arises to that course of life which is above his
nature.[143]

In the writings of some of the earliest monastic fathers of the Church of the East, we already have texts that suggest that the Christian mystic has access to a luminous body like that of Christ at the Transfiguration and at the Resurrection. Isaac of Nineveh, for example, states, "In the world to come, when people rise again from the earth to be clothed in the glory of the resurrection, there will no longer be interior or exterior, but rather their nature will be light."[144] Daidisho of Qatar (seventh century) taught, "Happy the soul whose eye has been purified from the troubles of the clouds of the world, and has been made simple and clear so as to perceive the Lord in a cloud of Light! His entire body will be luminous, the appearance of his face will glow with glory."[145] A remarkable text from Nestorius of Nonhadra in the eighth century discusses a paranormal phenomenon of colored light that is suggestive of the experiences of "tiglé" (spheres or nuclei of light) found in later dzogchen practices. He advises the monk to be careful of a vision of a disk of fire that appears during the time of prayer, sometimes accompanied by a delightful voice:

> [Instead] you must give your attention to the simple light that appears within you. In this simple light, moreover, a star will occasionally appear and shine, but later will hide itself and disappear: this is the mystery of the new world. The light is the color of the sky,[146] which is also the color of the nature of the purified soul. That color is the color of the firmament in which the intellectual insights of spiritual contemplation are situated like the stars. And when the light is that of crystal, the very light of the Holy Trinity shines on the soul as well, and the light of the soul project rays of fire which are the murmurings by which the soul glorifies God among the angels.[147]

Consistent with the Evagrian trajectory, these mystics teach a twofold set of spiritual stages: the life of active purification involving conversion, growth in the virtues, and attainment of purity of heart (freedom from the passions), followed by the truly contemplative life of altruistic love, contemplation of the spiritual essences of phenomena, contemplation of the divine mysteries, and supreme beatitude.

In the Syriac tradition, the twofold pattern is articulated by Berikhisho in accord with the tradition of the pseudo-Dionysius (also a Syriac author writing in Greek at the end of the fifth century). The first stage is the bodily stage, which involves the purification of material passions.

The second is the psychic stage in which the movements of the soul are purified. This process reaches completion with a return to the purity of the natural state, accompanied by contemplative insights about "all that is on earth, in heaven and in the depths." Between this stage and final perfection, there is a stage of clarity in which the soul is seen by itself ("the soul gazing on itself sees the divine light"), either resembling the sun, the moon, or the sapphire color of the sky. Finally, in the stage of true spirituality, the light of the Holy Trinity appears, such that the soul becomes like crystal. At that point, the monk may have visions of the trinity, judgment, providence, and so forth. In this vision of the clarity of the intellect, perfect union with Christ "through whom all things were made" takes place so that the ancient saying is fulfilled: "God has become man so that man might become God."[148]

Thanks to the research of Robert Beulay, we have ample access to the teachings of one of the greatest of the Christian mystics of the Syriac tradition, John of Dalyatha (ca. 690–786). Beulay has translated the surviving letters, homilies, and spiritual writings of this monastic father of the eighth century. What we find in John of Dalyatha is in continuity with the Evagrian trajectory as inherited in the Church of the East. Everything seems to revolve around the fundamental idea that human beings are called to illumination and perfection through union with God. The mysticism of John of Dalyatha is that of an experience of encounter with God, i.e., direct experience of God's presence in the heart (expression important for Evagrius, who uses the Greek term *nous*—the inner faculty of understanding—and his disciple John Cassian, father of the Western mystical tradition, who writes of *puritas cordis*—purity of the heart) and experience of the supernatural effects of this presence.[149] This is fairly traditional, as is his teaching on monasticism and asceticism. However, the entire system is grounded in the notion of a prior sense of calling, of a reality that is already present within the soul, which gradually emerges in the course of the practice of asceticism and love: "An elder told John of Dalyatha: 'For the duration of many days the use of bodily nourishment has become for me something superfluous; the vision of the beauty of my Lord fulfills my needs and casts from my mind this [food] preoccupation.... Another elder said: 'I already knew God before the worlds existed, because his knowledge was shining in my thought, the same knowledge that brought the worlds into being, and that knowledge preceded the knowledge that I have of all created existence.' And another: 'The mystery of the unity of Christ our savior is eternal and without beginning; this is why even his humanity itself is in the essential Gnosis,'"[150] which is a technical term in Syriac that resonates with the gnostic language of dzogchen, e.g., mind viewing mind, the basis (Tibetan: *gzhi*), awareness (*rig pa*), and so forth.

For John, the highest states of contemplation resemble the various kinds of *samadhi* that we find in a variety of Indic sources, both Hindu and Buddhist. In his homily 6, John sums up the effects of different stages of spiritual absorption on one's relationship with the outer world, up to the final state of contemplation. Thus, the vision of the soul by its own perceptive power leaves only a partial perception of the corporeal senses and of the phenomena of the world. Speaking psychologically, such a state of wonder interrupts and makes impossible the unbroken recitation of the daily Psalmody typical of Eastern Christian monastic observance, and also makes it useless to try to activate one's gaze toward the "remembrance" of God, because the attention is already fixed on the vision of the soul in itself, in which the divine light has made the soul transparent to itself in wonderment.[151] "As for the vision of the divine light in itself, transcending perception of that light present in created realities, once one has entered into the Cloud,[152] all vision, hearing, and knowing with regard to this world is abolished."[153] Thus, "The soul seeks refuge in the holy mountain of the Lord, which is the effusion of the light of His Being. The soul sees itself placed within torrential floods of light that bathe it on all sides."[154] Little wonder that the Christianity that evangelized Central Asia and China in this period was called "the religion of the light" (*jingjiao*).

Beulay assembles an astonishing number of quotations translated from the Syriac writings of this eighth-century master who lived towards the end of the eighth century, a contemporary of Padmasambhava, Vimalamitra, Manjushrimitra, Vairotsana, Shantarakshita, and Kamalashila: the Indian, Central Asian, and Tibetan masters who brought Mahayana and Vajrayana Buddhism to Tibet. One cannot but notice the contrast between these quotations, naturally framed in a Christian theistic language of contemplative prayer, and the aridity of the great work of the latter two Buddhist panditas, the *Tattvasamgraha*, which is a brilliant *summa* of scholastic Buddhism as it might have been taught at Vikramashila or Nalanda, the great north Indian centers of Buddhist teaching. All the more astonishing, therefore, to read the Syriac quotes and find them so close in style to pristine dzogchen: "Things may appear in a nondual way, such that each individual object appears without conceptual elaboration; having no thought for 'things as they are', whatever it is that makes its appearance corresponds to ultimate goodness; Then, since all is complete, one sets aside misguided efforts, and abides in the contemplative state."[155] This approach is developed in several extremely valuable texts found at Dunhuang.

That we are dealing with a transformative process that arises in a person who has already been doing a great deal of practice becomes clearer as we study these texts. Also, I think John of Dalyatha's description of wonderment or "stupor," which sounds very much like a state similar to yogic Samadhi, helps us understand the state of mind described by these dzogchen texts. It is not that one has altered the true essence of one's awareness; rather, through the experience of wonderment, one enters into the contemplative state that is itself always present, beneath and inseparable from ordinary consciousness. For this reason, we can speak of the appearance of things in a nondual way. Appearances are nondual only in a state of contemplative wonderment; otherwise, they seem to be phenomena outside the self-awareness of the perceiver who is working with ordinary sensory perception.

The teachings of John of Dalyatha (also known as John the Elder) go beyond this to describe the inner processes that he calls "supernatural" or the "work of grace" that connect his teaching with that of the New Testament experience of the resurrection. It also seems that the *Treatise on the Resurrection*, a supposedly gnostic work found at Nag Hammadi, has influenced this trajectory traceable back to Origen and Evagrius. Very much in the manner of the *Treatise*, John of Dalyatha states:

There is a work of grace that consists of something that falls into the heart of a monk like a burning coal; it inflames with its incandescence and sets afire even his body. This is the Spirit of adoption as a Son that we have received in Holy Baptism, the *arrhes* (the "down payment") of Eternal Life. This is the fire that will resurrect our bodies on the last day and will adorn them with incorruptibility and our souls with immortality. This fire consumes the body with love and the soul with delight.[156]

With this fire we also burn the beam that is in the eyes of our hearts, purifying the sight of our soul so that it may acquire the purity of its nature and the condition in which God created it in the beginning so that without obstacles it may comprehend that which it contemplates among the marvels of the laws of the Creator.[157]

By this fire, the soul attains the resurrection though still being in this life. It is in effect the power of the resurrection and the light of the saints.[158]

This body of teaching suggests that the body itself is to be transfigured into light. The body is thus not merely a vehicle for the liberation of particles of light as in Manichaeism and Jainism, nor is it only the mind that gazes upon itself as in Ch'an meditation.[159] The Syriac Fathers, basing themselves on the Gospel accounts of the transfiguration and the resurrection, discovered an experiential path towards spiritual transformation in the living human body, which is to become a body of light. The teachings of John of Dalyatha move the Christian imagination beyond poetic metaphors and symbols, to suggest substantial connections between the sacramental experience of the church, mystical contemplation, and embodied signs of spiritual realization.

Contacts with Buddhists, Daoists, and Manicheans: Jingjing and the "Jesus Sutras"

Perhaps the pinnacle of the Christian encounter with Buddhism and Daoism in the eighth century is *The Book on the Realization of Profound Peace and Joy*

(*Zhixuan anle jing*).[160] The manuscript represents very refined calligraphy and language; it is a luxury work intended to preserve a highly valued tradition in the Chinese community of the Syro-Oriental Church.[161] However, it is unlikely that this community would have sponsored the creation of this work at such a late date because by the time the caves at Dunhuang were closed, the Christian community was reduced to an insignificant minority in China. It is more likely, as Lin Wushu concludes, that the original text was composed just after the time of the famous stele of Xi'an, in the final decades of the eighth century (the reign of Emperor Dezong, 780–804), well before the Tang dynasty began to persecute foreign religions (in 845 under Emperor Wuzong).[162] Nicolini-Zani observes that this text may have been composed by the Christian monk, Jingjing, who was a quite competent master of literary Chinese, as can be seen in the Stele of Xi'an. The literary movement represented by this text and others that have been found at Dunhuang employed Buddhist and Daoist terminology to describe the Christian message. However, unlike earlier Chinese Christian texts that were translated from Syriac into Chinese, making use of Chinese religious terminology for the sake of convenience, these later works tend to *embrace* Buddhist and Daoist religious perspectives to the point of apparently downplaying more traditional Christian soteriology (such as the sacrificial death of Christ on the cross). In a certain sense, a dialogue and collaboration among Christian, Buddhist, and Daoist scholars gave rise to a common vocabulary and, for the Christians, an opportunity to create a theological approach that addressed the concerns of their dialogue partners. It was therefore not merely a question of the linguistic enculturation of Christianity in China but of the emergence of a distinctly Chinese Christian theology.[163] This could only have occurred if there had been an encounter on the level of an in-depth dialogue of spiritual experience. It is not enough to postulate a set of tendencies, questions, orientations present in Buddhist soteriology that were not (and still are not) addressed by traditional Christian theology. The urgency of the profound human questions of Buddhists and Daoists, and the possible validity of their responses, would only have been accessible to Christians who had had a deep experience of Buddhism or Daoism in practice. In this work on *Profound Peace and Joy*, we have a document that bears witness to the kind of creativity that can emerge from a dialogue of religious experience on the level of considerable depth. Given its composition in the late eighth century, this work places us in the world of emerging dzogchen in Tibet, and at times in contentious dialogue with north Indian Shaivism, pre-Buddhist oral teachings in Tibet, and with Chinese Ch'an Buddhism as well. Moreover, the *Book on Profound Peace and Joy* reflects the spiritual intensity of the great Syriac contemplatives such as Joseph Hazzaya and John of Dalyatha. Composed at a high point in the history of the Syro-Oriental Church in China and deposited in a cave at Dunhuang, this bold attempt at a synthesis between Chinese Buddhism and Christianity is a good candidate for the kind of text that may have influenced new trends in Tibetan Buddhism at the time of the first diffusion, or immediately thereafter in the time of fragmentation in the ninth and tenth centuries. Here is my translation based on the Italian of Nicolini-Zani, and used with his permission:

> ...When they heard those sublime words, within the ethereal hall[164] of supreme purity, [the Messiah] prostrated himself before all those who were gathered around him, to the right and to the left. Then his monk attendant[165] and [the other] followers rose up and drew near to him [and said]: "We human beings are confused,[166] [tell us therefore] what one truly ought to do so that all sentient beings[167] may be saved."[168] The Messiah replied: "It is well! If you seek to investigate the transcendent Law,[169] seat yourselves and discipline your spirit. All the species [of beings] have a nature [characterized by] peace and joy. Consider, for example, the moon in water: if the water is disturbed, it no longer reflects the image [of the moon]; or else consider, for example, the straw that is burned in fire: if the straw is moistened, one no longer sees the luminosity of the fire. The same is true for living beings[170] immersed in [ignorance]."[171]

The beginning of the text is a bit uncertain because the Chinese characters are faded.[172] It is most likely that Simon Peter, presented as a monk-attendant of Jesus the Messiah, bows respectfully and withdraws to one side, in the manner described in the early Buddhist sutras. It is not likely that the Messiah bows, as Nicolini-Zani's translation would suggest. In the teachings of the Messiah, we see the introduction of the notion of a "nature" characterized by peace and joy. The term "nature" in Indian and Chinese Buddhist texts refers to one of the dharmas of which the appearances of ordinary reality are composed. The idea of an original dharma, characterized by peace and joy, resonates with the "pure from the beginning" teachings of dzogchen with its emphasis on the primordial state. The imagery of the moon in water is widespread in Buddhist literature; it is one of the examples used much later by Longchenpa to illustrate wonderment and the spiritual breakthrough. In a text deriving from the traditions of Syriac monasticism, the "three stages of the solitary life," found at Turfan in a Sogdian translation,[173] we can see that the practices of the solitary life are meant to allow this inner "peace and joy" to emerge in the actual experience of the hermit.

> "Simon Peter,[174] in the first place, all of those who cultivate the transcendent way[175] are to abandon emotions and passions. [In fact] in the absence of emotions and passions, there will not even be desire or [mental] actions;[176] without desire nor mental action, one can be utterly pure;[177] being utterly pure, one can be enlightened (wu)[178] and realize the truth (zheng);[179] having been enlightened and having realized the truth, all of reality [in its true essence] is shown forth resplendent: having caused all the spheres of reality [in their true essence] to have become resplendent is truly the cause of peace and joy.[180]

Nicolini-Zani states, "The attainment of peace and joy, as described here, is therefore the entrance into the true essence of reality, characterized by a state of all pervasive luminosity."[181] This is the view expressed many times in the Buddhist tantras and of course in dzogchen. It is interesting that Simon Peter is the interlocutor of the Messiah. We should recall that Peter was considered the founder of the See of Antioch, the source of the theology of the Church of the East. The perplexity that he expresses reflects the experience of the Christians of the East in their difficult encounter with Buddhism and

Daoism. Not only are the soteriological systems radically different, even the fundamental questions and concerns of Buddhism and Daoism are almost unrecognizable to the Aramaic-Hellenistic world from which the Church of the East springs forth in its mission to Central Asia and the Far East. Only certain points of contact with the Evagrian contemplative trajectory seem to make a connection. Perhaps reminiscences of the *Gospel of Thomas*, *The Treatise on the Resurrection*, and other Christian apocryphal sources used by the Manicheans, enable the author of this text to construct a viable Christian response to the Buddhist concerns, opening up a place for them within Christianity. Does the text remain recognizably Christian? Does it match in skill and profundity the approaches being debated in Buddhism at that time in India, China, and Tibet? It is interesting that Jingjing, the supposed author of this text, translated the *Satparamita Sutra* in collaboration with the Buddhist monk named Prajna. Although we are told that this translation was not much appreciated by Chinese Buddhist critics, its existence does confirm that our author was in working contact with Mahayana Buddhists from Central Asia (Prajna was a *Hu*[182]), which is the same religious context from which the pristine dzogchen sutra anthologies emerged at this very time.

"Simon Peter, consider whether my body may have an extraordinary appearance and will [look?] different from [those of ordinary men]. The ten principles [that underlie reality][183] can be summed up in 'the four acquisitions.' The four acquisitions[184] are not known to me by means of [sensorial knowledge] and the ten principles I do not contemplate by means of an experience of [visual perception]. For the purpose of instructing human beings, [I now] make use of fictitious words.[185] What is one to do if one is unable to have cognition or vision of the true teaching [regarding the true essence of reality?] If there were cognition or vision, then there would be a body; if there were a body, then there would also be sentient beings; if there were sentient beings,[186] then there would also be desire and mental action: to possess that which one desires and that for which one acts is that which we understand to be emotions and passions. Those who have emotions and passions in fact cannot avoid finding themselves in every kind of suffering and anguish and are indeed very far from acquiring the fullness of peace and joy. This is why I affirm the absence of desire and the absence of mental action, abandonment of the sphere of corruption,[187] and immersion in the wellspring of the uncontaminated. Abandoning corruption,[188] one can become pure: this corresponds to emptiness,[189] emanating grace and light, it is possible to cause all of reality to become luminous. Causing all of reality to become luminous is that which is called the way of peace and joy.

The Messiah is presented as an appearance body of the Buddha, just as Garab Dorje is presented in the early eleventh-century biography. The use of "fictitious words" resonates with the Buddhist notion of using concepts as a skillful means as a way to move beyond concepts towards the realization of perfect truth. The distinction between cognition and vision [consciousness and sensory perception] reflects the Buddhist *Abhidharma* and *Vijnaptimatra* teaching on the five bodily senses, the internal "receptacle" (*ayatana*) that receives their perceptions and their coordination by a consciousness principle, *vijnana*. A sixth, coordinating consciousness principle—"mental consciousness"—is described by the mind-only philosophers as having three aspects: "A mental consciousness ascribes names to objects, perceives slightly hidden objects such as impermanence and emptiness, misconceives a difference of entity of subject and object, and so forth. The mind-basis-of-all (*alayavijnana*) does not cognize emptiness even though it has seeds with it that ripen and cause a mental consciousness to do so. The afflicted mind, seventh from among the eight consciousnesses, mistakenly conceives the mind-basis-of-all to be a self-sufficient person. Even though the mind-basis-of-all, because it is the transmigrating entity, is indeed found to be the actual person when one searches to find it, it is not a self-sufficient person. Thus, the seventh consciousness is described as afflicted by four mental factors: view of a self, obscuration with respect to a self, pride in a self, and attachment to a self. When these mental factors are overcome through their antidote—realization of selflessness—the untainted entity of the seventh consciousness remains. Then, when the conception of subject and object as different entities is destroyed totally and forever at buddhahood, the seventh consciousness is transformed into the wisdom of sameness cognizing all phenomena as equally free from a difference in entity between subject and object."[190] The notion that the objects of sensory perception do not truly exist reflects the view of Madhyamaka, the Middle Way philosophy of Nagarjuna. Much of the terminology in our text also reflects the teachings on perception, the senses, and the mind in the *Kephalaia Gnostica*, for which see the little anthology I have given above (pp. 156–166). In fact, this passage strongly resonates with both Christian contemplative and Buddhist views on the mind and on renunciation as a prerequisite for spiritual attainment. The term "sphere of corruption" in both Chinese (*ranjing*) and Tibetan (*'jig rten*) describes the world as the container of all that is composite and impermanent. The notion of making all reality luminous, as we have indicated, is close to tantric Buddhism, but it also reflects the Christians's self-understanding of Christianity as "the religion of light." Moreover, since the discourse is addressed to Peter, the passage suggests that we are on Mount Tabor where Christ showed his body transfigured in light, and thus as "not an ordinary human embodiment."

> "Simon Peter, I repeat what I said to you: I am in the heavens, but I am also on earth. I protect and sustain all beings by means of actions that are the cause of good [roots of virtue?]: those who on the way of God, and those who, on the contrary, are on the way of human beings; those who belong to my own kind and those who, on the contrary, belong to other kinds [of beings]; those who possess the [true] knowledge and those who, on the contrary, do not possess it.[191] I save and liberate all those who would otherwise be destined for chastisement for the evil [they have committed].[192] With regard to salvation and protection: in reality it is unheard of that these coincide with emptiness and the abandonment of merits. What of it? If there are merits, then there will also be fame; if there is fame, there will also be boasting; and if there is boasting, there is also a worldly mentality (Chinese: *xin*; Tibetan *sems*). Those who have a worldly mentality[193] will end up in every kind of pride and arrogance, without being able

to liberate themselves,[194] and they will truly be very far from the understanding[195] of profound peace and joy! For this reason I say: Those who do not have merits and fame, but who rather take on[196] a compassionate heart[197] towards all sentient beings, these shall be completely liberated. If they entrust themselves to my divine powers,[198] they can be enlightened regarding the precise truth, and to be enlightened regarding the exact truth is in itself the way of peace and joy.

It would seem that there is a mistake here, since the sentence "in reality it is unheard of that emptiness and the abandonment of merits coincide with salvation and protection," when the entire passage refers to the danger of merits, fame, and boasting. This might be the result of redaction on the part of the later copyist. The text probably read: "it is unheard of that salvation and protection coincide with clinging to emptiness and abandoning merits" since both clinging to emptiness and abandoning merits are mistakes of conceptualization that Vajrayana and dzogchen seek to rectify.[199]

> Simon Peter, I repeat it again for you: Thanks to my mode of visual perception, I can see every form without impediment; thanks to my mode of auditory perception, I can hear every sound without impediment; thanks to my mode of olfactory perception, I can smell every perfume; thanks to my mode of gustatory perception, I can distinguish among all flavors; thanks to my tactile perception, I can encompass every form; thanks to my mode of spiritual perception, I can pervade every object of knowledge without impediment. If these six modes of perception[200] were to be enacted fully, the results would be remarkable.
>
> My entire luminous and truthful teaching[201] has its origin in limitless[202] causes that have been accumulated in time without end. The merciful blessings[203] granted by my teachings are so abundant that they are in fact ceaseless and innumerable;[204] if one were to compare them to the King of All Mountains[205] [Sumeru], even if it should not reach the heights of these blessings, nonetheless

it would draw quite near to them. Because of that, all the good can adhere to the exact truth and therefore, thanks to their light and their grace, can shed light on everything; understanding in depth[206] [the true reality of everything], they can ascend to the land of peace and joy.[207] Once they have arrived [at this goal] and have realized the fullness [of knowledge], there is no longer any change of state.[208]

The nun-princess in the life of Garab Dorje, during her pregnancy dream, experienced this state of universal knowledge, transcending the senses. Jingjing's text relies on a Syriac term for mercy (*raḥmā*). The notion of ascending to a land of peace and joy sounds like entering the Pure Land; the permanence of this state could be interpreted a number of ways. One way is that those who attain peace and joy are on the "irreversible" eighth (unshakable) level of a bodhisattva. From a more radical tantric Buddhist approach, this would be to attain the primordial state, the "*samaya*" of remaining in the state of awareness at all times no matter what one is doing. However, there is also the risk that this could be a statement of "eternalism" in which a being remains in a high spiritual state without reaching the more dynamic view of the ongoing liberative process. The use of the term "no impediment" is another allusion to the *Abhidharmakosha* of Vasubandhu, who defines the element space as "that which does not impede," suggesting to the practice lineages the meditative experience of space-like awareness, encompassing everything. This is what Evagrius means by "essential knowledge" of the cosmos in the *Kephalaia Gnostica*.

Simon Peter, if it is thus, then the vast benefits conferred by the innumerable and merciful blessings are inconceivable to the mind. Therefore I reflect on this: if the mind cannot encompass this, what is there to say? If I speak of realizing something, and then cannot obtain that realization, then I cannot affirm that there are no obstacles.[209] Therefore I affirm the absence of desire, the absence of mental actions, the absence of merits, and the absence of realization.[210] If these four principles are sound, it would not be an exaggeration to state that it is possible to move beyond arguments regarding all the rest: being meek and humble, free and patient, and to have within oneself[211] great compassion. All those who do not have limitless passions will have full access to the law that governs all things[212] and will obtain that which is absolutely transcendent: to be able to obtain that which is absolutely transcendent is called the way of peace and joy.

This passage is a good example of how Buddhist proposals for perfect enlightenment and spiritual development were a challenge to standard Christian formulations of salvation. As if echoing the *Heart Sutra*, the Christian author balances Buddhist soteriological claims with Christian virtues, which is very much the strategy that many of the early dzogchen practitioners adopted to avoid debate with the reformists following Atisha, 'Brom Ston, and later critics such as Sakya Pandita and Bu ston.

In that moment, Simon Peter rose again to his feet, made a bow and broke forth in words of praise, exclaiming: "Great is the supreme and unique Venerable One![213] Truly great is the supreme and unique Venerable One! He is able to expound the mysterious transcendent law: this is in fact a profound mystery, inconceivable to the mind. I myself have not yet begun to realize the meaning of it. Therefore, I would like for you to instruct me again. You, O Venerable One, have affirmed the absence of desire, the absence of mental action, the absence of merits, and the absence of realization, and that these four principles are that which is called the way of peace and joy. But not having understood in depth the meaning of the question of the negation of existence, I ask, "How is it possible that there is joy in this?" The Messiah, the uniquely Venerable One, said: "An excellent question! Truly an excellent question! Since you wish to understand this question in further depth, I will explain it to you again. In effect, phenomena can only arise once existence has been negated.[214] If one affirms existence, then there can never be peace and joy. So what can one say? Consider the trees of a forest on an imaginary mountain: numerous branches and leaves are distributed among them offering their shade. However, this mountain forest does not seek out [of its own will] birds and wild beasts; rather, all the birds and the wild beasts spontaneously seek refuge in it. Or consider the waters[215] of the ocean: they are vast and limitless, and their depths cannot be plumbed. However the waters of the sea do not seek out [of their own will] the aquatic creatures; rather, the creatures of the seas live spontaneously in them. [On the contrary,] well-disposed[216] sentient beings seek out [with their own efforts] peace and joy, and do so insistently. They should rather pacify their minds, abiding in quiet, and constantly cultivating themselves. My teaching, in fact, does not seek out peace and joy [by willing it]; in this way, peace and joy arrive *spontaneously*. For this reason, I say that only by the negation of existence can things that exist[217] arise."

Here we can see the convergence of the Daoist *wu wei*—non-action—principle with the Buddhist notion of meditative tranquility. Dzogchen is called the way of effortlessness or the way of relaxation into the natural state, which is already present and from which all phenomena arise. Thoughts arise and dissolve spontaneously, and in meditation and post-meditation, they self-liberate (Tibetan: *rang grol*).

The Messiah went on to instruct Simon Peter and all the others, saying: "That which is expounded in this book is profound and difficult to understand. None of the teachings transmitted by various holy and virtuous men is based on this true and deep teaching. Let us give an example: Beings endowed with sight can travel and can see far ahead, thanks to the light of the sun. Simon Peter, the same is true of this book: both now and in the future, by means of this book it will be possible for beings endowed with a good heart to discern the way of peace and joy; it will therefore establish the foundations of all the teachings of all the sages. That being the case, when others hear this book preached, they will acquire delight; examining it closely, they will acquire alimentation; reciting it, they will acquire sustenance. You should also know that they and their fathers, they and their ancestors through all generations, are oriented towards the good by means of the bonds of good causes and conditions;[218] thus, in the past, good roots have been passed along across the generations, so that veneration for my teachings has grown; therefore, thanks to the benefits granted by it, it is possible to aspire to joy. For example, when the spring rains sprinkle and moisten the earth, all the plants gifted with roots produce shoots; if instead they lack roots, they cannot grow. Simon Peter, the same is valid for you: if you seek the transcendent law from me, it is because the numerous generations before you—fathers, ancestors, and relatives connected to you by marriage—have done good deeds in an excellent way, and this has been transmitted down to you."

This includes a teaching that emphasizes the ongoing blessing of God upon the human race, almost setting aside the notion of original sin; the idea here is that our human ancestors are to be honored for their virtuous actions, in accordance with the cult of ancestors typical of the Confucian tradition. In correspondence with the Buddhist notion of "roots of virtue," one's encounter with spiritual teachings in the present life is a result of an accumulation of virtuous actions in the past, not necessarily in previous incarnations but possibly in the extended family. It is to be noted, however, that honoring the ancestors was not entirely unknown to Christianity even in the West. A standard feature of many Romanesque cathedrals and abbeys in southern Italy was the incorporation of Roman funerary monuments prominently in the structure of the bell towers. It is as if these are our ancestors, we honor them, and the voice of the church bells is in some way their voice, urging us to be faithful to the new religion. Something similar is happening in this text, which presents itself as a kind of monument to the ancestors whose merits have been inherited by those who hear these words today.

Simon Peter, deeply moved, prostrated himself and again rose to his feet, made a bow and turned to the supreme Venerable One, asking: "Supreme and unique Venerable One, great in mercy and compassion,[219] having seen your power, please show yourself to be benevolent towards me, so that my foolishness may not lead me to distort your words, and so that I may not be led astray. If it is thus as you say, then our parents and hundreds of thousands[220] of previous generations—and thus not merely in reference to the present generation—have come to that which causes peace and joy[221] to arise for my benefit and for that of all people. Nevertheless, we have been for a long time drowning in confusion,[222] and even though we would like to save ourselves, we have not yet been able to do so in fact. We have not yet understood completely what is required to make progress towards that which causes peace and joy to arise." The unique Venerable One, the Messiah, said: "Thus it is, thus it is, just as you have said. Consider this exemplary narrative. Treasures shine forth on a mountain, such as pearls in their splendor, fruits on a forest of jade[223]: with their delightful fragrance they can satisfy hunger and extinguish thirst, as well as cure many diseases. There was once a sick person who, having heard of this forest in which such fruit can be found, became very attached to the thought of it by day and by night. Unfortunately, the mountain was high and the road leading there was very long, his body was feeble and his energy weak; moreover, having accumulated impure desires, his aspirations were not fulfilled. However, he could rely on a wise and virtuous relative who held the ladder for him and helped him to hold on, so that he could gather the desired fruit. In this way, the illness was cured.

"Now, Simon Peter, the hearts of many have been for a long time deceived and twisted: even though they have heard of this fruit, they do not desire it, though it is on the mountain of peace and joy; even though they have the idea to cultivate [their hearts], their faith is still rather weak. For this reason, if they could count on a friend[224] who serves the same purpose as the relative in the story, and he might instruct them with proper words that might become like the ladder in the tale, then they might be able to know the way,[225] and all the accumulated deceptions would be undone."

This part of the dialogue resembles the part of the tale of *Barlaam and Io-asaph*, chapter four, in which the young prince Ioasaph—locked away in a palace by his father to keep the knowledge of suffering and death far away from his thoughts—meets and converses with the disguised Christian monk Barlaam, who offers to show him the way out of suffering. This part of the story also most resembles the tales of the life of the Buddha Shakyamuni. It is interesting to have the conversation between the prince and the monk reworked as a dialogue between the Savior and St. Peter. The passage reiterates the concern of the Chinese Christians for the salvation of their ancestors and is thus an early example of a Christian theology of salvation for those outside the Church.

> For this is needed the doctrine of the ten realities to discern[226] the path of the gradual cultivation [of the heart]. And you will say: 'What do you mean by the doctrine of the ten realities to discern?'
>
> The first reality to discern: the lives of human beings, endowed with a physical body,[227] decline day after day, and cannot flee from death. It is like an inn that only offers temporary lodging and a roof over our heads, perhaps with refined foods to eat: how can these things occupy the attention of the guest, since he is not the true proprietor of the inn? Since he will soon have to leave that inn, he cannot long remain.
>
> The second reality to discern: human beings love their families, but at a certain point we all must go our separate ways; it is difficult to stay together. So it is with the leaves that all spring forth from the same tree: when the winds and the frost strike them, the branches are denuded of their leaves, which fall and are dispersed, and not even one remains.
>
> The third reality to discern: among human beings there are eminent and honoured persons; nevertheless, their glory and prosperity cannot endure for long. Just so is the moon at night, which sends forth light in all directions: when the fog comes up, and the new moon draws near, darkness replaces the light,[228] therefore, even if the moon may seem luminous, how can one entrust oneself to its light for the entire month?

The fourth reality to discern: among human beings there are those who are despotic and selfish; even if such a person thinks only of his own benefit, in reality, he is harming himself. So it is with the moth, who sees a fire in the night: it flies toward the fire, thinking it to be something good, not knowing that its own life will be destroyed in that very fire.

The fifth reality to discern: human beings accumulate treasures and riches; they expend great amounts of energy and tire themselves [for this purpose], but in reality all this is useless. It is like a small vase that can contain only a small quantity [of liquid]; should someone wish to pour all the waters of the rivers and the seas into that vase, it would only overflow, since it is not capable of containing more [than its capacity].

The sixth reality to discern: among human beings the passions constitute an obstacle; they originate in the nature of the human body, but they are the enemies of that bodily nature. It is like the worm[229] living[230] inside the trunk of a tree, which damages the life of the tree. It gradually eats away at the core of the tree, which then dries up and falls little by little to pieces.

The seventh reality to discern: when human beings drink inebriating beverages they are pervaded by a great feeling of happiness; however, once they become drunk and mentally clouded, they are no longer able to distinguish the real from the unreal. It is like a spring of pure water that can reflect everything that has a form as in a mirror that makes them visible; but if [that spring of water] is contaminated with mud, the reflected images disappear, and since the water has become very dirty, one can no longer see anything.

The eighth reality to discern: human beings divert themselves with such things as theatrical performances; in this way they both waste their time and tire out their spirits.[231] In the same way, it is like a madman whose eyes are clouded over in confusion and whose limbs[232] are frenetically agitated; not sleeping at night, his forces are diminished and at the end he can do nothing.

The ninth reality to discern: human beings following the variety[233] of doctrines merely place themselves at the service of apparent reality,[234] thus remaining far from the truth. In the same way a talented artist can paint cattle using splendid colors so that they appear to be real, but if these cattle were to be used to work the fields, they would certainly not yield any harvest.

The tenth reality to discern: human beings in seeking to cultivate goodness in themselves, in [reality] only seek to have the praises of others, mindless of the fact that in so doing they deceive themselves. It is like the oyster that contains a pearl; to obtain the pearl, the fisherman breaks the oyster, causing it to die; [the oyster's pearl] thus can ornament a person, who is not even conscious of the suffering [behind the fact of that pearl].

The division of a teaching into ten parts is attested in Hua Yen Buddhism because it is a common structural feature of the great *Avatamsaka Sutra*. It is important not to limit ourselves to Ch'an Buddhism when discussing Buddhist-influenced texts from the Tang dynasty before the persecutions of the 840s.

"Reflecting on these ten realities to discern, disciplining the body and the spirit, making our words and actions coherent, you will not err, and only in this way can you understand the following four transcendent principles. [But you will] ask: 'What are these four principles?'

The first is the absence of desire.[235] The emotions are in that which is called the interior spirit, which lead us to commit every kind of evil,[236] imagining these to be noble: for this reason, one should control them to the point of extinguishing them, not allowing them to reawaken. How is this done? One may consider a plant that has its roots hidden beneath the ground: if there is a disease in them, it is not externally visible; it is only recognizable when one sees the shoots of the plant drying out. It is the same with human beings: if there are passions in one's spirit, these may not be externally visible; nevertheless, a good wind-energy[237] (Chinese: *qi)* does not circulate in the four members and in the seven orifices [238] and therefore every kind of wickedness grows within, whereas peace and joy disappear. For this reason, one should put into practice in one's interior spirit the absence of desire.

The second principle is the absence of [mental] action.[239] Those things which are called exterior forms[240] have their proper movements and objectives, which do not follow the natural law and therefore unreal;[241] this is why one should hold them at bay, not allowing them to draw near. How does one do this? It is like a passenger on a ship that is crossing the ocean. The ship is shaken by the winds and battered by the waves; fearing that the ship will sink, the passenger is frightened. The same is true for every human being: one's exterior form has a kind of existence that hammers out its own worldly principles [of action]; only by making progress towards the cause of goodness, not counting the labor involved, can one forget about the striving in which one has been engaged. Because of this exterior form [and its demands], a human being should follow the way of the absence of mental action.

The third principle is the absence of merits.[242] If one has merits, one should not be complacent regarding the reputation [that derives from them], [but rather] one should display great mercy, seeking to lead every kind of [living being] to salvation;[243] thus, in the end, without being spoken about, one will attain that which was within one's capabilities. How can one attain this? If one considers the earth, for example, which makes everything grow according to its own nature and in accord with what belongs to each species, in such a way that each draws appropriate benefits: there are no words to describe this completely! The same is true of a human being: if one perseveres in the supreme transcendent law, puts into practice the luminous teachings, and leads other living beings to salvation, then one will become a participant in peace and joy in a wonderful way, without having anything that might attract praise. This is what is called the absence of merits.

The fourth principle is the absence of attainment.[244] It is not possible to understand the true reality of anything;[245] for this reason, forget [the false distinction] between that which is right and that which is mistaken, break through every [pre-conceived] structure, and abandon all merits. Even with regard to the sun, even if its existence seems to be an evident fact, [reflect on the fact that] its deeper nature is emptiness.[246] What should one do? One may consider a mirror that reflects everything: green, yellow, and all the other colors; that which is long, that which is short, and all other forms are all reflected in it, but one does not know how this happens. The same is true for a human being. To attain the nature of the true way,[247] to have peace and joy[248] in spirit, to examine the cause of everything, to be able to understand deeply[249] every reality—all these are things whose understanding[250] is completely gone, and nothing of it remains. This is what is called the absence of attainment.

This fourth principle reflects the spirit of the *Heart Sutra* and the attitude of the Ch'an School of Buddhist practice, with which the author may have been in dialogue. It also develops Evagrius's views on passionlessness (Greek: *apatheia*), freedom from misguided emotional attachments.

The Messiah continued: "Again, if someone enters the army, he needs armor to protect his body: if the armor is good, he will not fear the enemy. [In the same way] only the supreme transcendent law[251] of this luminous teaching can protect living beings from the enemy [forces] that afflict them, just as the abovementioned armor protects the body.

If someone crosses the ocean, he needs to be provided with a ship that can sail through the wind and the waves: if the ship is [*lacuna*],[252] he cannot reach the other shore. [In the same way] only the supreme transcendent law of this luminous teaching can ferry living beings across the ocean of mortality so as to reach the other shore [where one finds] peace, joy and precious fragrances."[253]

The image of a ship or raft is commonplace in Buddhist discourses on so-teriology. And the female bodhisattva Guanyin, an emanation of Avalokitesh-vara the Bodhisattva of compassion, is called the "ship of mercy." Ship images are employed in the stele of Xi'an and other Chinese Christian texts.[254]

> Whenever someone breathes the wonderful breath of the pre-
> cious fragrance that reawakens the soul[255] in a time of epidemic,
> in which many are ill and many more are dead, those dead return
> to life and illness will abate. [In the same way], only the supreme
> transcendent law of this luminous teaching can bring about the
> return to life of living beings [in which one has access] to the
> knowledge of the truth,[256] so that every form of sin and suffering
> may be eliminated.
>
> If a man or woman entrust themselves to my words, if they
> resolutely cultivate [this my] supreme law,[257] if they reflect [on it]
> day and night, if they abandon every form of corruption[258] [Skt:
> klesha], if they purify their true nature, arriving at deep and com-
> plete enlightenment, let it be known that these shall be liberated.
> Let it also be known that even the celestials[259] recognize the bene-
> fits that this book can bring, for not even they have arrived at the
> final understanding of ultimate reality.[260]
>
> Those who sincerely love [this teaching], who only rarely fail
> to cultivate proper conduct,[261] can travel along the way of radiant
> light; fearing no difficulties, they can travel in dark places without
> committing any evil, so as to arrive in a totally elevated place where
> they may long enjoy peace and joy. [Knowing these things], one
> should dedicate oneself decisively to cultivating [proper conduct].
>
> You disciples[262] and all those under the heavens who are lis-
> tening, put this my book into practice and you may become like
> a king who protects his territory. Consider for example a high
> mountain on which a great fire rages. All the inhabitants of that
> land will see it. The king and his ministers [who govern a coun-
> try] are comparable to that mountain, and the benefits that this
> my teaching [can bring] are comparable to that raging fire: if put

into practice, they will naturally enlighten [the leadership and the entire land], just like the light of that fire.

Simon Peter rose again to ask for further information, but the Messiah said: "It is better for you if I stop here without adding further words. Consider a well full of water, whose waters can never be exhausted, and a sick man who has just been cured, but is yet unable to drink very much: if one does not put a limit on the [quantity] of water to be drunk, it might cause new problems. Your situation is like his: since your good nature has just now been reawakened, listening to too many words might confuse you;[263] for this reason, it is better not to add anything more." Then everyone, having listened to these words, was full of joy, and, having been dismissed with deference, put them into practice.[264]

As in an *upadesha* of Milarepa that we have translated elsewhere,[265] the text concludes on a note of warning about trying to say too much; what can be said in words has been said. The image of the well with abundant water is found in St. Ephrem of Syria, one of the Fathers of the Church of the East, in reference to the meditative reading (*lectio divina*) of the Scriptures.

After the composition of this bold new theological vision, we know nothing of the rest of the life of Jingjing. The fact that his work was preserved with other Christian writings in Chinese in the Dunhuang cache indicates that these texts were treasured by the Syro-Oriental Christian community in that borderland between the Chinese and Tibetan empires of the Silk Road. This would also mean that there were Syro-Oriental Christians at Dunhuang as late as the end of the tenth century, in spite of their near disappearance in China after the persecutions of foreign religions mandated in 845. One is tempted to speculate that some restless members of the "religion of the light" might have sought refuge from the condemnation of Patriarch Timothy (in force from 787 to 823) and then again from the Tang disaffection with foreign cults, perhaps in some part of Tibet, or more likely along the northern branch of the Silk Road where there were more numerous Christian communities. Though some religions, like some species, have become extinct in the course of time, it is also true that nature and history seem to find unexpected ways of rescuing what might have been lost. Having found these treasures of an extinct part of the human adventure, it remains our present task to invigorate the creative theological task that has been left unfinished, buried by sands blown by the winds of the steppe.

IV

❧

Early Dzogchen:
Sources, Dialogues, and Reflections

Siddhah svatantrabhavah. The state of absolute independence
is already achieved.

—SHIVA SUTRA 3:13

In chapter two, we offered the reader a summary of the typical Nyingma scheme of dzogchen training and attainment, as it has evolved since at least the time of Longchenpa in the fourteenth century. Mindful of the many difficulties involved, we can now proceed to reflect more critically on the earlier history of this tradition. Dzogchen has undergone several periods of development that in many ways correspond to the history of Tibet. Having presented the most recent developments in chapter two, it becomes possible to examine the evidence for the earlier periods in order to appreciate the full range of dzogchen's development at the heart of Tibetan civilization. Dzogchen presents itself as a radical, nondualist approach to contemplative experience, an approach that is distinct from cultural accretions. As such, its modern exponents have argued for its transcultural character. However, in Tibet, the dzogchen lineages, Nyingma and Bonpo, always seem most closely allied with the archaic features of Himalayan culture and indeed have contributed much to the preservation of those features while at the same time developing the full spectrum of dzogchen practices that are claimed to prepare the way for the ultimate level of realization. Anne Klein expresses this with admirable clarity: "Dzogchen is sometimes even called a path without meditation because once one fully realizes one's own mind-nature or base there is no need for effort of any kind. Until then however, practice is necessary for clearing away the internal obstructions that prevent one from clearly experiencing the profundity of one's own being. Nyingma is the only Buddhist tradition in which dzogchen exists."[266]

TABLE III. EARLY DZOGCHEN HISTORY TIME PERIODS

Pre-Padmasambhava Tibet: 600–770s
Flourishing First Diffusion Buddhism: 770s–840s
Tibetan Empire dissolved, "Dark Age": 840s–970s
Renaissance and Second Diffusion of Buddhism: 970s–1250s
Mongol Ascendancy and Sakyapa Regency in Tibet: 1260s–1350s
Life of Longchenpa: 1308–1363
Phagmodru Ascendancy in Central Tibet: 1350s–1447 Civil War between Central Tibet and Southwest (gTsang), in various phases: 1490s–1640s Hegemony of the Gelugpa Order and the Dalai Lamas: 1640s–1950s
Phases of Dzogchen History:
Early assimilation of Buddhist teachings from China and Central Asia: 600s–770s
Foundation of Samye Monastery: 775
Council (?) of Samye against (?) Chinese Buddhism: 792–94
Era of "pristine dzogchen" within the First Diffusion: 770s–850s
Era of the lay tantrics (ngagpas); development of a nine-vehicles system: 850s–1100s
Tantric aspects of Buddhism acquire greater importance in dzogchen practice: 1000–1300
Longchenpa's (scholar, yogin, and terton) philosophical revolution: 1330–1360s
Age of the tertons (treasure discoverers, ritual specialists, and yogins): 1100–present day
Earliest tertons, eleventh century
Wu ru ton pa, Shakya Od: 1284–1339

| Ogyen Ling pa: 1329–1360/7 |
| Pema Lingpa, 1450–1521 |
| kLu Khang Temple in Lhasa: 1680s–1780s (illustrates the Pema Lingpa biography) |
| Jigmé Lingpa, 1730–1798 |
| Dudjom Rinpoche 1904–1987[267] |
| Dilgo Khyentse 1910–1991[268] |

It is possible to identify several periods of development for what came to be called dzogchen, the "ninth vehicle" of the Nyingma and Bonpo systems. There was a somewhat murky period at the start of Tibet's emergence as an imperial power in Central Asia in the seventh century when a variety of Buddhist teachings accompanied the monks, pilgrims, traders, and government officials along the Silk Road. In this period, the word dzogchen was not yet used, but already there were anthologies of sutra quotations[269] in circulation suggestive of the dzogchen approach to spiritual practice. This was followed by the arrival of Padmasambhava and other non-Tibetan masters during the reign of Trisong Detsen (742–797), at the height of the empire, during the period in which the monarchy was sponsoring Buddhism as the official religion of the Tibetan State. It was during this time that masters such as Vairotsana, Manjushrimitra, Vimalamitra, Padmasambhava, and others transmitted a number of foundational teachings associated with the dzogchen trajectory in subsequent centuries. Buddhist institutions flourished up until the reign of gLang Darma (Tri du dumten), to whom is attributed a "persecution" of Buddhism in about 842; in reality this so-called persecution seems to have been a policy enacted to severely restrict state support for monastic Buddhism.[270] The restrictions and "budget cuts" were a response to an economic crisis that arose when Tibetans—having embraced the pacific views of state-sponsored Buddhism—stopped expanding their empire. Following the assassination of Lang Darma, the empire experienced a number of rebellions (the first of these in 869)[271] and began to split up into a number of smaller states, each governed by regionally based aristocratic clans, some of whom were able to claim descent from the Yarlung dynasty, the dynasty of the imperial family. This period, which concludes the first diffusion (snga dar) of Buddhism, brings on what

Tibetan historiography calls the "dark age" or "age of fragmentation" because of the political disarray and the notorious proliferation of unorthodox tantric practices. It is claimed that, in this period from about 850 to 1000, the *ngagpas* (local tantric practitioners who were not monks) were employing the practices of Vajrayana Buddhism in the manner of sorcerers and shamans, promoting acts of violence, black magic, and sexual excess. As we know from the earliest biographies of Milarepa, it was in fact a regular feature of Vajrayana practice to employ magic for worldly ends, including revenge and intimidation. However, this should surprise no one because the original Sanskrit texts of such tantric cycles as *Hevajra, Cakrasamvara, Vajrakilaya* and other tutelary deities in fact contain magical rituals of this kind. Magic[272] is very much part of the traditions of South Asian religion, dating back to the *Artharvaveda* and most likely into the most archaic layers of human history. It was magic that gave rise to the "transgressive" dimension of tantric practice among the freewheeling mahasiddhas, and indeed it was magic that made these very mahasiddhas the objects of devotion and sponsorship by aristocratic circles in India and Tibet. The state needed the protective and exorcism rituals that tantric masters were able to provide. These were the rituals that Padmasambhava performed on behalf of the Tibetan state in order to remove preternatural opposition to the foundation of Buddhist institutions in a land dominated by archaic mountain deities. This same imperial period, as well as the subsequent "dark age" of disintegration, was crucial for the development of dzogchen as a distinctive approach within the traditions that later will be called Bonpo and Nyingma. As we shall see, not all was "dark" in this period.[273]

Purportedly as a response to the excesses of some ngagpa lineages, the royal line of Western Tibet, headed by Yeshe Od (959–1036), directed a group of young Tibetans to go to Kashmir[274] to study orthodox Buddhism, including the contemporary forms of Vajrayana practice, so as to spearhead a reform. The chief religious architect of this reform was the scholar-ritualist Rin chen zang po (958–1055).[275] The period of reform, which dates from the 990s and concludes with the mission of the Bengali master Atisha (982–1054), is considered the start of the second diffusion (*spyi dar*) of Buddhism in Tibet.[276] In contrast with the ngagpa traditions of the small towns and remote valleys of Tibet, the reform was characterized on the one hand by monastic foundations, and on the other hand by a new effort to import and translate previously unknown Vajrayana texts from India. Among these were new tantric cycles that included magical practices just as emphatically wrathful as any of the earlier tantras imported during the first diffusion. However, these new rituals were adapted for monastic use and excluded the ritual murders and sexual yoga[277] that had made them notorious. The wrathful and protective rituals were readily adapted, as they had already been throughout South and Southeast Asia, for the protection of the state and the sponsoring dynasties.[278] During this period, the dzogchen of the ngagpa practitioners evolved in competition with the newly translated tantras. This evolution seems largely to have consisted in adopting the characteristics of the more ritualistic and ghoulish tantric practices that David Germano calls "funerary Buddhism"[279] along with concerns about preparing for death and for transiting the intermediate state between death and rebirth. It must be said, however, that even in the first diffusion period, these concerns were present in the ritual matrix to which the dzogchen view was being applied as an interpretative perspective.

This is not to say that the newly translated tantras of the second diffusion were placed under a kind of ritual embargo controlled by state policy. Such an embargo did in fact exist in the first diffusion. Certain texts could only be transmitted in the context of the imperial court and allied clans, and not to the general public. In the second diffusion, there were many independent translators working on the new materials in the course of the eleventh century, such as rNgog Lo tsa ba Blo ldan shes rab (1059–1109) and Marpa Lhodrakpa (1012–1098?). Moreover, the older ngagpa traditions adapted to the new circumstances in ways that are crucial for understanding the history of dzogchen. Thus some of the second diffusion dynamism was reformist and monastic, whereas in other respects a kind of transmission typical of yogic and tantric lineages continued to be extremely important.

The life of Marpa, for example, illustrates quite clearly how an independent ngagpa could earn a considerable sum of money in the form of gold. Making good use of this wealth, Marpa was able to study with important Indian mahasiddha teachers such as Maitripa, Naropa, and many others during at least three journeys of spiritual research. Not only did Marpa translate key tantric texts, he also learned the commentarial tradition for each of them from distinct lineages associated with the Indian masters. As a result of the efforts of numerous Tibetan translators like him, the second diffusion involved the importation of texts, ritual cycles, and philosophical commentaries from the extant Indian Vajrayana lineages. There was no central state sponsorship of these activities across the length and breadth of Tibet because there was no centralized authority. A consequence of this lack of centralization was that the lineages gave rise to a great variety of institutional foundations, usually monasteries, to carry on the work of the yogis and translators who had succeeded in learning from the Indian Vajrayana masters. As these institutions acquired aristocratic patrons, they also became key players in the political history of Tibet in the twelfth and thirteenth centuries and beyond. This interplay between charismatic yogis, ngagpas, and monastic foundations gave rise to the complex features of Tibetan history up to and including the Mongol overlordship during the Yuan dynasty, which placed the Sakyapa Order[280] in the role of rulers of a *somewhat* united Tibet. Toward the end of the Yuan (Mongol) dynasty, the great Nyingmapa master Longchenpa presented his astonishingly brilliant philosophical writings inspired by dzogchen, which brought this school to a dazzling height in the intellectual history of Tibet.

TABLE IV. EARLY DZOGCHEN FIGURES[281]

Garab Dorje: late seventh century?
Manjusrimitra: early eighth century?
Vimalamitra: late eighth century
Vairocana, also spelled in Tibetan, Vairotsana, or Bai ro: late eighth century[282]
Padmasambhava: late eighth century
Sri Simha: eighth century
Buddhagupta: late eighth–early ninth century
Jnanasutra: eighth century?   Nyang Tingdzin Zangpo of eastern Tibet (Khams): late eighth century
gSal ba rgyal: late eighth–ninth century, Teacher of gNubs chen
gNubs chen: 840s–early tenth century

| Lharjé Zurpoché Shakya Jungné: late tenth–eleventh century |
| Zurchung Sherap Tra: eleventh century, one of the first to expound bodily dissolution (rainbow body) |

Before Longchenpa, however, during the eleventh and twelfth centuries, dzogchen practitioners began to discover hidden sacred objects and texts that were purportedly hidden by Padmasambhava, Yeshe Tsogyel, and other masters of the first diffusion. Some of these objects were found in or near some of the oldest Buddhist temples in Tibet. As time went on, however, the dramatic discovery of these "treasures" (*terma*) were often to occur in remote areas in the wilderness, thus connecting the discoveries and their discoverers (*tertons*) with the most archaic features of Himalayan spirituality and symbolism.

Seen in this sequence of historical developments, we can better understand the key features of dzogchen history prior to the great achievements of Longchenpa in the first half of the fourteenth century. Thanks to the work of Giuseppe Tucci as a pioneer,[283] Samten Karmay, Geoffrey Samuel, David Germano, Sam Van Schaik, Carmen Meinert, Anne Klein, Franz-Karl Ehrhard, Matthew Kapstein, John M. Reynolds, Namkhai Norbu Rinpoche, Lopon Tenzin Namdak Rinpoche, Donatella Rossi, Keith Dowman, David Templeton, Michael Walter, and others, we are able to glimpse something of the complex root system upon which later, post-Longchenpa dzogchen was able to proliferate in spite of numerous criticisms from some of the greatest Tibetan Buddhist theorists. What emerges from this mass of research and translation work is that the material we have presented in chapter two is a later systematization of what began as a very fluid set of meditation practices and spiritual insights used to interpret tantric Buddhism. There is little doubt that these practices and insights reflect the diversity of Buddhism across the great Silk Road: Central Asia and Persia, Kashmir and North India, western China during the Tang dynasty, Mongolia, and the Tibetan Empire. We are also able to suggest, in agreement with several of the scholars who have contributed to this research, that much of the diversity of Buddhism can be attributed to the very lively cultural exchange that characterized Central Asian civilization during the period that interests us. Once we have sorted out some of the key features of early dzogchen, it becomes possible to offer some observations about the emergence of the rainbow body as a sign of spiritual attainment in this system. All the evidence points to an early interest in miracles and wondrous signs, but the detailed modern emic Nyingma description of the practices associated with the attainment of the rainbow body (as reported in the account of the life and death of Khenpo A Chö) is hardly present at all in the earliest materials.[284]

Not a great deal is known, from a strictly historical perspective (and therefore etic in approach) about dzogchen in the time of the Tibetan Empire. A great deal has been read back into that period by Nyingma historians and hagiographers in order to support their claims of sacred continuity between the first diffusion of Buddhism and the later transformation of the ngagpa lineages into a perennially loosely organized school or order in Tibet. However, a great deal of historiographical progress has been made thanks to the Dunhuang manuscript discoveries and to recent studies[285] of the transitional figure gNubs Chen (Nupchen), who left a legacy of credible writings from the late ninth century. As Sam Van Schaik tells us: "The Great Perfection is a Buddhist approach to salvation, in a form only known to have existed in Tibet. From its earliest appearance in the eighth century it has survived to the present day. In the intervening centuries its literature grew into a vast range of texts, describing various different systems of the Great Perfection."[286] It is by no means easy to sort out this proliferation of texts, but we have prepared a small chart of some of the texts that seem relevant to the history we are tracing here. Sam Van Schaik, in a carefully argued article, "The Early Days of the Great Perfection"[287] is able to sort out many of the problems of language, transmission sequences, and interpretation.

TABLE V. EARLY DZOGCHEN TEXTS FOUND AT DUNHUANG
AND FROM THE NYINGMA CANON

The Six Vajra Verses (Cuckoo of Awareness: Rig pa'i khu byug)
The Small Hidden Grain, attributed to Buddhagupta (gSangs rgyas sbas pa)
Questions and Answers of Vajrasattva, by gNyan dPal dbyangs[288]
Gold Refined from Ore (rdo la gser zhun) "Primordial Experience" by Manjusrimitra.

Canonical Texts of the Nyingmapa[289]
Guhyagarbha Tantra
Kun byed rGyal po (Supreme Source)
Vairocana Five Original Transmissions from the rGyud 'bum of Vairocana
Three Statements of Garab Dorje
Accomplishing the Aim of Meditation
Lamp for Contemplative Seeing (bsam gtan mig sgron; also known as *rnal 'byor mig gi bsam gtan),* by gNubs chen.
Mind Series *(sems sde)*: the oldest dzogchen texts: *The Seventeen Tantras (rgyud bcu bdun)*[290] and the *Seminal Heart-Essence (snying thig ya bzhi)*
Space Series *(klong sde)*: rare transmissions involving mahayoga contemplative practices (completion stage style)
Instruction, or "Esoteric Precepts," Series *(man ngag sde)*: relatively late, overwhelmingly the best known, and widely promoted by the terma traditions. It is here that we find reference to trekchod, thodgal, and the rainbow body attainment.

Van Schaik, who is an expert in the Dunhuang manuscripts, describes the early competition of Buddhism during the first diffusion with "indigenous religious practices and local deity cults,"[291] which contributed to the difficulties that the ruling dynasty had to face with opposition from rival clans. Inevitably, a degree of tolerance was achieved through the assimilation of scholastic Buddhism on the level of state-supported monasteries such as Samye, founded in 775 by King Trisong Detsen (756–97), and of tantric Buddhism brought in by Padmasambhava and other non-Tibetan masters during the same reign. During this time, "civilized shamans"[292] laid the foundations for the kind of typically Tibetan religious practice that was quite possibly influenced by Buddhist importations from the semi-legendary kingdom of Shang Shung, the western part of Tibet, located on the trade routes connecting India with the main Silk Road across Central Asia.

To establish a teaching tradition based on Indian scholastic Buddhism, King Trisong Detsen invited the renowned scholar Santaraksita to become the abbot of Samye.[293] Thanks to the efforts of Santaraksita and his monk disciples, numerous Buddhist scriptures were translated into Tibetan. A serious effort was made to create a form of Tibetan that would accurately translate the Sanskrit originals. In this way, the philosophical range of Tibetan was greatly expanded. Buddhist literature was also translated from Chinese, with particular attention to the texts known to the schools of Mahayana Buddhism then flourishing in contemporary Tang dynasty China. Since tantric Buddhism was already present in China, it is not surprising that *yoga tantra* texts were among those translated into Tibetan in this phase of the first diffusion and were practiced by both monastics and laypeople."[294] Significantly, it was the lay tantric practitioner (*sngags pa*, Skt. *mantrin*) who would become the bearer of these earliest transmissions during the difficult times to follow.[295]

Van Schaik's expertise in the study of the manuscript cache found in the Central Asian monastic complex of Dunhuang enables him to give us one of the most reliable historical surveys of the earliest dzogchen texts, several of which were preserved in the caves sealed in about 1012. Van Schaik tells us:

> During the ascendancy of the Tibetan Empire, Dunhuang was under Tibetan control, although both Tibetan and Chinese lived there as monks and passed through as lay devotees. The Dunhuang texts contain some of the fundamental features of the Great Perfection that remain in most of its various later forms. These essential features owe much to earlier Buddhist literature, in particular the doctrine of emptiness (Skt. *shunyata*) set out in the *Prajnaparamita sutras* and the understanding of the nature of the mind set out in certain other sutras, such as the *Lankavatara*.[296]

Here is a typical example of a text from Dunhuang: "It does not matter whether all of the phenomena of mind and mental appearances, or affliction and enlightenment, are understood or not. At this very moment, without accomplishing it through a path or fabricating it with antidotes, one should remain in the spontaneous presence of the body, speech, and mind of primordial Buddhahood."[297]

Classic texts of dzogchen, in the period in which dzogchen was used as a method for interpreting yoga and tantra practices, teach meditation practices that direct the contemplative toward a "direct experience of the true nature of reality, which is immediately present."[298] The teaching and its result in practice "is held to be superior to all others, which are said to involve some level of intellectual fabrication."[299] In other words, whether the meditator is focusing on calming the mind (*shamatha*) or discerning the real nature of phenomena (*vipasyana*), or employing self-discipline in eliminating negative thoughts, dzogchen counters by pointing out that such methods are by their very nature conceptual, and therefore limited.[300] Dzogchen defined itself even in the earliest period as a supreme yogic approach to enlightenment (*Atiyoga*), and emphasized the ideas of "primordial purity, spontaneous presence, and nonduality" as found in the *mahayoga* tantras such as the *Guhyagarbha*.[301] Particularly in the later period (eleventh century), other tantric yogic and liturgical cycles were catalogued as lower methods, by using a scale of nine vehicles with dzogchen at the top.

In the earliest period, dzogchen "was used as an interpretive structure for the practices of the tantras," insisting for itself on the "rejection of any kind of path (*lam*), any conceptually fabricated form of practice."[302] Van Schaik's research enables him to bring some clarity to this apparently critical position by pointing out that the dzogchen teachings offer a viable approach to the very methods it seems to be rejecting. In this period, it is as if a new kind of spiritual intuition is coming into the world of tantric Buddhism. This intuition will become both a new kind of philosophy as well as a distinct vehicle of practice over the next three centuries (770s to 1100). For this reason, in the history of dzogchen, the "criticism is not to be taken as an injunction against engaging in the practices at all; rather the practices are contextualized within the higher perspective of nonconceptuality and nonduality."[303]

Dzogchen texts from the early period begin to be characterized by "a vocabulary that was later elaborated and developed into a technical terminology."[304] Examples of this vocabulary in the early texts are what Van Schaik translates as "gnosis" (*rig pa*, Skt. *vidya*), for ever-present nondual and nonconceptual awareness, and spontaneous presence (*lhun gyis grub pa*), indicating the immediate and unfabricated presence of "the body, speech, and mind of primordial Buddhahood." Equally important is the term primordial (*ye nas*), indicating that the awakened state has always been present, uncreated.[305] The earliest known dzogchen texts present the system as a "distinct yoga," referencing it to the Sanskrit word *atiyoga*, understood as the highest of the three "superior" yogas of Buddhist tantrism in the first diffusion systems of classification of *anuyoga*, *mahayoga*, and *atiyoga*. Most ritual tantras for the early school were of the *mahayoga* type. However, it is not until the eleventh century, when dzogchen is challenged by the new translations of Indian tantric texts, that the triad *anuyoga*, *mahayoga*, and *atiyoga* was clearly defined.[306]

While the earliest dzogchen teachings were taking root in Tibet, in the 840s one of Trisong Detsen's successors, Langdarma, began to limit the activities of monastic Buddhism, probably by implementing some severe budget cuts. A monk (possibly the abbot of Samyé, by then a Tibetan) assassinated the king in 842, precipitating an era of rebellion and disintegration for the Tibetan Empire. "In the following century and a half there was little or no monastic presence in Tibet, but it seems that the lay tantric practitioners flourished and maintained the transmission of the tantras and their associated practices, including "[307] dzogchen.

Thanks to Roberto Vitali and Jacob Dalton, we can link key figures from the first diffusion to the transitional figure of gNubs chen (who should probably be considered the real founding father of the Nyingma school) and then to the Zur masters in the crucial period of the troubled encounter between the Nyingma lineages and the second diffusion exponents in eleventh century Tibet. Vitali[308] gives cogent reasons for dating gNubs chen to 844–904, placing him well after the first diffusion. Dalton gives us a great deal of detail on the life of this important transitional figure during the "dark age" thanks to a careful piecing together of information gleaned from sources that ultimately reach back to some kind of autobiographical work. gNubs chen became a figure of controversy not only because of his dzogchen teachings but above all because he was accused of having created apocryphal tantric *sadhanas* (ritual manuals) based on teachings he claimed to have received during several visits to India and Nepal.[309] In fact, the biographical materials identified by Dalton were compiled by eleventh century masters in his lineage in order to defend his memory. Dalton shows both textual and geographical[310] reasons for connecting gNubs chen to the Zur clan. "Following the close of Tibet's age of fragmentation, Nupchen (Nupchen is the pronunciation; this spelling is often used in modern works in English on this topic) quickly became identified with the wrathful tantric rites of Shinjé-Yamantaka, through both his own spoken teachings, writings, and the later treasures he inspired. Love him or hate him, all seem to have agreed that Nupchen was a symbol for Tibet's age of fragmentation and that that symbol was a tantric and violent one."[311] He was thus the object of condemnation by the princely monk of Gugé, Pho-drang Zhiwa Od, and others in the late eleventh century.[312] His own lineage depicted him instead as "the lone hero of Tibet's dark age, a solitary Buddhist warrior, wandering the high mountain passes and fighting to save the Bud-dhist teachings from the chaos of his time."[313] As they did with Nupchen, the second diffusion critics also attacked the Zur lineage, Zurpoché, and Zur-chung and their writings. These lineages seem to have specialized in the kind of magical ritual texts that were useful on the village level and that we en-counter in the earliest biographies of Milarepa. In fact, one of the treasure re-vealers connected with Nupchen and the Zur lineage, Gya Zhangtrom, lived a generation before Milarepa.[314] Gya Zhangtrom's direct disciple, Nupchung, is believed to have been the young Milarepa's black magic teacher. From these biographical data, we can begin to understand something of the drama of the encounter between the old traditions dating back to the first diffusion and the impact of the new tantric and monastic reforms of the eleventh century. Strangely enough, the problem seems not to have been the seemingly radical assertions of pristine dzogchen such as those we find in *The Five Transmis-sions of Vairocana*: "Activity that is anathema or taboo, the five emotions and the five inexpiable crimes, on the path of purity deliver sovereign authority; nothing is rejected, not even sex."[315] Rather, it was the creative process of creating magical sadhanas on the basis of this viewpoint that bothered the second diffusion (or "*sarma*," i.e., "new transmission") critics. This leads us to suspect that the very notion of "pristine" versus "funerary" Buddhism may be of merely analytical validity, without corresponding to the actual early history of dzogchen in Tibet. Van Schaik's article takes this perspective, delicately preserving due respect for Germano's theory. Virtually every early dzogchen text, even the tersest and most "pristine," seems to make reference to tantric ritual, and as Van Schaik points out, the very term dzogchen arises in the context of the rite of tantric initiation, in which it signifies the moment of sublime ecstasy connected to sexual yoga. This is exactly the meaning of the other comparable term in Indo-Tibetan tantrism, *mahamudra*. Therefore, the distinction between dzogchen and Ch'an Buddhism, recognized by Nupchen (gNubs Sangs rgyas ye shes) in his *Lamp for Contemplative Seeing* (*bSam gtan mig sgron*) and reaffirmed many times in the contemporary writings of Chogyal Namkhai Norbu, lies in the distinction between the formless, spontaneous mindfulness practice characteristic of Zen, and the tantric view of the primordial presence of enlightenment requiring attuned recognition of the natural state. Moreover, the distinction between tantra and dzogchen lies in this same insistence on contemplative awareness: being present to the natural state of primordial purity, without pursuing the path of imaginative transformation typical of tantric ritual and meditation. However, dzogchen leaves the practitioner (*sadhaka*) free to explore the ritual sphere of religiosity in the manner of Buddhist tantra. It is precisely in this exploration that we may find the basis for the criticisms of the Nup and Zur lineages.

Moreover, once we have begun to get a feeling for this world of contemplative practice among freewheeling *ngagpa*s, we can also make the necessary connection between Milarepa and his contemporaries. The fact that Milarepa studied with the heirs of the Nup and Zur lineages, achieving horrific results in the practice of black magic, can now be seen as part of the criticism of the ngagpa lineages by the new or second diffusion (*sarma*) schools, especially the Kagyupa. The fact that Bre ston Lha dGa', the dzogchen teacher to whom Milarepa turned for a way of liberation "in one body, in one lifetime," was unable to transform Milarepa's mindstream in spite of his boast to be in possession of a teaching that should have succeeded "in a single day," can now be seen as a criticism of the "radical" dzogchen view of enlightenment. The new translation schools of the eleventh century were making the claim that their methods were superior to those of the earlier lineages precisely because they offered more vigorous kinds of skillful means for the transformation of even the worst moral offenders, something that dzogchen apparently was unable to accomplish.

It was only after some reorganization that the Nyingma lineages found a way to respond to the polemics that were directed at both their basic view of buddhahood and to their actual *sadhana* practices. In the eleventh-century time of inflamed contestation, we find the first instances of the terma tradition: treasure finders (tertons) who affirm the validity of the Nyingma teachings on the basis of rediscovering first diffusion texts that had been hidden by the masters of the eighth and ninth centuries. These termas claim to establish the continuity between practices transmitted in the great imperial period and the practices of the eleventh-century Nyingma lineages. Moreover, the biographies of various important figures also support the claim that Nyingma teachings are authentically Indian because they were transmitted by non-Tibetan masters such as Garab Dorje, Manjusrimitra, Sri Simha, and Padmasambhava to Tibetan translators such as Vimalamitra and Vairochana.[316] In the process, the Central Asian, Chinese Buddhist, and Shaivite/yogic aspects of these transmissions are moved to the literary background. We must not think that Tibet in the eleventh century was somehow a hermit kingdom isolated from surrounding civilizations. On the contrary, the trade routes and the highway of ideas were very much open at that time, and remained so for centuries, in spite of the Muslim conquests in northern India. The pressure to represent the Nyingma tradition as something uniquely linked to the earlier transmission of Buddhism was quite intense, a real "culture war" in which great minds on both sides contended, well aware of the accessibility of proof texts and living traditions on all sides.

David Germano's works make it clear that early dzogchen was already challenging scholasticism and the scholastic interpretation of tantra. The dzogchen authors seem to have been aware that Buddhist logic and the scholasticism of the successors of Nagarjuna and Asanga were radically challenged by other systems of thought that seemingly presented a more persuasive and dynamic vision of the absolute. Two of these systems were Syro-Oriental Christianity and the kind of Hinduism represented by the *Shiva Sutras*. Buddhism was collapsing in India because of its flawed anthropology, which was readily critiqued in debate by Hindu panditas such as Shankracarya.[317] The superficial notion of God as creator-absolute that we find in chapter two of the *Tattvasamgraha* of Shantarakshita and Kamalashila illustrates the problem: Buddhist scholasticism had become sclerotic and was unable to cope with a more dynamic notion of the absolute. In the meantime, Shaivism, Christianity, Manichaeism, and Islam had made major contributions to Indic and Central Asian culture. At the end of the tenth century the *Kalachakra Tantra* system sought to remedy the problem with a new form of tantric yoga influenced by the more sophisticated formulations of Kashmiri Shaivism. Dzogchen remedied the defects in Buddhist scholasticism with a nondualist, aesthetic/contemplative view that seems to affirm the self, to outline a universal process beyond karma, and to reach toward a formless attainment. Each of these three key anthropological and soteriological insights can be found in Shaivism and Syro-Oriental Christianity.

The Shaivite contribution is helpfully proposed by Michael Walter in his articles on "Jabir the Buddhist Yogi." In the third article,[318] Walter directs our attention to some little-known aspects of Central Asian Buddhism that eventually found their way into the Tibetan scriptures. Walter's articles challenge us to think in a much more flexible and practical way about yogic and alchemical activities among Himalayan tantrists. Walter states, "Many general comparisons have been made, and there is data suggestive of a much higher degree of mutual influence than has generally been accepted. In the current context, for example, we may ask whether the Buddhisms of northwest India and Central Asia were syncretistic. If so, the scenario here becomes probable, not merely feasible. Of course the testing of such a hypothesis cannot rest simply on examining texts—where they can be found—but must include plotting points of intersections where these religions have met, and upon what points they found a common interest."[319] It was not always easy or even possible for Buddhists to assimilate some of the known alchemical and yogic processes because there was no basis in Buddhist philosophy, especially as reorganized in the reformed monasticism of the Tibetan second diffusion, for these systems. However, in the Bonpo and Nyingma traditions, there was some room for flexibility, thanks to the independence that these traditions had enjoyed since the days of the first diffusion, and particularly after the fall of the empire. Walter cites metallic transmutational alchemy as one example of a practice incompatible with a Buddhist worldview. Another example he cites ties in to the biography of Garab Dorje and has to do with the transmutation of parts of a corpse into gold, called *vetalasadhana*, which alludes to the name of Garab Dorje as the "Good Ghoul" (Sanskrit:) or "Vampire."[320] Walter points out "Contrary to what has sometimes been asserted, teaching on 'rainbow body' yoga and its mention as a goal do not occur in the Tantra cycles brought into Tibet in the post-Imperial period, what Tibetans refer to as the 'later propagation' (*phyi dar*) of the Buddha's teachings; these include the *Kalacakra, Cakrasamvara,* and *Guhyasamaja tantras.* Rather … it entered at an earlier period, becoming the specialty of Rnying.ma and Bon yoga, and is justified as Buddhist by references from Sutra literature which are *ex post facto* and not temporally convincing."[321] It does seem, as the research of Germano, Dalton, Van Schaik, and others has shown, that there is no mention of the rainbow body or of the practices such as *thodgal* (direct transcendence, leap-over) in the early works associated with the beginnings of a dzogchen approach. It thus seems that the materials on alchemy and yoga studied by Walter came to have an impact on dzogchen practice well after the second diffusion was underway. In fact, I am inclined to read the history of dzogchen as a series of absorbed influences.

Dzogchen emerged as a special teaching in the imperial period, designed for a limited circle of people who had had spiritual experiences with tantric Buddhism but who found comparatively short sessions of meditation more congenial than ritual practice. This explains the "tethering" of dzogchen to tantric initiation, and its openness to some aspects of the Ch'an school, as shown by the Dunhuang texts studied by Carmen Meinert.[322] The work of gNubs chen Sangs rgyas ye shes (mid-ninth to early tenth century), *The Lamp for Contemplative Seeing*, attempted to revise these tendencies in the light of the purported debate in the eighth century between Kamalashila and the Chinese Chan master, Hva shang Mahayana. gNubs chen, one of the key figures in early dzogchen development before the second diffusion, presented the tantric ritual practices of Mahayoga in this same work, and then gave a very extensive exposition (204 folia) on the dzogchen teachings.[323] As both Germano and Van Schaik point out, dzogchen underwent a number of transformations in this period prior to the sealing (in 1012) of the famous Dunhuang cave containing so many manuscripts crucial for our study.[324] None of these transformations seems to contain mention of the rainbow body and its attendant system of practices. Dowman, too, in his translation of works attributed to Vairotsana, confirms that, at this early period, there seems to be no presentation of trekchod, thodgal, or the rainbow body.[325] In general, the "mind series" (*sems sde*) teachings lack these terms and practices.[326]

However, in the fourteenth century, Longchenpa commented extensively on these expressions and practices, indicating that something came into the picture between the first diffusion and the eleventh and twelfth centuries, well before Longchenpa, in the time when dzogchen was revising itself in part in the form of "treasure" discoveries (*terma*). Could the terma tradition have been the means by which non-Buddhist influences were assimilated into the dzogchen lineages and integrated with the Vajrayana?

By studying alchemy and contacts with other forms of Buddhism in the tenth century, Michael Walter hopes to propose a point of origin for the rainbow body teachings.[327] Walter himself tells us that the tantric cycles typical of the second diffusion do not teach about the rainbow body and do not contain the practices usually associated, in later dzogchen tradition, with that attainment. So where do they come from?

Walter indicates that Indian teachings on alchemy were received into the Tanjur portion (i.e., works not attributed directly to Buddha Shakyamuni, but to other masters, both Buddhist and non-Buddhist, writing in Sanskrit and other Indic languages) of the Tibetan Buddhist canon. Some of these works are attributed to the mysterious Iranian/Central Asian figure Jabir, a Nath yogin who authored a cycle of works that survives in Tibetan. Jabir transmitted medical recipes making use of mercury, other medical remedies from the Ayurvedic *rasayana* approach, methods of making amulets to prevent illness, and teachings for dealing with old age and sickness. The goal was to make it more possible for a yogi to attain liberation in this lifetime[328] in a body sustained and transformed by medical/magical practices. In Jabir's works, we encounter the presence of the Hindu deity Shiva in various forms and under various titles. In fact, Walter tells us that other Shaivite alchemical works of various origins can be found in the Tibetan *Tanjur*. Several of these works were used in Balkh and Swat in Kashmir where Shaivism developed a close relationship to Buddhism.[329] "Their use and interpretation by various groups of Buddhist yogis—in a variety of cultures, over centuries—seems to have been, at least in part, due to simple curiosity and a desire to experiment. Adhering to 'normative' doctrines were not compelling elements in their actions."[330] Walter proposes that the Islamic name Jabir be considered a "cover name for a syncretistic tradition utilizing Natha *hatha yoga* to enhance essence-extraction (*rasayana*), which in turn supports pursuing a final goal, achieving the 'rainbow body.'"[331] However, Walter is not able to find a connection between the light mysticism of these Jabir practices and later Nathist traditions. The most revealing material that he mentions is from a manuscript found in Turfan—most likely from the tenth century (though it may be a copy of an earlier work)—that gives detailed instructions on light visualization practices quite similar to *later* dzogchen practices. This work is replete with hints that actual yogic meditation practices, to a great extent derived from imagery in the later Mahayana sutras (such as the *Flower Garland Sutra*), were developed in Central Asia. I located one example in this *Yogavidhi* text rather easily, in a description of a visualization: "From other diamond thrones, Buddhas manifest themselves, gradually becoming visible from the topknots (*ushnisas*) of the Buddhas appearing before them; through the rays of sapphire light from their topknots, the whole world appears to shine."[332] Although the likelihood of a syncretic process is well developed in Walter's articles, in the end he is in as much of a quandary as we are in explaining the origins of the notion of a rainbow body. However, I think the light visualizations Walter mentions may be one of the key points of departure for the practices believed to culminate in that attainment. The most cogent presentation of the rainbow body as it enters dzogchen practice is in Samten Karmay's pioneering work on the great perfection, which we will survey below.

Continuing his exploration of Central Asian yogic traditions, Walter searches for a region where Buddhism might have interacted with other religions that gave a particular emphasis to *photism*—the mysticism of light in one form or another. Logically, this would have to be in the eastern part of the Iranian plateau, where he encounters Manichaeism. To support his syncretistic proposal, he is able to cite some valuable texts that have been found in archeological sites in areas under Iranian influence. These texts describe the luminous nature of the *skandhas* (the five components of a human person) and propose meditations on light of various colors.[333] The *Yogavidhi*, mentioned above, speaks of meditation on "sending out rays of rainbow light,"[334] a practice that receives some confirmation from the later Bonpo, *Zhang Zhung snyan rgyud* (eleventh century), which refers to the rainbow *method* (*gzha' tshon tshul*). What is it that turns this kind of purification practice into a method for altering the materiality of the body of the yogi? Although Walter gives us much that is helpful regarding Manichaeism and the light phenomena associated with the Buddha Amitabha, in fact the sources are chronologically out of sequence, and the practices quite different from what we know of *trekchod* and *thodgal* in the dzogchen systems. At best, we are given a possible source for the five colors cosmic symbolism in later, terma-based dzogchen, along with a helpful survey of the presence of Zoroastrian, Manichaean, Muslim, and Buddhist mysticism in Eastern Iran as far as Turfan. Both Bonpo and Nyingma traditions refer to this region in their myths of origin. In this region, and connected to the Jabir traditions, Walter suggests that the *thodgal* practice of staring at the sun at various times of the day comes from the practices of contemplatives in the Indo-Iranian borderland:

> On the basis of the natural luminosity of consciousness and the *skandhas* through them the *'ja' lus* is a natural expression for return to our origins in the first *bar do*, designated *'od gsal chos sku*, as well as being a generic, wished-for end of spiritual achievement, to be realized now or eventually. The rainbow body occurs so frequently in these contexts without any reference—even implied—to special practices for its attainment, that we can see its accomplishment rests on a passive acceptance of the photistic cosmogony formulated long before. Attaining a rainbow body in such contexts provides a basis for communication between past teachers and living disciples through visions.[335]

The total absence of reference to the Syro-Oriental Christian tradition in Walter's articles is something of a disappointment but not surprising. As already suggested in chapter two, we have been examining photism in this tradition, which continues the practice of light mysticism known in the early Christian church and among the monastic Fathers. In fact, this kind of mysticism of light was so important to the Byzantines that it became one of the central features of hesychasm, defended by Gregory Palamas in the fourteenth century,[336] at the same time as Longchenpa's philosophical exposition of dzogchen in Tibet. At all times, Christian light mysticism is connected to

the graces of the sacrament of baptism. The Eastern churches refer to this illumination as *photizmos*, based on several clear references in the New Testament
and Early Fathers, which also connect this light to the light of Christ's resurrection (II Corinthians 4:4,6; also Clement of Alexandria and Justin Martyr).
The same light is encountered in the other sacraments, and in each of them
it is understood to be the active presence of the risen Christ in the liturgical
rites of the church. The Manicheans, arisen from the experience of Mani in
the Elkesaite Judeo-Christian baptismal sect, not surprisingly continued to
make reference to this kind of sacramental photism. However, it is really only
in the Christian churches that bodily resurrection is connected to the illumination of baptism and the transformation of the body through sacramental
Eucharistic communion. Manichaean food rites for liberating the particles
of light entrapped in vegetables are not about creating a resurrection body of
light; whereas the Eucharist most certainly *is* about that.

The light mysticism of both Byzantine monasticism[337] and Syro-Oriental
monasticism, therefore, seems to provide a credible bridge that is lacking in
the Jabir alchemical materials and in the Manichaean texts as well.

David Germano, in an article on the theme of embodiment in tantric
Buddhism,[338] suggests ways by which tantrism sought to go beyond the basic
experiences of luminosity that we encounter in the Christian and Manichean
texts. Perhaps the Nyingma masters were responding to their Buddhist and
non-Buddhist challengers by developing a contemplative system that sought
to alter embodiment in a radical way, corresponding to the radicality of
dzogchen in general.

The rainbow body emerged as a yogic attainment during the culture war
period of the eleventh century, based possibly on earlier speculations on how
the human body might participate in the experience of enlightenment at the
time of death. As we have seen in the extremely attractive research of Michael
Walter, the history of the attainment of the rainbow body within the dzogchen tradition is not easy to establish. Samten Karmay, in his seminal work on
the history of dzogchen, shows that the eleventh-century theorists did in fact
base their ideas on Buddhist ideas of "nirvana attained without leaving any
remainder," i.e., understood at that time as to attain nirvana without leaving
behind any visible relics after cremation. The idea was that a practitioner of

Mahayoga tantra (in the series Mahayoga, Anuyoga, and Atiyoga, recognized as the highest three vehicles in dzogchen theory) "passes into nirvana either with the actual body or leaving it behind, but it must be mentioned that … the author he cites does not speak of this in connection with dzogchen."[339] The idea of the dissolution of the body emerges in dzogchen only after the "mind series" of texts has been assimilated by the lineages in the later period. Karmay tells us that the term *"phung po lhag med"* (the body without remainder) is discussed in the *klong sde*, the "space series" of teachings and, even more amply, in the *man ngag gi sde*, "the Instruction series" of dzogchen teachings. Since these treatises only go back to the eleventh century, we are constrained to that period for any discussion of this attainment. For the instruction series, "the internal elements vanish into their original place. The attachment to one's own body ceases and the body no longer appears with the actual flesh and blood. As the five external elements cease to exist, the appearance of earth and stone is no longer a coarse appearance, so nothing remains."[340]

From the eleventh century onwards, dzogchen treatises consistently use the term "without remainder" to designate a process by which the body of a deceased master ceases to exist, retaining its existence in the form of a body of light. When we come to Longchenpa in the fourteenth century, we find the following expression: "the exhaustion of the elements after the principle of the primeval purity has been finalized by means of the *khregs chod*, 'cutting off the rigidity' and the purification of the elements after the spontaneity has been finalized by means of the *thod rgal*, 'passing over the crest' are identical in their effectiveness for purifying the external and internal substances, but in the case of the *khregs chod*, when the atoms of the body vanish separately, the adept is instantly released to the primordial purity.… In the case of the *thod rgal* the adept assumes a luminous body and accomplishes the 'Great Movement.'"[341] Karmay notes that the conception of the rainbow body is not unique to dzogchen. However, the practitioner of dzogchen intends to attain such a body as a sign of the "return to the primordial state which is conceived to be in the form of light."[342]

Significantly, other Tibetan Buddhist schools severely and vigorously criticized this point of view, affirming that "the notion of the dissolution of the physical body into lights is totally extraneous to Buddhism."[343] These critics asserted that the rainbow body was a return to the pre-Buddhist idea of the ascent of the early Tibetan kings to heaven by means of a magical rope,[344] a topic that Tucci has also studied, and that we will discuss below. The eighth Karmapa, Mi bskyod rdo rje, pointed out that the rainbow body was the result of practices found among the Bonpo who teach methods "for watching lights and hold that if one's body enters into light one attains the 'eternal body.'"[345] These criticisms in the name of Buddhist orthodoxy suggest that there really was something alien about the rainbow body as a goal of spiritual practice. If we compare this notion with the original mind series teachings, we can also detect a certain dissonance because of the resistance of those "pristine" dzogchen teachings to the notion of attainments, stages, progress, purification, and striving. We also know that "watching lights" was a practice of the Tamil Siddha tradition several centuries prior to the eleventh-century explosion of dzogchen treatises, and it was also a practice of Central Asia Buddhists in the Vidhya yoga book found at Turfan.[346] These practices puts us back into the world of Manicheans and Syro-Oriental Christians along the great Silk Road.

In the final analysis, however, none of these traditions ever intended to resurrect or save the human body except one: the Christians. As Klimkeit points out, the Christians of Central Asia made the resurrection of Christ—and of humanity at the end of time—central and non-negotiable articles of belief. I have argued in chapter three that this is typical of all the Eastern Christian Churches, central to Christian monastic contemplative practice, and strongly supported by the relic of the shroud, known to the Byzantines who seem to have taken it from the Syriac Christians in the ninth century in order to safeguard it from the risk of destruction at the hands of the Muslim powers in Mesopotamia. Coinage from Byzantium,[347] in use throughout the trade networks of Asia, celebrated the shroud image of the risen Christ, as sindonology research has demonstrated statistically and iconographically. It would therefore seem reasonable to propose that the rainbow body was a Buddhist response within the embattled dzogchen lineages to the challenge of an encounter with Christians and Muslims, as well as to the infra-Tibetan culture war with the second diffusion reforms of monasticism and Vajrayana in the eleventh and twelfth centuries. The Christians referred to light phenomena occurring during meditation and prayer in their mystical writings, as in the cases cited in the works of John of Dalyatha. They also knew about states of samadhi, which they experienced as the cessation of thought in a state of wonder during the practice of psalmody.

What Christianity did not claim was that someone could attain the resurrection before the end of history. The dzogchen response was to incorporate the marginal practices known in Central Asia (possibly mediated by their Bonpo friends, as in the case of Milarepa's magic teachers) and among Shaivite yogis from Kashmir and from far-off Tamil Nadu—practices that were known to open the subtle body channels to light phenomena. Having already developed a powerful system of contemplative practices based on the primordial purity of the nucleus of enlightenment, conceived as dynamic within the mind-stream of the meditator, dzogchen practitioners may have surprised themselves when the legendary phenomena of "going to the heavens on a rope of white light" seemed to be attainable—in some form—with this synthetic new system of practice. What perhaps began as a polemical stance of self-defense might have emerged as an existential/contemplative reality in the practice experience of at least some highly motivated dzogchen yogis. I do not think this should surprise us, given the proliferation of other forms of mystical attainment in the dzogchen milieu during the second diffusion, particularly that of the tertons (Tulku Thondup lists more than thirty-three tertons for the eleventh century).[348] The description of the yogic-practice milieu around Longchenpa in the fourteenth century, as translated by David Germano and Janet Gyatso, also illustrates the kind of fervor and interactional energy present in such circles in which paranormal phenomena (dreams, possession, revelations, etc.) seem to have been the order of the day.[349] The fact that the terton phenomenon, with its self-defined connections to the days of Padmasambhava, and its inexplicable rediscovery of texts hidden in the Tibetan landscape, certainly suggest that a revival of the mystique of the imperial period was one feature of the Nyingma response to second diffusion criticisms.

Both Tibetan and Western scholars have noted the connection between the rainbow body attainment, and the notion of the ascent of kings into the heavens by means of a cable. Tucci observes,

"The summit of the sacred mountain is also the place of contact between earth and heaven. The connection between heaven and earth is a primeval article of faith for the Tibetan; in this connection one must recall the rope (*dmu thag*) which linked heaven and earth, but which was later cut, through the fault of man or as a result of a violation of the liturgical rules. As a result the two worlds have remained forever parted."[350] It was understood that the early Tibetan kings were sacralized by their relationship with both heaven and earth:

The power or *majestas* (Tib. *mnga' thang*) of the king rests above all upon his sacredness. Originally this was to guarantee purity and immunity against defilement by the evils threatening him and the kingdom. If a king is attacked by leprosy, or if he has a son born blind, then king and queen are buried alive, and the son cannot ascend the throne until he acquires the power of sight. If the king does not fulfill the requirements imposed on him then his *mnga' thang* is extinguished, the grass dries up and all goes to the bad.... There seems to me no reason to give up the opinion ... that the king renounced his power as soon as his son reached the age at which he could mount a horse, that is at thirteen years. This number expresses completeness and purity. Reliable indications are lacking concerning the further destiny of the old king. His ascent to heaven by means of the *dmu thag*, the rope of *dmu*, may indicate that he was removed by violence or exiled. In any case, the power went into the hands of the son, whose minister stood at his side.... Each new king completely transformed everything.[351]

Tucci provides us with a description of the origins of kingship as articulated in the legends of king Gri gum. The tale of this king suggests a typically Central Asian and Indo-European conflict between chthonic deities and sky deities, in which the king must act as a mediator, or lose his royal power:

It is well established that a significant break in funeral customs follow the death of Gri gum. Concerning the time before him the tradition speaks of an ascent of the king to heaven with the help of a cord connecting heaven and earth. In such a manner the dead king left no trace of himself behind; he vanished like a rainbow. At the time of King Gri gum, however, the cord broke, and the corpse was enclosed in a coffin and thrown in the river. The memory of the cord connecting heaven and earth is also found in other family histories, though various causes are given for its breaking.[352]

This notion of a cord linking heaven and earth, allowing for the disappearance of the king after death, is the *cultural* background for the claim of attainment of the rainbow body, and was cited by Tibetan native critics of dzogchen claims. However, a great deal of doctrine intervenes, and it is this doctrine and its history that should be examined in detail. Tucci was among the first to note that Shaivite and "gnostic" trends in the western Himalayas and in Central Asia seem to have contributed to the evolution of the Bon religion and the emergence of dzogchen teachings among Bonpos and Nyingma Buddhists.[353] More recent scholars, as we have shown above, have given even more persuasive indications of the syncretic environment in which myth, practice, and realization may have converged.

The doctrines of light and of bodily transformation are an integral part of the spiritual systems that emerge in the eighth century, and it is these doctrines that link developments in Tibet to Manichean, Shi'ite Muslim, and Christian practices, as well as to Kashmiri Shaivism and Vajrayana Buddhism. Bodies of light and vajra bodies are key features of the attainments claimed for the Buddhist tantras, but as Samten Karmay has pointed out, Tibetan Buddhist critics of dzogchen were particularly troubled by the claims of bodily dissolution. Nyingma apologists made such claims resonate with the scholastic Buddhist teaching on attaining "nirvana without remainder," i.e., without leaving relics behind, but their second diffusion-era critics were convinced that the rainbow body claims of the Nyingma did not correspond to this ancient teaching at all.

For the classic Vajrayana, the transformation of oneself into a divine being is common to all schools, although the liturgical procedures that bring it about through a series of stages vary in form. What is crucial here is that since the essence of a person is the light-mind, a notion inherited from the early Buddhist *Aggannata Sutta*,[354] one might be able to dissolve the material body into a body of light by using these Vajrayana techniques of transformation. Dzogchen, having intuited that the stages of creation and completion are in themselves artificial constructs, leading at best to a transformed way of perceiving and of being in the world, proposes a more radical solution: recovering direct experience of the primordial purity (*ka dag*) of all phenomena so that liberation can occur under any circumstances, without requiring the repeated rituals of transformation. The flux of life is itself perfect; the encounter with this flux is already contemplative absorption; all that the yogin needs to do is to orient him or herself on the basis of the disclosure of the natural state of awareness (conceded by the encounter with the dzogchen master) under any and all circumstances. The same light-mind is employed, but nothing is corrected or excluded. What arises is dealt with through the practices of cutting-through and leap-over, the two sets of practice that have been discussed in some detail in chapter two, and that must be now connected to the earliest dzogchen teachings that have come down to us.

It is good at this point to recall that Lama A Khyug stated insistently that in the encounter with the rainbow body, it is *sems* that counts, not visual perception (*mig*). Tucci's comments on tantra are also very helpful in understanding why Sam Van Schaik's early dzogchen[355] texts refer to an intense initiatic (ritual) experience when they make use of the term *rdzogs pa chen po* and not to a simple, formless moment of insight. So far no one has pointed out that the parallel term mahamudra, much used in the tantras of the second diffusion, refers to the same initiatic experience long before it was taken up as a description of the state of complete realization, particularly in a vast body of literature in the Kagyu and Gelug schools. By locating archaic dzogchen in a ritualistic context, it also makes more sense to interpret some of the earliest dzogchen advocates's insistence[356] that dzogchen is not Ch'an Buddhism. In fact, dzogchen has always been, as far as the Tibetans (including the Bonpos) are concerned, a form of tantric Buddhism—however atypical and perhaps unorthodox it may be. Michael Walter's study of the remarkable "syncretistic" figure, "Jabir the Yogin" helps us locate earliest dzogchen in a yogic, tantric, ritualistic milieu that was capable of incorporating features of the religious systems present to the west of Tibet. What seems to be missing in this mass of research, however, is a clear reference to a spiritual system that enhances the relationship between deep contemplative practice and bodily transformation. The usual candidates for this feature of dzogchen practice, leading to the "discovery" of the rainbow body, are Zoroastrianism with its early doctrine of the resurrection in the form of the generation of a heavenly body after death, Manichaeism with its food ritual to liberate elements of light, Daoism with its alchemical pursuit of bodily immortality, and Indian yoga and tantra traditions with their attention to the body as a vehicle for attaining siddhis. Hardly anyone takes seriously the possibility of a Christian influence on early dzogchen, but our previous chapter on the Evagrian trajectory in Syro-Oriental Christianity should make it clear that concerns with embodiment, resurrection, and light mysticism were abundantly represented in the writings of the Syro-Oriental mystics.

Early Dzogchen Practices and Teachings:
Reflections on the Historical Religious Trajectory Leading to Modern Rainbow Body Manifestations

One might conclude, on the basis of most scholarship on early dzogchen, that dzogchen is quite simply a logical development of the philosophical view and the practices of Vajrayana Buddhism. The Bonpo form of dzogchen could easily be attributed to adaptations that may have occurred in the eleventh century. At that time Nyingma and Bonpo masters worked amicably together, as we know from the story of Milarepa's youthful study of destructive magic and from an episode of "ecumenism" reported in the *Blue Annals*.[357] There is nothing in the earliest available dzogchen documents to assert definitively that we have a syncretic practice of some kind, although Walter's research on the interactions in Central Asia seem to demonstrate an exchange of ideas and methods across sectarian lines. The same suggestions of syncretism seem to emerge from a number of Dunhuang texts, such as the divination text, Pelliot Tibétain 351, which addresses the God Jesus Messiah who acts "like Vajrapani and Sri Sakyamuni." Jesus is described in this text as "judge at the right hand of God" as in the Nicene Creed, a copy of which in its Syro-Oriental form has been found in the Sogdian language at Turfan in a ninth- and tenth-century manuscript.[358]

The *Six Vajra Verses* attributed to Garab Dorje, or more accurately Vairotsana, and discussed in Namkhai Norbu Rinpoche's *Rigbai Kujyug* have a certain clarity and integrity of their own: "Even though the nature of diversity is nondual, in terms of individual things, it is free of conceptual elaborations (made by mind). Even though there is no thought of what is called 'just as it is,' these various appearances which are created are ultimately good (transcending relative good and evil). Since everything is complete in itself, abandoning the illness of efforts, one remains effortlessly with presence in the state of contemplation."[359] This text with a commentary by Vairotsana was found at Dunhuang, giving it a claim to considerable antiquity. Thus, Norbu Rinpoche can say confidently: "Now nobody can say that dzogchen is not authentic or is not an ancient teaching."[360] Of course, a teaching can be both ancient and authentic without being from one exclusive source of inspiration. And when we read the most ancient versions of the life of Garab Dorje, we begin to suspect that there is more to the origins of dzogchen than can be exclusively attributed to Buddhist Vajrayana. In fact, much recent research has demonstrated the very complex roots of Buddhist Vajrayana itself.[361] It is also true that many Tibetan lineages critiqued the dzogchen teachings as being wholly or in part non-Buddhist in origin, and to the present day, dzogchen theorists have sought to defend the Buddhist identity of their practices and doctrines.[362] Most typically, as in H. H. Dudjom Rinpoche's very extensive work, *The Nyingma School of Tibetan Buddhism* (1991), or in Dilgo Khyentse's *Zurchungpa's Testament* (2006), there are citations from canonical sources from early Buddhism, Mahayana sutras and shastras, and tantric works, all of which are made to concur systematically with dzogchen doctrines. Indeed, we are struck by the compatibility of these citations with the way that dzogchen authors describe their own unique system and find it difficult to imagine what it might have been that caused objections in the first place. One is reminded that, when we analyze the systematic arrangement of texts in any given tradition, we will find that the very process of winnowing a large body of texts for persuasive citations alters the meaning of the texts recovered from various sources. Moreover, a viewpoint that may have been present in a very rudimentary way in an ancient text can often acquire unexpected degrees of clarity and precision simply by being cited alongside other, similar texts.

Comparatively speaking, much of Christian theology has involved gleaning key texts from the scriptures and organizing them in a consistent schematic presentation for the purpose of defending certain doctrinal developments. The basic method of scholasticism, in any of the great traditions (there are Hindu, Buddhist, Muslim, Daoist, and Christian "scholasticisms"), is that of organizing citations from the basic sources of the tradition in order to demonstrate coherence, to present the teachings with credible clarity, and to subvert attempts to alter the basic dogmatic assertions that define the particular tradition. The methods employed are almost always the same: create an anthology of valid citations; define terms; resolve apparent contradictions among citations and previous commentarial materials; attempt to present a comprehensive view of spirituality, anthropology, and soteriology; and employ a hermeneutical scheme that persuasively supports the interpretation advanced by the particular author. The problem with scholasticism is that it is usually more effective as a teaching or apologetic tool than as a method for determining truth, particularly when challenged by entirely unexpected new data, or by previously unknown philosophical systems of interpretation.

With regard to Tibetan Buddhism, what we are proposing is even more challenging to a "canonical" scholastic approach to the tradition, because although it is relatively easy to see Buddhism in dzogchen, it is also possible to discover elements of other traditions that have been in dialogue with early dzogchen and, over time, were thoroughly assimilated to the Himalayan Vajrayana milieu in which dzogchen flourished. To do so, we will now examine the text of the biography of Garab Dorje in some detail. This narrative, probably composed in the eleventh century, is a kind of palimpsest of several traditions: Buddhism, Islam, and Christianity, with some possible influence from the Shaivism of Kashmir, accumulated over several centuries. It is as if the narrative itself reveals the territories both geographical and intellectual that were traversed in the emergence of what we now call dzogchen. We are reminded here of Michael Walter's comment that "Jabir the Yogi" may have been a literary expression for a process of transmission, more than the name of an individual. This line of research traces the history of dzogchen in order to discover moods, motivations, and exchanges that explain dzogchen origins and that may inspire further exchanges among contemplative practitioners in our own times.

Working with Tibetan historiography is by no means easy. The emic perspective of the written tradition frequently conceals more than it reveals, intentionally so. Blondeau's observations on Tibetan history and on the origins of Bonpo are helpful in sorting things out at least to some extent, and her work has been supplemented by scholars such as Matthew Kapstein, Geoffrey Samuels, Dan Martin, and others. The Bonpo reality in Tibetan civilization challenges us to rethink Tibetan religious history in surprising new ways. In some sources, Bon is presented as a syncretism of Indian and Iranian religion with some form of Central Asian Buddhism, bringing in as well the old royal cult and folk religion (*mi chos*), and perhaps shamanism. In Bonpo texts that have come down to us, we see Vajrayana Buddhism and Nyingma-style dzogchen brought together, with the names of the relevant deities changed. Vajrayana occupies the same ecological niche in Indian and Tibetan civilizations, and operates with many of the same syncretistic elements. We might ask at that point why Bon did not simply amalgamate with Nyingma. These two were, and are, very close in the gonpas of northern Nepal, Amdo, and western Tibet. Bon imitates the Buddhist system of monasticism and intellectual training (Madhyamaka, debate, etc.), and has done so apparently since the mid-fourteenth century. As we have seen during fieldwork in Dolpo and Mustang, the local gonpa maintained by ngagpa families works well for Bonpo and for Nyingma, especially if they are periodically in contact with the leadership of the respective monastic traditions. One wonders if the current profile of these communities on the "periphery" takes its origin from some time in the seventeenth century, once Gelugpa hegemony had been established at the center under the Great Fifth Dalai Lama. In that case, perhaps Bonpo exists as a persistent, archaic resistance to non-Tibetan forms of cultural hegemony.[363] In a certain sense, dzogchen practice within the Nyingma tradition establishes the same kind of counterpoint to monastic, institutional, and politically engaged forms of Buddhism. Without going too far into the question of "treasure finders," it does seem to be the case that, in practice, the treasure (*terma*) traditions articulate a firm commitment to archaic practices across a broad range of Tibetan cultural milieux, up to and including the great hierarchs, even the Dalai Lamas.

The historical account consistent with modern scholarship also has us thinking about why almost all the key defining moments in the official versions of Tibetan history are subject to doubt. When we actually study the oldest sources, Dunhuang documents, Chinese annals, Arabic sources, and archeological evidence, we discover that many of the later "official" Tibetan versions are not only inaccurate but also fail to report the conflicting evidence in what is available from primary sources. One of the reasons I find the *Blue Annals* so useful in spite of the limitations of the English translation is that its author, 'Gos los tsa ba gZon nu dpal (1392–1481) is often willing to question his own sources on the basis of what he considers better information. He is a good renaissance humanist in this regard! Official Tibetan history, apart from these exceptions, is often like the donation of Constantine, or the extravagant Christian medieval hagiographical tales that were meant to edify more than to inform. Many key themes of Tibetan history have been enshrined in persuasive and persistent myth, but historical research often contradicts the story: there may have been no royally organized Samye Debate; King Trisong Detsen may have been favorable to Ch'an Buddhism; Padmasambhava was not the primary source of dzogchen teachings; dzogchen ideas were not based on Chinese Ch'an Buddhism; local tantrism was not a riot of orgies and murder in the period after Langdarma, and Langdarma was not a remorseless persecutor of Buddhism (he seems to have merely cut the budget, and favored the ngagpas); furthermore, archaic sacrificial rites continued to be practiced under the Buddhist kings of Tibet, many of the termas were composed or created by the tertons who "discovered" them, Bon seems to have had a sophisticated meditational system before the arrival of scholastic Buddhism in the final decades of the eighth century; Padmasambhava's biographies are elaborately woven myths; it is by no means clear that the Ch'an monk Hwa Shang was expelled from Tibet because the royal family favored the Indian Buddhist scholastic tradition; the famous episode in which Atisha criticized the tantric meditation practices of Rin chen zang po may be apocryphal; in old age, Naropa, unlike the slender yogin depicted in his thangka portraits, seems to have been so enormously fat that he had to be carried around by disciples; gTsang smyon Heruka completely reinvented the historical Milarepa to suit his reform program at the end of the fifteenth century—among other things by switching Milarepa's hand from the left to the right ear in standard iconography, rewriting much of the poetry and reassigning roles to new heroes and villains in the biographical narrative—the list of fabrications is typical of Tibetan historiography. Many of the biographies of Tibetan saints are reinvented out of epic materials having little to do with the actual lives of these key figures. Time after time, idealized typologies replace historical fact by an acid process that devours the details that might otherwise interest and inspire the reader.

All of this conflict between myth and reality does not make it easy to write the early history of dzogchen. It is even more difficult to piece together a history of belief in the rainbow body, since few if any of the earliest authentic documents make mention of this phenomenon. For the history of dzogchen, as we have indicated above, there was a flourishing synthetic process in which ideas rooted in the kind of Mahayana abundantly present in Central Asia were being implemented by communities of yogins in areas to the west and north of Tibet (as in Michael Walter's studies of Jabir the Yogi). These yogins are identified typologically with the early dzogchen masters, even though the exact meaning of the word dzogchen in this period is not established, nor is there really a "dzogchen" school or order. Thus when David Germano asks about the origins and character of early or pristine dzogchen, we would like to suggest a response that refers to this Central Asian Buddhism now known to us in the fragments of sutras and paintings found in Silk Route oases by archeologists. This is the Buddhism that gave the Chinese some of the greatest translators of Sanskrit Buddhist texts—this Central Asian Buddhism created a bridge across the vast territories of Central Asia that arrived in China, supplanting the earlier translations that made their way from India to China. Mahayana insights are said to have entered Tibet via the figure of Hwa Shang, but it seems clear that they also arrived through the western route into the kingdom of Zhang Zhung. The transmissions are not easily datable. Some early form of Bon may have received these kinds of Buddhist teachings from Central Asian, Taoist, and Indian sources, well before the eighth century.

The texts translated by Giuseppe Tucci, which he and others thought were indicative of a Ch'an Buddhist origin for dzogchen, may just as easily be identified as inspirational teachings gleaned from the Mahayana sutras and shastras. These brief texts could have been copied by the disciples to keep in their meditation huts for guidance during meditation practice and expounded on in greater detail by a master in dialogue with disciples in a practice or retreat situation. What looks like pristine dzogchen in this form may have inspired some early yogins to compose original texts such as the Small Barley Grain, the Six Vajra Verses, and some of the other texts found at Dunhuang. These texts take their inspiration from the sutra anthologies, but they introduce pithy and creative forms of the teachings on practice, transmission, and philosophical viewpoint. Sam Van Schaik has shown that these texts are not to be read in contrast to the contemporaneous practice of the mahayoga tantras and the early atiyoga and anuttara yoga tantras (such as *Guhyagarbha*, which was a mahayoga tantra and the very early *Guhyasamaja*, which later tradition classified among the highest yoga tantras such as *Hevajra, Cakrasamvara, Vajravarahi, Mahamaya*, and so forth).[364] This would be the same kind of mistake as reading Buddha's Lions[365] as a polemical hagiographical collection seeking to promote spontaneous enlightenment over against the gradual approach, via scholarship and tantric ritual, to realization. Apparently the same authors were involved both in the production of short, pithy vajra verses as well as in writing tantric liturgies and commentaries, exactly as was the case in the later diffusion of tantric Buddhism in Tibet. In fact, the term "dzogchen," Van Schaik tells us, was used to describe the sublime moment of ritualized communion with the guru and consort during Vajrayana ritual initiation. Even early dzogchen, therefore, cannot be separated from its Buddhist tantric matrix.

The Six Verses (Cuckoo of Awareness) expresses the typical features of dzogchen theory and practice, attributed to a transmission from Garab Dorje,[366] whom we are identifying as a composite mythological figure from Central Asia: "What is perceived as diversity among phenomena is in reality nondual; particular phenomena are without conceptual complexity; that which is truly there is free of mental fabrications; the supreme buddha nature manifests in multiple forms; thus the yogin, indifferent to artificial approaches to meditation, knowing that realization is already spontaneously present, leaves perception exactly as it is."367 The key points in this teaching presume that a master is teaching an advanced yogin who has begun to glimpse realization. The teaching presupposes a long period of training that included study of Mahayana sutras and shastras, merit gathering activities, basic shamatha and vipasyana meditation brought to a high degree of perfection, and tantric ritual initiation. There is most likely a presupposition that the yogin has passed beyond monastic training and is engaged in a variety of tantric activities in a retreat setting. As a result of these practices, the yogin or sadhaka (someone engaged in a specific program of contemplative practice called a sadhana) has begun to experience profound changes in the way of seeing the world and its phenomena. Whatever this yogin perceives in the environment of practice and daily life is clearly understood to be a union between the organs of perception and their objects, exactly as taught in the *Abhidharmakosha* of Vasubandu, and further elaborated in Vasubandhu's later Mahayana works on the relationship between consciousness and perception. Thus the meaning of the term nondual in the Six Verses is not about ontology but about knowing through sensory perception: the act of perception is inseparable from the organs of the senses, their objects, and the interior structure of the perceiving consciousness factor in the mind of the perceiver. The absence of complexity is an assertion that the advanced yogin is no longer subject to emotional turbulence at the moment of perception because the memories of past experiences have been discharged through the practice of vipasyana meditation (mindfulness or insight meditation). The yogin no longer layers on interpretations and justifications for specific past actions, good or bad, and for emotional disturbances in the present. Thus having attained a degree of interior freedom (cf. Evagrius's passionlessness, *apatheia*), the yogin also knows that anything that appears among the phenomena of the flux of perception can in fact be allowed to appear without automatically arousing a flood of memory and interpretation, also known as conceptualization or mental fabrications (*prapañca*). Echoing the great *Heart Sutra*, the teaching goes on to remind the yogin that Samantabhadra—supreme buddha nature inherent in all phenomena (this is also called dharmata)—is encountered precisely in all phenomena as the dharmadhatu, the open sphere of all that is. Thus perception, free of conceptualization, directly and freely perceives the openness in every moment of encounter with the environment. At that point, all the mental training exercises have done their work, and there is no point in employing mentally constructed antidotes during meditation when purportedly negative thoughts arise. Instead, all thoughts become the "object" of open and free perception, the perfect attainment of continuous vipasyana, the meditative freedom that abides within the flow of all dharmas (the instantaneous appearances of the phenomena of perceived reality). For this reason, since the yogin is "already there," the perceptual flow of phenomena no longer needs to be corrected, altered, stopped, or improved. It is just what is, but at this point the yogin is both highly aware and highly sensitive, very close to full enlightenment, which will emerge appropriately at the right moment in the near future.[368]

This kind of teaching quickly leads us to identify a set of core values that persist in the dzogchen lineages: pure from the beginning; self-liberating perception; an existential component in which the true nature of mind and perception are glimpsed so that further practice is anchored in a remembered authentic experience. Thus, in the sphere of perception everything has always been pure, always rooted in the true nature of reality, and only defiled by interpretations, concepts and various emotional reactions—all of which are clouds in the sky of simple awareness. Once one has trained to perceive all the patterns of mental appearances as objects of the dissolving effect of vipasyana meditation, one immediately recognizes that every instant of perception (object, organ, consciousness as "one moment") is a moment of meditation, and thus one is always practicing. At that point, each "moment" dissolves of its own accord into perfect spaciousness, or "self liberates." This process should bring about enlightenment in a very short amount of time. Since the justification for the elaborate rituals of Vajrayana was to accelerate the bodhisattva path so as to reach enlightenment quickly, it is clear that the early dzogchen contemplatives were trying to accelerate the process even further by going directly to the essentials. However, they would not have even been able to conceive of around-the-clock awareness practice if the tantras had not already indicated a close rapport between liturgical rites, meditation periods, and post-meditation practice. The ritual Vajrayana approach and the great perfection approach as outlined in Buddhist and Bonpo treatises are inseparable as to inspiration and objective. This inseparability does not, however, exclude the possibility of other motivations for the elaboration of an accelerated system.

For example, since magical arts were and are widespread in the entire region, a master would need to accelerate his or her attainment of siddhis (magical attainments) to protect disciples from magical attacks of various kinds. Also, in the shifting political environments of Central Asia, China, India, and Tibet, it would have been important to have skillful means for protecting caravans from thieves, merchants from rapacious officials, princes from their dynastic enemies, and monasteries from invading armies. In addition, there would almost certainly have been a motivation to enhance Buddhist practice in the face of challenges from the other religions being promoted and discussed in Central Asia in this time period. We know that the influence of Vajrayana at the Mongol court in the thirteenth century depended on the Tibetans's superior skills in the magical arts. The hagiographical literature, time and time again, tends to confirm this particular aspect of Vajrayana. Let us return to the historical narrative.

The motivation for moving from milieux of scholarly monks living in well-ordered Central Asian monasteries (as described by Chinese travelers such as Hsuan Tsang)[369] may have derived from the following features of eighth-century cultural developments:

- ·⚬· The expansion and consolidation of a Muslim imperial hegemony in regions to the northwest of India, including those already exposed to Buddhism as well as Manichaeism, Nestorian Christianity, and Zoroastrianism(s).

- ·⚬· Dynastic and inter-imperial warfare in India and on all the borders of Tibet: warfare as a situation that may temporarily block exchange, but that may also favor exchange of ideas, goods, and territories. Tribes move after victories and defeats, as chronicled by Beckwith.[370]

- ·◇· Material decline of Buddhist institutions in India and Central Asia.

- ·◇· Flourishing of sutra-based Mahayana Buddhism in China; translations accomplished under Tang dynasty sponsorship, often by Central Asian scholars such as Kumarajiva.

- ·◇· Tantric Buddhism is emerging in various parts of India, in part stimulated by profound contacts with Shaiva and tribal mystical religiosity, in part by the needs of warring dynasties. Kingdoms in crisis are seeking protection from the magical and military assaults of their rivals; hence they turn to masters of magic and miracles such as the mahasiddhas.[371]

- ·◇· Even at Nalanda, the cult of Mahavairocana is established.[372]

- ·◇· Esotericism in China seems to surface in the 650s.[373] A century later, the Indian master Amoghavajra contributes to the spread of tantric Buddhism to Japan and Tibet.

- ·◇· A canon of tantric Buddhist scriptures is already known in the eighth century.[374]

- ·◇· Yogini tantras emerge in the period 720–730, again confirming the period as one of ferment, exchange, and dramatic developments in the forms of the spiritual life throughout the regions of China, India, and Central Asia. This is also the period when the Tibetan Empire is in expansion and the imperial dynasty is seeking to bring some form of Buddhism into Tibet as part of its advance into "civilization."

TABLE VI. THE VERY RICH AND COMPLEX INTERRELIGIOUS PANORAMA OF
CENTRAL ASIA

Zoroastrianism in the towns from east Persia to Samarkand and Dunhuang along the Silk Road, verified archeologically.
Manichaeism is particularly strong across the entire Silk Road.
Syro-Oriental Christianity, and other forms of Christianity have strong centers (dioceses and monasteries) along the Silk Road and seem to have been present in Tibet (as shown in Patriarch Timothy's letter about establishing a metropolitanate in Tibet, which would require the presence of at least six dioceses in Tibet by the 780s). Syro-Oriental Christianity produces some remarkable mystical literature in the trajectory of Evagrius of Pontus: Isaac of Nineveh, Joseph Hazzaya, John of Dalyatha ("the soul gazing upon itself,"-comparable to the dzogchen *trekchod* expression: "the mind looking into mind"), and in China the monk Jingjing, author of the Christian stele and the *Book on the Realization of Profound Peace and Joy*, and translator of a Mahayana sutra.
Vigorous Shaivite traditions especially in Kashmir and further northwest, but also well attested to in south India by the works of Tirumular. There is also evidence, difficult to pin down chronologically, of a connection between Tamil forms of Shaivism and Chinese alchemical traditions.
Mystical (Sufi), philosophical (Muktazalites under Caliph al-Mamun, late eighth century) and legalistic Islam are present in Central Asia after the conquest of Iran. Islam has been evolving rapidly as it encounters mystical Syriac Christianity and other religious traditions in Mesopotamia, Iran, India, and Central Asia.
The practice of meditation in caves is a common feature of spiritual practice throughout the region; John Moschus (ca. 550–619) knows of incorrupt bodies of hermits found meditating in caves in Syria and Palestine.
In the kingdom of Zhang Zhung, there is a well-developed synthesis of Buddhism and local spiritual traditions (proto-Bon?) including shamanism.

Returning to Germano and Van Schaik, we can now trace the stages of development from the late eighth century into the ninth century, during which Buddhism passed from a state-sponsored flourishing religion to a condition of serious persecution in both China and Tibet. The decline that was well under

way in Central Asia caught up with Buddhist institutions in both empires, leading to the survival of more modest, isolated, and local centers of spiritual practice. Thus, in China we have the survival of the ascetic, mountain-based Ch'an
lineages; and in Tibet we have the era of local ngagpa practitioners, both Bonpo
and Buddhist, attested to in the *Blue Annals* and in the biographies of Milarepa.
These ngagpas, or "mantra experts" would have been located in small temples
situated in the villages of Tibet. Usually married, they would perform a variety
of rituals for the local community and train promising youths in whatever skills
might be necessary to carry on the ritual traditions, again a phenomenon we
have seen in the early Milarepa biographies. In fact, even today in northern
Nepal, this is the form of Bon and Buddhism that prevails in most, if not all, of
the villages we have explored over the years. Unfortunately, the collective history of Tibet has branded these teachers with the emblem of "sex and violence,"
in order to explain why the king of Gugé in western Tibet had to sponsor a
reform of tantric Buddhism under the auspices of Atisha in about the 1040s.
His reforms were built on the previous four decades of revisions directed by Rin
chen zangpo in the west. The *Blue Annals* gives a more favorable presentation
of the lineages active in this period. It is here that we find the dzogchen pro-
moters discussed by Dan Martin, Sam Van Schaik, David Germano, Samten
Karmay, and Matthew Kapstein and others who have explored early dzogchen.
Thus we have gNubs and his lineage, and the Zur lineage, whose descendants
take us up to the end of the eleventh century. Other lineages are listed, with
short biographies, in Dudjom Rinpoche's *The Nyingma School*. What did these
masters do to create one or more dzogchen lineages? Sam Van Schaik presents
their achievements as an evolving process of creating liturgical and practice texts
that are increasingly systematized and harmonized with the earliest Nyingma
tantric cycles such as the *Guhyagarbha* and the *Kun Byed Gyalpo* (*The Supreme
Source*).[375] In the course of the eleventh and twelfth centuries, these lineages
absorbed the spirit and style of the newly introduced tantric cycles being translated by masters such as Marpa and the Shakyapa masters of this early phase
of the second diffusion. This process is what David Germano calls "pristine
dzogchen" being contaminated with "funerary Buddhism," by which he means
that the pithy practice-texts characteristic of the late eighth and early ninth centuries in these Buddhist-yogin circles begin to be accompanied by rituals and

practices typical of the larger world of Indian tantric Buddhism and Hinduism (Shaivite, mostly). These rituals dramatized the encounter between the mind and death by means of macabre symbolism, visualized cremation ground imagery, and erotic-wrathful divine representations. If Van Schaik is correct (and this would seem to be confirmed by Davidson's study of Indian esoteric Buddhism[376] contemporaneous with the early diffusion of Buddhism in Tibet), this kind of imagery was already present in the early period, although the primary forms were yoga tantra mandala deities and sexual yoga. Nevertheless, wrathful imagery was present because these liturgies were employed in the defense of various kingdoms threatened with invasion. Thus it would be a mistake to say that a pristine, purely contemplative form of dzogchen was at a later moment contaminated with funerary imagery. It was more a matter of a gradual development of a full-blooded tantric approach that drew on previously existing texts and practices known in all likelihood from the days of Padmasambhava, Manjusrimitra, Vimalamitra, Vairotsana, and other tantric masters of the first diffusion period.

In my opinion, the accelerated use of tantric practices of a funerary variety in eleventh and twelfth century dzogchen depends on the perceived need on the part of the masters of these old lineages (the foundational lineages of Nyingma) for a richer variety of skillful training methods for disciples. I think in part the failure of Bre Ston Lha dGa' to have an impact on the young sorcerer Milarepa, who had after all been trained by Nyingma and Bonpo experts in magical power and meditation, was a definite stimulus for the rapid evolution of dzogchen in this period. There may have been many talented young people like Milarepa coming to learn rituals and techniques from the old lineages. As a result, new training methods had to be devised. I suspect that the *ngon dro* practices (one hundred thousand repetitions of Refuge/Bodhisattva prayers and prostrations, Vajrasattva mantra and visualization, mandala offering, and a Guru Yoga liturgy) were designed to meet this need for more rigorous preparatory training. It is quite clear that even a very bright person needs certain kinds of yogic disciplines in order to prepare the mind and body for the demands of tantric ritual and more advanced meditation experiences, and these were being devised and implemented in the older as well as in the new lineages in the second diffusion period.

Along with *ngon dro* and other training regimens, the Nyingma and the Bonpo began to bring forward a variety of discovered texts and objects that purportedly had been hidden away during the time of Padmasambhava, King Trisong Detsen, Princess Mandarava, and Princess Yeshe Tsogyel in the eighth century. One famous instance of a hidden text is from the very old temple of Zha'i Lhakhang at the mouth of the valley leading to Drikung Til in central Tibet. In this case, a text was extracted from an ancient stele from the imperial period and deciphered. As time went on, other texts were discovered in more esoteric ways, described in Tulku Thondup's book, *Hidden Teachings of Tibet: An Explanation of the Terma Tradition of Tibetan Buddhism*.[377] In effect, these texts never claimed a prior authorized scriptural source in an Indian language. Rather, these were miraculously produced apocryphal scriptures, some of which emerged quite spontaneously in the minds of certain designated heirs of the Padmasambhava tradition who had reincarnated at the appropriate moment to communicate the content of the texts. Other texts arose in visionary experiences awakened upon the discovery of small objects or scrolls in rocks or caves.[378]

Subsequent to their discovery, usually as small scrolls or ritual objects hidden in rocks or pillars, the "treasures" or rather their accompanying entity guides (dakinis) inspired visionary experiences on the part of the treasure discoverers who then wrote down these experiences in the form of elaborate liturgical texts that included visualizations and mandalas. These rituals would then have been practiced by yogis in a retreat setting with the permission of the treasure discoverer, who was now recognized as the authorized tantric master at the head of a new lineage of practice.

After attaining realization during retreat, the yogis would take the same rituals into the lay tantric community, perhaps in a village setting or small temple, where the rituals would be used for a variety of purposes useful to the community (healing, exorcism, divination, initiation, blessing of new edifices or dwellings, spiritual guidance, etc.). The language of these rituals was closely affiliated with the traditional language of dzogchen, and could best be understood within the philosophical context of dzogchen. However, these rituals fulfill a variety of felt religious needs of the community that were (apparently) not adequately addressed in the earlier literature of dzogchen.

Although these religious needs tend to refer to concerns of daily life, the yogis found the new practices revealed in the treasures were of particular value in enhancing the spiritual development of the mind-body complex of the yogi. This enhancement should sensitize the yogi's ability to control and recognize the subtle flow of energy in the body-mind complex. Having attained this degree of control over energy flows, the yogi was better able to undertake the more advanced practices of dzogchen, such as trekchod and thodgal, which bear fruit in the various kinds of rainbow body attainment. Thus, the "treasure" tradition seems to be, at least in part, a recognition that the original insights of pristine dzogchen could not usually be achieved until certain preliminary changes had taken place with the yogi's mind-body complex. A partial confirmation of this conclusion can be derived from our conversations with Tamil Siddha yogis who told us that the body has to be prepared in various ways (including the use of herbs, minerals, meditation, and yoga) for the higher attainments in their system, including the body of light. That is, the coarse condition of the ordinary body-mind complex must be made more flexible and subtle.

I might also add that the claims of various authors that dzogchen and the rainbow body are much more ancient than the period of Tibetan history after the twelfth century are not supported by the historical evidence. However, many similar claims (most of which are relatively recent), especially those made about well known figures in Indian history (for example, Shankaracarya) whose bodies "disappeared," do suggest a broader cultural context for claims about yogic practices that make the body more elastic, with consequent postmortem phenomena of shrinkage or disappearance.

The eleventh and twelfth centuries is also the period when significant collections of texts were compiled under the name of Vimalamitra (*Bima snying thig*) and other early masters. It is here we find the earliest exemplar of the biography of Garab Dorje, which we will discuss below. Our analysis of this biography illustrates one of the key themes of this book, which is to suggest a wider (beyond Buddhism, beyond Tibet) cultural world for dzogchen origins. If there were no evidence for a larger setting within which the system that came to be called the "great perfection" came into being, there would be no point to our exploration of other, possibly related, systems.

The argument goes as follows: The earliest version of the biography of Garab Dorje, emerging just as dzogchen began to clothe itself in charnel ground ornaments, discloses crucial historical and ideological features of the origins of dzogchen. Other authors, lacking the evidence that we have been able to identify and correlate, have not entirely disclosed the nature, origins, development, and character of dzogchen. Each of the scholars we have cited has added a crucial piece to the puzzle of dzogchen origins and development. A close reading of the Garab Dorje biography provides us with a kind of road-map that traces many, if not all, of the traditions that flow together to give rise to dzogchen as it emerges in the eleventh century in Tibet, when the earlier forms of tantric Buddhism in Tibet were being challenged by the arrival of new tantric systems handed on by Indian masters to their Tibetan disciples.

We are fortunate to have access to research on the nature and character of the practice of the spiritual life in these vast regions in Western and Central Asia in this fertile period of history. Thanks to the work of Robert Beulay on Syro-Oriental Christian mysticism, we can enter the world of the mystics of the eighth century more securely. In this way, we can link the early Sufi movements[379] in Baghdad and Persia to the Syriac-Christian and Manichean ascetics who were flourishing at this time thanks to abundant financial support from the khans and merchants of the great Silk Road. We can also go farther afield thanks to Matteo Nicolini-Zani, to discover how Christians understood Buddhist and Daoist terminology in this period, particularly in the surviving writings of the prelate monk Jingjing who attempted to translate Buddhist scriptures alongside a Buddhist monk, and whose authorship of two key texts seems indisputable: the stele of 781 at Xi'an (a rare instance in this entire discussion of a true primary source: an original work carved in stone and dated, in contrast to a manuscript subject to copyists's errors) and the *Book on the Realization of Profound Peace and Joy* found at Dunhuang, which we have presented in the previous chapter. Another work in fragmentary form, *The Three Stages of the Hermit Life* in Sogdian from a Central Asian (Turfan) site, illustrates a Christian approach to progress on the spiritual path. This work links the Syro-Oriental Christian appropriation of the trajectory of Evagrius of Pontus through Isaac of Nineveh, Berikhisho, Joseph Hazzaya, John of Dalyatha, and others. The system of the three stages, a well-known feature of

Syriac ascetical and mystical teaching, lends itself to comparison with three-fold patterns of spiritual development in Vajrayana Buddhism:

TABLE VII. THREE STATEMENTS OF GARAB DORJE

The Testament:
To introduce a person's contemplative state directly.
To discover that state of "presence" without any doubt.
To integrate that understanding into all circumstances and continue in that state.
Vajrayana Approach:
The stage of generation of the deity visualization
The stage of completion: yoga of subtle body energy
The stage of mahamudra/dzogchen: formless bliss integrated into the on-going stream of awareness.
Syro-Oriental Christian Contemplation:
Bodily and mental purification of the passions
Psychic stage: return to the purity of the natural state of being
Spiritual stage: the soul sees itself as light and as divine image; has visions of energy, union, and divinization.

The Life of Garab Dorje:
An Analysis Illustrating a Turning Point in the History of Dzogchen

The early history of dzogchen has been told in a variety of ways. Gos Lotsa-wa, in the *Blue Annals*, gives a survey of the lineages of transmission for the great perfection. It is not always easy to follow the chronology in this chapter, which covers a period of disunity and decentralization in Tibetan history. In the early eleventh century, however, some of the dzogchen texts were collect-ed in a series associated with the name of Vimalamitra (Bi-ma in Tibetan), one of the scholar-yogis during the time of King Trisong Detsen in the eighth century. Among these documents, we have a biography of Garab Dorje, who is credited with the first dissemination of the dzogchen teachings in this world. This biography contains some disparate elements that seem to have been collected along the way; it reads as if a core narrative had been adorned with additional materials in successive editorial phases. What follows is my interpretation of this biography, which I take to be a narrative account of dzogchen origins in the *form* of hagiography, but that communicates much more between the lines.

In chapter three our research took us into the world of Syriac Christianity and Manichaeism giving us part of the general picture of Central Asian religions in our period of interest. We have noted that none of the Manichean documents available to us has anything like the life of Garab Dorje or the life of Jesus and Mary in surah 19 of the Qur'an. In spite of the very helpful research of Michael Walter on possible Manichean connections with dzogchen origins, I am not convinced of Manichaeism as the primary non-Buddhist source. Manichaeism focused on a soteriological system based on a sacred meal in which the lay "auditors" made offerings to the ascetic élite (the "perfect") who liberated particles of light by digesting the food that had been offered.[380] Yes, there is the language of luminosity. Indeed, Manichaeism in China, like Christianity, was named the "religion of light." However, in spite of Walter's claims of a system of yogic practice (not abundantly represented in the Central-Asian Manichean texts currently available), there is no evidence that the human body of the Manichean believer is being transformed into light, even metaphorically. In fact, the clearly Buddhist *Yogavidhi* text that Walter cites[381] is not Manichean, although it was found *near* Shorchuq, in Chinese Turkestan, where Manichaeism was present. Nevertheless, the text does have practices that engage the elements of the body with visualizations of colored lights in the manner of some later dzogchen practices that may have surfaced as termas. In fact, since most of the early dzogchen texts do not refer to a rainbow body at all, this particular text may acquire considerable value in tracing where this attainment may have arisen. The topic deserves further study, but in the present state of Manichean studies, I do not find a convincing argument connecting actual Manichean practices with dzogchen. However, Walter may have uncovered something useful in his research on

Central Asian alchemical practices, which do suggest a way by which a variety of spiritual traditions could blend.

If Manichaeism is not the primary inspiration for the contemplative system of earliest dzogchen, it makes sense to focus on the Islamic and Christian aspects of the biography of Garab Dorje to find more persuasive clues.[382] John M. Reynolds has already studied the Vajrayana aspects of the biographies that have come down to us; in my opinion he has been studying a *frame story*, designed to integrate dzogchen with Vajrayana, and not the essential narrative of the biography.[383] Note that the account in *The Golden Letters* is a complete translation, whereas the accounts in *The Supreme Source* and other recent dzogchen works are summaries. We need to use redaction and source criticism to arrive at this essential narrative, for which I ask the reader's patient indulgence. The life story of Garab Dorje contains some elements that reflect Qur'anic and Syriac Christian influences. For example, a story from the *Lalitavistara* tells of the visit of the child Buddha to a temple where he debates with the elders, as does the Child Jesus in the Gospel of Luke. The biography is truly a literary patchwork. The Qur'anic seclusion of Mary during her pregnancy is reported as being on an island in a lake where she lives in a grass hut, as does the princess-nun who is the mother of Garab Dorje. Garab Dorje's own long retreat in mountains and deserts is also in a "grass hut."

In reading Patriarch Timothy's precipitous condemnation[384] of John of Dalyatha, John of Apamea, and Joseph Hazzaya, one can see mystical teachings, such as the visibility of God, that might have resonated with a dzogchen view of the state of *rigpa*. In Beulay's work on John of Dalyatha, a key chapter "*La Vision de l'âme par elle-même*" (the vision of the soul by itself) examines the system of the Syriac mystics in detail[385] in such a way as to clarify these radical Christian contemplative teachings, which deeply disturbed the Baghdad Patriarch at the time. In a later homily the same author discusses of how the vision of the light in the soul leads the contemplative towards a vision of the divine.[386] These and other mystical teachings were condemned in the Synod of 786–87, a summary of which has been preserved in Arabic. One of the purported errors was the teaching on "the creature able to see its Creator."[387] Another view that earned condemnation was: "If you wish to receive the gift of the Spirit, do not remain faithful to prayer or the Divine Office, but flee to hide yourself in dark places in which you cannot hear even the voice of a bird." (Dark retreat?) And also: "When someone has attained perfection, he no longer has need of prayer, psalmody, reading, or labor, for he has become perfect." The mystical writers also asserted (following the logic of Ephesians 1:4) that the soul was not created in the beginning without a body, but it was present with God before [the creation of the body].[388] It would not take a great deal of effort to transmute these Syriac-Christian statements into statements compatible with the earliest texts of dzogchen. This becomes even clearer when we take note of the teachings of the Messiah in the "Peace and Joy" text attributable to the prelate-monk Jingjing, who was writing at the time of this synod. Thus the topics of the "Questions and Answers of Vajrasattva" such as nonduality,[389] freedom from effort, and the primordial, spontaneous presence of enlightened mind, can be seen in a Christian form in the Syriac mystics and in Jingjing's daringly original "sutra."

In both the works of Beulay and in the otherwise very disappointing book of Martin Palmer (*The Jesus Sutras*),[390] one encounters the richness of Syriac Christianity in Central Asia. Aside from the explicit and perhaps overstated need of Palmer (and of John M. Reynolds) to distance themselves from the themes and tendencies of traditional Western Christianity—particularly in its more Augustinian expressions, both Catholic and Protestant—one can find in their works some interesting insights into the roots of the dzogchen system. Reynolds has no use for any Christianity except Gnosticism. Unfortunately, he does not really understand Gnosticism very well, nor Eastern Christianity. Influenced by Jungian ideas, Reynolds goes far enough to see Christ and Garab Dorje as expressions of an "archetype"; but he does not ask himself what this term might mean beyond the framework of archetypal psychology. The perspective seems to reflect his discomfort with historical consciousness and the methods of research that accompany that way of seeing human development. Through the transformation of human consciousness from one civilization to another, myths and their underlying archetypal structures do indeed evolve. To speak of an archetype is not, as Reynolds might think, to exit from history into the confines of disparate instances of perception but rather to acknowledge that the human mind and spirit are in continual development in the course of history, from moment to moment. In the flow of moments of perception, certain mythic symbols acquire a persuasive power that persists over centuries and millennia, even as these symbols and their narrative expressions evolve with human culture. The fluid character of mind and perception that is so crucial to dzogchen training and realization seems quite compatible with at least some aspects of what Western thought sees as historical consciousness. Of course, I agree with Reynolds that historical consciousness cannot be absolutized, and in many ways it fails to account for the depths, discoveries, and persistence of what I would call "religious consciousness" (also loosely termed "spirituality").

The problem that any theory of religious studies or of historical consciousness must confront is that of the rapport between archetypes operating in the human psyche and life-changing encounters with real historical persons. All religions know that such encounters (in Tibetan, this is called *tendel*—the fulfillment of previous promises between master and disciple) contribute powerfully to the energetic force of the archetypes. A figure like Jesus of Nazareth had an enormous impact on his time and for centuries after. This is why there are so many accounts of his life and teachings.[391] He both embodied an archetype that was particularly evocative in his time, and he re-shaped the archetype in a way that had explosive impact on the cultures of the Mediterranean, the Middle East, East Africa, and Central Asia in the centuries between 100 and 1000 AD. Garab Dorje may have indeed been an historical personage, but he did not have this kind of impact. Only a few sayings are attributed to him by the oral tradition. The same tradition takes several centuries to canonize him with an elaborate biography. As in the case of "Jabir the Yogi," Garab Dorje may have been a remarkable master within a limited circle of disciples. He emerged as a key figure only later, when his archetypal presence could be evoked to sustain the dzogchen lineages in a time of crisis. The fact that only a few sayings and writings are attributed to him tends to support the theory that he was in some way an historical person—perhaps in the way Jabir was "historical." When one studies the biographies proposed for him, they can only be described as a pastiche of typologies and narratives borrowed from elsewhere. They are the kinds of biographies that "had to be that way" because "*c'est toujours come ça avec les saints*" (things are always like

that with the saints). We could just leave it at that, of course. The Garab Dorje biography in the *Golden Letters* is just another Buddhist tantric account of
a mahasiddha, rewoven out of elements borrowed from the *Lalitavistara*, the
Qur'an, the Gospel of Luke, some apocryphal gospels, and a variety of Indian charnel ground tantric sources. A strong Shaiva (from the *Shiva Sutras*)
influence is admitted even by Reynolds. The doctrines of dzogchen and the
practices of Shaivite and Nath forms of hatha yoga correspond closely to each
other. Moreover, there is the mediating role of the Bonpo tradition, which
leaves the dzogchen lineage open to further syncretistic tendencies. Loppon
Tendzin Namdak, for example, is convinced of Persian (Zoroastrian?) and
Central Asian influences on early Bon.[392] Placing the eleventh century Garab
Dorje biography in the context of the earlier Chinese Christian documents
helps to confirm Eva Dargyay's intuition about a possible connection between Jesus and Garab Dorje.[393] In the same context, we can recognize a
convergence between the doctrines of dzogchen and the spiritual teaching of
the Syro-Oriental Christian monks of Central Asia. It is as if those teachings
about Christ were carried within the surviving legend of Garab Dorje. But
what is more amazing is that the doctrines of dzogchen seem to converge, if
not to be coincident, with the spiritual teachings of the Syro-Oriental Christian monks in Central Asia, as if those teachings in some way were "carried"
by the legend of Garab Dorje.

For our purposes, this tendency to converge suggests something about the
history of spirituality that needs to be examined and appreciated in considerable detail. Our work on the rainbow body phenomenon has required us
to examine dzogchen practices and history. That body of research leads us to
the *Shiva Sutras*, late Indian Buddhist tantrism, the mysterious history of the
Bon religion, and to a variety of schools of yoga. However, it would be historically inadequate not to factor in the Christian and Manichean elements
in this equation of religious discovery. The Dunhuang Chinese Christian
and Manichean materials indicate clearly that west Asian religions in China
and Tibet were capable of profound syncretistic development. At the same
time the writings of John of Dalyatha and his associates indicate that Christian contemplatives from the other side of the Tibetan Empire had reached
remarkable, controversial insights into the nature of spiritual experience.

Placing these discoveries alongside the Shaivite yogic teachings and both Bon and Buddhist early dzogchen texts, we can suggest a strong case for the convergence and mutual influence of these various traditions. The Garab Dorje biography moreover seems to be emblematic of this convergence. It serves as a testimony to the coming together of a number of contemplative traditions in Central Asia, probably in the tenth or eleventh century, after centuries of experiment and exchange among the several traditions historically in contact with each other. This convergence brings in the syncretistic Islamic element as well, as Michael Walters was able to do with his study of Jabir the Yogi. As such, it would seem that this historical period was one of the most fertile for the development of very sophisticated spiritual practice systems and philosophies. Much of this material was suppressed or even destroyed in the centuries that followed, but we have an opportunity in our own times to revitalize this material as part of a wider dialogue of religions and cultures. Strange but true—the period often referred to as "the Dark Ages" turns out to be a fertile and enlightened era of spiritual discovery!

In reading Christopher Beckwith's epilogue to *The Tibetan Empire in Central Asia*,[394] I am struck by his strong arguments in favor of a re-evaluation of the period in question. He thinks that, given the technologies of the era, the great chain of empires from Tang China to Carolingian Europe, were mutually dependent components of Eurasian civilization. He confirms the evidence for both economic and cultural progress, and develops a persuasive case for the dynamics of trade and political exchange for this period. Building upon this historical study, we can contribute the detailed portrait of a spiritual revival that accompanied the economic and political trends of the period 650–1000. We need to do this because one of the most pressing questions that emerges in our research on the rainbow body is the comparative question: is the resurrection of Jesus an instance of the rainbow body? It is impossible to answer this question at face value, but it is possible to address the issues that this question raises by examining the contacts and connections among the civilizations of the Eurasian continent in the period in question.

None of the traditional spiritual systems of India were interested in bodily resurrection. Resurrection was always associated with black magic, vampires, and zombies (*vetali*). The Garab Dorje biography itself persists in this prejudice, by giving the resurrected child-teacher the name "The Happy Vampire." In the legends of the Indian Buddhist mahasiddhas, the attainment of enlightenment at times manifests in the form of some kind of bodily ascent to the realm of the deities. Chinese traditions propose the goal of immortality, attained by means of cinnabar alchemy. Similar proposals can be found in the Tamil Siddha tradition during the period that interests us.

It would in fact be the easy way out to say that the body of light is merely a Tibetan way of incorporating a Daoist/shamanistic idea of the body into a radical revision of Mahayana and Vajrayana Buddhism. However, the *actual practices* of Daoism, like those of Manichaeism, with the possible exception of alchemy (which brings in the Tamil Siddha tradition), seem to have little do with dzogchen, in either its eighth-century pristine form or in its later development as a distinct approach in Bon and Nyingma tantrism. The idea of a human body, perceived as a phenomenological unity with spirit and mind, becoming all-pervasive in the universe by returning to the primordial light from which the person was composed had to come from somewhere. And it seems that it comes from Christianity, where the doctrine of the resurrection precedes that of the ascension and where also the believer is supposed to participate in the life of the resurrection in this life.[395] True to its Semitic linguistic roots, Syriac Christianity placed a great deal of emphasis on embodiment, even in the higher states of contemplative prayer.[396] Once excommunicated, the monks around John of Dalyatha may have handed on their ideas to disciples who were willing to risk the excommunication that the decree of the Synod of 786–78 imposed on those who thought as he did. The excommunication remained in force for more than forty years, undoubtedly causing a great deal of perplexity in monastic circles. Finally, Patriarch Timothy's successor, Iso' Bar Nun (patriarch from 823–828), rehabilitated John of Dalyatha, thus reconciling the circle of the disciples with the Baghdad Patriarchate. As a result, the works of John of Dalyatha, under his name as John Saba the Elder, became rather quickly recognized as foundational to authentic monastic spirituality in the churches using the Syriac, Arabic, and Armenian languages.[397]

It is still a matter of speculation as to the extent of the Eastern Christian monastic contact with other spiritual systems developing to the east, in

Kashmir and Tibet, and whether there was any mutual influence on those new developments. These developments were based on the discovery that disciplined spiritual practice can heighten and intensify the experience of mind and spirit as all pervasive, primordial, a given and not something to be grasped at or attained—a state of awareness inseparable from the material world and quotidian awareness—and that this primordial given awareness the constant prevailing feature of a person who participates in the "divine nature." However, these views were being discovered at the same time by Shaiva masters, Bonpos, Manicheans, Vajrayana Buddhists, Sufis, and others as well. It was the perfect moment for a Christian view of transformation and resurrection to influence the development of new systems of spiritual practice in South Asia and Central Asia. Hence, what came to be called the rainbow body is the most sublime and persuasive manifestation of the entire synthetic process that took place in the heart of Eurasia in the seventh to ninth centuries. It is, in a very real way, a discovery dependent on the way Christian contemplatives had for more than six hundred years taken up the belief in the resurrection of Jesus. Monastic life was how Christian contemplatives lived the life of the resurrection, though this doesn't automatically mean that it was how Jesus of Nazareth lived, died, and rose again. The mystical appropriation of the "paschal mystery" within the way of life of Christian monasticism is enacted in the sacraments, above all in the Eucharist. Thus we can distinguish between Jesus's own death and resurrection and the lived experience of Christian communities through the centuries. Moreover, there are differences between the paschal mystery as lived by Christians and the set of practices that come to fruition in the rainbow body. Nevertheless, the Christian influence on the claimed dissolution phenomenon, its theoretical expression, and its manifestation in hagiography is highly likely. So far, none of the writers on the rainbow body have gone beyond the observation that a Christian connection is likely or possible. All recognize that a new feature such as survival of death in a luminous body has to come from somewhere; when the new feature is so persuasive, dramatic, and unprecedented, it is most likely not something invented out of some imprecise archetypal potpourri. It is more likely that this new feature came into the world of Himalayan spirituality from persons who themselves possessed all the indications of being highly realized spiritual leaders. The doctrines and practices advocated by these leaders must have seemed to confirm the tendencies already present in the Shaivite/yoga communities of siddhas and among the Vajrayana mahasiddhas. We thus take note of the shift from Vajrayana "transformation of circumstances" from impure to pure in order to attain liberation and the body of light, to the "primordially pure" view of dzogchen, the recovery of which through meditation on forms and formless light rays leads to the manifestation of the rainbow body. What did John of Dalyatha call his contemplative participation in the life of the risen Christ? *The "formless light."* If we enter the world of the Syriac mystics, we begin to discover a wealth of textual attestations to remarkable spiritual attainments, comparable to those claimed for practitioners of dzogchen.

The Life of Garab Dorje: A Commentary

Even the casual reader of the eleventh-century biography of Garab Dorje[398] might find it to be one of the most disconcerting and even bizarre biographies of a saint ever written in any tradition. Even for those familiar with mahasiddha biographies in a variety of Indian and Tibetan sources,[399] this tale is an astonishing compendium of strange events, disconnected among themselves and at times oddly in contrast to the documented teachings of the subject of the biography. Surely there is a great deal going on below the surface of this text, and it cannot be restricted to the impact of funerary or "charnel ground" imagery coming from the later Vajrayana, i.e., the "highest yoga tantras." An experienced reader, familiar with early Buddhist biographies, may note that Garab Dorje's mother conceives and gives birth under circumstances similar to Mayadevi, mother of Buddha Shakyamuni. Unlike Mayadevi, Garab Dorje's mother experiences both physical pain and mental anguish over the birth of this appearance-body of buddhahood. At an early age, the child Garab Dorje wishes to debate with five-hundred panditas; this resonates not only with well-known episodes in the *Lankavatara Sutra* and in the *Lalitavistara* but also with Luke 2:41-52 (the finding of the child Jesus in the Temple). Although we are still within Buddhist territory, narrative typologies from farther afield begin to appear. As in all hagiography, what matters is the message of the subject of the biography. Historical details turn up mixed with standard legendary typologies familiar to scholars of world folklore. In order to study this unusual, tantric biography of the human founder of the dzogchen lineages, we need to employ a number of tools. The first tool is the "first story" narrative identified by Christopher Beck with characteristic of Eurasian heroic sagas. The essential narrative elements or themes of the "first story" are given by Beckwith as follows: [400]

1. A maiden is impregnated by a heavenly spirit or god.
2. The rightful king is deposed unjustly.
3. The maiden gives birth to a marvelous baby boy.
4. The unjust king orders the baby to be exposed.
5. The wild beasts nurture the baby so he survives.
6. The baby is discovered in the wilderness and is saved.
7. The boy grows up to be a skilled horseman and archer.
8. He is brought to court but put in a subservient position.
9. He is in danger of being put to death but escapes.
10. He acquires a following of oath-sworn warriors.
11. He overthrows the tyrant and reestablishes justice in the kingdom.
12. He founds a new city or dynasty.

This "Eurasian" myth, which certainly resonates with other great heroic tales (David oppressed by Saul; Jesus; Muhammad; even Gesar and Milarepa), is easily adapted to both royal and religious applications. It forms the narrative core of many of the sagas of the Central Asian monarchs, conquerors, and heroes of our period of research; other typologies and historical elements are added by the bard as he or she recites the poetic version of the sage. [401] In the eleventh-century life of Garab Dorje, the human founder of the dzogchen lineage, we have a document that seems in many ways to correspond to the first story, applying the themes to a spiritual hero. At the same time, the dzogchen authors tell the story with a skillful use of narrative typologies colored by other great stories encountered along the way. The text resembles the Christian hagiographical romance of Barlaam and Ioasaph, whose latest version was probably produced in the same period (eighth century and eleventh century)[402] as the life of Garab Dorje, and that uses the same bardic methods of composition and redaction. It is particularly interesting how the doctrines of the great perfection—with its allusions that allude to the flow of change, the unpredictability of time, the openness of being, and the frailty of human error (cf. "imprecise compassion")—are illustrated by the very strangeness of the narrative.

Our second tool for examining the biography is the story of Jesus and Mary[403] as told in Qur'an surah 19 and in other parts of the Qur'an that refer to Jesus. It seems that the nineteenth surah had already entered the realm of legend and folklore and was ripe for becoming the core story of a new Buddhist story.

A third tool is to keep in mind elements of the life of Jesus and Mary as found in apocryphal gospels and other early Christian literature. This body of literature seems to have been passed through a folklore version of the nineteenth surah. However, there are some well-known features of the life of Jesus that are not in the Qur'an, which do turn up in the Garab Dorje hagiography.

A fourth tool of our research is to be aware of the view of the humanity of Jesus in the theology of the Antiochian school of early Christianity and the appropriation of that theology (so-called Nestorianism) by the Syro-Oriental Church of the East that was in contact with China, Central Asia, and Tibet in the period 600–1100. Antiochian Christianity de-emphasized the allegorical interpretation of Scripture, gave great importance to the literal meaning of the text, and kept the two natures of Christ (human and divine) separate without abandoning the soteriological vision of the ecumenical councils of the fourth century. The Church of the East went its own way after the fifth-century councils of Ephesus and Chalcedon. This church, also called the Syro-Oriental Church, spearheaded the ambitious project of evangelization that took the Christian message from Syria, Mesopotamia, and Asia Minor as far as Central Asia, Tibet, and China. The adaptability of Syro-Oriental theology is reflected in the remarkable documents that have been preserved in Chinese.[404] The spirituality of the Church of the East—especially that of its great contemplatives Isaac of Nineveh, Abraham of Kashgar, Joseph Hazzaya, and John of Dalyatha—certainly influenced Islamic mysticism as we can see in the writings of many Sufis, such as Ibn 'Arabi. It is this spiritual heritage that may have challenged north Indian and Himalayan contemplatives to reformulate their practices towards pristine dzogchen.

In the midst of the infra-Tibetan culture war of the eleventh century, a strange biography was written, that of Garab Dorje. Adhering to all the signs and symbols of funerary Buddhism, charnel ground imagery, and pristine dzogchen, it also slips a highly unexpected narrative into the Tibetan culture world: the biography of a saint from a western kingdom, containing unmistakable elements that refer to Jesus and Mary (both objects of polemics in Indo-Tibetan Buddhism at the time) by way of the nineteenth surah of the Qur'an. While telling an acceptably Buddhist Vajrayana story, the biography subtly reminds the astute reader that there is more to be told, but for the moment it can't be told because the primary concern of the author is to address the culture war that is underway at the time in Tibet. This culture war is amply attested to in the texts that have been preserved by all sides of the argument. It is interesting that, for what seems to have been a minority of local ngagpas, the dzogchen literature of the eleventh and twelfth centuries explodes with vigor and abundance. For example, the *Bi-ma snying thig* collection (referring to the first diffusion figure of Vimalamitra), in which the Garab Dorje biography is found, is clearly a response to a crisis.[405] The writing of a biography as a literary/doctrinal process not only returns to the debate theme of the eighth century—between a supposedly gradual versus spontaneous experience of enlightenment—but it also seems to work with the experience of real life as a village practitioner lived in dramatic contrast to the perfectionist or "virtuoso" approaches-to-enlightenment theme in earlier Buddhist literature. Buddhist tantrism addresses some aspects of the perfectionist theme by employing a system of interpretation based on the perfection of wisdom and "emptiness" doctrines. However, the tantras of both the first and second diffusion involve elaborate ritual procedures, many of which were not only reserved to a small circle of privileged disciples but also required a considerable outlay of wealth.[406] The ngagpa lineages sought to keep tantrism within the sphere of local village communities by creating new ritual cycles addressed to the concerns typical of the village life, as we can see in the Milarepa biographical tradition. Dzogchen teachings seem directed at an ever more radical interpretation of the same tantric themes that acquire central importance in all forms of tantra. This radical interpretation of "pure from the beginning" (*ka dag*) and a spontaneous introduction to the true nature of the mind and reality, allows the practitioner to access the states attributed to highest tantric initiations via contemplative relaxation and nonstriving, exactly the themes[407] that animate Jingjing's intentionally syncretic *Peace and Joy Sutra*. However, the dzogchen writers for the most part seem to evade the eschatological themes typical of theistic approaches. With the emergence of the *Kalacakra* as a preeminent tantra at the beginning of the eleventh century, however, it becomes necessary to address the question of the purpose of the universal process.[408] In fact, it seems that theistic developments in Central Asia, whether Manichean, Christian, Shaivite, or Muslim, force the great thinkers of Buddhist civilization to reexamine Buddhist teachings from top to bottom. The doctrinal and moral pillars of early Buddhism—spiritual progress toward enlightenment; altruistic compassion in the bodhisattva path; intense meditation training in shamatha and vipasyana; severe moral discipline both monastic and lay; deconstruction of the notion of a creator god; deconstruction of the stability of individual components of reality (dharmas) and of the self; denial of an origin and final purpose of the cosmic process; karmic retribution as inevitable and inexorable; extreme dualism between moral defilement and enlightened purity—all these key elements of a Buddhist worldview are challenged and reformulated in tantrism, and further subverted in dzogchen. This trend culminates in the brilliant philosophical synthesis of dzogchen that we find in Longchenpa, in which finally the universe does indeed seem to hold within itself the seed of enlightenment. That seed is the presence of manifestation from the very ground of consciousness, operating dynamically even within the cyclic bondage of beings down through the eons, moving consciousness in the direction of self-recovery or "recognition" that illuminates and liberates spontaneously. Thus the universal process itself is enlightenment working itself out in the very midst of darkness and confusion, and there is nothing that the contemplative practitioner need do but to allow this process to occur. In that way, as the translators of one of Longchenpa's works entitle it: *You are the eyes of the world*. Which is to say, the enlightened person is a manifestation of the original purity and enlightenment of the cosmic process itself, become conscious of itself. In the process of affirming this intuition based on the tantra known in English as *The Supreme Source*, the *Bodhicitta Tantra That is the All-Creating King*.[409] This is a composite work drawing upon the earliest dzogchen teachings. In the fourteeth century, commenting on this tantra, Longchenpa was able to articulate the basic understandings of his lineage on the attainments that accompany the ongoing practice-process of becoming the universe-conscious-of-itself, including the realization of the rainbow body. The rainbow body emerges as an attainment only during the culture-war period of the eleventh century in Tibet when it may have come forth from earlier speculations on how the human body might participate in the experience of enlightenment at the time of death.

We now turn our attention to the biography of Garab Dorje. The core story is as follows:

·◊· Three hundred and sixty years after the parinirvana of the Buddha Shakyamuni, we are introduced to a strange race of beings known as Koshana who live in the land of "Orgyan" to the west of Bodh Gaya. The term *kosha* means treasury or container, and in fact the koshana's intestines are said to be containers for tiny jewels. These beings are described in very positive terms as being very beautiful and adorned with gold, silver, and jewels; they have bear faces, human bodies, and iron bear claws. Their kingdom is adorned by a great temple connected to a network of shrines.

·◊· The king of the land is named Uparaja and his consort is Abhasvaravati; they bring a daughter into the world whose name is Kudharma.

Very early in life, Kudharma takes the vows of one who leaves behind the householder life; she then becomes a Buddhist nun. Kudharma withdraws to a marvelous island not far to the west of the great temple where she lives in a hut made of cane and rushes, attended by a dakini. There she engages in spiritual practices of the more ritualistic tantras associated with sublime purity.

·◊· In a dream, the princess is visited by a mysterious white-colored man who has a crystal lance and a crystal vase inscribed with the initiatic letters *Om Ah Hum Svaha,* referring to the five buddha families of the tantric mandala. Touched by this vase, from which rays of light emanate, she sees everything in the past, present, and future simultaneously. The dakini interprets the dream as an omen that an apparition body of a Buddha will be born.

·ᛇ· The princess wonders, "How this can be?" During her pregnancy she experiences bodily pain and mental discomfort. In the tenth month, a son with no father is born out of her right side. Being very ashamed of this situation, the princess-nun recites verses of lamentation.

Because she is so attached to the pure morality of a nun, she is consumed by shame. In her confused state of mind, she ignores the good advice of the attendant dakini and tosses the baby into the ash pit. However, lights and sounds emanate from the ash pit. After three days, she sees that the child in the ash pit has suffered no harm. Therefore, she cleans the baby and accepts him as being a holy apparition body, or "as a man who cannot die."

·ᛇ· From the sky above, the deities sing verses of blessing. Clouds of offerings emerge from a heavenly assembly of dakinis. The child, nurtured on sacred offering substances and divine medicines, grows rapidly.

·ᛇ· After seven years, the child asks permission to go visit the great teachers of the realm to discuss the Dharma; his mother is reluctant to let him go, but in the end allows him to visit his grandfather and the five-hundred panditas who serve him as Vedic priests in the great temple.

·ᛇ· The child visits his grandfather; although the child is respectful, he immediately points out that he is the king's spiritual superior. He asks the king's permission to meet with the Panditas. The king notes that the child has the bodily marks of a Buddha, realizes that he is an apparitional body, and grants his permission.

·ᛇ· The panditas are not pleased about this meeting, but the wisest among them has had an auspicious dream, so the meeting is accepted. The panditas are unable to confound the child, and they express their veneration for him, giving him the name Prajnabhava, "he whose nature is wisdom." The king also bestows upon him the name, Garab Dorje, the "vajra of supreme delight." His mother gives him the name "Teacher

Ashen Vampire," because he survived the ordeal of the ash pit and "came back to life." To the people he was known as the "Happy Vampire." At this time, he performed beneficial deeds for the good of others.

⬦ In a place of mountain solitude inhabited by hungry ghosts, he constructs a grass hut and practices contemplative absorption for thirty-two years. The effects of his efforts were seven earthquakes, sounds from the sky, and rainfalls of various flowers.

⬦ A theme of menace emerges when a voice from the sky says that the teachings of the non-Buddhists will deteriorate. The menace becomes serious when a non-Buddhist king is informed of the depth of meditation of Garab Dorje, thanks to a group of tattle-tale youths. The king sends two executioners to behead Garab Dorje, but they are unable to kill him. Instead, he ascends into the sky, the non-Buddhists begin to venerate him, and they convert to Buddhism.

⬦ After thirty-two years, Garab Dorje has mastered all the teachings of the previous buddhas, including the great perfection sutras, which abides in his heart. Together with two extravagant dakinis, he compiles the index to these sacred texts over a three-year period; he concludes his work with a commitment to protect these teachings and cause them to become established. The basic tale ends here.

⬦ The tale shifts location to the region of Bihar, near Bodh Gaya, to the cremation ground of Shitavana, the cool grove mentioned in Buddhist scriptures. The region is dedicated to a worldly deity and countless dakinis are present, engaged in grotesque, charnel ground activities. Out of compassion, Garab Dorje decides to go to the cremation ground, riding on a daughter of Vishnu, and the horrific creatures venerate him with offerings of fruit. Leaning against a stupa, he teaches the Dharma.

⬦ To the west of Bodh Gaya, the son a Buddhist Brahmanical family named Manjushrimitra hears a prophecy from the sky advising him to go to the Shitavana cremation ground in order to "attain Buddhahood in this physical body in one lifetime." Manjushrimitra goes to study with Garab Dorje for seventy-five years.

·◊· At the end of this period, the physical body of Garab Dorje disappears in order to manifest the way beyond all suffering. The earth shakes six times and masses of light and sounds appear in the sky. Manjushrimitra faints at this sight, but when reawakened he sees the Guru in the sky—seated in a mass of light—to whom he prays and laments. Garab Dorje reaches down and emanates a golden casket that circumambulates Manjushrimitra three times, only to fall into the palm of his hand. Inside the casket is the text of "The Three Statements that Strike the Essential Points," the testament of Garab Dorje.

·◊· The very act of seeing this object unites the master and disciple in perfect nonconceptual nonduality, causing the teachings to remain in the world for a long time. Manjushrimitra then divides the great perfection teachings into the "mind series," "the space series," and the "secret instruction series."[410] He also makes a summary of the oral transmission and writes an explanatory tantra on the great perfection. Not finding a suitable disciple to transmit these teachings to, he seals them up near Bodh Gaya under a boulder shaped like two crossed vajras.

·◊· To the west of Bodh Gaya there is yet another cremation ground with a stupa and to the northeast of the stupa is a lake; the beings near this lake include Matrika goddesses, demonic beings, cannibal entities, and Shaivite symbols. In the midst of these beings are also many yogins and yoginis. Manjushrimitra, adorned with the symbols of Buddhist realization, seats himself in the midst of this scene of violence and carnage and abid there for 109 years in Samadhi, in perfect equanimity. The story ends here.

We would like to propose the hypothesis that Tibetan scholar-contemplatives who had been left aside by the reform movements launched by Rinchen Zangpo (958–1055) and Atisha took a legend from the world-conquering Muslims's core document and re-worked it to tell a Buddhist story. The Tantric practitioners of the Nyingma and Bonpo lineages who were left out of the reform movement can be identified as similar to the teachers of magic whom Milarepa turned at the end of the eleventh century when he was in search of a way to avenge the injustices that his family had suffered. Milarepa's dzogchen teacher, 'Bre Ston Lha dGa', might well have studied with those who wrote the Garab Dorje biography. That biography, unmistakably a Buddhist story, brings Jesus, Mary, Muhammad, and the Central Asian first story into the Tibetan assimilation of a new spiritual worldview—that of the great perfection or dzogchen.

The biography is traceable to the eleventh century, but it reflects a process of transmission from the previous century. The new spiritual worldview called dzogchen had by then undergone considerable development, had become a lineage in its own right, and had penetrated Buddhist and Bonpo worlds of spiritual practice. Dzogchen had matured beyond its early use as a technical term for the bliss of tantric initiation to become the symbol for the supreme vehicle, in a system of nine vehicles of the Nyingma and Bonpo tantric systems. The biography of Garab Dorje reflects the tendency—under pressure from the western Tibetan reform movement, in the course of the eleventh century—to systematize and integrate dzogchen within the world of Buddhist Vajrayana. This procedure kept dzogchen alive at a time in which new tantric systems were being introduced into Tibet (the second diffusion) and monastic institutions were becoming repositories of the religious culture of the region. Like the later reform movement of the "mad yogins" at the end of the fifteenth century, dzogchen practice and theory seem to prefer the lay tantric to the monastic way of life, the solitary practitioner to the scholar-translator, and the people at the margins of society to the world of dynastic struggles.

The following is a paraphrase of the biography of Garab Dorje with comments linking the text to its possible sources:

> The biography opens 360 years after the parinirvana of Buddha Shakyamuni, which would have been some time in the seventh century BCE by traditional Buddhist reckoning.

COMMENTS

The number 360 is cosmological, referring to the lunar calendar of months with approximately thirty days per month; thus one day corresponds to one year. The region where the narrative takes place is called Dhanakosha (treasury of offerings) in the country of Uddiyana (in Tibetan, Orgyen), west of Bodh

Gaya (Vajrasana, the place of the Buddha's enlightenment). The location of Uddiyana (the Sanskrit adaptation of this name) has been the subject of numerous scholarly discussions. The general consensus identifies the location as a region of present-day Pakistan, the Swat Valley, where Buddhist archeological sites have been located. However, somewhat further north of this region is the former territory of Khwarizmia (Khoresmia),[411] whose capital was Urganč (in the report of Willem van Rubroek on the empire of the Mongols, this was called Organum[412]), a name that certainly resonates linguistically with "Örgyen." It is just south of the Aral Sea. The people of Khwarizmia spoke Sogdian, a language adopted by the Church of the East for the liturgy and for administration.[413] In the biography, the inhabitants of this exotic land are described as having human bodies but the faces and paws of bears. They are called Koshana, which means "treasure bearing" or "container" because their intestines are said to be full of tiny jewels! However, Koshana is likely to be a Sanskritization for Khoresmia. In any case, we are confronted with a geographical location that allows for an exchange of cultures, narratives, and religions. In this region, in fact, such exchanges had been going on for several centuries prior to the appearance of dzogchen in the Himalayas.

> The name of the king of this region is simply Uparaja, which means "a minor king". The king's daughter is Kudharma or Sudharma, i.e., "good religious practice," which suggests that she was born already endowed with spiritual gifts, attributable to accomplishments in previous incarnations.

COMMENTS

Like Mary the mother of Jesus, she is already "full of grace" (Luke 1:28) when the time for her miraculous conception is to take place. The dzogchen doctrinal point here is that everything is perfect (*rdzogs*) from the very beginning (*ka dag*). The atmosphere of this exotic Central Asian family is quite compatible with the first theme of the first story of what Beckwith calls the "Central Eurasian Cultural Complex," and thus further locates the narrative in its geographical setting in west Central Asia.

This princess becomes a Buddhist nun at a very early age and withdraws to a retreat setting on an island in a lake to the west of the main temple of her kingdom. She there engages in various meditation practices (identified by Reynolds as *yoga tantra*, abbreviated in the Tibetan term *dge sbyor*).

COMMENTS

In Christian Apocrypha such as the *Protoevangelium of James*, Mary is said to have been consigned to the Temple in Jerusalem as a small child (celebrated on the Feast of the Presentation of Mary) by her elderly parents Joachim and Anna. It is interesting that the traditional Muslim commentary on the nineteenth surah also makes an allusion to this tradition of the apocryphal gospels,[414] indicating scholarly Muslim familiarity with the legend. At the Temple Mary engages in pious practices and in the service of the rituals of worship in the Jewish tradition. The Qur'an recognizes her as a very special human being who is being prepared to become the mother of Jesus, the Anointed One; he is referred to as *al-Masih 'Isa ibn Maryam* (the Anointed One, Jesus son of Mary) on a number of occasions in the Qur'an. Surah 3:42-43 states: "O Maryam! God has chosen you and made you pure and raised you above all the women of the world. O Maryam, remain truly devout unto your Lord and prostrate yourself in worship and bow down with those who bow down [before Him]." It is important that the Qur'an 19:16-17 clearly shows Mary in retreat *before* her pregnancy: "And mention in the Book Maryam when she withdrew from her family to an eastern place, and kept herself in seclusion from them [for undisturbed worship]." This is one of the clues that the Garab Dorje text has been influenced more by the Qur'anic narrative, than by the Christian canonical or apocryphal gospels. Moreover, in the Yusuf Ali version of verse 19:17 we have the expression: "She placed a screen (to screen herself) from them," presumably from her family and relatives. The Buddhist term in our Garab Dorje account is *rab tu byung ba (pravrajya)*, which specifically means to leave behind "the householder's life." So the screen might be symbolic of separation from family life through the choice of celibacy. However, the Tibetan text refers literally to a hut canopied with kusha grass, or thatch (*'jag ma'i spyil po phub nas*: literally, of thatch; a hut; canopied/protected). In the *Buddhacarita*, we find the term "an awning" to describe a comfortable retreat setting—rather than a place of refuge as we have here—which was used to protect the mother of Buddha Shakyamuni. Both the Qur'anic exegetical tradition and the Christian apocrypha refer to Mary's retreat *within* the Temple, whereas Kudharma's retreat is one yojana[415] to the west of the great temple of the Koshana kingdom. Without overly interpreting the text, we might suggest that the reference to retreat "outside the temple" is a figure for the revelation of "something new." The same motif is used in the case of Christ, crucified "outside the holy city" in order to open up a new sacred dispensation. A number of features of this dzogchen narrative suggest that "something new" is being revealed. It is also of interest that a very famous Sufi treatise on retreat practice, Ibn 'Arabi's *Journey to the Lord of Power* (*Risalat al-Anwar*), develops the idea of withdrawal and anonymity for the Sufi mystic in terms that derive directly from this one verse of the Qur'an.

> She becomes pregnant through the intervention of a heavenly being: a white man holding a lance and bestowing tantric empowerments. The princess encounters this being in a dream.

COMMENTS

This is almost a direct restatement of the first theme of the first story. It is also a feature of the narratives of holy conceptions in world literature. The Qur'an describes the event again in surah 19:17: "Then We sent to her our angel, and he appeared before her as a man in all respects," which caused Mary consternation. As in Luke 1:26-38, the mysterious visitor is Gabriel (Arabic: Gibril), an angelic messenger and the event is called "the annunciation." The messenger is not the agent by whom the conception takes place; in fact, Mary indicates in no uncertain terms that she wants nothing to do with any violations of her chastity. "How shall this be since I do not know man?" (Luke 1:34) and: "She said: 'I seek refuge from thee to [God] Most Gracious: [come not near] if thou does fear God ... She said: 'How shall I have a son, seeing that no man has touched me, and I am not unchaste?'" (surah 19:18, 20)

In the Garab Dorje account, the dream is replete with tantric Buddhist ritual symbolism: The white man is adorned with a crystal lance and a headdress consisting of a crystal vase. The initiatic empowerments of the five buddha families of the tantric mandala are represented by the sacred syllables, *Om Ah Hung Swa Ha*. Rays of light emanate from the vase, which is touched to the head of the princess three times. In her dream, she was instantly able to see the three realms (past, present, and future). However, upon awakening, she is surprised by what has happened and recounts the dream to her attendant, who is understood to be a dakini with a different name from the previous dakini.

> The nun-princess is in pain during the pregnancy and is ashamed of the child once it is born from her right side. She refers to the child as "this fatherless boy" (*pha med bu 'di*) in several verses of lamentation. In spite of a more positive interpretation from the attendant who says that the child is "a son of the Buddha" (*sangs rgyas kyi sras gcig*), the princess orders the baby to be thrown into the ash heap.

COMMENTS

Thus the child is in danger of death (themes 3 and 4 of the first story) and begins his destined heroic unfolding. The birth from the right side is reminiscent of the birth of the Buddha in *Lalitavistara* and the *Buddhacarita*. Along the lines of dzogchen doctrine, the verses of lamentation suggest that the Princess is in psychological pain because she is ashamed of being thought of as unchaste: "I only desired to liberate beings through purity, but now I will be slandered for having sinned." Her attachment to the concept of good reputation has become an obstacle to her spiritual development. In spite of her shame and the real crime of trying to kill the child, rays of light and melodious sounds emanate from the ash heap (in accord with theme 3 of the first story); the child, in spite of everything, is truly marvelous. In total contrast to the birth of Buddha Shakyamuni, the birth in this story is a cause of great pain and anguish. The theme of shame and distress appears quite clearly in the Qur'anic account of the birth of Jesus, and it is Mary who must endure extreme physical pain (surah 19:23) while in solitude, since Joseph is not explicitly mentioned in the Qur'an (however, there is an allusion to the betrothal episode in the *Protoevangelium of James* in Surah 3:44). "Ah! Would that I had died before this! Would that I had been a thing forgotten and out of sight!" The desire to be forgotten and out of sight resonates with the princess's command (theme 4 of the first story: here the princess takes the part of the evil usurper king), "put this [the baby Garab Dorje] into the ash pit and stir up the ashes to hide it," but it is interesting that explicit slander from other people is lacking in both accounts. In the Gospel of Luke, there is no hint of criticism or slander; Mary quickly goes to visit her cousin Elizabeth (Luke 1: 39-56) and is hailed as the Mother of my Lord. In the Gospel of Matthew, it is Joseph who is concerned about the pregnancy and wishes to divorce Mary, but an angel in a dream warns him not to do this. One is tempted to see in the Qur'an a carry over of the Nestorian limitations on the veneration accorded the mother of Jesus. In any case, among the Syro-Oriental Christians, and also in the Qur'an, Mary is highly regarded, though not called "*Theotokos*" (the God-bearer). During her delivery, her pain is eased by a miraculous voice, she is fed from a date palm tree, and a spring appears beneath her to provide water. It is only when she brings the child back to her family that she becomes the subject of criticism and slander: "They said: 'O Mary, truly an amazing thing hast thou brought! O sister of Aaron, thy father was not a man of evil, nor thy mother a woman unchaste!'" (surah 19:27-28) Which is to say that Mary's maternity brings shame on a Jewish priestly family. Mary is unable to reply (verse 29), but the child himself replies: "I am indeed a servant of God: He hath given me revelation and made me a prophet" (verse 30).

> After three days, the child is still alive and emits rays of light and sound (theme 3: the child is marvelous); the child is rescued (theme 4).

COMMENTS

The notion of resurrection on the third day comes directly from the Christian creed. The child Garab Dorje is taken out of the ash pit, washed in milk and perfumed water, and placed on a white, stainless silk piece of cloth. These "corrections" on the part of the princess resemble the attempts to embalm the body of Jesus on the Sunday after his death. The princess continues to "think" too much; now, she conceptualizes that the baby is the appearance body of a Buddha "or else this is the behavior of some man who cannot die." Even her attempts to interpret the events surrounding the birth of the child, though conceptual and misguided, do not impede the delivery of Garab Dorje's message. At the risk of speculating too much, the reference to the white cloth *(slar dar dkar po dri ma med)* seems to connect this story to the relic of the shroud, which was certainly known to the Church of the East, since it had been kept until the ninth century in Edessa, one of the key centers of these Syro-Oriental Christians.[416] In any case, the allusion to embalming tends to connect this part of the story to the strange names that the child will be given further along.

> The child is nourished by clouds of medicines provided by Rishis and other heavenly beings (somewhat in the manner of the feeding of the heroic child in the first story by wild beasts out in nature: themes 5 and 6). The child grows rapidly, in a miraculous fashion that resonates more with the Qur'anic account of a baby Jesus who speaks like a prophet while still in infancy than the child in the Gospel of Luke, who only becomes loquacious at age twelve and who, "grew in wisdom, stature and favor before God and men"(Luke 2:52).
>
> The child Garab Dorje begins to demonstrate precocious abilities. Unlike the Central Asian hero, however, his gifts are not military but intellectual. The child wishes to debate the Dharma with his grandfather and the circle of scholars who serve the royal court. The child literally commands his mother to grant him permission, in contrast to the obedient child Jesus of Luke 2:51. Opposition to the child's charisms is expressed by the king of Koshana and his five-hundred panditas, but the child overcomes their objections.

COMMENTS

This theme is found in the First Story (Themes 7 and 8), as also in the Life of the Buddha as recounted in the *Lankavatara Sutra, Lalitavistara,* and the *Buddhacarita.* There are of course resonances here with the child Jesus debating with the rabbinic scholars in the temple (Luke 2:41–52). In surah 19, on the other hand, the debate is not with scholars at the time of Jesus's birth. Instead, the narrative anachronistically has the child criticizing the theological debates of Jews and Christians—debates that developed in the centuries between the life of Jesus and the appearance of the Qur'anic narrative six centuries later (surah 19:34–40). Nevertheless, the miraculous child in each case is sent into the world to set to rights erroneous religious thinking.

The biography of Garab Dorje gives the child several new names as a consequence of his victory over the panditas in debate. These include: "He whose nature is wisdom," "Vajra of Supreme Delight," the Master "Ash-Colored Vampire" (or "Zombie," since he has died and come back to life), and "Master Happy Vampire," since it is understood that his consignment to the ash heap was a death sentence. The miraculous child thus "rises from the dead" to carry out his mission.

Like Jesus after his baptism in the Jordan (Matthew 3:13–17) and retreat of forty days in the desert (Matthew 4:1–11), Garab Dorje also goes into retreat in a demon-infested wilderness where, like his mother, he builds a hut of cane and rushes (*'jag ma'i spyil phub*, the same words are used here as for the nun-princess's hut); here the text resonates with the Gospels by giving the length of the retreat as thirty-two years (two more than the familiar, if erroneous, thirty for the age of Christ at his baptism) rather than forty days.

After Garab Dorje concludes the retreat, a threat emerges from a *tirthika* (non-Buddhist) king (first story themes 2 and 9), similar to the opposition of Herod, Herod the Tetrarch, Pharisees, and Saducees to Jesus. As in the case of Jesus, the danger provoking opposition is the purported radicalism of Garab Dorje's religious message.

As in the Qur'an, the Jews were unable to kill Jesus, so also the *tirthikas* cannot kill Garab Dorje; like Jesus, he ascends without dying (see Qur'an surah 4:157–158).

Garab Dorje now, having meditated on all the Buddhist scriptures for a period of thirty-two years, reveals the dzogchen scriptures. With the help of a dakini, a Sophia/wisdom gnostic figure mounted on a dragon and adorned with lightning bolts, he compiles the scriptures and their indices in a three year period. The text makes references to oral teachings that are entrusted not to human beings but to dakinis. The text concludes here by referring to the "shorter lineage of transmission."

After an ambiguous reference to "special sources" of the Buddhist teachings, the text resumes with the imagery of cremation grounds, in this case at a distance of five *yojanas* northeast of Bodh Gaya. After describing a stupa, the text presents an apocalyptic scene of perversion, worldliness, and evil; out of compassion, Garab Dorje resolves to convert the denizens of this corrupt location with the help of another female wisdom personage.

Garab Dorje acquires his only mentioned disciple, a saintly Brahman Buddhist practitioner named Manjushrimitra, who is destined to attain liberation in one lifetime. The whole purpose of the narrative seems focused on the transmission from Garab Dorje to this one figure.

Garab Dorje attains the rainbow body of the complete exhaustion of the elements: "Having caused his physical body, together with its pollutants [to dissolve and] disappear, demonstrated the method for the complete transcending of suffering."[417] This is one of the earliest known literary references to the rainbow body attained by "exhausting the elements."

Manjushrimitra faints, but then has a vision of the ascended Garab Dorje like a mass of light in the sky (cf. Acts 9; Galatians 1, the conversion of St. Paul), and receives the transmission of the teachings, including the "the three statements that strike the essential points."

Manjushrimitra then sets up the three series of dzogchen teachings: "The mind series" (*sems sde*), "the space series," (*klong sde*) and "the secret instruction series" (*man ngag gi sde*), thus constituting the "founding of a dynasty or city" in the form of a sacred transmission. Strangely, there is no one to whom these teachings can be bestowed.

Another long cremation ground section, repeating descriptions of the perverse atmosphere previously encountered; here Manjushrimitra abides in a multistoried house, surrounded by yogins, yoginis, and dakinis. He continues to abide in samadhi for 109 years in a state of equanimity, as if to say, he attains realization, does not actually die, and remains in equanimity in the midst of the chaos of this world and of the ordinary mind.[418]

Like the well-known tale of *Barlaam and Ioasaph*, the life of Garab Dorje tells more than one story. *Barlaam and Ioasaph* is the tale of the Buddha's life and conversion, embellished with elements of Manichean, Muslim, and finally Christian spirituality, presented as an integral part of the corpus of Christian hagiography. It was D. M. Lang who, having traced the complex history of the text, was able to conclude, "The resemblance between the ethical system of the book of *Barlaam and Ioasaph* and the teachings of the Buddha is not complete in every respect, particularly since the Manicheans of Central Asia, the Arabs of Baghdad, and then the Christian translators, all worked over the text in their turn, and adapted it to fit the dogma of their particular faith."[419] Lang goes on to trace the history of the legend making use of texts recovered from Turfan in Old Turkish, and a Manichaean Turkish version of an episode that appears in the later Shi'ite version of the tale of Yudasaf (or Budhasaf).[420] This material, traceable to Manichaean propaganda during the Caliphate of Mahdi (775–785), influenced later Sufi groups in Mesopotamia.[421] The Arabic version of the tale ended up in Spain, where it was translated into Hebrew about 1220.[422] The tale was handed on in Persian as well, where it was part of the oldest (early tenth century) poem in classical Persian. The first Christian version is traceable to an eleventh-century manuscript in Georgian; the Greek version is a translation of this work. The old attribution of the *Barlaam and Ioasaph* tale to St. John of Damascus is unsustainable because in fact there is no mention of this tale among Greek-speaking Christians for three centuries after the Damascene, who died in 749. The Greek version is attributable to Abbot Euthymius, a Georgian on Mount Athos, who died in 1028,[423] but was probably further embellished by the great Byzantine hagiographer Simon Metaphrastes before it came to the attention of a Latin translator in 1048.[424] From there, the legend passed into European medieval literature in many languages. This itinerary of the story of Buddha Shakyamuni illustrates the kind of multi-layered redaction a tale in this period might undergo. If a Buddhist tale might travel westward to Manicheans, Muslims, and Christians, it is quite possible that a Christian or Muslim tale might have found its way eastward to Tibet.

Garab Dorje's story, we might venture to say, is the story of dzogchen itself—a spiritual practice system that attempts to harmonize and correct all that has come before, by disclosing the most fundamental realities of consciousness, presence, and perception. In this effort, the story of Garab Dorje and the system it represents occupy a niche similar to that of the *Bhagavad Gita* in Indian religious history. For it is in this particular section of the epic *Mahabharata* that we have Hindu responses to and elaborations of all previous schools of spiritual discipline. Garab Dorje's odd biography impresses us with its free form, its contempt for any semblance of logical narrative structure, and its numerous allusions to other legendary sources. It uses its sources quite freely, as do other similar works such as Barlaam and Ioasaph. However, there are moments in which the Garab Dorje biography is aware of the details of its sources and their meaning. The authors of the Garab Dorje biography altered the meaning of their narrative sources when it suited the purpose of telling a dzogchen narrative of origins. In particular, we note the dramatic contrasts between this biography and the extravagances of the *Lalitavistara* account of the Buddha Shakyamuni's birth and life. Where the *Lalitavistara*, and to a lesser extent the *Buddhacarita*, emphasizes the purity and perfection of the appearance of Shakyamuni in this world, the biography of Garab Dorje seems to emphasize a climate of emotional turmoil, opposition, incomprehension, and risk. The characters in the narrative appear and disappear exactly the way thoughts and appearances manifest during a session of meditation. Their disappearance suggests that even in the narrative text itself, the reader is not to fall into the habit of conceptualizing everything he or she reads! The cremation ground imagery, which at first glance seems to indicate the eagerness of the twelfth century authors to insert dzogchen into the historic moment of the second diffusion of Vajrayana Buddhism in Tibet, on further reflection, seems to contrast with Vajrayana imagery. Unlike the descriptions of sacred sites in the *Vajrayogini*, *Hevajra*, and *Cakrasamvara* tantras, these "apocalyptic" scenes are not suggestive of ritual mandalas of peaceful and wrathful deities in yab-yum union. More than anything, they conjure up the impression of a mind at meditation, assaulted by thoughts that manifest in consciousness, arising from memory and from the body itself. In this way, the narrative places itself in the genre of an upadesha, an oral teaching, meant for the committed practitioner. It is not simply an edifying tale or an account of legitimation for a lineage that has been subjected to criticism. In fact, the most ferocious critical responses to dzogchen had not yet been written. [425] The narrative is an embodiment of the teacher and of the teachings, flowing playfully around the figures of princesses, dakinis, the Joyful Zombie, the Buddhist Brahman, and the Shaiva-like retinue that occupies the charnel ground geographies in which revelation takes place. Personages are like figments of rainbow dissolving into the sky, narratives trail off like clouds in a sunset, apocalyptic nightmares vaporize with the rosy morning rays of the rising sun, and numerology taunts the reader with temptations of interpretation. Time and library-cataloguing roll on together, suggesting that the upadesha also involves the disciple in the process known as "tradition": handing on what has been received in mind-to-mind transmission. Handing it on only in credible, authentic relationships between master and disciple, in which mind-to-mind, word and symbol mediate an understanding rooted in previous long searches, frustrations, terrors, and rages. All these moods, quite similar to Indian nine-rasa aesthetics, are encountered in the story. In the life of Garab Dorje, the main character disappears more than once; the narrative ends by telling us about someone else!

All of this suggests that the full verbal account of anyone's life and liberation cannot be written. The tale was lived, as we must live, in the conditions in which we find ourselves. No one is there to retell it all, nor to observe it and make connections and corrections for us. We are left to our fleeting perceptions, self-liberating in the body-mind's own light, gaining strength we know not how. Even if we were, like Mahler in the tenth symphony, to scream and become shrill with anxiety over not having said or sung all that we might have wished to have said or sung, we are still assured in the view of things, that there are some connections that matter more than others. These connections flash forth from the ground of consciousness, make themselves present, stir up wonderment, and spontaneously place us in our primordial state of being aware.

For all that we have researched and read, translated and interpreted, the great question of Hamlet, "To be or not to be," remains at the heart of dzog-chen, of Buddhism, and of any contemplative path. If "to be" means to be a thing, a someone, an object, automatically the question emerges: "in this moment you are that? In the next moment, are you still that, or are you something else?" The temporal dimension automatically deconstructs the notion of a permanent something that has a nature or identity. Ironically, Hellenistic thought proposed the notion of substance as the marker by which something retains its identity in the flux of time. The problem then moves automatically to the question of "And how do you know that the identity you had a second ago is the same as the identity you might claim now as we ask this question?" And by the time we have asked the question, the moment has slipped away! At the same time, "not to be" suffers from the same limitations, leaving us with the suspicion that "to be or not to be" are two sides of the same coin, or question. People who spend a great deal of time in prayer and meditation notice that there is a normal tendency to move from complex forms of words and ritual gestures towards greater simplicity. Moreover, in the experience of suffering, which both Christians and Buddhists recognize as having enormous motivating force, we experience a gradual purification and simplification of our grand designs and desires. If one combines the experience of the dark nights that purify and simplify our self-consciousness with the "to be or not to be" question, it is difficult not to arrive at the Heraclitean "everything flows" (panta rhéi) perspective.[426] We realize that all the philosophy we may have studied takes us only so far—it gives us a somewhat useful vocabulary for discussing important questions with others—but in the end it is understood to be provisional. If taken as the absolute truth, our philosophical language always disappoints. The question of being and the question of knowing both self disclose as a paradoxical and disconcerting encounter with an eternal now about which one cannot speak because in speaking, the moment flees inexorably into nonexistence and unknowing—substituted by another exceedingly mobile "eternal now," and another, and another. The discipline of meditative recollection makes this fluidity all the more apparent and may even show us the gaps between moments of simple awareness. We may begin to realize that focused attention, set free from any fixation on a state of consciousness of one sort or another, may actually be highly energizing and life affirming when directed to these fleeting moments of intense awareness. The moment becomes the "object" of our meditative concentration; the moment's enormous, indeed limitless, ability to escape fixation—because it disappears, allowing the next moment to take place—begins to teach us profound lessons about our own nothingness, our humility, our inability to verbalize the phenomena that are in continuous movement in and around us. We may be tempted to seek refuge in the "gaps" between thoughts, but by their very nature, these gaps cannot be described, and are as fleeting as anything else. At best, the gaps may disclose a kind of awareness that is distinguishable from the ordinary discursive thoughts that dominate our usual way of being "ourselves" and defining our nature. Therefore, the enlightened mind is simply present, effortlessly, alert, and clear as phenomena enact their dance.

If we compare the approach of the Evagrian contemplative trajectory with the Mahayana and dzogchen approaches to the flux of awareness, keeping in mind the obvious differences in philosophical language that the respective authors employ, we are struck by the evidence we can glean from the texts (always within the limits of what a text can tell) that there is a very strong degree of convergence. There is more to this convergence, however. The type of contemplative practice that comes to be called dzogchen arises from two strands in Buddhist thought: the Perfection of Wisdom sutras and related shastras (treatises), and the highly ritualized tantras with their strong connections to Indic religiosity. At a certain point in the practice of the generation stage and completion stage of tantric practice, some sadhakas (tantra practitioners) seem to have run into the paradox of time and being, of moments of awareness and their fleeting nature. At that point, a kind of purification must have taken place in which the notion of employing what is essentially a religio-magical ritual with visualizations and mantras to obtain certain kinds of paranormal powers and effects, suddenly seems to be not only futile but counterproductive. What Keith Dowman says so startlingly seems also to have dawned on a group of highly sensitive people in Tibet in the eighth century: there is something wrong with "prostituting" the present moment[427] in order to obtain "something" in some future moment. Since the present moment is all that presents itself from the ground of awareness and being, it must be within that momentary nucleus of awareness that "everything" must be found. The seed of buddha nature (*tathagatagarbha*) is to be seen contemplatively in the heart of the momentary instant of consciousness that the meditator encounters as flux—and not as a perpetual metaphysical "something" that underlies everything else. This is the real meaning of nihsvabhava, which is awkwardly translated as "no self nature" in so many English renderings of Buddhist literature.

What is utterly fascinating about this Buddhist perspective is that it so closely converges with the Christian contemplative fascination with a single verse (3:10) of the Letter to the Ephesians: "the pluralistic (*polypoikilos*) wisdom of God." This word polypoikilos means "many-colored, various, manifold, multiform" and in the context of Ephesians, it means "the wisdom of God has shown itself in Christ to be varied beyond measure and in a way which surpasses all previous knowledge."[428] How could the tiny, marginalized Christian community of the first century have made such a radical claim unless they had hit upon a way of seeing and knowing reality that in some dramatic way undermined both the ordinary ways of thinking of people bustling about that enormous (250,000 population estimate for Ephesus in the first century) port city, and the philosophical claims of Platonists, Stoics, and others thinkers at that time? They seem to be saying that the creative wisdom of the divine, having entered the human sphere in Jesus Christ, has enabled them to see reality in a completely new way, and in fact, to have access to that experience of reality. Thus in I Peter 4:10, this "manifold" (poikilos) grace of God is something dispensed and enacted among them. This text refers to the "charismata"—the paranormal gifts of the Holy Spirit that characterized the way of life and of prayer of first century Christians. In other words, once one touches reality in its moment-to-moment incarnate immediateness, the moment bursts open to reveal a plurality of remarkable qualities that transform human life, consciousness, choices, discernment, action. Fast forward to what Longchenpa will say more than twelve centuries later, and we begin to see conditions for the possibility of a profound encounter between two drastically different religious cultures.

Moving on to Evagrius of Pontus, we find that the Ephesians 3:10 verse is quoted seventeen times in his most esoteric work, the *Kephalaia Gnostica*. a work written to guide advanced contemplatives in refining their conscious awareness in the Egyptian hermitages of the late fourth century. The lineage of Christian desert contemplatives continues eastward from Egypt with Pseudo-Macarius, Abraham of Kashkar, Isaac of Nineveh, Babai the Great, Joseph Hazzaya, Philoxenus of Mabbug, John of Dalyatha, and so many others whose works are now locked away in tattered manuscripts in Syriac, Arabic, Armenian, and Sogdian. Finally we come to the threshold of Tang China for the Buddhist-Christian encounters of the seventh and eighth centuries, culminating in the works of the monk-prelate Jingjing, such as *The Sutra on the Realization of Peace and Joy*.

In a work of this kind, which so extensively employs Buddhist terminology, one cannot help but detect a long period of conversation on a very deep level between the Christian author and one or more Buddhist interlocutors. We know the name of at least one of these, the monk Prajna, of Central Asian origin. We also know that what Prajna and Jingjing did in translating one of the Perfection of Wisdom sutras was to provoke a denunciation to the imperial throne by Buddhist monks offended by the implicit syncretism of their combined efforts. Chinese Buddhism at the end of the eighth century was not amenable to the counsels of Ashoka, emperor in India in the third century before Christ as inscribed in rose granite as the Twelfth Rock Edict of Ashoka:

> The beloved of the gods, the king Piyadassi, honors all sects and both ascetics and laymen, with gifts and various forms of recognition. But the Beloved of the Gods does not consider gifts or honors to be as important as the advancement of the essential doctrine of all sects. This progress of the essential doctrine takes many forms, but its basis is the control of one's speech, so as not to extoll one's own sect or disparage another's on unsuitable

occasions, or at least to do so only mildly on certain occasions. On each occasion one should honor another man's sect, for by doing so one increases the influence of one's own sect and benefits that of the other man; while by doing otherwise one diminishes the influence of one's own sect and harms the other man's. Again, whosoever honors his own sect or disparages that of another man, wholly out of devotion to his own, with a view to showing it in a favorable light, harms his own sect even more seriously. Therefore, concord is to be commended, so that men may hear one another's principles and obey them. This is the desire of the Beloved of the Gods, that all sects should be well-informed, and should teach that which is good, and that everywhere their adherents should be told, "The Beloved of the Gods does not consider gifts or honor to be as important as the progress of the essential doctrine of all sects." Many are concerned with this matter....[429]

Nevertheless, there was something that inspired Jingjing and Prajna to work together in the old Ashokan style, and indeed the Tang dynasty seems to have favored the various religions throughout the empire, up to the tragic events of the 840s when Buddhism, Christianity, and Manichaeism were proscribed and persecuted as "foreign cults." However, our question remains: What inspired the Buddhist-Christian dialogue of the eighth century? We are forced to use our imaginative faculties to reconstruct this encounter, but fortunately the texts that have come down to us allow us to see that certain themes held in common by Mahayana Buddhism, Syriac contemplative Christianity, and early or pristine dzogchen imply a dialogue of inner experience.

If we look at the vocabulary of the Christian texts given in chapter three, we can see the challenges presented by the encounter with Buddhism. How can one explain the Gospel and its soteriology in Buddhist terms? Indeed, what might be the reason for attempting to make use of Buddhist terms to describe Christian salvation? Clearly, there is a conversation going on in which Christians are attempting to make their beliefs understandable to Chinese Buddhists. The remarkable extent of Jingjing's knowledge of the terminology of Chinese Buddhism reflects what was obviously a long period of study and, most likely, meditation practice. These are some examples extracted from our translation of Nicolini-Zani's footnotes:[430]

1.	Confused (*Mihuo*): A composite expression that describes the misguided being, someone confused by something. In Buddhism, the term indicates the deception of illusions that lead far away from the true nature of reality.
2.	Beings (*Youqing*): This word translates the Sanskrit word *sattva*, sentient beings.
3.	Saved (*Jiuhu*): It literally means to save and to protect, a Buddhist expression.
4.	Transcendent law (*Shengfa*): This expression is used frequently in this text. Its original meaning in Buddhism is *abhidharma*, but it can also mean the law that transcends description and intellectual understanding. To attain this cognitive reality is to realize the true essence of reality, buddhahood.
5.	Living beings (*Hansheng*): Buddhist word that is used synonymously with *youqing* and *zhongsheng*, for sentient beings in general.
6.	Ignorance (*Chenmai*): It literally means immersed in the cycle of birth and death, drowning in ignorance.
7.	The transcendent way (*Shengdao*): The way that leads to the realization of the true essence of reality.
8.	Mental action: Emotions (*dong*), passions or desires (*yu*), yearning (*qiu*), and mental actions that generate attachment to existence (*wei*), are seen as the four principal obstacles on the way to peace and joy.
9.	Pure (*qing*): It translates the Sanskrit term *amala*, limpid, synonymous with Chinese *jing*, which translates the Sanskrit *vimala*, both terms widely used in Buddhist texts. Compare *qingjing*, which translates *parishuddhi* or *vishuddhi*, to designate a mental state free from evil and defilements.
10.	Illuminated (*Wu*): A key word for Buddhism, meaning to be enlightened, to be awakened, to be realized.

11. The Truth (*Zheng*): In Buddhism, this term indicates the experience of the realization of the truth upon which one enters buddhahood. Like *wu* it is a key term in Chinese Buddhism.

12. Peace and joy (*Anle yuan*): The attainment of peace and joy is here described as entering into the true essence of reality, characterized by the presence of all-pervasive luminosity.

13. Fictitious names: Since the world accessible to the senses is mere appearance without inherent existence, the names given to sense data only serve to comprehend the fictitious, unreal aspect of phenomena (Sanskrit, *prapanca*), which is to be overcome in any case.

14. Sentient Beings (*Huai shengxiang*): These are beings possessing life and thought.

15. Emptiness (*Xukong*): Translates the Sanskrit term *shunyata*, the void or open nature of all phenomena.

16. Deep understanding (*Yuantong*): Buddhist term for total penetration (*vipasyana*) of the true nature of all things by means of an enlightened mind.

17. Compassionate spirit (*Beixin*): It seems to translate the key Mahayana Buddhist term *bodhicitta*, understood here as a heart-mind intent on compassion (Sanskrit: *karuna*).

18. Divine powers (*Shentong*): These are the supernatural powers (*siddhi*) of a Buddha.

19. Modes of perception (*Liufa*): The power of the Messiah to overcome obstacles tied to the world of forms and sensory perceptions is described here in typically Buddhist terms. In Buddhist *Abhidharma* psychology, there are six senses (*liuru*): the eye, ear, nose, tongue, body, and mental perception. Just as the fully awakened one is the the Buddha, so also the Messiah is free of the obstacles (*wuai*; Sanskrit: *apratihata*) and limits encountered in the phenomenal world. Underlying this phrase is the notion of *abhijna*, or *siddhis* (*liutong*), consciousness of all phenomena free of distortions, including magic power, the divine eye, the divine ability to hear, knowledge of the thoughts of others, remembrance of previous rebirths, and knowledge about how to overcome human passions.

20. The law that governs all things (*Zhufa*): Buddhist term (Sanskrit *sarvadharma, sarvabhava*) referring to the multiplicity of phenomena and their relationships (compare Ephesians 3:10 and Evagrius of Pontus: *polypoikilos*, multiform, variety).

21. The ten realities to discern (*Shizhong guan fa*): The key term here is *guan*, which is used to translate the Sanskrit *vipasyana* or v*idarshana*: contemplation involving attentive discernment of reality using the mental faculties in order to discriminate between that which is illusory and that which is real. This contemplation is the means by which one penetrates and one comes to understand the real essence of things.

22. Phenomenal realities (*Youwei*): Buddhist technical term that indicates all that is immersed in samsara, hence all changeable phenomena tied to the karmic process. In the final analysis, it refers to the unreal world as opposed to absolute reality.

23. Absence of realization (*Wuzheng*): The conscious ascetical renunciation of becoming involved in the nature of appearances and contradictory phenomena.

24. Can understand nothing (*Juezhi*): Common Buddhist word to indicate the comprehension of the true essence of things, thanks to bodhi, to awakening, to enlightenment.

25. Emptiness (*Xukong*): *shunyata*.

26. The true way (*Zhendao*): This expression indicates the way of peace and joy, understood as the equivalent of the way that leads to the realization of the true essence of reality.

27. Penetrate the depths (*Tongda*): Like two other expressions used in this text (*yuantong* and *xuantong*), this Buddhist word indicates the total penetration of the true nature of everything by means of an enlightened mind.

These terms also resonate repeatedly with early dzogchen terminology. In the "Cuckoo of Awareness" (*Rigbai Kujyug*), in the "Small Hidden Grain,"[431] and in the "Questions and Answers of Vajrasattva."[432] We can find the same concerns as those in the *Peace and Joy* text. The very teachings attributed to the Messiah and that cause a great deal of difficulty for the disciples's understanding are found in the "Six Verses" in a terse and unmitigated form:[433]

The intrinsic nature of variety of phenomena is nondual
Whereas complexity is absent in particular manifestation;
That which is transcends conceptualization, but
Samantabhadra manifests in appearances.
One already has realization, so striving is to be abandoned;
Being spontaneously present, things remain as they are!"

It is interesting that this text is attributed to the yogin Vairotsana, who is said to have translated it from teachings given him by Shri Simha in Oddiyana; the Tibetan name for the Buddha Vairocana is *rNam par sNang mDzad*, found in the line "Samantabhadra manifests in appearances" (Tibetan: *rnam par snang mdzad kun tu bzang*), which can also be translated "Vairocana is Samantabhadra," that is, "multiplicity is entirely, primordially good." If we compare this insight, which is at the very heart of dzogchen realization, we can see that it resonates forcefully with the text of Ephesians, "the multiform wisdom of God." In a Semitic linguistic setting such as the thought of St. Paul, and even more so in his Syriac-speaking heirs, divine wisdom, the gnostic Sophia and multiplicity of manifestations would be familiar and indeed foundational expressions of both cosmology and soteriology: "wisdom varied beyond measure in ways that surpass all previous forms of knowing."

The Tibetan of the second line can mean, "complexity is absent in particular manifestations" (*cha shas nyid du spros dang bral*), or "in terms of individual things, that diversity is free of conceptual elaborations (made by mind)" in John Reynolds's translation.[434] This refers to what is going on from moment to moment in our conscious awareness; the contemplative practitioner perceives individual phenomena without inventing the explanatory elaborations that Nagarjuna called "conceptualizations" (*prapañca*). Thus, for the dzogchen practitioner, all previous forms of knowing are abandoned because of the inherent limitations of conceptualization, evaluation, and explanation. "The meditator being spontaneously present (in the state of contemplative awareness), things remain as they are!" (Tibetan: *lhun gyis gnas pas bzhag pa yin*).

The "Small Hidden Grain" attributed to Buddhagupta, has the advantage of interlinear notes that purport to explain the meaning of the original

Tibetan text. The text emphasizes the pristine approach, a mode of interpreting tantric experience:[435]

> To what extent does a profound nonconceptual state
> Appear as an object of the intellect?
> Since an experience of profound nonconceptuality
> Is experience, that is not the case.
> Debate over the characteristics of Suchness
> Is teaching that does not penetrate the Dharma.
> So, however profound the words that one speaks,
> How could they measure up to the true meaning?
> In the accumulation of merit and wisdom,
> Meditation and purification of karmic traces,
> There exists the 'peg of fixation'.
> In the ungraspable sky there is no artificial improvement.
> And all bodily artificiality
> Arises from attachment to the idea of the body.
> In the sky without karma, there is nothing to improve.
> Sky-like primordial presence
> Has no crossed legs or straight posture.
> Being naturally present in the sky
> Is not the basis for alteration in the sky.
> The nature of mind, the sky-like sphere of Enlightenment,
> Is not the basis for attaining enlightenment.
> The nature of mind, without base or root,
> Is not found by searching for it, like the sky.
> In enlightenment, which is free from generation,
> Causes or effects of enlightenment are completely absent.

If these verses seem to resonate with the "Peace and Joy" text, the interlinear notes go even farther to speak of "the nondual mind of enlightenment," "discernment of each thing," "great nonconceptuality," "great emptiness," "the teaching on obscurations and obstacles," "the extreme of subject-object fixation," "free from effort and striving," absence of "virtue and nonvirtue," absence of "both cause and result of great enlightenment," the sky as "great expansiveness," the sky as "wisdom of discernment," the basis as "free from conceptual elaboration," the mind as "the reality of the universal ground," and various metaphors such as "fire extinguishing water" or "a wild animal seeking a mirage."[436]

Jingjing seems to be responding[437] to this kind of perspective by insisting on affirming "the absence of desire, the absence of mental actions, the absence of merits ... being meek and humble, free and patient, and to have within oneself great compassion ... to be able to obtain that which is absolutely transcendent is called the way of peace and joy." Thus, in this Christian sote-riology, the attainments of Buddhist meditation are linked to the Sermon on the Mount by allusions to both sets of scriptures. The Messiah also says: "I affirm the absence of desire and the absence of mental action, abandonment of the sphere of corruption, and immersion in the wellspring of the uncon-taminated. Abandoning corruption, one can become pure: this corresponds to 'emptiness'; emanating grace and light, it is possible to cause all of reality to become luminous. Causing all of reality to become luminous is that which is called the way of peace and joy." Here we can see the Christian contemplative doctrine of luminosity, already present in the New Testament, affirmed by the Egyptian monastic traditions, and strongly asserted by the Church of the East. This is the same vocabulary adopted by the Manicheans to unite Bud-dhist and Christian terminology in their own attempt to explain their beliefs in China. Although the Manicheans had many advantages over the Christians in their mission to the East, it is also true that the trajectory we are describing did not have to encounter either Manichaeism (it did, in fact, in the writings of Ephrem of Syria in the fourth century, who wrote a work against the Mani-cheans) or Buddhism to develop its theory of contemplative *photism*. Instead, this photism arises directly from baptismal theology in which it was under-stood that the newly baptized Christian participates in the light of the risen Christ, called "*photizometha*" or illumination (New Testament, Justin Martyr, and Clement of Alexandria). The Pseudo-Macarius, a monastic writer of the fifth century, writes: "at the resurrection, everything will become luminous, everything will be immersed in light and fire and will be transformed."[438] Evagrius took the risk of asserting that this kind of contemplation occurs during the lifetime of the monk: "When the rational beings in their intellects shall have attained the contemplation that is truly noetic, then too shall the material nature of their bodies be taken away, and thus the contemplation of the nature of bodies will become immaterial" (*Kephalaia Gnostica* II.62) based on Origen, *On First Principles* (Book II, Chapter III). With Hans-J. Klimkeit's work on the Christian-Buddhist encounter in Central Asia, we note the persistence of the theme of the resurrection in the Christian documents.[439] This idea, as he rightly points out, is in total contrast to Buddhist soteriological notions. It is only during the eleventh century, however, that we find the Buddhists expressing strong resentment against Christian, Muslim, and Manichaean teachings. For example, both the *Kalacakra Tantra* and the *Insadi-Sutra* polemicize against Christian and Muslim figures and hope that Maitreya will soon appear on earth to overcome the kingdoms of Bagdad and Byzantium.[440]

At the time of Jingjing, however, it was still possible for Christians and Buddhists to work together for mutual understanding, and for the Christians to develop a unique set of theological solutions to the problems raised by their dialogue with the Buddhists of Central Asia and China. The resurrection idea, and the notion of luminosity, however, created challenges for Buddhist thinkers. It is true that the cult of Amitabha already existed, and the Hua Yen school—based on the brilliant *Avatamsaka Sutra* of the Mahayana canon—was flourishing in China in the seventh and eighth centuries. However, there is no evidence at this period for any claims about a rainbow body. In fact, the Christians are not really pressing for a realization of the body of the resurrection in this life, only for a kind of increased mental and bodily subtlety in anticipation of the full participation in the resurrection at the end of time. Moreover in the period before the eleventh century, the non-dzogchen schools of Buddhism, even those tantric schools that speak of a subtle body or a light body, do not make any claims that would be equivalent to the rainbow body. Later apocryphal "treasure" literature (*terma*) does make such claims, but none of the Dunhuang documents refers to this kind of attainment. For these reasons, we are tempted to say that the rainbow body manifestation emerged along with other Buddhist writings in Tibet during a time of crisis and change to express the "myth of religious superiority." Other tantric schools, we repeat, did not accept this teaching. Only the dzogchen school presents itself as the way to attain this particular manifestation of buddhahood, and only at the start of the second diffusion at a time when it is in a weak position. This is also a time in which the caves at Dunhuang are closed. Christianity in this period seems to have overcome the crushing devastation of the 840s in China, and to have spread during the tenth century among the northeastern Turks, the tribes of the Ongut and Kerait. Even more conversions occurred in the eleventh century when the Keraits carried Christianity to some of the Mongols.[441] This is exactly the period in which Tibetan dzogchen masters began to take stock of their situation and systematize their teachings. The Dunhuang texts indicate a lively exchange between Christians, Manicheans, and Buddhists during the same period. The strange biography of Garab Dorje is written soon after the sealing of the Dunhuang caves, bringing us to the threshold of a new kind of hagiographical tale in which the charnel ground imagery of the Buddhist tantras is combined with Muslim and Christian narratives to create a remarkable contemplative master born of a virgin, who rose from the dead, worked in thirty-two year cycles, ascended into heaven in a body of light, and transmitted the dzogchen teachings to Manjushrimitra and apparently others associated with the first diffusion of Buddhism in Tibet. All of this points to a new, more polemical kind of exchange between Christians and Buddhists in Tibet, taking place in the milieu of the ngagpa masters placed under scrutiny by the reforms of Rinchen Zangpo and Atisha in the first half of the eleventh century.

Once we have examined the early history of dzogchen, we come to a crucial watershed in the eleventh century. The reforms of Rinchen Zangpo and Atisha reintroduced scholastic, philosophical, and monastic styles of Buddhism into Tibet. Given the political and geographical situation, however, the role of the lay lama—the village ngagpa—did not die out so easily. In fact, it would seem from the life of Milarepa that there were accomplished ngagpas both Buddhist and Bonpo in the central Yarlung Valley and throughout the Himalayas, as discussed in Dan Martin's articles on the early education of

Milarepa and on lay Buddhist movements in this period, and my own article on the religion of Milarepa before his "conversion."[442]

Of greater importance for our discussion than the teachers of destructive magic, however, is the story of 'Bre ston Lha dGa'. Dan Martin[443] is not sure if he was a Bonpo or a Nyingma. He lived in the valleys though which rivers flow south toward Gyantse. The fact that he failed to awaken spiritual attainment in Milarepa, who was after all not a mere victim nor a mere ordinary deluded person but a sorcerer already experienced in a number of tantric traditions, shows that at least one approach to dzogchen was in crisis in the late eleventh century: the claims made for dzogchen are very great, but the results are less convincing. Hence, Lha dGa''s intention to study the six yogas of Naropa may be taken as a cultural statement of the crisis of dzogchen in its pristine form. In other words, pristine dzogchen, even when practiced assiduously, was not able in all cases to bring disciples to realization. The second diffusion tantras owed their acceptance and success in Tibet to the remarkable impact that their practitioners, e.g., Marpa and Milarepa among many others, had on their contemporaries. This impact is formalized in the bKa' gdams pa master Gampopa, who founded the bKa' brgyud pa monastic lineages by uniting the two streams of Kadampa scholasticism and ngagpa tantrism, fathering the four elder bKa' brgyud pa orders. This is exactly the crisis that David Germano's dzogchen masters of the eleventh and twelfth centuries are trying to resolve, and it is why they increasingly turn to the tantric rituals and yogas that pristine dzogchen had seemingly downplayed. Hence we find, according to Germano, the emergence of funerary Buddhism among the dzogchen masters, expressed in terms of bardo teachings and charnel ground tantric imagery. At the same time, the early Milarepa corpus manifests the same concerns. In fact, we can find Bonpo and dzogchen teachings and terminology in Milarepa's earliest songs and oral teachings. Just because he had Marpa as his main guru does not exclude the ongoing influence of other masters and their teachings in the transmissions that Milarepa himself took in hand. Thus, the life of Milarepa and the early sources we have studied elsewhere, help us to depict the evolution of dzogchen just as Germano suggests that we should do.[444]

Our description of the early days of dzogchen takes us up to this particular threshold: here we emphasize—more strongly than previous scholarly research—the Christian component in the transformation of early dzog-chen into a "supreme vehicle" that brings the yogin to the attainment of the rainbow body, as described in detail by Longchenpa. The kinds of pho-tism that we find highly developed in the fourteenth-century works of this Nyingma master indicate a brilliant synthesis that has taken place between the early 1000s and the late thirteenth century, during which the *trekchod* and *thodgal* practices are fully developed. These practices seem to have bor-rowed much from the Siva Sutra traditions of Kashmir and from the Tamil Siddha teachings of alchemy. Many of the trekchod practices seem to align well with the *Vijnana Bhairava* practices for "stopping the mind."[445] Some of the photism of thodgal seems to have been taught by Jabir the Yogi, but his teachings probably weren't actually practiced within the Tibetan lineages that nevertheless preserved his texts. The visions of spheres of light described for thodgal, are already suggested in such gnostic texts as the "Treatise on the Resurrection"[446] and in the descriptions of meditative states found in John of Dalyatha.[447] These experiences might have been enhanced by the kind of pranayama practices cultivated by the Nath yogis, allowing Buddhist contemplatives the opportunity to forge a new vehicle out of both pristine dzogchen and other forms of contemplative practice, including that of the Syro-Oriental mystics.[448]

Lama Norta, relative and disciple of the Khenpo

V

※

Concluding Reflections:
Answering Unanswerable Questions

*There are more things in heaven and earth, Horatio, than are
dreamt of in your philosophy.*

—HAMLET

If we were to return to our village-gossip question, "*Che fine ha fatto?*" we
may find ourselves a new frame of reference from which to propose some
concluding thoughts, keeping in mind that there is a double meaning to that
infamous question. The "end" of the subject of the gossip might be a good
or bad death, but it might also be a successful career, perhaps as a well-paid,
dysfunctional bureaucrat! So it goes, in the *vox populi* of the village piazza.
Classic South Asian cultural anthropology has studied the interaction between the "great tradition" and the "little, or village tradition."[449] The great
tradition is that of the panditas, of Sanskrit culture, of the great temples and
the six darshanas (philosophical perspectives) of classical Hinduism. The little
tradition is that of folk religion, local festivals for local deities, unorthodox
yogis, visionaries possessed by deities—all the habits of the heart to which the
small rural or tribal community clings, oblivious to historical pressures and
social engineering.[450] Anthropologists may be so impressed by the survival of
the little tradition that the undeniable presence of history and of the great
tradition on the local level may be eclipsed in the written account of one's
research. In the same way, the scholar of textual traditions easily ignores the
village culture that colors the procedures of the most orthodox temple liturgies. In our research in Tamil Nadu among the *Siddhar* medical practitioners,
themselves advocates of bodily transformation and attainment of the body of

290

light, the two tendencies are in constant dialogue. The great tradition and the little tradition are in some cases lived as if they were one seamless view of life, as indeed from an emic perspective, they are. The distinction between "great" and "little" is not absent in emic perspectives, but its dynamism in living communities of discourse is not well served by accentuating that distinction. The relational model of "difference in identity" applies with full persuasive force when we report on what is actually believed and performed.

In our local village culture here in the Molise region of Italy, we cannot help but be struck by the opposite tendency. That faith that the local cultures cling to is most certainly not that of the professors of theology in Naples, Rome, or Chieti, not to forget Milano. It is the religion of folk magic, herbal healing, *maghi* and fortunetellers, of gypsies and elderly women not all of whom are wise, who promise solutions for life's little and great moments of anguish. Sometimes the solution is *lo sfogo*—letting off steam precisely by paying someone else to put a curse (la fattura; il maleficio) on one's enemies. We are back with Milarepa and his mother in eleventh-century southern Tibet, "If you are many, make war, if you are few, cast spells." And so it goes. There are also the processions, the novenas, the feasts of the saints and even the feasts of the Catholic liturgical year, and above all the prince of all feasts: death, in which the longest and most elaborate rites are demanded. Here, "great and little" share an uneasy compromise in the piazza, the church, cemetery, and home—not just on the Day of the Dead (popularly conflating the Feast of All Saints on November 1 with that of All the Faithful Departed on November 2) but at each and every funeral, its eighth day, its thirtieth day, and so on for years on end. One is struck by the facility with which significant feast days can be preempted by funerals, or by the preferred local saint. In one local village, on the feast of the Assumption of the Blessed Virgin Mary (August 15), her vespers and procession are preempted by the procession of San Rocco (whose feast is August 16). The Feast of the Transfiguration of Christ (August 6) is preempted in the provincial capital by the lesser liturgical feast of the Madonna della Libera (which is August 5, and is officially the feast of the dedication of the Basilica of Santa Maria Maggiore in Rome). Many towns still celebrate Santa Filomena—a century after the Vatican published archeological evidence that there never was a Santa Filomena. The same with

Santa Barbara, for whom there is no evidence before the ninth century. A statue of Saint Agnes, dressed exactly like the goddess Diana, is celebrated in the cold of January with panegyrics and great devotion in the town of Longano, above Isernia. Examples could be multiplied, but suffice it to say that the Catholicism of the Catechism of the Catholic Church is somewhere in the "Cloud of Unknowing" up here in these mountain territories.

What is more, the power of shamanism is as strong as it ever was among our ancestors in the steppes of Central Asia. Holy women communicate with the dead—as do the delogs[451] in Tibet—and then indicate how many prayers and masses are to be said to liberate the souls from Purgatory. Holy men and women spend their entire lives at the sickbed of the incurable, communicating revelations from the other world. Thousands make the pilgrimage to the latest shrine where the Blessed Mother delivers her message to visionary children or youths. Exorcisms, with or without the approval of the local bishop, are performed by charismatic friars whose message closely adheres to those of their Pentecostal and Fundamentalist rivals. The evil eye is regularly diagnosed with an egg and oil on the surface of a bowl of water. Stories of miracles are told to any who will listen. Those who sing louder on pilgrimages through the mountains are esteemed, if not always imitated.

In the course of our research on the rainbow body, we have seen how the great and the little traditions converge in a figure such as Khenpo A Chö. In fact, his ability to wear the yellow hat of the Gelugpa and the red hat of the Nyingmapa is the liturgical embodiment of his great skill in uniting two of the great streams of Tibetan spirituality. At the same time, thanks to his unique biography and "happy ending," we catch a glimpse of the real place of the Nyingma tradition in Khams. It rests in the voice of the village tradition, the charismatic world of local cults and devotions. The impression that we have had in the West from fervent, emic Buddhist practitioners is that the tradition of dzogchen, especially of the termas, is a highly respected "great" tradition in Tibet. This opinion dislocates the experience from its lived reality, as so often happens in scholarship and in apologetics. The real beauty of the Nyingma tradition is precisely its closeness to the village tradition, to ordinary people, marginalized yogi practitioners, and the married ngagpas, with their dreadlocks and chöd drums, wandering next to traders and brigands along the precipitous mountain trails.

Lama Norta greets Lama Piyok in the stockade, Khenpo A Chö hermitage.

To understand the jargon of the ngagpas, however, one must enter their emic world, that of esoteric practitioners, which is par excellence a closed community of discourse. While translating Khenpo Tsultrim Lodro's[452] account of the dissolution of the body of Khenpo A Chö, a Tibetan friend exclaimed: "This is the way practitioners speak, this is the way my elderly parents speak. It is a world unto itself, it is not in any way compatible with a scientific worldview. You must understand this." Once again, we return to Lama A Khyug's aphorism: "The rainbow body is a matter, not of the eyes, but of the heart-mind," a view that mirrors Henry Corbin's citations of Iranian Sufism in his masterful essay on "Divine Epiphany" in the Eranos Yearbooks.[453] As students of South Asian languages and cultures have observed—on both the great and little—levels, the language of esoteric discourse relies heavily upon nuance, allusion, and citation. It is an aesthetic expression of what people in a particular culture believe to be more profoundly true than chronology. One must return frequently to the early work of Mircea Eliade to remind ourselves that the religious perspective invests certain phenomena with a "saturation of being" in order to speak of the "really real," of that which is of ultimate importance. What is seen by the eyes and timed with a wristwatch is not saturated with being the way contemplative experience of is.

The problem extends beyond the sphere of the strictly religious. It is a fact that every time Western scholars have tried to ascertain the historical facts about Tibet; its empire; its religions; its more recent polity; its perennial conflicts; the chaos and backwardness that opened the way for Imperial Chinese, British, and later Communist intervention, we have run into the emic/etic problem. In other words, the native sources tell one story, and other sources tend to indicate that the native sources are not accurate. In spite of the fact that Tibetan sources (analogous to Chinese annals) are more concerned with history and chronology than, by comparison, Indic sources, for the most part the way they tell the story is not really shaped by the same humanistic values of Western historiography. If a scholar is too allied to the emic Tibetan view, he or she will tell us that there was a debate at Samyé in which Indian Buddhist scholasticism triumphed (the Great Tradition) over Chinese Ch'an Buddhism and related Tibetan schools (supposedly, early dzogchen). In fact, there is no hard evidence for an historical debate at the monastery of Samyé, and there is Chinese evidence that the Tibetan court actually favored the Ch'an approach to Buddhism and not the scholasticism of Shantarakshita and Kamalashila.

When we move into the world of the termas, the emic temptation is to say that these are in some sense actual documents hidden by Padmasambhava (or disciples) in the eighth century, foreseeing the persecutions[454] of Langdarma in the ninth century. These hidden teachings are said to be guarded by esoteric forces, only to be revealed at the right time in order to refresh, authenticate, and renew the Nyingma (or Bonpo) tradition in future moments of decline.[455] In reality, the termas are certainly taken as dramatic signs of renewal when they are discovered. As practice texts, they introduce new liturgical forms in strict continuity with Nyingma and Bonpo tantric ritual traditions. What seems to be authenticated is not so much the tradition as the terton and his cultural message in a particular moment of Tibetan history. As Michael Aris has shown,[456] the termas are the literary or artistic products of these visionary individuals whose motivations were very often sectarian and political. The tertons at times represent an effective rebellion of the "little tradition" over against the imposition of imperial and religious hegemony. Tertons and their apocryphal revelations evidently sustain elements of the ngagpa Buddhism associated with the first diffusion under the Tibetan Empire of the seventh and eighth centuries. At the same time, the many dzogchen teachings and tantric rituals are also in evident harmony with the ngagpa style that survived the post-Langdarma period. It is this freer, more local, magical, esoteric, and lay-oriented tradition to which the great theorists of dzogchen belonged: the sNubs lineage, the Zur lineage, and even Bre ston Lha dGa', Milarepa's failed dzogchen teacher. It is the ngagpa form of Nyingma Buddhism and Bon that had to confront the second diffusion Buddhism of the new Indian tantric cycles introduced in the eleventh and twelfth centuries: Cakrasamvara, Hevajra, Vajravarahi, and above all Kalacakra, the so-called funerary Buddhism discussed by David Germano.[457] The vitality of the ngagpa lineages and of the kind of dzogchen that failed to liberate Milarepa in one lifetime can be seen in the remarkable life of Longchenpa.[458]

Thanks to David Germano, we have an image of Longchenpa as the scholastic master of a "great tradition" lineage, the philosophical prince of dzogchen, especially in his translation[459] of the *Treasury of Precious Words and Meanings*. However, in his and Janet Gyatso's wonderful translation of another work, Longchenpa and the Possession of the Dakinis,[460] we seem to be a wholly other world. Here we have Longchenpa as a tantric master in retreat, surrounded by male and female disciples, some of whom are possessed during practice and liturgical sessions by a variety of female deities or dakinis. During possession, these entities critique the master, propose revised relationships with other masters, and affirm the authenticity of what has thus far been taught. Here we cannot help but see analogies with esoteric societies, especially of the little tradition, all over the world and in every era of human history. What could be more chilling, and convincing, than to observe the altered behavior of the possessed, and to receive the "mysterium tremendum et fascinosum" of their untrammeled critiques? Are we at a coven of medieval European witches? At a Pentecostal healing retreat? At an exorcism in a counter-reformation Capuchin friary? Among neanderthals preparing for the hunt in a darkened cave? Among marginal yogis and street people at a charnel ground in Bihar? Or perhaps with the slightly daft healer women studied in Sri Lanka by G. Obeyesekere in the 1970s?[461] In the end we are left with the question: is Nyingma Tibetan Buddhism the true voice of the village tradition, and as such, should it not be allowed its own voice, unencumbered by biases and expectations of those seeking "scientific" outcomes accessible to video recorders? Our rainbow body research would tend to support the "traditionalist" approach in religious research, in which each tradition is allowed to speak in its own voice. Each tradition is appreciated for what it says and does with regard to the promotion of the spiritual and moral life among its adherents. The appreciative observer does not have to be converted to the views expressed. In any case, conversion would inevitably distort the integrity of the cultural setting and the originality of its self-expression. It is useless to adopt a pseudo-emic perspective as if this were some kind of objective, scientific, literal truth. The two categories, "scientific" and "saturated with being" are complementary, not coincident.

The cottage industry of finding the themes and insights of modern physics[462] in the mystical teachings of China, Tibet, and India, has a tendency to confuse categories of human thought and experience that should be kept distinct. For example, the entire set of categories that quantum mechanics uses as a basis for research has in fact nothing whatsoever to do with the categories that sustain a life of contemplative practice. There is no way in either science or in spiritual disciplines to explain coherently how meditating on spheres of light or various sounds might have an effect on the proto-plasm of the cells: the cause- and-effect efficacious connection between science and spirituality is invisible to all currently available methods of research. Researchers at the Mind and Life Institute and the IONS (Institute of Noetic Science) have made some interesting suggestions,[463] but they also have the advantage over many other researchers on the relationship between brain and consciousness in that at least some Mind and Life people are also trained philosophers. However, even with these comparatively open-minded scientists, there are moments in which there is a profound confusion of categories between natural science (studying phenomena by means of measurable phenomena) and the spiritual quest per se. Certainly, I am not opposing further research in this area—on the contrary. I am only cautioning that we do not yet have adequate methodologies corresponding to the claims being made for this kind of research.

In many ways, our research on the rainbow body and body of light has indicated that at the present time our knowledge and our methodologies are at a point similar to that when the first full size photographs were made of the Shroud of Turin in 1898.[464] At first, scientists were simply astounded by the photographs, which revealed an object displaying unsuspected features unlike anything seen previously. As time went on, a number of hypotheses were proposed to explain the historical meaning of the image and how, physically speaking, the image may have been formed. Over 115 years of debate and research on this subject have given us a prudent model to follow in our future research. To study the shroud, researchers have had to rely on atomic isotope dating, archeology, paleography, studies in ancient legal procedures, religious history, biblical interpretation, optics, numismatics, botany, chemistry, and linguistics.[465] The debate continues, with new data emerging every few years in publications and international conferences.

It is for this reason that my responses to the kinds of questions that may have led the reader to this book may not be entirely satisfactory. In a famous interview, it was Sigmund Freud who observed: "my discoveries may have been perceived by some as unsavory. "Undoubtedly some readers, wedded to emic or etic fixed positions, may have the same opinion of this research. It would be untrue on my part to say that I had no extraordinary experiences in the course of this research. At many points along the way, the journey seemed guided by more than just good planning on my part. Moreover, as we were told by the Japanese-Burmese monk Cealo, from an emic or esoteric point of view, we would not have been asking these questions if we were not in some sense already "within" the world of discourse as spiritual practitioners and seekers. If that were not enough, over the past fifteen years I have been inspired to produce a significant number of works of art by certain inner experiences that accompanied the years of research on the body of light in various cultures.[466] I hope to publish these works and their interpretations in another literary format.

The very first steps of this research were, in fact, an act of "guru yoga" offered to my main teacher, Brother David Steindl-Rast, O.S.B. He was convinced that I had had a number of experiences supported by a long enough personal history of spiritual practice to be able to carry out this project. I have tried to respectfully guide this research without excluding critical thinking. For this reason, I am inclined to object to those bloggers who are out to show that various preternatural phenomena are fakes. Time after time, these essayists demonstrate their biases, and ignore serious scientific research when it disagrees with their prior convictions. As such, "hunting down fakes" seems to be an apology for pseudo-science, seriously lacking in critical thinking. It is one thing to seek out explanations for preternatural phenomena within the boundaries of legitimate scientific research, it is quite another to misuse scientific information selectively to support some other agenda. This happens frequently both among believers and would-be exposers of fakery. It is bad enough when we confuse theological or philosophical thinking with experimental science; the websites in search of fakery tend to reflect a lower category of thought.

In my research on the rainbow body over the past fifteen years, I have found the problem to be insufficient skepticism among Western converts and a lack of scientific methodology for undertaking serious research.

Following the lead of Sindonology, I have tried to outline what that research might require.

One great difficulty in discussing the rainbow body has been to bridge the apparent gap between pristine dzogchen, which is adorned with many multicultural and interreligious possibilities, and dzogchen after the second diffusion of Buddhism in Tibet, in both Bonpo and Nyingma traditions. The later dzogchen systems seem to be characterized by features that reflect moments of identity crisis within Tibetan civilization that developed less as a result of outside influences. It is this later or "contaminated" or "funerary" dzogchen that shows signs of internal reconstruction, brought about by exasperated attempts to sustain the claim that dzogchen is an exclusively Buddhist practice with roots in Indian Vajrayana, comparable to the anuttara yoga tantras. This revision of pristine dzogchen seems to have arisen in response to typically Tibetan categories of criticism, such as the later history of the "Samyé debate," the repudiation of supposedly Chinese influences in Tibetan Buddhism, the shen-tong/rang-tong debate,[467] beliefs about terma and tertons—and for that matter any "apocryphal" Buddhist or Bonpo texts. A great deal of effort seems to have gone into aligning dzogchen with second diffusion Buddhism and distancing it from Chinese and Central Asian religious experiences. Nevertheless, like fossils in a mass of limestone, we can still detect the earliest flashes of spiritual insight that gave rise to a remarkably different way of construing the contemplative life. "You are the eyes of the world" is light years away from "All is suffering, the fruition of negative karma and deceptive perceptions." Nevertheless, as Sam Van Schaik points out, the earliest texts from Dunhuang clearly indicate that dzogchen originally meant the most intense spiritual moment of realization to be attained during the ritual of initiation in first diffusion Tibetan Buddhism. The term "dzogchen" came to characterize a complete system of spiritual practice (indeed, a "ninth vehicle") only during the eleventh and twelfth centuries. According to Van Shaik, the term dzogchen was not used in the earliest sources to refer to a kind of primordial spiritual attainment detached from ritual practices, in spite of the survival of this kind of rhetoric in texts such as Vairotsana's *Five Transmissions*.[468] Both Van Schaik and Germano have attempted to articulate various resolutions of this discrepancy.[469]

We can attempt to summarize the characteristics of the great perfection after early dzogchen as follows:

⬦ After Longchenpa's magisterial contributions to the philosophy and practice of dzogchen, philosophical creativity seemed to go into decline. Not only does Longchenpa represent a pinnacle, his is a pinnacle that is rarely if ever reached by the subsequent history of the lineage. Instead of building upon the dramatic shift in consciousness that his work articulates, the tradition simply incorporates the cautious approach of a gradual path.[470]

⬦ The increased focus on the *terma* tradition tended to emphasize rituality, sectarianism, and funerary Buddhism in the manner of second diffusion Vajrayana. Sectarianism in this sense is also linked to increasingly nationalistic tendencies such as the revival of the symbolism of the early Tibetan empire in those clan polities that sponsored some dzogchen yogins. Thus, dzogchen becomes, like early Indian Vajrayana, a magical system used to sustain the interests of the state. Usually this persists among small, local polities. However, in the case of the Great Fifth Dalai Lama, we encounter the terton tradition at the very pinnacle of the hegemonic state.[471]

⬦ We see other lineages such as Karma Kagyu, and of course the Nyingma, taking up dzogchen in its funerary, tantric form, probably because of the inherent persuasive power of the shamanic form of practice typical of the ngagpas. All these lineages emphasize the state of contemplative consciousness as being the proper frame of mind in which the yogin carries out the rituals. Many Kagyu and Nyingma authors assert the convergence of dzogchen and mahamudra, the two most frequently used terms for the state of contemplative absorption that is the matrix for appropriate ritual conduct.

⬦ The rainbow body attainment *gradually emerges* in hagiographic narratives as a manifestation of dzogchen realization alone. This articulation is fiercely defended by both Bonpo and Nyingmapa authors. Other forms of postmortem bodily dissolution are discounted, including the light body, the illusory body, incorruption, and "flying off to the land of the *dakas*" as in the biographies of the mahasiddhas. However, 'Gos Lotsawa—a Kagyu master strongly favorable to dzogchen—preserved the earlier, more inclusive tradition, in his compilation of early dzogchen biographies in chapter three of the *Blue Annals*.

·👁· Some proponents of dzogchen seem to be responding to the criticisms of Sakya Pandita, the Gelugpa heirs of Tibetan scholasticism, and certain Kagyu reformers such as gTsang smyon Heruka. At this point, dzogchen becomes more than a "way of practice"—it becomes a kind of sectarian position over against other systems, as articulated especially in hagiographic and *terma* literature. We should not underestimate the importance of the Lha dGa' episode[472] in the life of Milarepa as provocative of a series of dzogchen responses. The failure of a dzogchen master to deliver liberation in one lifetime to the sinful sorcerer Milarepa required some kind of explanation. In my opinion, this failure is the hagiographical reason for dzogchen's incorporation of practices along the lines of the graduated path typical of second diffusion Buddhism.

·👁· As a symptom of the need for a gradual path, we detect an increasing forgetfulness of the earliest dzogchen teachers, who taught effortlessness and primordial enlightenment as already present, and an enormous growth in the cult of Padmasambhava, especially promoted by the tertons. The cult of Padmasambhava required elements compatible with a path involving guru yoga rituals, visualizations, mantras, and lengthy preliminary practices as preparation for dzogchen initiation.

Thus, the body-of-light attestations in other tantric literature are sharply distinguished from the rainbow body attainment for sectarian purposes, to the point of emphasizing the attainment of the "rainbow body of great transformation"[473] by Guru Rinpoche as a kind of unique and almost unrepeatable realization. In the modern literature of the Nyingmapa, such as the *History of the Nyingmapa* by Dudjom Rinpoche, this tendency is accentuated. Even Western scholars of the tradition, such as Jean Luc Achard and John Reynolds, offer a stout emic defense of the authenticity and uniqueness of dzogchen in particular with reference to the rainbow body attainment.[474] These sectarian polemics are accentuated by the widespread devotional habit among Western Buddhist practitioners to believe almost anything a Tibetan lama or text says, often accompanied by belabored efforts at concordism (artificial attempts to harmonize religious teachings with scientific findings) with the Western scientific worldview, or by tenuous claims that Buddhist scriptures in one way or another anticipated the discoveries of quantum physics, astrophysics, and so forth. In some Tibetan Buddhist circles, it is naively believed that to think scientifically might be a breach of the sacred bond of devotion between disciple and the guru.

These attempts mirror the labors of progressive rabbis in nineteenth century Judaism to make the claim that the kosher laws anticipated the discoveries of microbiology, or of early twentieth century Christians trying to harmonize seven days of creation with billion-year blocks of time in the evolutionary cosmic world picture. As such, all forms of "concordism" are sectarian expressions of modernity in the form of religious apologetics, polemics, and proselytism. Literary proselytism takes a number of forms, accentuated in recent decades by the use of the internet. There is the fervent, devotional "lama-knows-best" approach, which at least has the virtue of affectivity. Thus we find Western Buddhists expressing themselves with fervent devotion for Padmasambhava that mimics Christian confessions of conversion and faith in Christ[475] for which see the testimonies in the appendices of Sogyal Rinpoche's *The Tibetan Book of Living and Dying*). Soka Gakkai Buddhism's great popularity in the West is another example, in which the proselytizing styles of neo-Protestant movements are taken up by a Japanese new religion that venerates the thirteenth-century reformer Nichiren apparently more fervently than it venerates Shakyamuni. Modernizing may take retrogressive doctrinal forms (traditionalism), or perhaps more insidiously, it may attempt to reconstruct a religion in order to make it palatable to modern audiences. Donald Lopez devastatingly exposes these apologetic and proselytizing trends, localized in both popular and scholarly literature, in his insightful *Prisoners of Shangri-La*. Similarly, Michael Aris's book, *Hidden Treasures and Secret Lives,* allows us to enter sympathetically into the world of pious deception and devout fantasy that seems to have a long history in Tibetan religion. Sympathetic or not, eagerness to believe can get in the way of an authentic search for truth in any field of research. Even 'Gos Lotsawa was aware of the existence, in the fifteenth century, of "spurious accounts" of the life of Milarepa, which he set about correcting in accord with his own principles of hermeneutics.

Keeping all these cautionary tales in mind, and distancing myself from any desire to write a polemic or to condemn the legitimate religious beliefs of anyone, I would like to address the problem at the heart of my own research on the rainbow body. In many of the messages I have received from readers over the years, it is obvious that people find the rainbow body phenomenon highly compelling. The reason people are curious is that the human mind does seek out the truth, and in particular there is a search for truth that goes beyond the data accessible to the senses. We also need to be aware that some modern people are still in some way searching for a religion in which they can believe. Islam, Judaism, and Christianity have failed many people by not living up to their own best ideals. Those who have been hurt make no secret of the fact and have written extensively across every imaginable literary genre about the purportedly demonstrable immoral behaviors sponsored by these "monotheistic" or "Abrahamic" religions. Modern Hinduism, with the exception of popular yoga and some forms of Vaishnavaism, sets up numerous barriers to conversion. Buddhism has many appealing features for modern Westerners, but being highly ascetic, philosophical, and peculiarly nontheistic, it lacks decisive mass-persuasive power. Some popular forms of Buddhism try to appeal to human needs and desires: recite the title of a sutra as a mantra, and you will receive various worldly benefits. The one Buddhist claim to a persuasive paranormal phenomenon, however, is that of the rainbow body. To the general reader, it seems that if one does the practices of dzogchen under the guidance of a living master of the lineage, after death one's body should dissolve into manifestations of rainbow light. This aspiration might be stated in terms that sound suspiciously like cookbook magic. In this one phenomenon, a number of ancient problematic challenges are resolved:

·◊· What Christians claim for Jesus alone is shown to be possible to any serious yogin who follows the recipe offered by a still-viable religious tradition.

· What modern science says is impossible turns out to be possible and within the reach of experience, and even of observation, thus satisfying those who object to the intellectual hegemony of natural science.

· What seems to be appealing if unbelievable in Buddhist philosophy is verified by physical evidence. This is the classic basis for the "prisoners of Shangri-La" problem: a mysterious civilization, hidden away beyond the Himalayas for centuries, has preserved intact an ancient, superior, pre-scientific system of knowledge.

· The rainbow body attainment provides the ultimate vindication of the spiritual quest; a life dedicated to meditation and altruism is confirmed by a verifiable postmortem "seal of approval."

· For atheists who still find "spirituality" attractive, here there is no need for a god; if one practices within the environment of an authentic dzog-chen lineage, complete realization and liberation are within one's reach. This also liberates a psychologically sensitive atheist from whatever guilt complex may arise from having repudiated the theistic cultural heritage of Western civilization. It is interesting that the *Supreme Source*, transla-tion of the *Kun byed rGyal po* dzogchen tantra, has a fervent disclaimer that the "*rgyal po*" (king) who "created everything" (*kun byed*) should not be confused with the idea of a creator god.

· Even infra-Buddhist polemics and sectarianism are resolved in favor of one particular lineage of practice, which claims to be the pinnacle of all other vehicles of the tradition. This lineage is endowed with many affective features, such as guru-yoga, that can substitute for devotional theism and for the Christian belief in the Incarnation.

However attractive these solutions may seem, problems remain unresolved:

· There is so far no scientific evidence for the rainbow body attainment. True, there are some suggestive photos[476] and interviews. There are the shrunken bodies yet to be examined by forensic experts with experi-ence in the study of natural and artificial mummification. However, accounts of skeptics present at such manifestations are nonexistent to the best of my knowledge. This means that there is no control group for establishing the veracity of "believer" observers, or testing for various methods of falsification. It is significant that even a practitioner like Matthew Kapstein displays caution in his essay, "The Strange Death of Pema the Demon Tamer." He does state that his own teacher, Serlo Khenpo Sanggye Tenzin (1924–1990) was deeply affected by the dissolution of the body of another lay yogin in eastern Tibet. As a result of this manifestation, the man's son found "his world had been quite overturned, and he had long ago abandoned a mainstream monastic vocation in favor of the more eccentric life style of a yogin and adept of the great perfection system."[477] Kapstein covers much of the same ground that we have examined in this book, without having sounded the depths of the Syro-Oriental Christian, Manichean, and Tamil Siddha evidence. The examples of rainbow body accounts that he gives are all from after the eleventh century, and therefore from the period in which the tertons's revelations have become a key feature of dzogchen. He points out that the exclusive claim to the rainbow body "has become an important aspect of Nyingma apologetics."[478] He also takes note of the case of Khenpo A Chö, from a newspaper account from the People's Republic of China that disagrees with our eyewitness accounts.[479] Kapstein's caution, along with a similar proposal to our own for a sympathetic view of the emic accounts, is evident in his conclusions, in which he also dutifully offers some possible natural explanations.[480] However, most helpful are the following comments:

We have become accustomed in recent years to speaking of experiences as culturally constructed or, better, as mediated by the constructions of language and culture. Nothing that I have presented here would refute that view. But we should be wary, lest we come to speak of cultural constructions themselves as the rigid repetitions of culturally specific paradigms. What culture constructs can at best be described as a malleable field in which received tradition and the lived experiences of individuals enter into dialogue and through their dialogue form and reform one another.... We have seen, for example, that even if we hold that the entire phenomenon of the rainbow body to be a Tibetan cultural construction, it was nevertheless one that could be in important respects contested in Tibet itself....The problem that we confront here, of course, is that, unlike many types of claimed religious experience, such as visions and more mystical experiences, that can be interpreted as events occurring within the subject's consciousness alone, the rainbow body purports to describe a physical event. It belongs to the class of miracles. Who are we to say that it never occurs?[481]

·⟡· Kapstein concludes with a suggestion that since "intensive visions and experiences of light are regularly associated with some types of yogic and contemplative practice," something like the dissolution of the body into spirit may become plausible. As we have indicated in our research, the same may be said of the Syro-Oriental Christian mystics, the Daoist search for immortality, and in the light mysticism of the Tamil Siddha tradition. What remains to be demonstrated is whether the rainbow body as a *physical* manifestation is a "miracle" that cannot be studied scientifically, or a result of following a certain recipe of spiritual prac-tices, which at least in theory can be repeated scientifically. By the same token, the nature of the act of perception of an eyewitness to this phe-nomenon also needs to be scrutinized systematically, if sympathetically and with respect for the religious character and cultural integrity of the dzogchen community.

·⟡· The most studied "miraculous" relic of all time, the Holy Shroud of Tu-rin, believed to be the burial shroud of Jesus, offers a large body of sci-entific evidence gathered in the face of repeated attempts to falsify the literal historicity of the relic. The more the shroud is studied, the more evidence accumulates to indicate that this is not only a true relic but also a mysterious testimony to the reality of both the sufferings of Jesus and of his resurrection. In fact, the shroud is a testimony of the unique-ness of the Christian doctrine of the resurrection, particularly in view of the various attempts to analyze the formation of the image on the fibers of the linen cloth. There is no comparable physical evidence for the rainbow body. There are, however, several extant shrunken corpses of Tibetan masters who have passed away in recent years, such as Dudjom Rinpoche and Lama A Khyung. There are also numerous instances of post-cremation relics of unusual properties. However, these relics have not been subjected to detailed forensic tests.

·⚬· For the rainbow body as described in the traditional accounts of Bonpo and Nyingma yogins, there is not even a scientifically credible hypothesis, much less material evidence that can stand up to tests of falsification, as the internet skeptic bloggers will happily remind us. Although the rainbow body attainment is claimed for a limited number of yogins in every generation, in fact the manifestation is unpredictable, defies consistency, and leaves no evidence, at least nothing comparable to the shroud. As I have shown above, so far we have good interviews of eyewitnesses and the sincere faith and devotion of serious practitioners in the tradition.

The experience of millions of serious Buddhist meditators over the past 2,500 years does not seem to confirm the uniqueness, availability, or verifiability of the rainbow body attainment. Explanations restricting the attainment to the dzogchen lineages fly in the face of the hagiographical and yogic claims of other lineages. Such accounts attest to an internal atmosphere of polemics among the various lineages. There seems to be no viable hypothesis that might enable even an emic critic to put different traditions of practice to a test of authenticity. Many of the dzogchen practitioners were undoubtedly very serious and even learned, but there is a significant tradition of rainbow body attainers who seem to have followed a regimen of extremely simple practices that would have been available to other Buddhist followers of other lineages who never claimed this particular attainment.[482] The pieces of the puzzle do not fit with the evidence from other Buddhist lineages. At the same time, there are claims of bodily dissolution in some forms of Hindu mysticism, Ch'an, and Taoism. Finally, the sympathetic account of the early dzogchen lineages in the *Blue Annals* does not actually attest to the attainment of the rainbow body at all. In fact, the author of the *Blue Annals*, 'Gos Lotsawa, does not mention the exclusively dzogchen practices of trekchod and thodgal. Since these practices were known to Longchenpa, it may be a question of leaving unsaid something that was still considered sealed in secrecy within the lineages. 'Gos Lotsawa does attest to paranormal attainments among dzogchen practitioners such as levitation, moving through solid materials (rocks, earth, and mountains), walking on water, manifesting divine forms within mandalas visible to the general public, multiplication of food and drink, reading minds, producing miraculous harvests, passing one's hand through a stone column, being unhurt by an avalanche, and so forth. Interestingly, Lha rje sGro sbug pa, a master born in 1074 to whom 'Gos Lotsawa attributes the power of levitation, makes the claim that he will attain the abode of the rigdzins ("holders of contemplative awareness") at the time of death, but the report of his death only mentions some miraculous signs accompanying the rites of cremation. None of these manifestations goes beyond any of the miraculous deeds reported for Milarepa, and none of them corresponds to the self-arisen cremation fire that is said to have occurred at Milarepa's death rites.[483] Matthew Kapstein, in his article "The Strange Death of Pema the Demon Tamer," takes these ambiguous elements into account in his discussion of the claims of bodily dissolution in eastern Tibet, very much along the lines we are pursuing in these essays on the rainbow body phenomenon—but Kapstein did not have access to the interview materials that we were able to collect in eastern Tibet and at Mindrolling gompa.

Historical evidence in the form of the Dunhuang documents, steles, and archeological discoveries calls into question many of the claims made by traditional Tibetan *chos 'byungs* (religious chronologies) about the authenticity of the standard accounts of certain lineages of transmission. If anything, the evidence points in the direction of the far more interesting creativity, originality, and adaptability of the Tibetan yogins. Even native Tibetan historians critiqued apocryphal scriptures, fabricated hidden treasures, and created spurious accounts of miraculous deeds. Scholars have repeatedly encountered confused personal identities, sectarian bias, altered points of emphasis, disappearing categories, repetitions of previously established mistaken interpretations of the sources, incomplete use of sources, and polemically motivated alterations of the inherited biographical traditions. These habitual failures of disclosure render all Tibetan religious narratives suspect, requiring independent verification from non-Tibetan sources.

In the case of Khenpo A Chö, we have testimonies from his disciples and religious superiors that he was a man of consummate humility, altruism, and commitment to practice. Both before and after his training at Khandzé and Lhasa as a Gelugpa scholar, he followed the dzogchen teachings that had been widely disseminated in Nyingma circles since at least the ris-med movement of the nineteenth century. His high degree of spiritual realization is testified to in the spiritual qualities observable among his many disciples—male and female, lay and monastic. If his body did indeed dissolve as described by eyewitnesses, this accomplishment was the fruit of a life of intense spiritual practice that might have taken any number of forms including spontaneous ignition. The idea that this attainment is restricted only to a certain lineage, that the rainbow body is not the same as the light body or the illusory body of the six yogas traditions, or that the Khenpo only attained a dissolution of the atoms of the body and not even the rainbow body as one commentator asserts[484] is indicative of sectarian speculation. Early dzogchen accounts make no mention of these distinctions; the rainbow body is never compared to other yogic attainments; in fact, the notion of the rainbow body is hardly mentioned. Only in sources from much later in Tibetan history (post sixteenth century) do we find the divisions into categories and degrees of attainment.[485] Similar observations could be made with regard to other lineages that make claims of bodily dissolution, such as the bKa' brgyud pa. The extent that the rainbow body attainment is claimed exclusively for Bonpo and Nyingma dzogchen practitioners, and not for other Vajrayana Buddhist practitioners, suggests that what counts is the practice of dzogchen. To be fair, though the style is Vajrayana, the insider perspective is that dzogchen is a unique and unsurpassable view that integrates all others, precisely by being superior to them.

Surely these literary accounts have the earmarks of hagiographical formulae devised for sectarian purposes—possibly recycling the early, pre-Buddhist legends of the *dmu thig*, the cable connecting the early kings with the realm of the sky—with the intention of asserting a uniquely Tibetan character to this set of attainments. As such, the formulaic rainbow body contributes to a broad range of nationalistic tropes within Tibetan history, including the struggle for sovereignty between "red hats" and "yellow hats" and the endless struggles over center and periphery—little tradition and great tradition—down through the centuries.

The narrative of the rainbow body is a description in hagiographical terms of a centuries-long debate about authenticity and sectarian identity, with strong political overtones. In the case of Khenpo A Chö, as in the writings of the Great Fifth Dalai Lama, we can see an example of an irenic approach in which a Gelugpa re-assumes a nationalistic set of practices in order to be of service to a community undergoing massive cultural stress and dislocation. It is interesting that, during their interviews with me, the Gelugpa confrères of the Khenpo avoided discussing the rainbow body at all, probably in order to avoid the no man's land of sectarian polemics. It is important to recall that both the Great Fifth and the present Fourteenth Dalai Lama are unusual in being open to Nyingma spirituality, dzogchen, and even the terma traditions, but this openness is in contrast to prevailing trends among historical Gelugpa masters.

Khenpo A Chö was a Gelugpa master, in touch with the highest and most traditional representatives of his order, but he was born and raised in a Nyingma milieu. That he could unite Nyingma and Gelug in his own person as he pursued the highest spiritual attainments is a message for the world far more noble, credible, and universal than the paranormal dissolution of his corpse—and certainly more worthy of imitation. In the end, nature dissolves the body in any case, and the question of "*Che fine ha fatto?*" devolves into a set of poetic reflections on faith, devotion, and holiness among those left behind. This was precisely what we experienced with the joyous, but nostalgic, nuns at Kandzé.

Key Questions and Responses

Alas, sometimes a conclusion is not a conclusion, no more than an "end" is a final judgment on anything or anyone. The following are the kinds of questions that readers bring to this body of research, with the kinds of responses that I feel are respectful to the limits and possibilities of the data.

Is There a Connection between Dzogchen and Syriac Christianity?

Is there a connection between dzogchen and Syriac Christianity? In my opinion, with all due caution because the research is necessarily inferential, there must have been a connection. The argument in favor of a connection relies on the following highly probable human interactions during the relevant period of history (eighth–ninth centuries):

·֎· We know that there were collaborative connections between Central Asian Buddhism and Christianity. The Mahayana Buddhist translation project(s?) of the Buddhist monk Prajna and the Christian monk Jingjing, author of the Stele of Xi'an of 781 and other Syro-Oriental Christian works, has critically reliable historic attestation. In fact, the project was considered highly irregular and threatening by the Chinese Buddhist establishment, who sent a memorandum to the throne in protest. However, Jingjing knew enough about Daoism and Buddhism to be able to write elegant Chinese sutras presenting Christian teachings in the manner of the great religions of China. Although we know nothing about other Syro-Oriental Christian initiatives involving collaborative sutra translations, the Dunhuang manuscripts (probably datable to the late tenth century, two centuries after they were composed) are of such high quality that the existence of an ongoing Chinese Christian school of theologians can be inferred.

·֎· These Christian sutras demonstrate conceptual connections between Chinese Syro-Oriental Christianity and Ch'an and Hua Yen Buddhism. These are the Chinese Mahayana Buddhist schools most likely to have influenced the original pristine form of dzogchen as attested by the Tibetan documents found at Dunhuang, such as the *Six Vajra Verses* (*The Cuckoo of Awareness*) and *The Small Hidden Grain* by Buddhagupta.[486] I have indicated the connections to Daoism, Ch'an, and Hua Yen in my commentary on the Christian book on the "Realization of Peace and Joy." It is important to keep in mind that Chinese sutra translations after Kumarajiva (ca. 334–413) followed the rigorous approach of Central Asian Mahayana Buddhism. This is the kind of Buddhism that would have been practiced by the "western" monk Prajna, the collaborator of the Christian monk-prelate (*chorepiscopus*) Jingjing. It is also true that this same Prajna is thought to have worked with the Japanese tantric Buddhist Kukai, founder of the Shingon School, and to have translated tantric works.[487] The evidence for this is slender, but persuasive. In any case, Prajna did translate two Mahayana works crucial to Hua Yen and Ch'an Buddhism: *The Flower Garland (Avatamsaka) Sutra* and the *Heart Sutra*. The vocabulary and structural elements present in these sutras turn up in the works of Jingjing.

·◊· Both Tibetan dzogchen and monastic Syro-Oriental Christianity adhere to a highly convergent notion of spiritual life including the notion of primordial purity, visualizations of spheres of light, mind gazing on mind (soul gazing on soul) as light, three similar phases in the path of practice, and bodily transformation as an outcome (resurrection, body of light), without asserting that this literally happens at the time of death. Both traditions, along with Daoism and forms of Chinese Buddhism, assert that the masters may leave incorrupt bodies at death. In addition, there are strong notions of bodily immortality in these traditions. These claims are usually supported by relic production and incorruption of the venerated corpses of saints. Immortal beings are perceived by the heart of the disciple (perhaps in visionary experiences), not by the physical eye.

·◊· There are geographical connections that connect definite places with a mythical itinerary for the spiritual teachings relevant to the body of light. Although the Swat Valley is identified many times in later literature as the homeland of Padmasambhava, in reality there is little archeological support for the presence of tantric Buddhism in this area.[488] What has been found is compatible with discoveries in Maharashtra, for example at Ajanta and Ellora. However, the name "Urgyen" as a form of Oddiyana suggests the region south of the Aral Sea, where one of the main cities of Khwaresmia[489] was named Urganč (Organum).[490] Syro-Oriental Christian, Manichean, and Zoroastrian sites have been excavated in this region. In our commentary on the Garab Dorje biography, we have indicated why this legendary geography connects developments in Tibetan Buddhism along the lines of dzogchen with the Christian mystical teachings practiced in centers along the Silk Road. In effect, the Garab Dorje legend serves to reveal the tracks of these connections, by concealing what is basically the story of Jesus and Mary from the nineteenth surah of the Qur'an inside a literary jewel-box narrative based on Indian tantric liturgies and narratives. A comparable literary process can be seen in the well-known legend of *Barlaam and Ioasaph* in which the life of Buddha Shakyamuni undergoes extensive redactions in the course of many centuries, turning up at last as a Byzantine hagiographical account of Christian hermits.

·◇· A mass of documentary and archeological evidence would tend to support the otherwise rather obvious fact that along the Silk Road there was a great deal of debate, conversation, and exchange of ideas related to religious practices and beliefs. Where else in human history do we find so many prosperous cultural centers where several religions were practiced?[491] Manichean, Christian, Zoroastrian, Daoist, Buddhist, Sufi, and shamanic traditions were well known and accessible along this route that transported a great deal more than silk.

I'd like to add a highly speculative observation on possible links between dzogchen and the Syro-Oriental Christian appropriation of Evagrius of Pontus's ideas into the heart of Syriac Christian mysticism: Evagrius takes the term "variety" (Greek: *polupoikilos*, which may also mean "vast, infinite") from Ephesians 3:10 and quotes this verse more than seven times in the *Kephalaia Gnostica*—it appears more than any other verse from the New Testament. The verse is pregnant with mystical significance, which we can see by starting our citation from part of verse nine: "now shedding light on the concealed intention that was to come to pass; this mystery hidden in God the Creator of All for eons, so that now, by means of the Church, the immensely varied [i.e., infinite] wisdom of God might be made known in the heavens to the Principalities and Powers." In the first place, the reference to "light" (Greek: *photisai*) is a term specific to baptismal initiation, which meant participation in the divine light by which Christ was raised from the dead. The concealed intention in this verse specifically refers to the mission of the Church not only throughout the world but even beyond it among beings dwelling in the heavens (in this case, the text is referring to angelic powers assigned to assist the political authorities on earth). The author (St. Paul or a disciple) wants to articulate in the most superlative terms that the conversion of non-Jews to Christianity is a key moment in the unfolding of the revelation granted to believers in Christ. That the wisdom (which could be the capitalized Sophia of Proverbs 8, the feminine architect of the universe who assisted in the creation of all things) is multifarious, indeed, infinite and vast, corresponds to the objective of the passage. That is, the entire mission of the Church is empowered not by a motive of conquest and extirpation but of inclusion and reconciliation. This is exactly what the Syriac mystics experienced in their contemplation of the essence of all phenomena, again following Evagrius's system, and it is also the precise motivation for the Syro-Oriental Church's mission to the East, as expressed in the composition of mystical, synthetic sutras. Is this not also the meaning in Buddhist tantrism of Vairocana, the *infinitely variegated* Buddha at the center of the yoga tantra mandalas?[492] Matthew Kapstein points out that the fourth verse of the *Six Vajra Verses* refers to Vairocana Buddha by using the term "*sna tshogs rang bzhin*": a term usually translated as the "inherent nature of things in their variety." In the Dunhuang manuscript (IOL Tib J 647) translated by Karen Liljenberg,[493] the author of the text is identified with the name Vairocana as well. The text emphasizes the same Evagrian themes of nonduality, primordial purity, spontaneous presence, awe in nonconceptual experience, and inner simplicity[494] that we have seen in the texts cited from the *Kephalaia Gnostica*. Is this mere coincidence? A common set of contemplative archetypes? Or the result of profound conversations between masters whose degree of attainment would be difficult for us to measure? Fortunately, we do have these splendid texts, and our own experience as a first step towards understanding them.

Is There a Connection between the Rainbow Body and the Resurrection?

Is there a connection between the rainbow body and the resurrection of Jesus and indeed of all persons? This question, which gets at the crux of the problem, is the question that motivated Brother David to ask me to pursue this research in the first place.

We can begin with the oldest New Testament witness to the resurrection, which is mentioned not in the gospels but in the letters of St. Paul. I am going to emphasize I Corinthians 15, which was probably written in the period

50–52 AD, about twenty years after the death of Jesus of Nazareth, rather than I Thessalonians, the oldest surviving Christian document.[495] "I am transmitting to you the tradition that I myself received, that Christ died for our sins in accordance with the Scriptures, that he was buried, and that he was resurrected on the third day in accordance with the Scriptures, that he was seen by Peter (Kephas), then by the Twelve, and later seen by over 500 of the brethren. Later he was seen by James and by all the apostles. Last of all, he appeared also to me." (I Corinthians 15:3–8). The reference to the scriptures underlines the importance of continuity between the faith of ancient Israel (in the form of the Greek translation of the Old Testament, and *not* the Hebrew version that has been handed down as the Masoretic version) and the faith of Christians of both Jewish and Hellenistic backgrounds. The death for sin was therefore a confession of faith in a sacrificial death on the part of the Messiah (Christ) by which sins would be forever forgiven. We now know, thanks to the shroud research, that Jesus was buried in a special shroud made of the kind of linen that would have been worn by priests in the Temple in Jerusalem, the garb that would have been used on the Day of Atonement (Yom Kippur). It was not the usual procedure to bury anyone, much less a condemned criminal, in such linen. It is thus an interesting part of the tradition handed down that Jesus's death was a sacrifice for sin, just like the rites of Yom Kippur. Somehow, the facts of Jesus's burial included this ritual aspect, in spite of the horrendous circumstances under which the trial, execution, and burial took place. In spite of the use of the Greek word *egegertai* for "resurrect," it is not accurate to say that the resurrection is the same thing as resuscitation of a body, or the healing of a sick person. The Greek verb is used in the earliest formulations of the resurrection account (e.g., I Cor 15, 3–5), but this is a good example of how a word has many valences, many nuances of meaning. In describing a *new mode of being*, the authors used words that had a fixed set of meanings (to rise up, to arouse, to awaken, to rise up from a recumbent posture, to restore to health, to rebuild …) in the manner of Koiné Greek, in order to express a polyvalent faith experience that goes beyond the set of fixed literary meanings that dictionaries give us.

Apparitions are an effect caused on the perceptions of the visionary persons, but it still remains to seek to understand what may have caused the perceptions. Depending on what philosophical system we are working with, there is a perceiver and something perceived; subsequently there is interpretation and action. The action reveals to some extent the intentions of both perceiver and the one perceived, if only because the one perceived does not randomly appear and deliver messages all the time to everyone. Granted, in a nondualistic system, perceiver, act of perception, and the one perceived are considered unitary—a moment in a flow of perceptions. Perception, too, is linked to the notion of the perceivable attributes of a particular phenomenon. One of the ways to deconstruct the notion of a phenomenon's "existence" is to argue that once the attributes are removed, there is no phenomenon. Thus, there is thought to be no need for a metaphysical substrate to which attributes might "adhere." In any case, this is a classic Buddhist argument. Nevertheless, when an action takes place subsequent to a moment of perception, conditioned by that act of perception, even a nondualist system will have to acknowledge a flow of causality at least on the relative level. This analysis of course proves nothing, but it does suggest that the interpretation of a phenomenon depends on reflection, knowledge of what system we are using to interpret it with, and what intention we are advancing in our interpretation.

In the writings in which St. Thomas Aquinas seeks to interpret the Pauline texts on the resurrection, it is clear that resurrection is transformation into *an entirely different mode of being*. In the Pauline writings, this is called a *soma pneumatikos* (a body endowed with spirit, or "wind").[496] Paul also strongly emphasizes the connection between Christ's resurrection and the resurrection of all the dead (I Corinthians 15:12–20). It is useless for only one person to rise from the dead if there is no soteriological connection between that person and others who, by faith, have come to participate in the new mode of being of the resurrected person. The relationship between the risen Christ and the believer is analogous to the relationship between all human beings and the first man, Adam; Christ inaugurates an entirely new mode of being human. From verse 35 to 57, Paul goes on to explain in analogous ways how the resurrection may occur. It is quite clear from this passage that the resurrected body, whether of Christ or of the believer, is definitely in a new mode of being and is spiritualized, without precisely being "dematerialized." The embodied life of the children of Adam is transformed into the spiritual body of the man of heaven, Christ. The embodied life is radically changed: "We shall not all die, but we shall all be changed, in a flash, in the twinkling of an eye, at the last trumpet call … the dead will rise imperishable, and we shall be changed." (I Corinthians 15:51–52).

At the same time, the Catholic tradition affirms that in some irreducible way, the dead will rise, "with their bodies which they have now." (Fourth Lateran Council, 1215 CE) A considerable debate occurred about to what extent the resurrected body would be materially "the same" as that buried in the tomb, especially given the obvious fact that bodies can completely decay into dust in a few years after burial in certain locations. Two theologians in the fourteenth century, Durandus of S. Porciano and John of Naples, held that the identity of the soul alone is sufficient for the identity of the resurrection body with the person who had lived on earth.[497] This view seems to have been rejected by the majority of theologians in the scholastic period, and in modern times belief in a separable, immortal soul has also waned, largely because of a misunderstanding of ancient Israelite beliefs about the afterlife. Modern theology prefers to speak of the integrity and unity of body and soul, without however denying that after death there is the particular judgment of the individual soul. Saints can work miracles after death, both through their relics and by intercession in their purely spiritual nature—their immortal souls—abiding in union with God. However, the scripturally defined spiritual character of the resurrected body remained part of Catholic teaching under Scholasticism. Thomas Aquinas articulated the four qualities of the risen body in the *Supplement to the Summa Theologiae* Questions 82–85: *impassibilitas* (not capable of further suffering); *subtilitas* (subtlety, can pass through walls); *agilitas* (agility, can move easily and at great speed); and *claritas* (luminosity), since this body is free from sin or defilement it will be radiant as the transfiguration of Jesus. The bodies of the damned lack these qualities; however, they will be both incorruptible and immortal so as to undergo the punishments of eternal hell. As is typical of his theological project, Aquinas preserves the core meaning of Catholic tradition with great attention to equilibrium, wherever possible reconciling divergent views by a skillful use of reason.

In her book on the resurrection of the body, Caroline Bynum discusses in detail the belief that the bodies of the resurrected have to be materially the same as their bodies at death; however, she looks only at a particular (though admittedly very important) strand of theological tradition in a particular period of human history. The reason for this belief is that the sacraments are received in a particular body, and it is through the grace of the sacraments that we participate in the spiritual transformation that *is* the resurrection, transmitted by Jesus to us through the Church. However, this is not the only way to understand the resurrection of the body. The sacramental part of the teaching is very important. This human body bears the graced impact of its reception of the sacraments. When Paul speaks of receiving baptism for the dead (I Corinthians 15:29), he is connecting the teaching on the resurrection with the teaching on baptism. This also ties in to some very profound spiritual teachings in the Eastern Churches.[498] It is how relics are believed to work miracles, since the bodily relics of a saint carry the sacramental consecrations of all the sacraments that a person received while alive.

However, it is also possible to imagine theological developments in the light of scientific discoveries in our own times. We no longer think of protoplasm in the same way that we did a thousand years ago; microbiology and biochemistry have completely altered our knowledge of bodily processes, and even our idea of what a human body is; we now need to take into account microorganisms and even organelles, such as mitochondria, that have their own DNA and evolutionary history. From this perception what rises on the last day is in fact a community of living beings, symbiotically supportive of the self-emergence of consciousness, in accord with a physical, scientifically accessible genetic program. To the believer, this program is a "close fit" with the plan of God so magnificently praised in the theological hymn of Ephesians 1:3–23.

Does the Rainbow Body (or Any Other Paranormal Postmortem Phenomenon) "Really" Happen?

The Tibetan Buddhist faithful make a point to look for various signs at the time of death of great lamas.[499] For example, the abundant production of small spherical relics (*ringsel*) during the process of cremation is one of the signs that a monk at Khopan in Nepal manifested a few years ago.[500] Such unusual post-cremation relics have been reported for a number of Tibetan lamas. Also quite well known is the postmortem phenomenon of the body of a master who remained in meditation position, with the area around the heart still warm (*thugdam*), and incorruption lasting for as long as three weeks. At the time of death, after the *thugdam* ceases, the bodies of high lamas are preserved with salt and camphor, a process that clearly promotes the desiccation of the flesh. However, on rare occasions, there is shrinkage not only of the flesh of the deceased, but also of the bones; this typically occurs in the forty-nine-day period between death and cremation of the great lamas. Dilgo Khyentse is reported to have manifested this kind of shrinkage, and a number of years ago a Drikung Kagyu master reportedly did the same. Similarly, Dudjom Rinpoche's shrunken body has been preserved in a stupa in the Nyingma monastery near Boudha in Nepal. In the case of Khenpo A Chö, the entire body dissolved without leaving any relics. Rainbows and other light phenomena appeared at the time of his death. The dissolution took place under a piece of yellow cloth that had been placed over his body at the time of death. Disciples saw the gradual shrinkage of the body under the cloth over a seven-day period of time. No signs of decomposition occurred.

It would seem that something remarkable does occur in the bodies of certain yogis/practitioners of meditation in the dzogchen tradition(s), and possibly in others. There seems to be general agreement that the practices that lead to these kind of physical manifestations need to be done assiduously over a long period of time. In the case of Christian hermits and contemplatives, there are numerous instances of incorruption in both Catholicism and Eastern Orthodoxy, and a few rare cases of bodily dissolution (reported mostly in the Middle East and centuries ago, so they are hard to verify).[501] However, reports translated from Syriac and Arabic into French by Robert Beulay, a Belgian Carmelite priest who did research in Iraq, indicate degrees of realization comparable to those of dzogchen among Syro-Oriental Christian monks in the seventh through ninth centuries in Central Asia, at exactly the time period when dzogchen was emerging in Tibet. These kinds of information allows us to begin to hypothesize that ascetical lifestyles, assiduous contemplative practice, and visionary experiences create the conditions for the possibility of postmortem phenomena of various kinds.

The case of Jesus's resurrection presents some important contrasts with the cases of rainbow body attainers: most attainers (here Khenpo A Chö is exceptional) didn't have disciples and in fact were not learned or monastics—usually they were married lay folk living a humble, hidden lifestyle. The body of potential rainbow body attainers cannot be seen or touched after death (Jesus was embalmed and his body was handled in various ways after his violent death on a cross). The rainbow body strictly speaking should occur instantaneously—although in many reports it requires over about a week—but Jesus's resurrection took place (based on the evidence of the Shroud of Turin) within thirty-six hours, and there were no reports of light phenomena or rainbows. Rainbow body manifestations do not leave a high-energy imprint on cloth, but Jesus somehow managed to leave a kind of image of himself on the linen of his own shroud. The differences between the rainbow body and the resurrection in my opinion sustain the thesis that contemplative practice is essential, but that a particular sect or lineage is not.

We have also examined some historical materials to suggest that the modern dzogchen teachings on the rainbow body may represent a consolidation of a variety of much older, and less sectarian, practices and claims. Some of these practices have Christian origins, others seem to come in via Shaiva and Nathist practices. Others, more difficult to verify, may have come in via Manichean rites of eating and liberating particles of light bound within vegetable foods. The Tamil Siddhas's bodily transformation (*kayakalpa*) practices are also likely to be contemporary with early dzogchen and to have had some connection with China. The same limits with regard to tradition, history, and advances in science apply to the so-called rainbow body as they do to the Christian notion of resurrection. The "rainbow body" is a technical term only used in dzogchen. Even there, the dissolution into atomic particles is explained as a lower form of the phenomenon, not as the rainbow body. When it is said that hair and nails remain, the claim is that these are "impurities." What about the contents of the intestines? Many other questions remain. Why was there no image on the cloth that covered the body of Khenpo A Chö? The disciples covered the body with a cloth and offered prayers and circumambulations while the light phenomena continued for a week. When they removed the cloth, which I am told is now venerated in a chapel in the kLu ma gompa temple, there was nothing there, no stains, no marks, no image, and neither hair nor nails. Many scholars and anthropologists whom I have interviewed are convinced that the rainbow body accounts are to be taken as devotional hagiographical accounts intended to glorify the memory of the deceased. In some cases, it seems that the rainbow body accounts are a kind of apologetic strategy for the Nyingma and Bonpo traditions, which have experienced a number of periods of violent persecution in Tibetan history. It is interesting that the oldest accounts of dzogchen practice do not mention a rainbow body, although there are various accounts of miracles, some of which (having the power to stop blood flowing from a wound) seem to have natural explanations.[502] However, the case of the Bonpo monk who began to manifest signs of dissolution after death in 2001 seems to suggest that something paranormal does occur that merits further research. Recall that this episode has verisimilitude precisely because it ended in police intervention and the embarrassment of the monk's family. If nothing had happened at all, why would the family have called attention to the event? It would have been quite simple to compose a hagiographical account in the traditional manner, without any need for verification or eyewitnesses.

How Should Further Research Be Done?

Researchers need to examine, more critically and in greater detail, the kind of methodology needed in order to study the rainbow body phenomenon, and related end-of-life vindications. Since these phenomena are complex, we have used the methods of cultural anthropology in order to gather data. It is so far impossible to do laboratory experiments to verify or falsify the claims that certain highly realized masters manifest the dissolution of the body at death.

We have already mentioned the Shroud of Turin in our discussion of the resurrection of Jesus Christ. The great advantage that the shroud phenomenon has over the rainbow body is that it has now been studied for over a century by some of the most talented and critical scientific and historical researchers of modern times. It would seem that the methods that have been fruitful in studying the shroud could be adapted to study the rainbow body. In this way, an "impossible" preternatural phenomenon could come within the scope of critical research without necessarily invading the territory of a strictly theological or soteriological [i.e., infra-religious] approach. The research on the rainbow body is at a comparable point of development as shroud research in 1898—at the time of the first photographs of the Shroud of Turin. The scientific world was astonished by this extraordinary image by the Italian photographer Secondo Pia. No one expected that the shroud would have contained an image so completely unlike any other image of the crucified Christ. Even more astonishing, the negatives of these early photos showed that the image on the cloth was darker in those areas in which the body of the crucified man was in closer contact with the cloth than in those areas in which the cloth would not have been in contact. This meant that the image was formed in an unknown way by direct contact. In some way, the proximity of the cloth to the body of the crucified man determined the accuracy of the image produced on the fibers of the linen cloth known as the Shroud. This observation, confirmed in later studies—time after time—was completely unexpected. The Shroud image was neither a pious fraud fabricated by a medieval artist, nor a devotional image conforming to the expectations of Christian believers. Subsequent research made use of the following disciplines:

- The study of ancient textiles
- Art history
- Numismatics
- Botany, for the identification of plant silhouettes and pollen traces
- History of the Byzantine Empire
- Paleography of the Roman Empire
- Greco-Roman epigraphy (the study of inscriptions)
- Church documents preserved in various manuscripts in Greek, Latin, Aramaic, etc.
- Study of the religious beliefs and practices of the Jews in antiquity
- Archeology, including methods for dating ancient artifacts such as Carbon 14
- Forensic medicine related to the study of wounds and the decomposition of the human body after death

- ⟡ DNA testing of ancient blood samples, etc.
- ⟡ New Testament studies; study of the apocryphal Christian writings

Research on the rainbow body has a long way to go before we can claim such a complete roster of methods. In order to approach the level of Sindonology, we would need to have critical studies in the following areas:

- ⟡ History of dzogchen, particularly the terma traditions
- ⟡ History of Tibet; Tibetan mythology and linguistics
- ⟡ Study of yogic methods of spiritual practice in India, Tibet, Central Asia, and China
- ⟡ Forensic medical studies of extant Buddhist relics
- ⟡ Postmortem accounts of phenomena connected with yogins, Tibetan lamas, Chinese Buddhist, and Taoist masters, etc.
- ⟡ Research on postmortem incorruption, shrinkage, delayed decay, mummification, spontaneous bodily combustion, and the like
- ⟡ Research on Himalayan death rituals and customs, including the methods used for determining death and for the time to dispose of the body
- ⟡ Epigraphy and textual criticism in Tibetan, Chinese, Sanskrit, and other Asian languages
- ⟡ Repeated interviews over a long period of time with eyewitnesses and practitioners in the relevant traditions
- ⟡ Interviews with representatives of the traditions critical of the claims of those who present the rainbow body as a supreme spiritual attainment
- ⟡ Examination of police records regarding the deaths of persons claimed to have attained the rainbow body
- ⟡ Study of Tibetan apocrypha, *terma*, and other peripheral documentation including hagiography and epic
- ⟡ Quantum physics in relationship to human biology, including studies on bioluminescence
- ⟡ Scientific study of consciousness, meditation, end of life, and spiritual practice in the broadest sense (ritual, belief systems, hierarchical relationships, etc.)

Obviously, we are not at this point as yet, although there are a number of valuable publications available in Western languages in these fields. In the present book, what have we accomplished? We have presented the eyewitness accounts and discussed the probability of their veracity. We indicated the cultural anthropological parameters involved in this research. We presented the latest findings on the history of dzogchen, including evidence for reformulations of the notion of the rainbow body over the past 1300 years. We proposed some preliminary criteria for generating a scientific hypothesis on preternatural postmortem phenomena in Buddhist cultural settings, with the intention of offering a proposal for further scientific research in this field. We proposed some phenomenological approaches that might offer a critical control on the claims of believers without invading their belief system(s). Now it is time for other researchers to continue the investigation, whether from an emic or from an etic perspective, mindful that no one program of research can exhaust the data or finalize the interpretation of the data.

We have frequently employed the terms emic and etic in this research. In religious studies, one can take an emic, insider perspective and describe one's own religion or culture. Otherwise, one can take the position of the outsider, the observer from another point of view, an etic perspective. The etic perspective is not necessarily skeptical, but its criteria for evaluating truth claims will certainly be different from those of the emic perspective, even if the writer is a believer within some other system. In practice, the etic perspective is an adopted voice whose purpose is to communicate observations made in one cultural setting in order to inform and educate members of another cultural setting.

One of the risks of religious studies and anthropology generally is to forget that one participates inevitably in some kind of emic perspective. Thus, a "scientific" explanation for a particular anthropological or religious phenomenon needs to meet the criteria that "believers" in such perspectives (i.e., scientists and those who place their trust in them) will understand and respect. We are always translating, we are always describing an observed set of phenomena to a group of persons (a community of discourse) that for various reasons understand reality in ways that are distinct from the ways by which a particular society or religion understands reality. The task of the scholar is to translate[503] without betrayal, in other words to translate in terms that are faithful to the data gathered in the act of observation. This fidelity can be limited, however, by the set of assumptions that the scholar brings to the task of translation. Observation can be more or less accurate, depending on the extent to which the observer is thinking about how it might be possible to describe the experience of observation to an audience that has never had an experience of this kind. In other words, it is a major distraction during observation to pass from being the emic observer to the etic describer. The full-blooded participant observer attempts as complete an immersion as possible in the experience to be described. Shortly afterwards assisted by the work of other observers, the accuracy of recordings and photography, and the precision of one's own memory, the trained observer attempts to describe the experience. Only later upon further reflection, does the participant observer attempt to reformulate the written description in "scientific" terms that are composed in the literary forms acceptable to academic, scientific discourse. The emic observer must contend with other restrictions. If the emic observer is writing for the community of faith of which he or she is a part, the description needs to meet the criteria of accuracy respected in that community. The description may need to be cleared by the leadership of the community; even to write about certain reserved matters may require special permission. The writer may expect criticism from members of the community who may not agree with particular nuances or interpretations advanced in the published description. The observer-believer may omit features of the experience that do not correspond to the doctrines of the religion, or may enhance elements that promote the religion in order to encourage readers to become more observant, or to encourage nonmembers to become believers. Thus both emic and etic observers may be limited by an inner and outer set of screening processes and motivations. It might be helpful for the two kinds of observers to work together, or at least to exchange critiques of the reported observations, in order to achieve a higher standard of accuracy both in description and in interpretation.

In my experience as an observer, I attempted to gain a partially emic perspective by presenting myself always as I am—a Catholic priest who is knowledgeable about various world religions and who has studied some of the languages of South Asia. However, I have maintained a largely etic perspective in interpreting the data, always checking with believers to be sure that I have not slanted my interpretations with my own biases. At times, it is impossible to avoid the bias. It is certainly impossible to avoid the desire to communicate one's discoveries with a readership that is not restricted to Tibetan Buddhists or academic scholars, without at the same time restricting oneself to a readership that tends either to believe too much or too little of the "other"! One of the reasons some of the religious teachers from South and East Asia have complained about what they perceive to be the limits of the English language to translate the terminology of their religious systems may in fact not be about the limits of the language, as much as about the limits of academic criteria of acceptable discourse on religious topics. I have attempted to go beyond those limits, without becoming credulous or completely skeptical. At the same time, I have been candid about my personal religious perspective in this research.

I was directed to this project by my spiritual father, Brother David, and I felt a noteworthy component of paranormal "guidance" in the course of the work. Moreover, in the long interval between the interviews, over ten years ago, and this writing, I have had time to assimilate those experiences of inner guidance and to start to express myself along the fault lines between emic and etic; I have been personally engaged in both an insider process, as manifested in certain of my works of art since 1999 and in this body of research, which I have attempted to ground in cultural anthropology.

Obeyesekere's study of rebirth and karma suggests some interesting approaches to the relationship between myth and history. He is aware that myth often preserves a set of ideas over a comparatively long period of time in cultural history, enabling the writer to suggest that some elements of the "original" form of an idea may have been carried forward in time. He is also aware of the paradoxical nature of historiography, in which the tone is one of accuracy, a chronicle of actual events—when in reality, the sources used to support this perspective may in fact contain much that is mythic, interpretative, and of dubious origin. Not only does one need to know why an ancient writer might have been advancing a particular agenda, but one also needs to analyze why a particular manuscript or set of documents might have been allowed to survive. Then, there is always the question of the impact of an anonymous copyist who introduces interpolations that need to be checked against other similar documents. Historiography is an artful cultural exercise, seeking to make plausible use of materials that have been subjected to critical analysis and weighted in accord with their verisimilitude. But myth may always slither past our criticism, and it may do so precisely because myth often functions better than chronicles and annals as a bearer of plausible human motivations. Thus, when we say that the Tibetans often seem to prefer the myths of their own history to the chronicles and annals, we are simply stating something widely recognized in historiography, even in Enlightenment Europe.

Obeyesekere's essay *Karma and Rebirth*, a fruit of his mature research and reflection, directs our attention to Native American, Hellenistic, and Buddhist insights about death, karma, and rebirth. It is an investigation into some of the most fundamental representations of the human condition ever conceived. These representations have become archetypes lodged within the collective imagination of many surviving cultures. They also influenced the development of the cultures we refer to in our study of the encounter of religions in Central Asia. One of our concerns will be to sort out the "*Che fine ha fatto?*" question from the more intimate question of what a real flesh and blood human being must confront in the subjective environment of his or her own interiority. In other words: there is the public space in which a person's life is evaluated, and there is the interior space in which a person lives more or less conscious of the flux of thoughts, choices, and emotions.

One of the great insights of some contemplative traditions that correspond to modern phenomenology and existentialism is that the experiences of the inner person are in constant movement, and that it is impossible to postulate a human life entirely without psychosomatic fluctuations. Thus, the ancient claim of Patanjali that "yoga is the cessation of mental fluctuations" (*cittavrttinirodha*) may in fact be illusory, even for those who practice in that tradition, especially if the cessation is understood as anything other than temporary. Even if one were to go into a prolonged state of samadhi (as in the case of Gampopa, for example, in his encounter with Milarepa), that state must come to an end, and one must again contend with the realities of communal and social life. One must also contend with one's own thoughts about such experiences, and that contending often constitutes the true path to wisdom wherein the "self" is gradually eroded by the forceful discovery of inner freedom. What is particularly interesting for our study is that those contemplative traditions that recognize fluctuation and movement as a manifestation on the human level of higher consciousness are also those traditions that posit bodily transformations as a set of signs that confirm spiritual attainment. Whether in the form of resurrection or in the body of light, the vehicle is not separable from the attainment.

However the narrative may be rationalized, the attainment on the subjective level is evaluated above all between guru and disciple; the bodily signs are structured to include the wider community in this evaluative dialogue. Thus the Buddhist biographies speak of the hope that a realized master will leave behind relics to sustain the spiritual practice of the community. Leaving behind relics as a postmortem sign is recognized as a point of tension with the manifestation of the complete dissolution of the body—itself a supreme sign of inner attainment. For this reason, some dzogchen masters teach that a practitioner who accepts disciples will not attain the complete dissolution of the body but will instead leave relics behind for the sake of the disciples who survive him or her. Complete dissolution is usually encountered in the case of persons who practiced assiduously in secret. Such persons were often thought of as marginal, unintelligent, unpromising, and even eccentric. In their case, the dissolution of the body after death is a reply to the cynical side of the question *"Che fine ha fatto?"*

However, in the case of Khenpo A Chö, and in several other recent instances, the absence of relics left after death seemed part of a narrative of attainment in the context of the political situation of occupied Tibet—with its destruction of monasteries and retreat centers, imposition of a materialist worldview, and marginalization of Buddhist practitioners, along with the culture, religion, and society. Thus humbled, the practitioner can manifest complete bodily dissolution in order to communicate hope to a seemingly hopeless situation, the fact remains that overarching explanations should be understood flexibly and as not inexorable truths. For this reason, we open up our methodology to narratives and oral histories, each one of which is complete in itself even when accompanied by the mandala of its own community of discourse and belief. Each saint is unique; each hagiography is necessarily unique if it is to be true to the saint and to the process of sanctification in a particular tradition. In fact, "a tradition is a world," as L. Lhalungpa stated it so well in his translation of the Milarepa biography,[504] but we must keep in mind that each world of tradition is a dynamic process. To hand on the teachings means to keep them alive in the irreducibly unique lives of those who hand on and of those who receive, practice, and attain them.

Obeyesekere's comments on Plato further assist us in a critique of a purely "rationalist" approach to death and its accompanying narratives.

> ... Plato was not interested in conversion, but he addressed his message to those willing to listen, which for the most part meant the members of his academy. Nevertheless, like us he had to persuade his listeners and interlocutors to agree with him, and, like the Buddha, he did it through a form of dialogical discourse with dramatis personae who acted as strategic interlocutors. But unlike those of any other thinker that we have dealt with, Plato's doctrines of rebirth derived their force through the human faculty of Reason. I want to contrast this apotheosized Reason of the Greek Enlightenment with the 'Buddhist Enlightenment', in which reason is only given secondary place. All forms of Buddhism subscribe to the distinction between conventional and ultimate truths (Pali: *sammuti sacca* and *paramattha sacca*); ultimate truths are apprehended through penetration (*prativedha*), that is, through meditational ascesis and not through reason.[505]

This important insight contrasting Buddhist methods for attaining to truth with Platonic reliance on reason articulates one of the most important fault lines in the history of Western philosophy. The contemplative approach to the realization of the full potential of a human being was not unknown to the West. Certainly we find it in Plotinus and his school, in the various incarnations of Manichaeism, and in monastic Christianity. The great debate between St. Bernard of Clairvaux and the father of Scholasticism, Peter Abelard, is a watershed in Western thought that has resonated for nine centuries. In fact, the problematic aspects of some Western interpretations of Buddhism (signaled by Obeyesekere), seem to have their roots deeply entrenched in this debate.

For example, the Buddhist term "*catur-arya-satya*" is regularly translated as "the four noble truths," thus translating the middle term, arya, as an adjective and not as a noun. In fact, it is a noun that refers to a specific set of persons, "the noble ones," not necessarily members of the Aryan tribes in northern India, but rather those meditators who have discovered the highest spiritual truth following the Buddha's teachings and implementing them in a specific kind of meditational practice, which Obeyesekere calls "ascesis" (Greek for discipline or training). Thus, the four truths pertain to that which the noble ones have discovered through ascesis; the authentic meaning of the four truths (suffering, the cause of suffering, the suppression of suffering, and the eight-fold path that leads to liberation) is accessed only by those who meditate deeply and assiduously. Only these are "noble," or saints. Thus there is a specific kind of élite at the very core of the Buddhist sangha, whose identity is grounded in contemplative practice and attainment. Merely understanding the words used to list the four truths does not in any way constitute a person as a member of the noble ones. Debates over semantics, the logical consistency of statements, and the structure of grammar does not make one an Arya. Not even presenting a detailed analysis of the ways by which truths are known makes one an Arya. Only spiritual attainment, analyzed in various degrees (stream enterer, once returner, arhat, etc.), makes one a noble one.

Similarly, for St. Bernard, a coherent dialectical exposition of the meaning of various biblical and theological statements may be useful for understanding the language employed by the church to guide believers to salvation, but the exposition in itself does not gain salvation for the expositor. Only long hours of contemplative prayer, liturgical prayer, *lectio divina*, penance (ascesis), and physical labor over many years of faithful monastic commitment will disclose the true meaning of Christian salvation and sanctification. Wisdom is not attained in the time it takes to parse a line from the Apostles's Creed; wisdom reveals herself to those whose entire way of life is dedicated to her service. Abelard's radical rationalistic approach attacked the contemplative way of life; he sought to resolve the tensions he discovered in discordant sentences of scripture and theology using logic, reasoning and subtle semantic distinctions. Abelard's methods lent themselves to an academic environment in which people studied for a limited number of years, not always to complete a degree but simply to become familiar with the terminology and the rationale of the disciplines taught in the medieval universities. It seemed that his was the fast track to truth, eliminating years of perplexity and doubt for many, if not for all, spiritual seekers. In the expanding population of twelfth- and thirteenth-century Europe, the need for clergy, magistrates, administrators, physicians, and teachers was acute. Talented men attended lectures for two or three years before being employed by a feudal lord, a bishop, a monastic administrative bureau, a hospice for pilgrims, and so forth. Only those destined to teach formally in the universities would actually take the degrees of bachelor, magister, or doctor. There was clearly only a limited amount of time in which to gain knowledge, and Abelard's method was tailored to the needs of the times. Fortunately, St. Bernard's approach was upheld even within the universities by those religious orders that sent their members for studies. However, the very birth of modernity required the exclusion of the contemplative approach from the universities.

Only in recent years have attempts been made to rediscover contemplative approaches to consciousness and knowledge, usually in the form of studies of the brain function of people who practice forms of Buddhist meditation. The traditional Christian contemplative disciplines, East and West, are, if not extinct, better known through literary studies than through actual practice. The fact that these methods are known only to specialists in medieval literature is an indication of how difficult it will be to apply a knowledge of such methods to further study on the rainbow body and the resurrection.

In a recent speech inaugurating the new term (September 2014) at his Rangjyung Yeshe Shedra, H. E. Chokyi Nyima Rinpoche took up the task of demonstrating, from a Buddhist perspective, the validity of St. Bernard's monastic and contemplative approach to cognition. Of course, Rinpoche knows little or nothing of St. Bernard, but he articulated the issues with a rhetorical style tailored to the minds of his listeners, just as St. Bernard would have done with his students from the University of Paris in the twelfth century. Naturally, it is my hope that Christians, Muslims, Hindus, and Buddhists who are aware of the issues at stake might work together in a search for truth, as Emperor Ashoka advised in his Rock Edicts of the third century B.C.[506]

Returning to the quote from Obeyesekere, we note that the dialogical method known as the Socratic Method was geared to persuade. Plato reports on how Socrates would ask his students or interlocutors leading questions in order to prod the inquirer to look more deeply into the implications of his previous assertions. In a Platonic/Socratic dialogue, flawed assertions are rectified by depicting likely outcomes of such assertions under various circumstances. The persuasive formulation of an imaginative model in which errors are exposed on the basis of their consequences and force of reason in these discussions takes on the students's opinions in order to arrive at the truth is established on the basis of desired outcomes. The articulation of truth requires the dialogue, or debate, between differing models of what is desirable, until one or the other model gives way to the approach that seems most fitting (to the transcendental criteria of beauty, goodness, and truth). It is important to note that here reason is a model constructed in the imagination and debated with words. As in Platonic thought generally, the imaginative model or archetype is constructed so as to establish an abstract principle of that which is true. In other words, an abstraction or model is a generalization, tested by comparing likely outcomes.

Buddhist philosophers were, and are, also perfectly capable of critical analysis and debate. The doctrine of the "two truths"—conventional truth and ultimate truth—is foundational for Buddhist reasoning: Conventional truth (*samvrtisatya*) is in fact true in relation to the observable world; this kind of truth is attained through a critical, dialectical process that employs reason at least as rigorously as Plato, Socrates, or Aristotle would have done. However, superior to this kind of truth is an ultimate truth that can be determined only by following the gradual path of meditation experience (*bhavana marga*). Meditation experience may be discursive or nondiscursive in character and should not be reduced to a discursive attempt to derive conclusions by inference or deduction. The Western problem of metaphysics after Kant arises precisely at this point: the refusal to engage with the contemplative methods of any tradition confines the Western philosopher to reasoning about and within the sphere accessible to sense data. Anything that might be imagined or implied by an intuitive or aesthetic experience, or inferred on the basis of a broad spectrum of perceptions, but that cannot be tested materially is automatically set aside as "metaphysical" or "mystical." As a result, as far as a Buddhist or for that matter St. Bernard might be concerned, these restrictions are a strait jacket, impeding epistemological penetration (Sanskrit: *prativedha*) of the most profound truths of existence. Thus a philosopher strictly within the confines of Western notions of "reason" can never be an Arya, because such a person will never be a yogin, with the possible exception of a true Neo-Platonist.

Buddhism, and other South Asian spiritual traditions (as well as contemplative forms of Christianity, Islam, and Judaism), assert that by means of yogic/meditative processes, an ascetic penetrates to the true nature of reality in a way that is not merely subjective. The discovery of a higher or deeper level of truth is asserted by all the great traditions when they speak of ultimate reality, and it is precisely this assertion that post-Kantian thought excludes from the sphere of reason. Thus, it has become impossible to recover from Peter Abelard's point of view, not because metaphysics is wanting in logic, but because the processes of human transformation are blocked by the prevailing insistence on conventional truth. To put it another way, people are not allowed by the prevailing worldview to connect existentially with their innermost sense of being. The problem is not about language or the capacity of the discursive rational mind to discern and to perceive; it is about denying human beings a faculty that they already have—a faculty that has been nurtured for millennia by some of the most remarkable people who have ever lived. This is the price our world has paid for its material progress.

It is with a sense of irony that one returns to Plato with a critical perspective. Consider that many of the positions that seemed "rational" to Platonists down through the ages (including Aristotle, the Arab commentators, Aquinas, the later scholastics down to Leibnitz) are no longer accepted as reasonable or true. Conventional truth is just that: conventional, agreed upon, and therefore mutable. In fact, the process of determining conventional truth is endless and can produce results that are at least as self-contradictory as the statements that Abelard was trying to rectify.

Even the so-called scientific method may be identified with the method of Platonic "reason." Science is a system that responds to a set of observable data with a hypothesis, which is essentially an imaginary model whose purpose is to generalize the data into mathematical constructs that may or may not be useful in predicting or evaluating other sets of data. Scientific discoveries may be falsified by experimental data. Then the scientists return to the computer to generate new, hopefully more accurate models. Otherwise, experimental data are subjected to further tests, which can be thought of as an exercise in persuasion, designed to establish the veracity of a particular hypothesis. As such, science can usefully be seen as a cultural product designed to critique and persuade. Scientific paradigms or laws are in effect models that have undergone a process of cultural assimilation through experimental testing, itself a cultural activity. Experimental testing is subject to critical analysis with regard to the reliability of the data obtained, the refinement of the experimental procedures, the accuracy of the interpretation of the data in published reports of the experiment, and finally their replication in other laboratories.

The neglected scientific laboratory of the *bhavana marga* (practicing meditation) leading to *prativedha* (noetic insight), might usefully be revisited. Practicing meditation systematically over a long period of time could be conceived as a kind of experiment to discover whether it is possible to open up human awareness to higher, deeper, more reliable dimensions of consciousness than those accessible through discursive reason. Going beyond phenomenological studies of empathy, insight, intuition, and aesthetics, this kind of research could deconstruct the impasse that exists between contemplative epistemology and post-Kantian restraints on human knowing.

Practically the entire history of Western philosophy has been a narrative of this fundamental problem of the separation between the contemplative practices that elicit the discovery of a higher dimension of consciousness and the use of the discursive intellect to understand or to explain observable phenomena. Yoga is set against *pramana* (spiritual discipline versus inference). Some forms of modern phenomenology have tried to overcome the bifurcation in Western thought, and hence we have Guenther's use of Heidegger[507] in a skillful attempt to translate Buddhist philosophy into Western literary forms. I think that Guenther's approach enables us to move beyond the foundationalism and substance/nature discussions of the Hellenistic heritage, into a more dynamic, dialogical, and evolutionary form of philosophy. In effect, we are coming to discover the human person as a subject irreducibly in dialogue with inner and outer environments across the span of a conscious lifetime, which is exactly the perspective of meditation-focused traditions as well. Here is an example in the journals of Thomas Merton of the breakthrough that can occur when an astute contemplative, sensitive to philosophical issues, arrives at a nonfoundational, nonsubstantial insight about the self as process:

> The time has probably come to go back on all that I have said about one's "real self" etc. etc. And show that there is after all no hidden mysterious "real self" other than or "hiding behind" the self that one is, but what all the thinking does is to observe what is there or to objectify it and thus falsify it. The "real self" is not an object, but I have betrayed it by seeming to promise a possibility of knowing it somewhere, sometimes as a reward for astuteness, fidelity, and a quick-witted ability to stay one jump ahead of reality. However, the empirical self is not to be taken as fully "real." Here is where the illusion begins.[508]

The key point here is that our construction of death may feed this illusion of the self: it is as if to die well were to confirm (and to die badly to deny) the basic truth of the personified "self," and that by having abandoned behaviors associated dualistically with some notional false self one has been a better, or worse, expert in constructing a "true self." The journal entry shows how such a crucial insight might emerge in a serious practitioner: in this case a practitioner of the contemplative tradition descending from St. Bernard. It also helps us understand Merton's interest in Buddhism as more than academic; it is as if he were already practicing under a Buddhist master simultaneously as he continued his Christian monastic practice. This background certainly prepared him for the encounter, four years later, with Tibetan Buddhist leaders in exile in India. What is also important is that the journals recount the kind of spontaneous experiences[509] that orient a person towards the *bhavana marga* and of the phenomenal breakthroughs that occur in the course of maturing the *marga* through assiduous practice. One does not usually get this kind of insight by an exercise in logic or dialectics. St. Bernard, John of Dalyatha, Vairotsana, Nupchen, and Longchenpa were onto something.

Khenpo A Chö hermitage: two elderly women disciples

I now give Gerard Manley Hopkins the final word of resurrection:

> Man, how fast his firedint, his mark on mind, is gone!
> Both are in an unfathomable, all is in an enormous dark
> Drowned. O pity and indignation! Manshape, that shone
> Sheer off, disseveral, a star, death blots black out; nor mark
>   Is any of him so stark
> But vastness blurs and time beats level. Enough! The Resurrection,
> A heart's-clarion! Away grief's gasping, joyless days, dejection.
>   Across my foundering deck shone
> A beacon, an eternal beam. Flesh fade, and mortal trash
> Fall to the residuary worm; world's wildfire, leave but ash:

In a flash, at a trumpet crash,
I am all at once what Christ is, since he was what I am, and
This Jack, joke, poor potsherd, patch matchwood, immortal
   Diamond,
         Is immortal diamond.[510]

NOTES

Introduction

1 John Lukas, *At the End of an Age* (New Haven: Yale University Press, 2002), 98.

2 Lukacs, ibid., 98.

3 Lukacs, ibid.

4 Lukacs. ibid.

5 Lukacs, ibid., 99.

6 Pier Luigi Luisi, *Mind and Life: Discussions with the Dalai Lama on the Nature of Reality*. (New York: Columbia University Press, 2009), 30–32.

7 Eloise Meneses, Lindy Backues, David Bronkema, Eric Flett, and Benjamin L. Hartley, "Engaging the Religiously Committed Other: Anthropologists and Theologians in Dialogue," *Current Anthropology* 5:1 (February 2014), 82–104. A recent example from the debate between science and Protestant Christianity can be found in this article.

8 www.isites.harvard.edu/icb. This site presents a succinct summary of the emic/etic distinction.

9 Tiso, "Research notebook," August 23, 2002.

10 *Aggañña Sutta,* "On Knowledge of Beginnings," verse 10, in *The Long Discourses of the Buddha: A Translation of the Digha Nikaya,* Maurice Walshe, trans. (Boston: Wisdom Publications, 1995), 409–410.

11 "Examination of the Doctrine of God" in *The Tattvasangraha of Shantaraksita with the Commentary of Kamalashila*, vol. I, trans. Ganganatha Jha (Delhi: Motilal Banarsidass, 1986). This is an attempt to prove that such a being cannot be the cause of phenomena. This philosophical work is a collaboration between the two scholastic Buddhist masters who were invited to teach in Tibet in the second half of the eighth century.

12 David Francis Germano, "Poetic Thought, The Intelligent Universe, and the Mystery of Self: The Tantric Synthesis of rDzogs Chen in Fourteenth Century Tibet," PhD diss., University of Wisconsin, 1992.

13 Ibid., 18.

14 Ibid., 17–18.

15 Merrill Peterson and Kennard Lipman, trans., *Longchenpa: You are the Eyes of the World* (Ithaca: Snow Lion, 2000).

16 Patanjali, *Yogasutras* I, 2. *Cittavrttinirodha*, as the definition of yoga.

17 In post-colonialist analysis, emic and etic are reducible to two emic perspectives, one of which tries to reduce the other to a subaltern status. Thus,

academic materialism and scientific reductionism try to assert their perspectives as objectively "etic", over against "emic" religious consciousness, represented as collective manifestations of human confusion, alienation, fear, lack of semantic coherence, and guilt.

18   The five-hundred-year war against contemplative institutions in Western Europe is an example of how history written by the "victors" can suppress unpleasant truths. In this case, the consequences of the suppressions under Protestant and Enlightenment-inspired regimes continue to resonate in the practices of European bureaucracies and in the textbooks used in European schools. Unfortunately, knowledge of the facts is restricted largely to ecclesiastical circles. The ruined hermitages and "tourist site" monasteries are quite in evidence, however, to those willing to travel off the beaten path. The same history is being enacted in our own times in Tibet.

19   Matthew Kapstein, "The Strange Death of Pema the Demon Tamer" in Matthew T. Kapstein, editor, *The Presence of Light: Divine Radiance and Religious Experience* (Chicago: University of Chicago Press, 2004).

20   Interview with Loppon Tenzin Namdak in Kathmandu, March 11, 2001.

21   Sanskrit, *siddhi*. The related term *siddha* means one who has attained "*siddhi*"; *siddhi*s include lesser miraculous abilities as well as the higher attainments of enlightenment or liberation, such as liberation while still in the embodied state: *jivan-mukta*.

22   David Gordon White. *The Alchemical Body: Siddha Traditions in Medieval India.* (Chicago: University of Chicago Press, 1996).

23   B. Natarajan, ed., *Tirumular's Tirumantiram* (Mylapore, Madras: Sri Ramakrishna Math, 1991).

24   In this verse, we can see the sinuous aesthetic of Tamil poetry: Tamil: *Anbenum uyirolir arive/ Anbenum anuvul amaindhaper oliye/ Anburuvaam para Sivame.*

25   T. R. Thulasiram,. *Arut Perum Jothi and Deathless Body: A Comparative Study of Swami Ramalingam with Sri Aurobindo and the Mother and Tirumoolar,* vol. I . (Madras: University of Madras, 1980), 15.

26   Ibid., 413–420.

27   Namkhai Norbu, oral commentary on *Rigbai Kujyug: The Six Vajra Verses,* ed. Cheh-Ngee Goh. (Singapore: Rinchen Editions, 1990).

28   Author's interview in Pondicherry with Tulasiram, February, 2003.

29   See chapter two in this book.

30   There are in fact some aspects of the biography of Ramalinga that resemble biographical episodes reported for the ancient Greek philosopher Empedocles.

31   James L. Kugel, *Traditions of the Bible: A Guide to the Bible as It Was at the Start of the Common Era* (Cambridge: Harvard University Press, 1998), 104–05, 325.

32   Mary Boyce,. *Zoroastrians: Their Religious Beliefs and Practices,*. (London: Routledge and Kegan Paul, 1979), 14–15, 27–28.

33   The Tamil Siddha tradition represented by Tirumular is quite in contrast with Patanjali's *Yoga Sutras*, given that Patanjali is considered to have been a Tamil. For example, his image may be found among the sculptures on the great temple of Chidambaram.

34   David Gordon White, *The Alchemical Body*. This use is extensively reported under "mercury" and "rasayana".

35   Manjusrimitra, *Primordial Experience: An Introduction to rDzogs-Chen Meditation*, trans. Namkhai Norbu and Kennard Lipman with Barrie Simmons. (Boston and London: Shambhala, 1987), xii–xiii.

36   Ian A. Baker and Thomas Laird, *The Dalai Lama's Secret Temple: Tantric Wall Paintings from Tibet* (New York: Thames and Hudson, 2000), 144.

37   Jason David BeDuhn, *The Manichaean Body: In Discipline and Ritual* (Baltimore: Johns Hopkins University Press, 2000), see esp. chaps 4 and 6.

38   Ibid. See also, Michael Walter, "Jabir the Buddhist Yogi, Part III. Considerations on an International Yoga of Transformation," *Lungta* 16 (Spring 2003): 21–36.

39   Livia Kohn, ed.,. *The Taoist Experience: An Anthology,* (Albany: State University of New York Press, 1993).

40   Thomas Cleary, trans., *The Secret of the Golden Flower: The Classic Chinese Book of Life* (San Francisco: HarperSanFrancisco, 1991). The translator hints that this syncretic work is from the late eighteenth century, the time of Jigmé Lingpa, the Tibetan terton, among other luminaries.

41   Approximately 750–850 for the first diffusion; 850–1000 for the "dark age," or "age of fragmentation."

42   B. A. Litvinsky, Zhang Guang-Da, R. Shabani Samghabadi, eds., *History of Civilizations of Central Asia, vol. III, The Crossroads of Civilizations A.D. 250 to 750* . (Delhi: Motilal Banarsidass, 1999).

43   Matthew T. Kapstein, *The Tibetans,* (Oxford: Blackwell Publishing, 2006), Chap. 3;. Christoph Cüppers, ed. *The Relationship Between Religion and State (chos srid zung 'brel) in Traditional Tibet,* (Lumbini, Nepal: Lumbini International Research Institute, 2004). For greater detail, see these works.

44   Matteo Nicolini-Zani, *La via radiosa per l'Oriente* (Magnano, BI: Edizioni Qiqajon, 2006). This work includes outstanding translations and a large bibliography.

45   Ronald Roberson, C.S.P., *The Eastern Christian Churches: A Brief Survey*, 3rd ed. (Rome: Edizioni Orientalia Christiana, 2008), Appendix I, 185ff.

46   William Dalrymple, *From the Holy Mountain,* (New York: Henry Holt, 1997).

Chapter I

47 Composed by Tshophu Dorlo, also known as Pema Gyurmé Gyamtsho. Translated by Yaroslav Kormatovsky and Francis Tiso.

48 The reader will note that the account weaves back and forth seamlessly between Gelugpa and Nyingma communities of practice.

49 The abbreviated form of the local monastery in the town where, at the end of his life, he attained the dissolution of the body.

50 One of the early translators of dzogchen teachings during the imperial first diffusion period, end of the eighth century.

51 At the moment of his death, the Khenpo was reciting *Om mani padme hung,* the mantra of Avalokiteshvara.

52 *Yidam* is the Tibetan word for one's tantric tutelary deity, the principal deity of the mandala of a particular tantric liturgical cycle.

53 According to my research assistant, the term'"body of light" is used here by mistake, most probably because our author felt the prophecy had to be fulfilled in some way. From a strictly Nyingma scholastic point of view, what Khenpo A Chö attained was actually not the body of light but disintegration of the body into atoms. The tradition mentions four types of bodily dissolution: if one attains the body of light, others see his body instantly turning into a mass of fire. In the case of Khenpo A Chö, the body gradually disappeared. Attainment of the authentic body of light is an inseparable part of attaining the great transference. The Nyingma scholastic tradition says that this is one of the rarest of special attainments, much less commonly reported than the atomic dissolution of the body.

54 Sonam Phuntsok (bsod nams phun tshog), *The Chariot That Pulls the Sun of Faith and Devotion,* supplement to the biography of the great abbot Dorje Chang Lopsang Ngawang Khyentse (*mkhen chen rdo rje 'chang blo bzang nga dbang mkhyen brtse'i snang bad pal bzang po'i rnam par thar pa'i kha bskangs dad gus nyin byed 'dren pa'i shin rta.*)

  And by the same author: "*The Chariot That Pulls the Sun of Faith and Devotion.*" This is a supplement to the biography of the great abbot Dorjechang Lopsang Nagwang Khyentsei Nanwa Pel Zangpo (*mkhan chen rdo rje 'chang blo bzang ngag dbang mkhyen brtse'i snang ba dpal bzang po'i rnam par thar pa'i kha bskangs dad gus nyin byed 'dren pa'i shin rta zhes bya ba*)

  Tshophu (mtsho phu rdor lo), *alias* Pema Gyurmé Gyamtsho (pad ma 'gyur med rgya mtsho). *The Song of the Queen of Spring Coming from Afar, Ornament of the Vajra Vehicle of the Old Translation School, Sole Jewel of Jambudvipa.* The condensed biography of the precious abbot A Chö, whose body dissolved into atoms without remainder on the seventh day of the seventh lunar month of the Year of the Earth-Tiger of the seventeenth rabjung in Nyagrong in Khams (*Khams nyag rong du rab byung bcu bdun sa stag lo'i zla ba bdun pa'i tshes bdun la gzugs sku rdul phran lhag med du deng bam khan rin po che a chos kyi rnam thar snying bsdus dpyid kyi rgyal mos rgyang glu snga 'gyur rdo rje theg pa'i khyad chos 'dzam gling brgyan gcig.*)

_____. *Those Persons in Tibet whose Aggregates turned into the rainbow body due to the practice of dzogchen.* (*bod du rdzogs pa chen po nyams su len pas phung po 'ja' lus su gshegs pa*).

Tupten Chokyi Wangchuk (thub bstan chos kyi dbang phyug). *Biography of Tshewang Rigdzin, the Great Abbot who accomplished the Rainbow Body ('ja' lus ba mkhan chen tshe dbang rig 'dzin gyi rnam thar*).

55 Particularly of the type in which a person is to make a representation of the Three Jewels in some form so as to be liberated from bad rebirths, according to the *Tsig mdzod chen mo,* a large Tibetan language dictionary

56 "Mo" divination involves tossing a rosary in the air, catching it with two hands, and counting the number of beads between both hands. The resulting count is evaluated in accord with Tibetan numerology.

57 The key term "view" refers not only to the doctrinal assertion of nonduality between perceiver, object perceived, and the act of perception but also to the state of awareness or of contemplation in which this nonduality is experienced directly.

58 Lama A Khyug did manifest paranormal phenomena at death, leaving a greatly shrunken body relic, which has been part of the Buddhist relic tour sponsored by Lama Zopa in recent years.

59 Prophesy has an important place in Tibetan Buddhism. On the basis of promises made in former lifetimes, a future spiritual encounter may be predicted. Also, Tibetans make extensive use of divination to assess events and confirm prophetic claims made about particular individuals, especially tulkus.

60 So it might have taken less than seven days.

61 This probably refers to Kundun Rinpoche, His Holiness the Dalai Lama.

62 Yongdzin Lopön Tenzin Namdak, *Masters of the Zhang Zhung Nyengyud: Pith Instructions from the Experiential Transmission of Bönpo Dzogchen,* Carol Ermakova and Dmitry Ermakov, eds. (New Delhi: Heritage Publishers, 2012).

63 Lopon Tenzin Namdak, *The Dark Retreat According to Shardza Rinpoche,* John M. Reynolds, ed.and trans. (Bischofshofen, Austria, transcript, April 1991).

64 For example, Dilgo Khyentse and Dudjom Rimpoche. Recently, a photograph of the shrunken relic body of Lama A Khyug has appeared on a website related to Lama Zopa's relic tour.

65 Marion H. Duncan. "The Kingdom of the Dead," in *Customs and Superstitions of Tibetans*, (Delhi: Book Faith India, reprint 1998).114, 117. Duncan mentions shrunken bones of an ordinary person and the use of mummification for high lamas.

66 Charles Ramble, "Status and Death: Mortuary Rites and Attitudes to the Body in a Tibetan Village," *Kailash*, (1982): 333–54.

67 Matthew T. Kapstein, "Strange Death of Pema the Demon Tamer," in *The Presence of Light: Divine Radiance and Religious Experience* (Chicago: University of Chicago Press, 2004), 119–56. Compare Kapstein's chapter, which covers much of the same ground as this chapter. Kapstein concludes with a reference to a news report on Khenpo A Chö.

68 Robert R. Desjarlais,. *Body and Emotion: The Aesthetics of Illness and Healing in the Nepal Himalayas.* (Philadelphia: University of Pennsylvania Press, 1992).

69 Rinpoche lived with the Benedictine monks on Cauldey Island for several years.

70 Khenpo Tsultrim Lodro, *dPal bla rung gi mkhan po tshul khrims blo gros kyi gsung 'bum bzhugs so// deb dang po,* (1996), 289–97.

Chapter II

71 Sam Van Schaik, "The Early Days of the Great Perfection," *Journal of the International Association of Buddhist Studies* 27 (2004): 1:166–206, 182–90.

72 David Germano, "The Funerary Transformation of the Great Perfection (Rdzogs chen)," *Journal of the International Association of Tibetan Studies* 1 (October 2005), THDL #T1219.

73 Michael Aris, *Hidden Treasures and Secret Lives: A Study of Pemalingpa (1450–1521) and the Sixth Dalai Lama (1683–1706)* (Delhi: Motilal Banarsidass, 1988), 104–06.

74 Aris, Ibid., 113. For the wall painting, see Ian Baker and Thomas Laird, 204.

75 Janet Gyatso, *Apparitions of the Self: The Secret Autobiographies of a Tibetan Visionary* (Princeton: Princeton University Press, 1998). Jigmé Lingpa's (1730–1798) life is presented here.

76 Ibid, 143–44; E. Gene Smith, *Among Tibetan Texts: History and Literature of the Himalayan Plateau*, ed. Kurtis R. Schaeffer (Boston: Wisdom Publications, 2001), section VI. See this work for a description of the *ris-med* (nonsectarian) movement which was deeply influenced by Jigmé Lingpa.

77 The basic research for this section was contributed by the talented Russian translator and practitioner, Slava Komarovsky, who also tutored the author in literary Tibetan in 1997. In this highly technical section, key Tibetan terms are given in Wylie transliteration.

78 In this book, lower case "dzogchen" stands for the entire tradition of non-transformational realization of the natural state, from its earliest manifestations to the present day, including all its literary and institutional aspects. Specific documents within the tradition are indicated in accord with their sectarian affiliation.

79 Van Schaik, "The Early Days of the Great Perfection," 182, shows that an early form of the "nine vehicles" formula already exists in certain Dunhuang manuscripts, thus dateable to the late tenth century.

80 Tiso, *Liberation in One Lifetime* (North Atlantic Books, 2014).

81 Ibid, 189–90.

82 Ibid, 291-92.

83 Chokyi Nyima Rinpoche, *Union of Mahamudra and Dzogchen* (Hong Kong: Rangjyung Yeshe Publications, 1989), for a discussion of this topic.

84 Baker and Laird, *The Dalai Lama's Secret Temple,*. 85–86

85 Nalinaksha Dutt, *Early Monastic Buddhism* (Calcutta: Firma KLM Private Ltd., 1981) 191–92.

86 Tiso, *Liberation in One Lifetime*, 280.

87 Jigmé Lingpa, *Chariot of Omniscience* (*rnam mkhyen shin rta*) vol. 4, 35.

88 In chapter three, we will see how the Syro-Oriental Christian monk-prelate, Jingjing, turns this insight into a teaching of Jesus.

89 That is, a lasting metaphysical substrate that sustains the identity or nature of a thing.

90 Francis V. Tiso and Fabrizio Torricelli, "The Tibetan Text of Tilopa's *Mahamudropedeśa*," *East and West* 41 (1-4) (IsMEO, 1991): 205–29.

91 Keith Dowman, *The Flight of the Garuda: Teachings of the Dzokchen Tradition of Tibetan Buddhism* (Boston: Wisdom Publications, 1994).

92 Jigmé Lingpa (*'jigs med gling pa*). *Chariot of Omniscience* (*Rnam mkhyen shing rta*). In *The Collected Works of Kun-mkhyen 'Jigs-med-gling-pa*, vol. 2, Sonam T. Kazi, ed.Lhasa Edition Gangtok, India: Ngagyur Nyingmay Sungrab), 122–877.

93 In fact, dzogchen systems also make use of a program of extraordinary preliminary practices analogous to those of Vajrayana. These practices seem designed to bring disciples burdened with negativity towards a level of purity and sensitivity that will allow them to benefit from dzogchen practice. In this way, they will avoid the failure experienced by Milarepa in his early training in dzogchen.

94 See Baker and Laird, *The Dalai Lama's Secret Temple*, 146. Here the Vajra chains are depicted like beads on a rosary, p. 146.

95 Kongtrül Yönten Gyamtsho (*kong sprul yon tan rgya mtsho*) / Lodrö Tayé (*blo gros mtha'yas*).Limitless Ocean of Knowables (*Shes bya mtha' yas pa'i rgya mtsho*), vol. 3. (Peking: Mi rigs pe skrun khang, 1982).

96   Ibid.

97   Tiso, *Liberation in One Lifetime*, 245–46.

98   Kongtrül Yönten Gyamtsho, ibid.

99   Tiso, *Liberation in One Lifetime*, 259–73, for a translation of *The Biography of Vajradhara* by rGyal Thang pa.

100   As we were told emphatically by Lama A Khyug during our interview in 2000.

101   The consensus of biblical scholars is that I Thessalonians, Galatians, Philippians, Romans, I and II Corinthians, and Philemon are authentic. Ephesians and Colossians are either by Paul or a close disciple. I and II Timothy, II Thessalonians, and Titus are by a disciple; and Hebrews is by another author with some connections to the circle of Paul's disciples.

102   As usual, a google search of these items will turn up a variety of sources, not all of which are reliable. I have visited the Bolsena and Lanciano Eucharistic miracles personally, and find the Lanciano episode historically problematic but scientifically convincing. The Buenos Aires miracles of the 1990s seem to be convincing, but I do not have direct evidence for their authenticity, other than what is reported on-line. As I will discuss in the next chapter and in the conclusions, I find the Shroud of Turin convincing, but have reservations about the Manupella image. Moreover, I will discuss some personal experiences linking bodily and mental mystical states in the conclusions.

Chapter III

103   Syriac is the liturgical language of a number of ancient Christian Churches in the Middle East and India. It is a form of Aramaic, an ancient Semitic language that was used throughout the Middle East for centuries. Aramaic is related to Hebrew and Arabic, and is reputed to have been the spoken language of Jesus.

104   The Monastery of Bose, in the town of Magnano in northern Italy, was founded by Enzo Bianchi in the 1960s. There are now over seventy monks and nuns in the community, and at least five new foundations in other parts of Italy. The community offers retreats to people in all walks of life. It is also active in ecumenical work and scholarship, with an outstanding publishing program on which I have relied for much of this research.

105   Scott Brodeur, *The Holy Spirit's Agency in the Resurrection of the Dead*, (Rome, Editrice Pontificia Università Gregoriana, 2004), 141. "What does Paul mean when he says 'let us also bear the image of the one like heaven'? (I Cor. 15:49) He certainly cannot be urging them to put on the spiritual body, since this will happen only at the end of time…This will happen only at the general

resurrection of the dead, when the natural body is changed into the spiritual one."

106   Based in part on Apocalypse 20:4-6, and on the end-time parables of Jesus, Matthew 24:40-41.

107   Their feast day was formerly observed on July 27.

108   *Evangelii gaudium*, paragraph 254, www.vatican.va.

109   Margaret Barker, *The Great High Priest: The Temple Roots of Christian Liturgy* (London & New York: T & T Clark Ltd, 2003), with much on Enoch traditions, 120ff.

110   James L. Kugel, *Traditions of the Bible* (Cambridge: Harvard University Press, 1998), 861–63.

111   This is based on the date of the proconsulship of Gallio in Corinth, which he held probably for a brief period in 50.

112   Scott Brodeur: *The Holy Spirit's Agency*. For a brilliant exigetical study of these issues in I Corinthians 15 and Romans 8, see Brodeur's work.

113   It is instructive to compare our knowledge of Buddhism and Christianity in their earliest phases of development in order to relativize the extreme conclusions that some scholars propose for the latter. Christianity has a very strong historical basis. Christian graffiti from the first century have been catalogued; there are manuscript fragments attributable to the first century and many that are certainly attributable to the early second century; the most numerous of all ancient manuscripts to have survived from the second and third centuries CE are Christian canonical and noncanonical scriptures; institutional continuity is reasonably secure from the late first century; key figures are dated, their tombs known, non-Christian sources refer to early Christian writings and authors, there is massive archeological evidence for early Christian institutions. In contrast, there are no known Buddhist manuscripts from before the fifth century CE (i.e., one thousand years after the lifetime of the Buddha). All the dates for the life of the Buddha, the earliest councils, and the earliest Buddhist writers remain difficult to establish with precision. Debates on the historical dates of the Buddha in the scholarly literature are exstensive. The earliest language of the Buddhist scriptures was neither Pali nor Sanskrit but probably a type of Prakrit spoken in Madhyapradesh; none of these materials survives except in rare fragments usually from Central Asian archeological sites. There are few archeological discoveries related to Buddhism before the era of the Emperor Ashoka (third century BCE). At best, some of the relics in the Ashokan stupas may be authentic and show evidence for a cult of the relics of the Buddha going back to the time of his parinirvana. Since the early Buddhist viharas were constructed of wood, none have survived the climate of India; we only know

of them through the Pali sources and later inscriptions when viharas were constructed of stone or brick.

114   James M. Robinson, ed., *The Nag Hammadi Library in English*, 3rd ed. (San Francisco: HarperSanFrancisco, 1990).

115   "Because of the common meaning of 'physical/bodily' in modern English, I do not think the resurrection of Jesus means this. Physical/bodily means fleshly, molecular, protoplasmic, corpuscular existence." From the website of the recently deceased Marcus J. Borg, a dialogue partner of Brother David whose ideas stimulated this research project: Marcus Borg, www.marcusjborg.com. Also see, Stephen C. Barton, "The Transfiguration of Christ According to Mark and Matthew in Christology and Anthropology," *Auferstehung: Resurrection: Wissenschaftlichen Untersuchungen zum Neuen Testament,* Friedrich Avemarie und Hermann Lichtenberger, eds. *135,* (Tübingen, Mohr: Siebeck Publishers, 2001) 231–46. Barton's recent article challenges the misuse of hermeneutics to arrive at these kinds of conclusions.

116   John Walsh, *The Shroud* (New York: Random House, 1963).

117   Emanuela Marinelli, *La Sindone: Testimone di una presenza* (Cinisello Balsamo, MI: Edizioni San Paolo, 2010); Pierluigi Baima Bollone, *Sindone: Storia e scienza* (Scaramagno, TO: Priuli & Verlucca, 2010); Barbara Frale, *La Sindone di Gesù Nazareno* (Bologna: Società editrice il Mulino, 2009).

118   Keith Dowman, trans. *Radical Dzogchen: Eye of the Storm: Vairotsana's Five Original Transmissions*, (Kathmandu: Vajra Publications, 2006).

119   Larry W. Hurtado: *Lord Jesus Christ: Devotion to Jesus in Earliest Christianity*, (Grand Rapids, MI: William B. Eerdmans, 2003).

120   Armand Veilleux, "Monasticism and Gnosis in Egypt," in *The Roots of Egyptian Christianity,* B.A. Pearson and J. E. Goehring eds. (Philadelphia: Fortress Press, 1986), 271–306.

121   Jacques É. Ménard, editor and translator. *Le Traité sur la Résurrection* (NH I,4) (Québec: Les Presses de l'Université Laval, 1983), 43-57, my translation from French and Coptic into English.

122   Tiso, *Liberation in One Lifetime*, 213; a translation of a thirteenth-century biography of Milarepa.

123   The St. Thomas Christians claim a history in India going back to the mission of St. Thomas in the first century. They are members of the Church of the East whose presence in South India is attested historically since at least the fourth century.

124   Reynolds *The Golden Letters*, p. 183

125   Nicolini-Zani, *La Via Radiosa;* Ian Gillman and Hans-Joachim Klimkeit, *Christians in Asia Before 1500* (Surrey: Curzon Press, 1999); Hans-Joachim

Klimkeit, "Religion in a Pluralistic Society: The Case of Central Asia," in Ugo Bianchi, ed. *The Notion of Religion in Comparative Research: Selected Proceedings of the XVI IAHR (1990)* (Rome: L'Erma di Bretschneider, 1994); G. Uray, "Tibet's Connections with Nestorianism and Manicheism in the Eighth–Tenth Centuries," in Ernst Steinkellner and Helmut Tauscher eds., *Contributions on Tibetan Language, History and Culture, Proceedings of the Csoma De Körös Symposium, Velm-Vienna, 1981* (Wien: 1983).

126 Religions unknown to earliest Christianity, though extant in the first century include Hinduism, Buddhism, Taoism, Confucianism, and Central Asian Shamanism. Early Christians knew about Judaism, Egyptian religion, Hellenistic theurgy, Zoroastrianism, Samaritan religion, and possibly the older religions of the Middle East.

127 A. M. Casiday, *Evagrius Ponticus* (London: Routledge, 2006). See this work for a biographical and bibliographical survey, with key texts in translation.

128 A fruitful comparison could be made with David Germano's interpretation of Longchenpa's philosophy (1992) in chapter five: "The First Adamantine Topic: The Ground and Ground-Presencing," pp. 60ff. "This topic thus deals with the character and dynamics of that Ground in its self-contained interiority, as well as the nature of its initial spontaneously present transition from this pure self-contained interiority into actualization or "presencing," as it breaks out of its seamless enclosure to evolve into a complex hierarchically organized integrated cosmos resonating with luminosity and intelligence."

129 Francis Tiso: "Evagrius of Pontus and Buddhist *Abhidharma*," 2006, *Religion East and West*.

130 Jeremy Driscoll, The *Ad Monachos* of Evagrius Ponticus: Its Structure and a Select commentary (Roma: Studia Andeliana 104, 1991).

131 Ibid.

132 The quotations are my own translation. I used the following French translation to check the known Greek fragments: Antoine Guillaumont trans., *Les Six Centuries des "Kephalaia Gnostica" d'Evagre le Pontique*, Patrologia Orientalis Tome XXVIII, Fascicule 1 (Paris: Firmin-Didot e Cie, Imprimeurs-Editeurs, 1958). I worked mainly with the Syriac version that seems most closely to follow the original Greek. However, in my selection I tried to cite those texts that were *least* re-worked by Babai the Great in his Syriac version of the text, which is the version most likely to have spread among Syro-Oriental Christians on the Silk Road.

133 Ronald Roberson, C.S.P., *The Eastern Christian Churches, A Brief Survey,* 7th Ed. (Rome: Edizioni Orientalia Christiana, 2008), 141–44; 185–92.

134 *Ecumenical,* that is, convoking the entire "household" of mainstream Christians

135 Such as the great Theodore of Mopsuestia (ca. 350–428).

136 Jedin, *History of the Church*, vol. II, 464.

137 By this time, many Christians from Syria had been deported by the Persians, so that the Syro-Oriental Christian Church was composed of bishops, priests, deacons, monks, nuns, and laity from a variety of theological perspectives. For this reason, recent scholarship has abandoned the use of the term "Nestorian" to designate this Church.

138 Jedin, ibid., vol. II, 468.

139 Sabino Chialà, *Abramo di Kashkar e la Sua Comunità* (Magnano: Edizioni Qiqajon, 2005).

140 Nicolini-Zani, *La via radiosa per l'oriente*, 197–8. This is from his translation of the Stele of Xi'an, also known as the "Stele Recounting the Spread of the 'Da Qin' Religion of Light in China," in which Da Qin refers to the eastern provinces of the Byzantine Empire. The text was written in early 781, probably by the monk-prelate Jingjing, who also wrote the *Book on the Attainment of Peace and Joy.*

141 Nicolini-Zani, ibid., 116.

142 Under the Caliph, Al-Mamun, the Muktazalite "rationist" philosophers revolutionized Islamic thought. Eventually, this movement arrived in Muslim Spain from which it profoundly impacted Catholic Scholasticism in the twelfth and thirteenth centuries.

143 Nicholas Sims-Williams in *Orientalia Christiana Periodica* 47 (1981), 441–46.

144 Robert Beulay, *Lumière sans forme: Introduction l'Étude de la Mystique Chrétienne Syro-Orientale* (Chevetogne, Belgique: Éditions de Chevetogne, 1987), 72.

145 Ibid., *Lumière sans forme*, 71.

146 The color sapphire-blue was already part of Jewish mystical lore; it passed into the works of Evagrius and resurfaces here among Syro-Oriental Christians. The same sapphire color and crystalline seats of Buddhas and Bodhisattvas appear in a visualization in the Buddhist yoga manual found at Turfan and published by Dieter Schlingloff as *Ein Buddhistisches Yogalehrbuch* (Berlin: Akademie-Verlag, 1964), 125.

147 Beulay, *Lumière sans forme,* 220.

148 Beulay, ibid., 223.

149 Beulay, *Jean de Dalyatha, Mystique Syro-Orientale*, 63, fn. 8.

150 Beulay, *Lumière sans forme*, 226.

151 Beulay, ibid., 226.

152 For which see St. Gregory of Nyssa on Moses and Philo of Alexandria's *Life of Moses.*

153 Beulay, ibid., 227.

154 Ibid., 19.

155 My translation of the "Cuckoo of Awareness," i.e., *The Six Vajra Verses* attributed to Garab Dorje.

156 Beulay, *Lumière sans forme*, 66.

157 Ibid., 67.

158 Ibid., 68, 69ff.

159 Carmen Meinert, "Chinese *Chan* and Tibetan *Rdzogs Chen*: Preliminary Remarks on Two Tibetan Dunhuang Manuscripts," in *Religion and Secular Culture in Tibet, Tibetan Studies II,* Henk Blezer ed. (Kathmandu: Vajra Publications, 2010), 289–307.

160 "Text E" of the Chinese Christian Documents, my translation from the Italian of Matteo Nicolini-Zani, *La via radiosa per l'oriente* (Ed. Qiqajon, 2006), 285–302. Nicolini-Zani has prepared this translation following the suggestions of Lin Wushu, who corrected the transcription of P. Y. Saeki (1934), and recovered the work of Haneda Toru in 1929. He also used the photographs of the original manuscript (at the present time inaccessible to scholars because of the wishes of the current private owner) published in 1958. Lin Wushu dated the manuscript, Pelliot 3847, to the late tenth-early eleventh century [and thus a generation before the hypothetical dates of the biography of Garab Dorje] in the *Lo rgyus chen mo* by Zhang ton Tashi Dorje (1097-1167).

161 Nicolini-Zani, 164–65.

162 Ibid.,. 163.

163 Ibid., 171–78.

164 The expression "celestial hall" (*tiantang*), occurring frequently in Buddhist texts to indicate the place of bliss where desire and consequent suffering are extinguished, has been borrowed by the Christians to designate what is in all probability the paradise of heaven, as can been seen in the Sino-Christian documents of the Tang dynasty that have come down to us. In this immaterial environment, the Messiah teaches his disciples in this text.

165 Attendant monk: (*shijia*): In Buddhism, this is the term used for the disciple closest to the Master to take loving care of him. In the case of the Buddha Shakyamuni, this would have been Ananda.

166 Confused (*mihuo*): A composite expression that describes the misguided being, someone confused by something. In Buddhism, it indicates the deception of illusions that lead far away from the true nature of reality.

167 Beings (*youqing*): This word translates the Sanskrit word *sattva*, sentient beings.

168 Saved (*jiuhu*): Literally, to save and to protect, a Buddhist expression.

169 Transcendent law (*shengfa*): This expression is used frequently in this text. Its

original meaning in Buddhism is *abhidharma* but can also mean the law that transcends description and intellectual understanding. To attain this cognitive reality is to realize the true essence of reality, buddhahood.

170 Living beings (*hansheng*): Buddhist word that is used synonymously with *you-qing* and *zhongsheng*, for sentient beings in general.

171 Ignorance (*chenmai*): literally, immersed in the cycle of birth and death, drowning in ignorance.

172 Li Tang's translation is very cautious, non-committal.

173 Nicolas Sims-Williams, "Syro-Sogdiana I: An Anonymous Homily on the Three Periods of the Solitary Life," in Orientale Christiana Periodica 47 (1981): 441-446, a translation of a Christian document found in Turfan.

174 Simon Peter: *cenwen sengjia*: This expression seems to be composed of elements of non-Chinese origin. On the basis of a hypothetical phonetic reconstruction, it seems to be the Tang era pronunciation of the Sogdian term *Samghon sang*, a name that is translated as Simon Peter in Sogdian Christian literature. Cf. Text B, Nicolini-Zani, which gives the names of the saints and of key scriptures in the canon of the Church of the East, in which this name means Simon Peter.

175 The transcendent way (*shengdao*): The excellent path that leads to the realization of the true essence of reality.

176 Mental action: Emotions (*dong*), passions, or desires (*yu*), yearning (*qiu*) and mental actions that generate attachment to existence (wei), are seen as the four principal obstacles on the way to peace and joy. The term reflects Yogacara Buddhist psychology as outlined in the *Abhidharmakosha* of Vasubandhu.

177 Pure (*qing*): Translates the Sanskrit term *amala*, limpid, and synonymous with Chinese *jing*, which translates the Sanskrit *vimala*, both terms widely used in Buddhist texts. Compare *qingjing*, which translates *parishuddhi* or *vishuddhi*, to designate a mental state free from evil and defilements.

178 Illuminated (*wu*): A key word for Buddhism, meaning to be enlightened, to be awakened, to be realized.

179 The Truth (*zheng*): In Buddhism, this term indicates the experience of the realization of the truth upon which one enters buddhahood. Like "*wu*" it is a key term in Chinese Buddhism.

180 Peace and joy (*anle yuan*): The attainment of peace and joy is here described as entering into the true essence of reality, characterized by the presence of all-pervasive luminosity.

181 Nicolini-Zani, *La via radiosa,* 287, fn. 15.

182 "Hu" was the Chinese word, during the Tang dynasty, for any Central Asian nationality. Sometimes translated "westerners."

183 The Ten Principles underlying reality (*shiwen*): It seems that this expression is synonymous with *shizhong guan fa*, the "teaching on the ten realities to be discerned" which appears later in this text.

184 Four Acquisitions (*sida*): This abbreviated expression seems to anticipate the "four transcendent principles" (*sizhong shengfa*, abbreviated as *sifa*) that appear later in this text.

185 Fictitious Names: Since the world accessible to the senses is mere appearance without inherent existence, the names given to sense data only serve to comprehend the fictitious, unreal aspect of phenomena (Sanskrit, *prapanca*), which is to be overcome in any case.

186 Sentient beings (*huai shengxiang*): Beings possessing life and thought.

187 Corruption (*ranjing*): This term indicates that part of the world of living things that undergoes corruption in the cycle of birth and death. Ran means contaminated or corrupt, the opposite of *jing*, which means pure.

188 Corruption (*ranjing*): This term indicates that part of the world of living things that undergoes corruption in the cycle of birth and death. Ran means contaminated or corrupt, the opposite of *jing*, which means pure

189 Chinese: *xukong*; Skt.: *shunyata*; Li Tang says this form of the word derives from Daoist usage, which suggests the "fasting of the mind" of which Chuang Tzu speaks, in other words, inner openness, receptivity and intuition. See page 174, "empty of or ceases from constant prayer."

190 Jeffrey Hopkins, *Meditation on Emptiness* (London: Wisdom Publications, 1983), 384–85.

191 Dyadic images that are meant to suggest the divine and human natures of the Messiah. They seem to indicate something of the Syro-Oriental Christology, but also to hint at the simultaneity of samsara and nirvana in Mahayana Buddhism. In the *Uttaratantra*, for example, buddhahood is all-pervasive, neither confined to nirvana nor restricted by samsara.

192 Good and bad actions are here contrasted in their effects. Good actions (*shanyuan*) produce good effects; bad actions produce negative consequences at the time of karmic retribution (*ebao*).

193 Spirit (heart-mind; *xin*): All the Buddhist schools accentuate *vijnana*, consciousness, the fifth skandha of the psychosomatic composition of a being. The Chinese term *xin* includes the intellect and the seat of all mental activity as well as the emotions associated with the "heart". The decision to translate this term as "spirit" was dictated by a desire to be consistent throughout the translation of this text. It is always to be read in its dual mind-heart, connotation.

194 Liberate (*dutuo*): Buddhist soteriological technical term to refer to a being that has been brought to freedom from the cycle of transmigration.

195 Deep understanding (*yuantong*): Buddhist term for total penetration (*vipasyana*) of the true nature of all things by means of an enlightened mind.

196 Assume, take up a compassionate spirit: Literally, "accept responsibility for."

197 Compassionate spirit (*beixin*): Seems to translate the key Mahayana Buddhist term *bodhicitta*, understood here as a heart-mind intent on compassion (Sanskrit: *karuna*).

198 Divine powers (*shentong*): Paranormal powers (*siddhi*) of a Buddha. Compare the divination text, Pelliot tibétain 351 from Dunhuang, which refers to Jesus Messiah as having such powers. See earlytibet.com December 2, 2007, with comments by Sam Van Schaik.

199 *The Eye of the Storm: Radical Dzogchen*, by Keith Dowman. See for a discussion of this issue

200 Modes of perception (*liufa*): The power of the Messiah to overcome obstacles tied to the world of forms and sensory perceptions is described here in typically Buddhist terms. In Buddhist *Abhidharma* psychology, there are six senses: (*liuru*): the eye, ear, nose, tongue, body and mental perception. Just as the fully awakened one, the Buddha, so also the Messiah is free of the obstacles (*wuai*; Sanskrit: *apratihata*) and limits encountered in the phenomenal world. Underlying this phrase is the notion of *abhijna*, or *siddhis* (*liutong*), consciousness of all phenomena free of distortions, including magic power, the divine eye, the divine ability to hear, knowledge of the thoughts of others, remembrance of previous rebirths, and knowledge about how to overcome human passions.

201 The Luminous Teaching (*jingjiao*): The name for Syro-Oriental Christianity in China during the seventh to the ninth centuries; it occurs five times in this text.

202 Originates in infinite causes: Literally, without beginning or end.

203 Merciful (*luojimei*): This term appears twice in the text. It seems to be the Tang era phonetic transcription of the Syriac term *rahma* (or *rehmta*), which means mercy.

204 Innumerable: literally, a billion.

205 Imperial mountain (*dishan*): It is not clear to which mountain this refers. It might be Sumeru, the *axis mundi* of Buddhist mythology. Compare Chinese *fadi*, "emperor of the Dharma."

206 Deep understanding (*xuantong*): An expression similar to *yuantong*, above.

207 Land of Peace and joy (*anle xiang*): the goal of the way (*dao*) of peace and joy.

208 Unchanging: Seems to suggest the idea that samsara is brought to an end.

209 Obstacles: the idea is that of that which is "unimpeded" (a characteristic of buddhahood and of the element "space" or sky).

210 Absence of desire (*wuyu*), absence of mental action (*wuwei*), absence of merits (*wude*), and absence of realization (*wuzheng*): a list of the four principles that

will be explained in detail later in the text. These expressions resonate persuasively with assertions of early dzogchen.

211 To possess in themselves. Literally, to bear in their own depths.

212 The law that governs all things (*zhufa*): Buddhist term (Sanskrit: *sarvadharma*, *sarvabhava*) referring to the multiplicity of phenomena and their relationships.

213 Supreme and Unique Venerable One (*wushang yizun*): Buddhist epithet, here applied to the Messiah.

214 Generating phenomena (*youti*): Buddhist philosophical term indicating anything that has a real or mental form. The "natural state" *is* emptiness.

215 Waters: literally means "springs of water".

216 Well disposed (*youyuan*): Buddhist term that literally means "having a causal connection" and often refers to beings who become believers in the Dharma having been deeply touched (in this life, or in a previous one) by an encounter with the Buddhist teachings.

217 Existing things (*youfa*): Buddhist term for things that exist, in contrast with non-existent things (*wufa*).

218 Positive causes (*shan jieyuan*): Technical term from Buddhist soteriology indicating a concatenation of positive actions that produce good results including liberation in the future.

219 Mercy and compassion (*daci dabei*): Terms used to describe Buddhas and Bodhisattvas, especially in our period for Guanyin and Maitreya.

220 Hundreds of thousands: Literally one hundred, a thousand and ten thousand, an expression indicating a huge number.

221 *Anle yuan*: the cause of peace and joy.

222 Sunk in confusion (*hunzhuo*): The term means ignorance and corruption.

223 Mountain of treasures, forest of jade: Places and images from Buddhist mythology. The mountain of treasures (*baoshan*) might refer to Sumeru, or another of the nine mountains sacred to Buddhism.

224 Count on a friend: *shan zhishi*, a Buddhist term referring to a learned disciple well versed in the sacred texts. *Kalyanamitra*.

225 To know the way (*wudao*): To be enlightened about the knowledge of the way of peace and joy.

226 The Ten Realities to discern (*shizhong guan fa*): The key term here is *guan*, which is used to translate the Sanskrit *vipasyana* or *vidarshana*: contemplation involving attentive discernment of reality using the mental faculties in order to discriminate between that which is illusory and that which is real. This is the means by which the truth is penetrated and one comes to understand the real essence of things.

227 Physical body (*roushen*): body of flesh.

228 Darkness takes the place of light: Literally, this means "the last day of the moon and the first day of the moon change places." The last day of the moon refers to the night of the new moon (the darkest night) and the first day of the moon refers to the full moon night.

229 Larva (Nicolini-Zani gives *hechong*, perhaps *xiechong*?): A particular type of insect larva that lives in tree trunks, destroying them from the inside.

230 Living inside (*huasheng*): A verb used specifically for those insects that pass through life cycle transformations, from egg to larva, from larva to cocoon, and from cocoon to moth or butterfly.

231 Spirit (*jingshen*): The spiritual part of man, as distinct from the physical body; it can indicate the spirit, the vital energy, the mental faculties, etc.

232 Limbs: literally, hands and feet.

233 Various doctrines (*zajiao*): This expression refers to the wide range of teachings that human beings follow, suggesting however that these are for the most part false teachings in contrast to the true doctrine.

234 Phenomenal realities (*youwei*): Buddhist technical term that indicates all that is immersed in samsara, hence all changeable phenomena tied to the karmic process. In the final analysis, it refers to the unreal world as opposed to absolute reality.

235 Desire (*wuyu*).

236 Evil (*eyuan*): A negative cause that produces negative effects in accordance with the doctrine of karmic retribution.

237 Breath (*qi*): Traditional Chinese (Daoist) term for vital energy on every level of the cosmos, in particular in the vital breath or energy-wind of the human body.

238 Four members and seven openings (*sizhi qiqiao*): The four members mean the hands, feet, arms, and legs. The seven openings (of the head) refer to the ears, eyes, nostrils, and mouth.

239 Absence of mental action (*wuwei*): classic Daoist concept of "non-action," natural, spontaneous.

240 Exterior forms (*waixing*): apparent realities.

241 Unreal (*xuwang yuan*): cause of falsehood, in the sense of unreality, as opposed to reality, *shi*, or *shixiang*.

242 Without merit (*wude*).

243 Leading to salvation every species of living being: This passage brings to mind the ideal of the bodhisattva who, motivated by compassion (*karuna*) and guided by the perfection of wisdom (*prajnaparamita*), vows to help other sentient beings to reach enlightenment.

244 Absence of realization (*wuzheng*): That is, the conscious ascetical renunciation of becoming involved in the nature of appearances and contradictory

phenomena. In Ch'an, to be so perfectly enlightened that one leaves no trace of having realized enlightenment.

245 Able to understand (*juezhi*): Common Buddhist word to indicate the comprehension of the true essence of things thanks to Bodhi, to Awakening, to Enlightenment (*pratisamveda-yāti, anubudhī*), to awaken to or understand.

246 Emptiness (*xukong*): *shunyata*.

247 The true way (*zhendao*): As indicated in note 10, this expression indicates the way of peace and joy, understood as the equivalent of the way that leads to the realization of the true essence of reality.

248 Peace and joy (*anle xin).*

249 Penetrate the depths (*tongda*): Like two other expressions used in this text (*yuantong* and *xuantong*), this Buddhist word indicates the total penetration of the true nature of everything by means of an enlightened mind.

250 Comprehension (*jueliao*): Like the term already found in this text, *juezhi*, this too is a Buddhist technical term that means to be clearly and completely enlightened about the true nature of things.

251 Supreme transcendent law (*shengshang fawen*): Variation on the expression *shengfa* and *shengshang fa*, also used in this text.

252 A lacuna in the manuscript. Possibly meant a damaged boat.

253 Peace, joy, and precious perfumes: Salvation is here described explicitly in terms used by Buddhists. The mission of the Buddha was to lead conscious beings to enlightenment, helping them to cross over the ocean of human existence, *shengsi hai*, in his ship (the Dharma); he brings human beings from the shore of terrestrial existence immersed in samsara, to the farther shore of liberation, nirvana. Also Guanyin (Avalokiteshvara), the bodhisattva of mercy, is called the "ship of mercy" in Buddhist traditional devotional texts. These images are also found in the text of the stele of Xi'an and in other Christian Chinese texts.

254 Nicolini-Zani, 300–301, fn 83.

255 Precious perfume that awakens the soul (*fanhun baoxiang*): There is an allusion to this particular type of perfume in the stele of Xi'an in which the region called *Da Qin* (that is, the eastern provinces of the Roman Empire) is described as its source. This is the land of origin of the Syro-Oriental Christian missionaries.

256 Knowledge of the truth (*zhenzhi*): Buddhist term that means true wisdom or knowledge of the ultimate truth (*prajna*).

257 Reflect on the supreme law (*siwei*): In Buddhist lexicons, it means the act of attentively reflecting on something, with discernment as to whether the object of consideration is real or mentally constructed.

258   Every type of defilement (*ranwu*): In Buddhism, the term means everything that is contaminated, false, misguided because of attachment to illusory appearances. It translates the Sanskrit term, *klesha*, which signifies defilement and corruption arising from attachment to sensual pleasures, to false interpretations of reality, to severe austerities as a means of attaining liberation, to belief in the real existence of a self which is nothing more than the cause of suffering, etc

259   Celestial creatures (*tian*): In Buddhist literature, it means the *devas*, divine beings categorized in hierarchical order

260   Ultimate reality (*zhenji*): Technical term in Buddhism for the ultimate truth (*paramarthasatya*), the domain of the truly real.

261   Cultivate one's own conduct (*xiuxing*): This idea, frequently repeated in our text, is also found in Buddhist texts to mean ethical discipline, action, or conduct (Sanskrit: *carya*) in conformity with the Dharma. By extension, it refers to one who practices in this way, i.e., a disciple of the Buddha.

262   Disciples (*dizi*): Typical term in Buddhist scriptures for the disciples of the Buddha (*shravakas).*

263   Listening to too many words might confound you: Literally, "might cause doubts to arise in you."

264   Departing with deference, they put the teachings into practice: The text concludes in a manner similar to many Buddhist sutras.

265   Tiso, *Liberation in One Lifetime*, 291.

Chapter IV

266   Anne Carolyn Klein, "Assorted Topics of the Great Completeness by Dodrupchen III," in David Gordon White, ed., *Tantra in Practice* (Princeton, NJ: Princeton University Press, 2000), 557.

267   Author of the authoritative work, *The Nyingma School of Tibetan Buddhism: Its Fundamentals and History,* Gyurme Dorje and Matthew Kapstein, ed., trans., (Boston: Wisdom Publications, 1991).

268   Tulku Thondup Rinpoche, *Hidden Teachings of Tibet* (Boston: Wisdom, 1997), 189–201.

269   Giuseppe Tucci, *Minor Buddhist Texts, Part I & II* (Delhi: Motilal Banarsidass, 1986), 428–59.

270   Kapstein, *The Tibetans* (Blackwell, 2006), 81.

271   Ibid., 82.

272   In this context, "magic" can be defined as the acquisition of paranormal abilities chiefly concerned with advancing this-worldly aims. Magic, i.e., acquiring *siddhis*, is distinct from the attainment of the full enlightenment of a Buddha.

However, in the vast array of "skillful means," magical displays and siddhis of various kinds constitute part of the compassionate action of a Bodhisattva. The "magic versus religion" debate arose in religious studies from entirely different premises.

273 The *Blue Annals*, written in the 1460s, gives a more favorable interpretation of the lineages operative in this period in, "The Early Translations of the Mantrayana Tantras."

274 Kapstein, *The Tibetans*, 91.

275 Giuseppe Tucci, *Rin-chen-bzang-po and the Renaissance of Buddhism in Tibet Around the Millenium*. (New Delhi: Aditya Prakashan, 1988).

276 Ibid., 96–99.

277 Sexual yoga was practiced as a visualization in the "stage of generation" (*utpattikrama*) in which the yogin self-represents as a deity with attributes in union with a divine consort. Some Dunhuang texts indicate that this more tame approach was already known before the second diffusion.

278 Geoffrey Samuel. "Tantra and the State," in *The Origins of Yoga and Tantra: Indic Religions to the Thirteenth Century* (Cambridge, UK: Cambridge University Press, 2008), chap. 12. . See also: Ronald M. Davidson, *Indian Esoteric Buddhism: A Social History of the Tantric Movement* (New York: Columbia University Press, 2002), especially Chap. 4, "The Victory of Esotericism and the Imperial Metaphor."

279 David Germano, "The Funerary Transformation of the Great Perfection."

280 See Kapstein, *The Tibetans*, 110–16.

281 Sam Van Schaik, "The Early Days of the Great Perfection"197 et passim; Dudjom Rinpoche, *The Nyingma School of Tibetan Buddhism, Its Fundamentals and History*, vol.I (Boston: Wisdom Publications, 1991). See these for lineage biographies.

282 His biography: *Bai ro' dra 'bag chen mo, The Replica*, translated as *The Great Image*, attributed to Yudra Nyingpo, and completed in the twelfth century

283 Giuseppe Tucci "The Debate of *bsam yas* according to Tibetan Sources." in *Minor Buddhist Texts Part II*, chap.1. Tucci's, work on dzogchen, including a comparison with Ch'an and citations of early canonical sources can be found here. Tucci, *Religions of Tibet*, 72–87. A good introduction to dzogchen may be found in his section on the rNyingmapa School.

284 Tucci, *Minor Buddhist Texts*, 363. He refers to the *Blue Annals'* report that the body of a disciple of Vimalamitra, Ting nge 'dzin, disappeared upon the perfect purification of his mind. Also see John M. Reynolds, *The Golden Letters* (Ithaca, NY: Snow Lion, 1996), 139–173. It is also interesting to see how the rainbow body, *trekchod,* and *thodgal* are extracted from the very old "Three

Statements of Garab Dorje," a commentary based on sources from the twelfth and thirteenth centuries, purporting to transmit teachings from Vimalamitra in the early ninth century

285 For example, Dylan Esler, "The Exposition of Atiyoga in gNubs-chen Sangs-rgyas ye-shes' bSam-gtan mig-sgron" in *Revue d'Etudes Tibétains* 24 (October 2012): 81–136. The entire issue is dedicated to the "mind series" teachings, particularly in the early period.

286 Sam Van Schaik, *Approaching the Great Perfection* (Boston: Wisdom Publications, 2004), 3.

287 Van Schaik, "The Early Days of the Great Perfection," 165–206.

288 Ibid., 190.

289 See Tulku Thondup, *Hidden Teachings of Tibet*, (Boston: Wisdom Publications, 1997).

290 David Germano, "Poetic Thought, The Intelligent Universe, and the Mystery of Self," 3.

291 Van Schaik, *Approaching the Great Perfection*, 4–10.

292 Geoffrey Samuels, *Civilized Shamans: Buddhism in Tibetan Societies* (Washington, DC: Smithsonian Series in Ethnographic Inquiry, 1995).

293 Van Schaik, *Approaching the Great Perfection, 4.*

294 *Ibid.*

295 See Dudjom Rinpoche, Jikdrel Yeshe Dorje, *The Nyingma School of Tibetan Buddhism, Its Fundamentals and History.* vol. I (Boston: Wisdom Publications, 1991), 523.

296 Van Schaik, *Approaching the Great Perfection*, 4.

297 Ibid.

298 Ibid., 4–5.

299 Ibid., 5.

300 See Milarepa's discussion in the *gdams ngag mdzod*, in Tiso, *Liberation in One Lifetime*, 278–80.

301 Van Schaik, "The Early Days of the Great Perfection," 200.

302 Van Schaik, *Approaching the Great Perfection*, 5.

303 Ibid., 5 and 325.

304 Ibid., 6.

305 Ibid.

306 Ibid.

307 Ibid.

308 Roberto Vitali, *The Kingdoms of Gu.Ge Pu.Hrang*, (Dharamsala, India: Tho. ling gtsug.lag.khang lo.gcig.stong 'khor.ba'i rjes.dran.mdzad sgo'i go.sgrig tshogs.chung, 1996), pp. 546–4v8.

309   Jacob P. Dalton, "Preliminary Remarks on a Newly Discovered Biography of Nupchen Sangyé Yeshé," in *Himalayan Passages: Tibetan and Neware Studies in Honor of Hubert Decleer,* Benjamin Bogin and Andrew Quintman, eds. (Boston: Wisdom Publications, 2014), 149, 153.

310   Dalton, "Preliminary Remarks," 155–5.

311   Ibid., 158.

312   Ibid., 149–50.

313   Ibid., 159.

314   Ibid., 156. See also: Dan Martin, "Early Education of Milarepa", 1982.

315   Keith Dowman, trans. *Eye of the Storm: Vairotsana's Five Original Transmissions* (Kathmandu: Vajra Publications, 2006), 32.

316   Interesting to find, among the disciples of Padmasambhava, Pelgi Yeshe, a Sogdian (see *The Nyingma School,* pp. 605-606), who taught Nupchen in the latter part of the ninth century.

317   See Gregory J. Darling, *An Evaluation of the Vedantic Critique of Buddhism* (Delhi: Motilal Banarsidass, 1987) Shankaracarya and other Hindu masters showed the flaws in Buddhist reasoning about the soul and the absolute. As a result, the intellectual position of Buddhism in India gradually declined and various forms of theistic Hinduism prevailed.

318   Michael Walter, "Jabir the Buddhist Yogi," Part III. Considerations on an international yoga of transformation," *Lungta* 16 (Spring 2003): 21–36.

319   Michael Walter, Ibid. 22. Walter only alludes to the long prior history of Hellenistic contacts with Central Asia and especially Buddhism from Ashokan times to the Gupta Empire of the fifth century CE. See Georgios T. Halkias, "When the Greeks Converted the Buddha: Asymmetrical Transfers of Knowledge in Indo-Greek Cultures," in *Religions and Trade*, Peter Wick & Volker Rabens, eds. (Leiden: Brill, 2014), 65–116.

320   Walter, Ibid, 23.

321   Ibid., 24, fn.10.

322   Carmen Meinert, "Chinese Chan and Tibetan rDzogs Chen: Preliminary Remarks on Two Tibetan Dunhuang Manuscripts," in Henk Blezer, ed., *Religion and Secular Culture in Tibet, Tibetan Studies II, PIATS 2000, Leiden.* (Kathmandu, Vajra Publications, 2010), 289–308.

323   Ibid., 290–91, fn. 4.

324   David Germano, "The Funerary Transformation of the Great Perfection," (2005). Sam Van Schaik, "The Early Days of the Great Perfection," 165–206.

325   Dowman, *Eye of the Storm*, xxvi ff.

326   The earliest dzogchen system, the "mind series" of practices. See Van Schaik *Approaching the Great Perfection*, 8.

327 Walter, "Jabir the Buddhist Yogi," Part III, 22.

328 Ibid., 24.

329 Ibid., 12, which gives a survey of geographical regions in Central Asia.

330 Ibid., 25.

331 Ibid., 26.

332 Dieter Schlingloff, *Ein Buddhistisches Yogalehrbuch* (Berlin: Akademie-Verlag, 1964), p. 125.

333 Walter, "Jabir the Yogi," Part III, 27.

334 Ibid.,. 33–34, citing Schlingloff, *Ein buddhistisches Yogalehrbuch.*

335 Ibid., 35; Cf. Reynolds, *Golden Letters*, 34 and 140.

336 See Gregorio Palamas: *Difesa dei santi esicasti*. Introduzione di Renato D'Antiga (Padova: Edizioni Messaggero, 1989), and the final volume of the Slavo-Byzantine *Philokalia*, trans and ed. G.E.H. Palmer.

337 Where it is an all-pervasive theme, closely connected with the hesychastic experience of seeing God with the eyes of the heart. In fact, it is also found in the Prologue to the sixth-century monastic *Rule of St. Benedict*, "let us open our eyes to the deifying light"—*deificum lumen,* a theme that comes to the Latin West via John Cassian, who was a main disciple of Evagrius of Pontus in Egypt.

338 David Germano, "The Shifting Terrain of the Tantric Bodies of Buddhas and Buddhists from an Atiyoga Perspective," in Ramon Prats, ed., *The Pandita and the Siddha: Tibetan Studies in Honour of E. Gene Smith*, (Dharamsala: Amnye Machen Institute, 2007).

339 Samten G. Karmay, *The Great Perfection (rDzogs Chen)* (Leiden: E. J. Brill, 1988), 193.

340 Ibid., 193.

341 Ibid., citing Longchenpa's *gNas lugs mdzod*, 193.

342 Ibid., 194.

343 Ibid., 195.

344 Ibid., 195-6, citing dPal mang dKon mchog rgyal mtshan, 196, fn. 90.

345 Ibid., 195.

346 Dieter Schlingloff, *Ein Buddhistisches Yogalehrbuch* (Berlin: Akademie-Verlag, 1964).

347 Pierluigi Baima Bollone, *Sindone: Storia e scienza*, (Torino: Priuli & Verlucca, 2010). Plate 1, opposite page 176, shows a fine example of a Byzantine gold *solidus* of this kind, dated to 692.

348 Tulku Throndup, *Hidden Teachings of Tibet*, 189–201.

349 "Longchenpa and the Possession of the Dakinis," in David Gordon White, *Tantra in Practice*, chap.14

Ibid., 223–25.

350 See Tucci, *The Religions of Tibet*, 246.

351 Tucci, ibid., 236–37.

352 Ibid., 223–25.

353 Ibid., 80ff.

354 *Dighanikaya-Atthakathatika Linatthavannana*, Vol. III, Edited by Lily De Silva (London: Pali Text Society, 1970), XXVII, 45–64.

355 Van Schaik, "The Early Days of the Great Perfection," 182–84.

356 For example, the crucial ninth-century figure of gSnubs Sangye Yeshe, in Van Schaik's helpful blog on Ch'an and Dzogchen, earlytibet.com.

357 George N. Roerich, trans., ed. *The Blue Annals* by 'Gos Lotsawa (Delhi: Motilal Banarsidass, 1979), 112–13.In addition to the stories about Milarepa's practice of black magic, learned from both Bon and Nyingma masters, there is the more "ecumenical" episode in Book III in which three masters, a tantric (*ngagpa*), a Buddhist monk, and a Bonpo are called upon to consecrate a temple.

358 Sam Van Schaik tells about these texts in his blog, earlytibet.com, on December 2, 2007, and cites the various French and German publications relevant to the documents he describes in English.

359 John M. Reynolds trans. *Golden Letters*, 19.

360 Cheh-Ngee Goh, ed. *Rigbai Kujyug: The Six Vajra Verses, An oral commentary by Namkhai Norbu, December 1985, Merigar, Italy* (Singapore: Rinchen Editions, 1990), 4.

361 Geoffrey Samuels, *The Origins of Yoga and Tantra: Indic Religions to the Thirteenth Century* (Delhi: Cambridge University Press, 2008); Ronald M. Davidson, *Indian Esoteric Buddhism: A Social History of the Tantric Movement* (New York: Columbia University Press, 2002); Christian K. Wedemeyer, *Making Sense of Tantric Buddhism* (New York: Columbia University Press, 2012).

362 See some of the classic arguments in the *Blue Annals*, Book III, 119, 130.

363 Some recent works on Bon: Bru-sgrom rGyal-ba g.yung-drung (1242–90), *The Stages of A-Khrid Meditation: Dzogchen Practice of the Bon Tradition,* Per Kvaerne and Thupten K. Rikey trans. (Dharamsala: Library of Tibetan Works and Archives, 1996). Namkhai Norbu, *Drung, Deu and Bön: Narrations, Symbolic Languages and the Bön tradition in ancient Tibet*, Adriano Clemente and Andrew Lukianowicz trans.(Dharamsala: LTWA, 1995); Geoffrey Samuel, "Shamanism, Bon and Tibetan Religion," in Charles Ramble and Martin Brauen, *Anthropology of Tibet and the Himalaya.* (Kathmandu: Vajra Publications, 2008).

364 Van Schaick, *Approaching the Great Perfection,* 6.

365 J. B. Robinson, trans. *Buddha's Lions The Lives of the Eighty-Four Siddhas. Caturasiti-siddha-pravritti* by Abhayadatta. (Berkeley: Dharma Publishing, 1979).

366 *Rigbai Kujyug*, 1.

367 My translation of the Tibetan text edited by Karen Liljenberg, www.zangthal. co.uk 2010 from the British Library Dunhuang Manuscript IOL Tib J 647.

368 *Asian Journal*, November 16, 1968 (cf. *The Other Side of the Mountain*, p. 278-279). Chatral Rinpoche called Merton a "*rangjyung sangyé*," a self-arisen Buddha, in this famous conversation between two hermits.

369 Also spelled Xuan Zang (602–664).

370 Beckwith, *The Tibetan Empire in Central Asia*,

371 R. Davidson, *Indian Esoteric Buddhism*, 115; 121–23.

372 Ibid., 149, fig. 5.

373 Ibid., 116 f.

374 Ibid.,145, 152.

375 Van Schaik, *Approaching the Great Perfection*, 4–8; and "The Early Days of the Great Perfection." See for discussion of the harmony between dzogchen and Nyingma tantras of the early period.

376 Davidson, *Indian Esoteric Buddhism*

377 Tulku Thondup, *Hidden Treasures of Tibet.*

378 See Namkhai Norbu, *The Crystal and the Way of Light: Sutra, Tantra, and Dzogchen*. John Shane ed. (New York: Routledge & Kegan Paul, 1986), 51–52. I myself found an interesting cave in the Molise, Italy, at Frosolone, with a silhouette that seems to be Padmasambhava, a kind of long-distance *terma*.

379 Muhyiddin Ibn 'Arabi, *Journey to the Lord of Power: A Sufi Manual on Retreat*. Introduction by Sheikh Musaffer Ozak al-Jerrahi, Rabia Terri Harris trans. (New York: Inner Traditions International, 1981). See also: Henry Corbin, "Divine Epiphany and Spiritual Birth in Ismailian Gnosis," in *Man and Transformation: Papers from the Eranos Yearbooks, Bollingen series* XXX.5 (Princeton: Princeton University Press, 1964).

380 Jason David BeDuhn, *The Manichaean Body: In Discipline and Ritual* (Baltimore: The Johns Hopkins University Press, 2000), 257–59.

381 Walter, "Jabir the Buddhist Yogi, Part III" 27.

382 Matthew Kapstein, "The Strange Death of Pema the Demon Tamer,"138. Kapstein also argues for influences coming from all three religions, as well as Daoism. The article gives a good survey of the sources for the rainbow body in dzogchen tradition.

383 David Germano, "The Funerary Transformation of the Great Perfection (Rdzogs chen)", and "The Shifting Terrain of the Tantric Bodies," in *The Pandita*

and the Siddha. David Germano writes convincingly about the "charnel ground imagery" of on funerary Buddhism and early dzogchen).

384 The Patriarch, who is also noted for having mentioned Tibet in at least two letters, and who nominated a metropolitan archbishop for Tibet, was a friend and dialogue partner of the Muslim Caliph, Al-Mamun. Both men were aligned with the rationalist tendencies of the time. In the case of Al-Mamun, the Caliph preferred the views of the philosophical Muktazalites, in opposition to the Muslim jurists and the mystical Sufis. Similarly, Timothy seems to have been wedded to a highly rational, Antiochean approach in Christian theology, and downplayed the mystical element in monastic spirituality.

385 Robert Beulay, *L'Enseignment spiritual de Jean de Dalyatha, Mystique Syro-Oriental du VIII siècle* (Paris: Beauchesne, 1990), 323–39.

386 Ibid., 511–14.

387 By which is meant that one is to discern that the soul is the image of God, and by recognizing the image, one becomes what one sees. Even before Evagrius of Pontus, the great Saint Anthony wrote: "Those instructed by the Holy Spirit know themselves according to their own intellectual essence. He who knows himself knows God; he who knows God is worthy to adore him as he should." See: Paolo Bettiolo, ed., *Evagrio Pontico: Per conoscere lui* (Magnano: Qiqajon, 1996), 35–36.

388 Robert Beulay, O.C.D., *La lumière sans forme: Introduction à l'étude de la mystique Chrétienne Syro-Orientale* (Chevetogne, Belgique, 1987), 229–30.

389 The first line of the *Kephalaia Gnostica* (I, 1) of Evagrius states "In the Absolute, there are no distinctions".

390 Martin Palmer, *The Jesus Sutras: Rediscovering the Lost Scrolls of Taoist Christianity* (New York: Ballantine-Wellspring, 2001).

391 Wilhelm Schneemelcher and Edgar Hennecke, *New Testament Apocrypha,*. Vol. One, *Gospels and Related Writings*. R. McL. Wilson trans. (Philadelphia: The Westminster Press, 1963).

392 Conversation at Swayambhu, Kathmandu, 2001.

393 Eva M. Dargyay, *The Rise of Esoteric Buddhism in Tibet*, (Delhi: Motilal Banarsidass, 1977), 20. The legend has some similarity with the legend of Sophia and the story of Christ's life. We, however, do not want to speculate as to whether reciprocal influences and dependencies exist beyond the parthenogenesis.

394 Christopher I. Beckwith, *The Tibetan Empire in Central Asia: A History of the Struggle for Great Power among Tibetans, Turks, Arabs, and Chinese during the Early Middle Ages* (Princeton: Princeton University Press, 1987).

395 The *locus classicus* for this is the use of the present subjunctive, *echéi* in John 6:40, "anyone who sees the Son and believes in him, has eternal life, and I will raise him up on the last day." The immediacy of the attainment of eternal life

was troubling to Patriarch Timothy of Baghdad, but had been sustained long before by St. Cyril of Alexandria in his Commentary on the Gospel of John, Book 11, 11; and by St. Leo the Great in his sermon on the passion of Christ.

396   See *Syriac Fathers on Prayer,* 122ff.

397   Sabino Chialà, ed., *Mostrami la tua bellezza,* (Magnano: Edizioni Qiqajon, Monastero di Bose, 1996), 4–5.

398   John M. Reynolds, *The Golden Letters,* 177, a translation of the Tibetan text in the *Bima snying thig.*

399   *Buddha's Lions; Women of Wisdom;* the works of the Mad Yogin of gTsang and his disciples; the Nath biographies, etc.

400   Christopher Beckwith, *Empires of the Silk Road,* (Princeton and Oxford: Princeton University Press, 2009) 12.

401   See Albert B. Lord, *The Singer of Tales,* (Cambridge: Harvard University Press, 1960).

402   John Damascene (attributed), *Barlaam and Ioasaph.* G. R. Woodward and H. Mattingly, trans. introduction by D. M. Lang (Cambridge MA: Harvard University Press, 1983, Loeb Classical Library, 34).

403   Barbara Freyer Stowasser, "Mary," in *Encyclopedia of the Qur'an,* vol. 3, Jane Dammen McAuliffe, ed (Leiden-Boston: Brill, 2003), 288–95.

404   Nicolini-Zani, *La via radiosa.*

405   "The *Bima Nyingtig* is said to have been concealed in the eighth or ninth century and rediscovered in the eleventh, yet it is not strictly classified as a treasure text …" Van Schaik, *Approaching the Great Perfection,* 9.

406   See Gampopa's biography of Marpa and Milarepa in Tiso, *Liberation in One Lifetime,* 247–58.

407   Dalton Esler, "The Exposition of Atiyoga in gNubs-chen Sangs-rgyas ye-shes bSam gtan mig sgron," *Revue d'Etudes Tibétaines* #24, (2012). Esler also goes into considerable detail on the persistence of these themes during the late ninth century.

408   David Germano, "Shifting Terrain of Tantric Bodies …," 53.

409   *The Supreme Source: The Kunjed Gyalpo, The Fundamental Tantra of Dzogchen Semde,* translated by Chogyal Namkhai Norbu, Adriano Clemente, and Andrew Lukianowicz (Ithaca: Snow Lion Publications, 1999). This dzogchen tantra, known in English as *The Supreme Source,* lists the five root tantras of the dzogchen mind series of teachings. This earliest dzogchen work was literally entitled *The Bodhisattva Tantra That Is the All-Creating King;* "*Sarvadharma-mahasantibodhicittakulayaraja*"is the Sanskrit title of this work.

410   This passage is a clue to the actual date of the text, some time in the eleventh century.

411 E. E. Nerazik and P. G. Bulgakov, in "Khwarizm," *History of Civilizations of Central Asia,* vol. III, B. A. Litvinsky, ed. (Delhi: Motilal Banarsidass, 1999), 207–32.

412 Nicolini-Zani, 50.

413 Nicholas Sims-Williams in *OCP* 47 (1981):441–46. Compare *Manuscript C,* the Christian Sogdian manuscript from Turfan.

414 Cf. Yusuf Ali version of the Qur'an, fn. 2471.

415 Yojana is an Indian measure of distance, approximately 8 kilometers or 5 miles.

416 The date of the transfer of the shroud relic to Constantinople was August 15, 944. A tenth-century manuscript in the Vatican Library contains the account of this event written by Gregory, archdeacon of the basilica of Santa Sophia, who was an eye witness. The relic was acquired from the Arab rulers of Edessa for 12,000 argentei (coins of Byzantium), and taken to the imperial chapel on the island of Pharos, where it became a symbol of divine protection for the city of Constantinople. Compare the accounts in Barbara Frale, *La Sindone di Gesù Nazareno* (Bologna: Società editrice il Mulino, 2009), 41–43, and in Pierluigi Baima Bollone, *Sindone: Storia e scienza* (Scarmagno, Torino: Priuli & Verlucca, 2010), 26–29, where it is clear that the three Christian communities (Chalcedonians, Jacobites, and Nestorians) in Edessa objected to the transfer. Each of these three church communities possessed a copy of the relic, which represented for them an authentic image of Christ crucified and resurrected. Thus, again in the period that interests us, a major symbol of the resurrection was the object of veneration and the subject of controversy in a way that would have been known throughout the Christian communities of Central Asia.

417 John M. Reynolds, *Golden Letters,* 187.

418 This is the complete text of the surah: the narrative of the life of Mary (Maryam) and Jesus (Isa) in the nineteenth surah of the Qur'an: Sūra XIX: Maryam, or Mary:

16. Relate in the Book (the story of) Mary when she withdrew from her family to a place in the East.

17. She placed a screen (to screen herself) from them; Then We sent to her our angel, and he appeared before her as a man In all respects.

18. She said: "I seek refuge From thee to (God).Most Gracious: (come not near) If thou dost fear God."

19. He said: "Nay, I am only a messenger from thy Lord, (to announce) to thee the gift of a holy son."

20. She said: "How shall I have a son, seeing that no man has touched me, and I am not unchaste?"

21. He said: "So (it will be): Thy Lord saith, "That is easy for me: and (We wish) to appoint him as a Sign unto men and a Mercy from Us": It is a matter (so) decreed."

22. So she conceived him, and she retired with him to a remote place.

23. And the pains of childbirth drove her to the trunk of a palm-tree: She cried (in her anguish): "Ah! Would that I had died before this! Would that I had been a thing forgotten and out of sight!"

24. But (a voice) cried to her from beneath the (palm-tree): "Grieve not! for thy Lord hath provided a rivulet beneath thee;

25. "And shake towards thyself The trunk of the palm-tree: It will let fall fresh ripe dates upon thee.

26. "So eat and drink and cool (thine) eye. And if thou dost see any man, say, 'I have vowed a fast to (God) Most Gracious, and this day will I enter into no talk with any human being.'"

27. At length she brought the (babe) to her people, carrying him (in her arms). They said: "O Mary! Truly an amazing thing hast thou brought!

28. "O sister of Aaron! Thy father was not a man of evil, nor thy mother a woman unchaste!"

29. But she pointed to the babe. They said: "How can we talk to one who is a child in the cradle?"

30. He said: "I am indeed A servant of God: He hath given me Revelation and made me a prophet;

31. "And He hath made me blessed wheresoever I be, and hath enjoined on me prayer and charity as long As I live;

32. "(He) hath made me kind to my mother, and not overbearing or miserable;

33. "So Peace is on me the day I was born, the day that I die, and the day that I shall be raised up to life (again)!"

34. Such (was) Jesus the son of Mary: (it is) a statement of truth, about which they (vainly) dispute.

35. It is not befitting to (the majesty of) God that He should beget a son. Glory be to Him! When He determines a matter, He only says to it, "Be," and it is.

36. Verily God is my Lord and your Lord: Him therefore serve ye: this is a Way that is straight.

37. But the sects differ among themselves: and woe to the unbelievers because of the (coming) Judgment of a momentous Day!

38. How plainly will they see and hear, the Day that they will appear before Us! But the unjust to-day are in error manifest!

419 See D.M. Lang, Introduction to *Barlaam and Ioasaph*, p. xiii; cf. also: Joseph A. P. Wilson, "The Life of the Saint and the Animal: Asian Religious Influence in the Medieval Christian West." *JSRNC* 3.2 (2009): 169–194, equinoxonline, for additional hagiographical observations, including everything in Lang.

420 Lang, xvii–xviii.

421 Ibid., xix.

422 Ibid., xix.

423 Ibid., xixff.

424 Ibid., xxxi.

425 Samten Karmay, "On the Doctrinal Position of rDzogs-chen from the tenth to the thirteenth Centuries," *Journal Asiatique,* 273 (1975):147–156.

426 See Christopher Pramuk, *Sophia: The Hidden Christ of Thomas Merton* (Collegeville, MN: Liturgical Press, 2009), 137–42, for a discussion of this aspect of Herakleitos in Merton's key transitional work, *The Behavior of Titans.*

427 Keith Dowman, *Eye of the Storm,* 29.

428 Gerhard Kittel and Gerhard Friedrich, eds., *The Theological Dictionary of the New Testament,* translation by Geoffrey W. Bromiley (Grand Rapids, MI: Wm. B. Eerdmans Publishing Company, 1968).

429 Twelfth Rock Edict, Romila Thapar, *Asoka and the Decline of the Mauryas* (Oxford: Oxford University Press 1997), 255.

430 Nicolini-Zani, *La Via Radiosa,* 285–302.

431 www.zangthal.co.uk, Karen Liljenberg trans., 2007, from the British Library Dunhuang Manuscript IOL Tib, J, 594.

432 Jacob P. Dalton, "The Questions and Answers of Vajrasattva," in David Gordon White, ed. *Yoga in Practice* (Princeton: Princeton University Press, 2012),185–203

433 The Six Verses are presented as my own translation from the Tibetan original. The source of the Tibetan is *Rigbai Kujyug: The Six Vajra Verses.* An Oral Commentary by Namkhai Norbu.

434 *Rigbai Kujyug,* 19.

435 www.zangthal.co.uk, Karen Liljenberg, "The Small Hidden Grain."

436 Ibid., Karen Liljenberg's notes on "The Small Hidden Grain," 4–5.

437 Or else Buddhagupta is responding to Jingjing, depending on when the "Small Hidden Grain" was written.

438 Pseudo-Macario, *Spirito e fuoco,* Lisa Cremaschi ed., trans. (Magnano: Edizioni Qiqajon, 1995), 190. Translated from Italian by Francis V. Tiso.

439 See Hans-Joachim Klimkeit, "Christian-Buddhist Encounter in Medieval Central Asia," in *The Cross and the Lotus: Christianity and Buddhism in Dialogue.* G.W. Houston, ed. (Delhi: Motilal Banarsidass, 1985), 9–24;. See also

Nicolini-Zani, 66, where he points out that the Christian Sogdian texts display a certain insistence on the theme of the resurrection, to contest the Manichean "docetic" beliefs about the resurrection of the body.

440 Klimkeit, typescript, 8.

441 Klimkeit, typescript. Sam Van Schaik, in his blog (December 2, 2007), has discussed a Dunhuang fragment, IOL Tib J 766, that contains a sketch of a Syro-Oriental cross alongside writing in Tibetan and Uighur or Sogdian script. The cross has the three "beads" that make it a symbol of this Christian tradition (see the Iranian silver bowl—ciborium or chalice—in the National Museum of Oriental Art, Rome, Palazzo Brancaccio). The same kind of cross is found at the top of the X'ian stele of 781; the stele was probably written by the same Jingjing who wrote "Peace and Joy."

442 Dan Martin, "The Early Education of Milarepa," *Journal of the Tibet Society* 2 (1982):52–76; Francis Tiso, "The Religion of Milarepa Before His Conversion", Ugo Bianchi, editor, *The Notion of Religion in Comparative Research: Selected Proceedings of the XVI IAHR Congress,* 1990 (Rome: L'Erma di Bretschneider, 1992).

443 Martin, "Early Education of Milarepa," 61.

444 David Germano, "The Funerary Transformation of the Great Perfection" (2005).

445 *Vijnanabhairava: La conoscenza del tremendo*, Attilia Sironi, trans. (Milan: Adelphi, 1989).

446 James M. Robinson, ed. *The Nag Hammadi Library in English* (San Francisco: HarperSanFrancisco, 1990), 52–57.

447 Ibid., chapt. three.

448 From John of Dalyatha's twentieth homily, in which the author addresses Christ as the Divine Sophia of the Father, "Since the time when I thought that I found you within me, I have come to see that you abide in all things, as a whole, without division, in completeness." (Homily 20, V, 349b), And in Homily 25: "O Lord, may your holy light make the beauties of your mysteries appear in the deepest heart of my mind, as in the minds of the [angelic] Powers of your Holiness, who ceaselessly fix their gaze on those resplendent rays." My translation from Beulay's French translation.

Chapter V

449 Milton Singer, *When a Great Tradition Modernizes* (New York: Praeger Publishers, 1972).

450 G. Obeyesekere, *Medusa's Hair.* (Chicago: University of Chicago Press, 1981). And: Robert R. Desjarlais, *Body and Emotion: The Aesthetics of Illness and*

Healing in the Nepal Himalayas. (Philadelphia: University of Pennsylvania Press, 1992).

451 A person who has apparently died and gone to the land of the dead, only to return to tell the tale, including who is in one of the hell realms "doing time."

452 Khenpo Tsultrim Lodro, *Gsung 'bum. Deb dang po.* Mi rigs dpe skrun khang, 2006. 289–297.

453 Corbin, "Divine Epiphany," in Joseph Campbell, ed., *Man and Transformation: Papers from the Eranos Yearbooks.* "His exterior (… his exoteric self as he appears to the noninitiate) typifies the exterior of a closed Door. His interior (… esoteric self) is a light from the veil of the Merciful and Compassionate. When a veil hides thee from the eyes and the person shines through the heart of his splendor of Light, thou seest how much of it thou art capable of assuming …" See especially 153–4, refering to the Imam: his text is a theistic version of the message of Lama A Khyug .

454 Recent historical scholarship has made Langdarma into less of a villain than the native sources. It seems he was more concerned about balancing the imperial budget than with extirpating Buddhism from Tibet. His descendents in Western Tibet were later to sponsor the revival of Buddhism in the late tenth century. See Kapstein, *The Tibetans* (2006), 77–95.

455 Tulku Thondup Rinpoche. *Hidden Teachings of Tibet* (Boston: Wisdom Publications, 1997), 62–63.

456 Michael Aris, *Hidden Treasures and Secret Lives* (Delhi: Motilal Banarsidass, 1988);. Cf. Janet Gyatso, *Apparitions of the Self,* (Princeton: Princeton University Press, 1998).

457 David Germano, "Funerary Buddhism" (2005).

458 David Germano, *Poetic Thought* (1992).

459 Ibid.

460 David Gordon White, ed. *Tantra in Practice,* 239–65.

461 G. Obeyesekere, *Medusa's Hair.*

462 As in Fritjof Capra's *Tao of Physics.* Cf. attempts to correct this approach in David Steindl-Rast, Thomas Matus, and Fritjof Capra, *Belonging to the Universe* (San Francisco: HarperSanFrancisco, 1991).

463 Pier Luigi Luisi. *Mind and Life: Discussions with the Dalai Lama on the Nature of Reality.* (NY: Columbia University Press, 2009).

464 Emanuela Marinelli. *La Sindone: Testimonianza di una presenza.* (Cinisello Balsamo: Edizioni Paoline, 2010), 20–26; 127–128.

465 See citations of the works of Pierluigi Baima Bollone, E. Marinelli, Barbara Frale, Giulio Fanti, Saverio Gaeta, and others in the Bibiliography. There are innumerable websites, to be used with caution because of the strongly

apologetic intent of their authors. However, the STURP website is reliably scientific. www.shroud.com; see also www.stlouisshroudconference.com.

466   www.francistiso.com See also: Museo Nazionale d'Arte Orientale (MNAO) "*Divysamprayoga*": a group art show in Rome, May–July 2013.

467   See Shenpen Hookam, *The Buddha Within*, for a discussion of this debate between two interpretations of the experience of emptiness in Tibetan Buddhism (Albany: State University of New York Press, 1991).

468   Van Schaik, "The Early Days of the Great Perfection,

469   See especially Van Schaik, "The Early Days of the Great Perfection," And his book, *Approaching the Great Perfection*. Also, David Germano, "The Funerary Transformation of the Great Perfection."

470   See Van Schaik, *Approaching the Great Perfection*, 8–10.

471   See Samten Karmay, *Secret Visions of the Dalai Lama*, (London: Serindia Publications, 1988), 4–5, in which it is clear that the Great Fifth conceived of his role as head of state as that of a ritual hierophant performing wrathful sadhanas to subdue rebellion and defend the boundaries of Tibet.

472   *The Life of Milarepa*, Lobsang P. Lhalungpa, trans. (Boston & London: Shambhala, 1984), is the version by gTsang Smyon Heruka, written at the end of the 1400s. Pages 41–43 describe Milarepa's plight, having followed Nyingma and Bonpo ways of sorcery, and his disastrous failure to attain anything by means of dzogchen. See Tiso, *Liberation in One Lifetime*. Earlier versions of the biography indicate that there was indeed a problem about the ineffectiveness of dzogchen as far as Milarepa the sorcerer was concerned.

473   *'ja' lus 'pho ba chen po*.

474   The same fiercely sectarian voice reaches its most shrill culmination in the polemical writings of Trinley Norbu, son of Dudjom Rinpoche. In his book *A Cascading Waterfall of Nectar*, (Boston: Shambhala, 2006) Trinley Norbu assails, among other things, dialogue with non-Buddhist religions and secular philosophies. He insists that a serious Buddhist practitioner must believe literally in the cosmology of *Abhidharma* and *Kalacakra* texts, including the "flat earth," while distancing oneself from any form of scientific view of the universe.

475   See the testimonies in the appendices of Sogyal Rinpoche, *The Tibetan Book of Living and Dying*.

476   Anne Klein presents some interesting photographs of Adzom Rinpoche during a teaching session (plates just before page 167), in which it seems that he is dissolving into light. See Anne Carolyn Klein, *Heart Essence of the Vast Expanse: A Story of Transmission* (Ithaca, NY: Snow Lion, 2009). A similar photo of the Sixteenth Karmapa circulates on the internet.

477 Matthew Kapstein, *The Presence of Light*, 120.

478 Ibid., 148.

479 Ibid., 149–50. The newpaper report says that hair and nails remained, but this was denied by our interviewees.

480 Ibid., 151–52.

481 Ibid., 151.

482 See David Germano, who raises this issue in "The Shifting Terrain of the Tantric Bodies of Buddhas and Buddhists from an Atiyoga Perspective," in Raimon Prats, ed., *The Pandita and the Siddha: Tibetan Studies in Honour of E. Gene Smith*,(Dharamsala: Amnye Machen Institute, 2007).

483 Tiso, *Liberation in One Lifetime*, 29–42, on the death of Milarepa in various accounts.

484 Ibid., chap. II. Because it was not instantaneous but took about seven days.

485 David Germano, "Tantric Bodies."

486 For Dunhuang Manuscript IOL Tib J 647 and IOL Tib J 594. www.zangthal. co.uk

487 Chen Huaiyu, "The Encounter of Nestorian Christianity with Tantric Buddhism in Medieval China," in Dietmar Winkler and Li Tang, eds, *Hidden Treasures and Intercultural Encounters.* (Berlin: LIT Verlag, 2009).

488 Some evidence for the cult of Tara and of the yoga tantra figure of Vairocana has been found, but even Tara and Vairaocana correspond to contemporary sculpture at Ellora, and to the interests of Central Asian and Chinese Mahayana Buddhism.

489 Litvinsky et al., eds., *History of Civilizations of Central Asia*, vol. III. , chap. 9. See also: Nicolini-Zani, 50.

490 In the well-known six-line hymn to Padmasambhava, the location of his birth is pronounced "Ürgyen."

491 Litvinsky et al eds., *History of Civilizations of Central Asia*, vol. III, chaps. 17 and 18.

492 For Vairocana images in Central Asia: Simone Gauier, Robert Jera-Bezard, and Monique Maillard, *Buddhism in Afghanistan and Central Asia* (Leiden: Brill, 1976), plates 37, 38, 39,40. An elegant ninth-century Vairocana from Central Tibet can be seen in Pratapaditya Pal, *Himalayas: An Aesthetic Adventure* (Chicago: Art Institute of Chicago, 2003), plate 109, p. 170. For the spectacular Vairocana chapel at Gyantse, see Franco Ricca and Erberto Lo Bue, *The Great Stupa of Gyantse* (London: Serindia Publications, 1993), 116–20. For the cosmological aspects see Akira Sadakata, *Buddhist Cosmology: Philosophy and Origins* (Tokyo: Kosei Publishing, 1997), 151–57.

493 *The Cuckoo of Awareness* by Vairocana. Karen Liljenberg, trans., 2010, version 1.2 Zang Thal, "Translation of Texts into English", www.zangthal.co.uk, files /The_Cuckoo_of_Awareness.pdf.

494 An accompanying commentary tells us: "All phenomena on the relative level are 'variety.' But in their essential sameness they are non-differentiable," referring to the open and interdependent nature of all phenomena, so-called voidness.

495 I Thessalonians 1:10 reiterates the reason for the conversion of the Thessalonians, from idolatry to the service "of the living and true God, and to wait in expectation for Jesus our redeemer, whom [God] raised (Greek: *egeiren*) from the dead, to return from heaven." I Thessalonians 4:14 is an explicit statement of faith: "We believe that, as Jesus died and rose again (Greek: *anestê*), God will also bring to Jesus those who have died united to him." These are the oldest known statements of belief in the resurrection of Jesus and of Christians.

496 Scott Brodeur, *The Holy Spirit's Agency in the Resurrection of the Dead* (Rome: Pontificia Università Gregoriana, 2004), takes up this topic in exegetical detail.

497 Caroline Walker Bynum, *The Resurrection of the Dead* (New York: Columbia University Press, 1995), see especially chap. six.

498 Sebastian Brock, ed., *The Syriac Fathers on Prayer and the Spiritual Life.* (Kalamazoo: Cistercian Publications, 1987), see especially, xxi–xxxiv.

499 Conversation with Jetsunma Tenzin Palmo, June 20, 2014. Jetsunma is an Englishwoman belonging to the Drukpa Kagyu Order. She has founded a large monastery for women in northern India.

500 Tenzin Zopa, comp., Robina Courtin, ed., *The Thousand Buddha Relic Stupa: Commemorating the Great Mahasiddha Geshe Lama Konchok.* (Kathmandu: Kopan Library, 2003).

501 *The Spiritual Meadow* mentions a number of incorrupt monks, such as #87 John the Humble, an anchorite found incorrupt who tomb emanated light and #89, an anchorite of Mount Amanon whose intact body was found fifteen years after death. See also #120 and 121. In #122, two monks appear to be naked, but their bodies in reality have the power to disappear. William Dalrymple reports on an anchorite whose body is said to have disappeared after death: William Dalrymple, *From the Holy Mountain* (New York: Henry Holt, 1998). John Moschus, *The Spiritual Meadow*, translated by John Wortley (Kalamazoo, MI: Cistercian Publications, 1992).

502 For example, I found an herb in Helambu (a mountain region north east of Kathmandu) that rapidly stops blood flowing from a wound (leech wounds, but also others).

503 In Italian, there is the notorious saying: *Traduttore traditore!* (The translator

betrays!) Translation always falls short of a recognizable representation of the truth of the "other" culture or language.

504   *The Life of Milarepa*, L. P. Lhalungpa trans., (1977) xviii.

505   G. Obeyesekere, *Imagining Karma* (Berkeley: University of California Press, 2002), chap. 6, 249 ff.

506   Rock Edicts of Ashoka, XII.

507   Germano, "Poetic Thought," IV, 1.

508   *Dancing in the Water of Life: Seeking Peace in the Hermitage,* Robert E. Daggy, ed.(San Francisco: HarperSanFrancisco, 1997).

509   *The Other Side of the Mountain: The End of the Journey*, edited by Patrick Hart, (San Francisco: HarperSanFrancisco, 1998), 322–23, describing the visit on December 1, 1968 to the granite statues of Buddha and Ananda at Polonnaruwa, Sri Lanka. "Looking at these figures I was suddenly, almost forcibly, jerked clean out of the habitual, half-tied vision of things, and an inner clearness, clarity, as if exploding from the rocks themselves, became evident and obvious."

510   "That Nature is a Heraclitean Fire and of the Comfort of the Resurrection." W. H. Gardner, ed. *Poems and Prose of Gerard Manley Hopkins* (Baltimore: Penguin Books, 1968), 66.

BIBLIOGRAPHY

Tibetan Texts

The Biography of the Ist, IInd, IIIrd & IVth Dodrupchen Rinpoche. Gangtok, Sikkim: Pema Thinley Sikkim National Press, 2000.

'Gos Lotsawa Gzhon Nu Dpal. *The Blue Annals*.Reproduced by Lokesh Chandra from the collection of Raghu Vira. New Delhi: International Academy of Indian Culture, 1974.

'Jigs Med gLing Pa'i rnam thar. *Life of Jigmé Lingpa (1730–98)*. N.D. circa 2000. ISBN7-5409-1921-3/K.161 (Lhasa)

Klong-Chen-pa Dri-Med-'Od-zer. *Snying Thig Ya Bzhi*. Vol 9, Prt 3, *Bi Ma Snying Thig*. New Delhi: Trulku Tsewang, Jamyang and L. Tashi, 1970.

Kunsang Rinpoche. *Special Teachings on thod rgyal in dzogchen practice. Shin tu gsang ba chen po tho rgal snyan brgyud kyi zin bris kun tu bzang po'i dgongs rgyan yig med u pa de sha mkha' gro'i thugs kyi ti la ka zhes bya ba bzugs so*. Padma las 'brel rtsal/ Zangs mdog dpal ri par khang, N.D.

Mkhan po Tshul Krims Blo Gros. *Gsung 'bum*. Vol. 2, *Mi Rigs dpa skrung khang*, 2006.

rTsa rLung 'phrul 'Khor. ISBN 7-5409-4353. 1992, Lhasa.

Traleck Khenpo Tenzin Oser. *Seed of Faith: The Life Story of His Holiness Chadrel Sangye Dorji Rinpoche*. Gangtok, Sikkim: Pema Thinley Sikkim National Press, 2000.

The Christian Traditions

Avemarie, Friedrich, and Hermann Lichtenberger. *Auferstehung=Resurrection: The Fourth Durham-Tübingen Research Symposium—Resurrection, Transfiguration, and Exaltation in Old Testament, Ancient Judaism, and Early Christianity* (Tübingen, September 1999). Tübingen, Ger.: Mohr Siebeck, 2001.

Aquinatis, Thomae. *Summa Theologiae. Cura Fratrum eiusdem Ordinis*, V: Supplementum. Indices. Madrid: Biblioteca de Autores Cristianos, 1958.

Bollone, Pierluigi Baima. *Sindone: Storia e scienza.* Scarmagno, Torino, It.: Priuli & Verlucca, 2010.

Barker, Margaret. *The Great High Priest: The Temple Roots of the Christian Liturgy.* London: T & T Clark, 2003.

Barsanufio e Giovanni di Gaza. *Spiritualita' dei Padri del Deserto: Lettere di Barsanufio e Giovanni di Gaza.* A cura di Maria Teresa Lovato. Roma: Citta Nuova Edizioni, 1980.

Beulay, Robert. *L'enseignment spirituel de Jean de Dalyatha, Mystique Syro-Oriental du VIIIe siècle.* Paris: Beauchesne, 1990.

———*La Lumière sans forme: Introduction l'étude de la mystique Chrétienne Syro-Orientale.* Chevetogne, Bel.: Éditions de Chevetogne, 1987.

Brock, Sebastian, ed. and trans. *The Syriac Fathers on Prayer and the Spiritual Life.* Kalamazoo, MI: Cistercian Publications, 1987.

Brodeur, Scott. *The Holy Spirit's Agency in the Resurrection of the Dead: An Exegetico-Theological Study of I Corinthians 15, 44b–49 and Romans 8, 9–13.* Rome: Editrice Pontificia Università Gregoriana, 2004.

Brown, Peter. *The Body and Society: Men, Women and Sexual Renunciation in Early Christianity.* London: Faber and Faber, 1991.

———. *The Cult of the Saints: Its Rise and Function in Latin Christianity.* Chicago: University of Chicago Press, 1981.

Burton-Christie, Douglas. *The Word in the Desert: Scripture and the Quest for Holiness in Early Christian Monasticism.* New York: Oxford University Press, 1993.

Bynum, Caroline Walker. *The Resurrection of the Body in Western Christianity, 200–1336.* New York: Columbia University Press, 1995.

Casiday, A. M. *Evagrius Ponticus.* London: Routledge, 2006.

Chiala', Sabino. *Abramo di Kashkar e la sua comunita'.* Magnano, It.: Edizioni Qiqajon, 2005.

Clark Elizabeth A. *The Origenist Controversy: The Cultural Construction of an Early Christian Debate.* Princeton, NJ: Princeton University Press, 1992.

Cyril of Jerusalem. *Lectures on the Christian Sacraments: The Procatechesis and the Five Mystagogical Catecheses.* Edited by F. L. Cross. Crestwood, NY: St. Vladimir's Seminary Press, 1977.

Delehaye, Hippolyte S.J. *The Legends of the Saints*. Notre Dame, IN.: University of Notre Dame Press, 1961.

Driscoll, Jeremy. *The 'Ad Monachus' of Evagrius Ponticus: Its Structure and a Select Commentary*. Rome: Edizioni Abbazia San Paolo, 1991.

Evagrius Ponticus. *Le Gnostique ou a celui qui est devenu digne de la science*. Traduction par Antoine Guillaumont et Claire Guillaumont. Sources Chrétiennes. No. 356. Paris: Les Éditions du Cerf, 1989.

———— *Sur les pensées*. Édition du texte Grec, Traduction par Paul Géhin, Claire Guillaumont, et Antoine Guillaumont. Sources Chrétiennes, No. 438. Paris: Éditions du Cerf, 1998.

————. *Contro i pensieri malvagi*. Magnano, It.: Edizioni Qiqajon, 2005.

———— *Per conoscere lui. Esortazione a una vergine-ai monaci-Ragioni delle osservanze monastiche-Lettera ad Anatolio-Pratico-Gnostico*. Traduzione a cura di Paolo Pettiolo. Magnano, It.: Edizioni Qiqajon, 1996.

———— *The Praktikos: Chapters on Prayer*. Translated by John Eudes Bamberger. Kalamazoo, MI: Cistercian Publications, 1978.

Fanti, Giulio, and Saverio Gaeta. *Il mistero della Sindone: Le sorprendenti scoperte scientifiche sull'enigma del telo di Gesu'*. Milano: Rizzoli, 2013.

Filosseno di Mabbug (Philoxenus). *I sensi dello spirito: Lettera a un suo discepolo; Lettera parenetica a un ebreo diventato discepolo*. Traduzione a cura di Sabino Chialà. Magnano, It.: Edizioni Qiqajon, 2000.

Frale, Barbara. *La sindone di Gesù Nazareno*. Bologna, It.: Societa' Editrice il Mulino, 2009.

Gillman, Ian, and Hans-Joachim Klimkeit. *Christians in Asia before 1500*. Surrey, UK: Curzon Press, 1999.

Grégoire, Réginald. *Manuale di agiologia: Introduzione alla letteratura agiografica*. Fabriano, It.: Monastero San Silvestro Abate, 1987.

Gregory of Nyssa. *The Soul and the Resurrection*. Translated by Catharine P. Roth. Crestwood, NY: St. Vladimir's Seminary Press, 1993.

Grillmeier, Aloys S.J. *Christ in Christian Tradition*. Vol.1, *From the Apostolic Age to Chalcedon (451)*, Atlanta: John Knox Press, 1975.

————. *Christ in Christian Tradition.* Vol. 2, *From the Council of Chalcedon (451) to Gregory the Great (590–604).* Prt. 1, *Reception and Contradiction: The Development of the Discussion about Chalcedon from 451 to the Beginning of the Reign of Justinian.* Atlanta: John Knox Press, 1987.

————. *Christ in Christian Tradition.* Vol.2, Prt. 2, *The Church of Constantinople in the Sixth Century.* London: Mowbray, 1995.

Guillaumont, Antoine. *Les 'Képhalaia Gnostica'd'Évagre le Pontique et l'histoire de L'Origénisme chez les Grecs et chez les Syriens.* Paris: Éditions du Seuil, 1962.

————. *Les Six Centuries des "Képhalaia Gnostica" d'Évagre le Pontique.* Patrologia Orientalis, Tome XXVIII, Fascicule 1. Paris: Firmin-Didot e Cie, 1958.

Hausherr, Irénée, S. I. *La Méthode d'Oricuaison Hésychaste.* Roma: Pont. Institutum Orientalium Studiorum, 1927.

Hennecke, Edgar. *New Testament Apocrypha.* Edited by Wilhelm Schneemelcher. Translated by R. McL. Wilson. Vol. 1, *Gospels and Related Writings.* Philadelphia: Westminster Press, 1963.

Hodges, Richard. *Goodbye to the Vikings? Re-reading Early Medieval Archaeology.* London: Gerard Duckworth & Co., 2006.

Hurtado, Larry W. *Lord Jesus Christ: Devotion to Jesus in Earliest Christianity.* Grand Rapids, MI: William Eerdmans Company, 2003.

[Damascene, John (attribution)]. *Barlaam and Ioasaph.* Translation by G. R. Woodward and H. Mattingly. Introduction by D.M. Lang. Cambridge, MA: Harvard University Press, 1983.

Kugel, James L. *Traditions of the Bible: A Guide to the Bible As It Was at the Start of the Common Era.* Cambridge, MA: Harvard University Press, 1998.

The Lives of the Desert Fathers. Introduction by Benedicta Ward. Translated by Norman Russell. Kalamazoo, MI: Cistercian Publications, 1981.

Louth, Andrew. *The Origins of the Christian Mystical Tradition: From Plato to Denys.* Oxford: Clarendon Press, 1981.

Marinelli, Emanuela. *La Sindone: Testimone di una presenza.* Cinisello Balsamo, It.: Edizioni San Paolo, 2010.

Maximus the Confessor. *The Ascetic Life. The Four Centuries on Charity.* Translated and annotated by Polycarp Sherwood. New York: The Newman Press, 1955.

McEvedy, Colin. *The Penguin Atlas of Medieval History*. Middlesex, England, 1976.

Ménard, Jacques É. ed. *Le Traité sur la résurrection* (NH I, 4). Québec: Les Presses de l'Université Laval, 1983.

Meyer, Robert T., trans. *Palladius: The Lausiac History*. Westminster, MD: Newman Press and Longmans, Green, and Co. 1965.

Nicolini-Zani, Matteo. *La via radiosa per l'oriente: I testi e la storia del primo incontro del cristianesimo con il mondo culturale e religioso cinese* (secoli VII-IX). Magnano It.: Edizioni Qiqajon, 2006.

di Ninive, Isacco. *Discorsi ascetici: Terza collezione*. A cura di Sabino Chiala'. Magnano, It.: Edizioni Qiqajon, 2004.

————. *Discorsi Spirituali: Capitoli sulla conoscenza, preghiere, contemplazione sull'argomento della gehenna, altri opuscoli*. Traduzione a cura di Paolo Bettiolo. Magnano, It.: Edizioni Qiqajon, 1 985.

Origen. *Treatise on the Passover and Dialogue of Origen with Heraclides and His Fellow Bishops on the Father, the Son and the Soul*. Translated by Robert J. Daly. Ancient Christian Writers, No. 54. New York: Paulist Press, 1992.

Ortiz de Urbina, Ignatius. *Patrologia Syriaca*: Altera edition emendata et aucta. Roma: Pontificium Institutum Orientalium Studiorum, 1965.

Palmer, G.E.H., and Philip Sherrard, Kallistos Ware, trans., ed. *The Philokalia: The Complete Text,* Vols 1 and 3. Compiled by St. Nikodimos of the Holy Mountain and St. Makarios of Corinth. London: Faber and Faber, 1979.

Palmer, Martin, with Eva Wong, Tjalling Halbertsma, Zhao Xiao Min, Li Rong Rong, and James Palmer. *The Jesus Sutras: Rediscovering the Lost Scrolls of Taoist Christianity*. New York: Ballantine Publishing Group, 2001.

Parmentier, Michael. "Evagrius of Pontus 'Letter to Melania I'"in *Forms of Devotion*. Edited by Everett Ferguson. New York: Garland Publishing Company, 1999, 272–309.

Peña, Ignacio. *La straordinaria vita dei monaci siri,* Secoli IV-VI. Cinisello Balsamo, It: Edizioni Paoline, 1990.

Pseudo-Macarius. *Discorsi e dialoghi spirituali/ Macario-Simeone*. A cura di Francesca Moscatelli. Bresseo di Teolo, It.: Edizioni Scritti Monastici, Abbazia di Praglia, 1988.

————. *Spirito e fuoco: Omelie spirituali* (Collezione II). A cura di Lisa Cremaschi. Magnano, It.: Edizioni Qiqajon,1995.

Roberson, Ronald C.S. *The Eastern Christin Churches: A Brief Survey*, 7th Edition. Rome: Edizioni Orientalia Christiana, 2008.

Saeki, P. Y. *The Nestorian Documents and Reliacs in China.* Tokyo: The Toho Bunkwa Gakuin: The Academy of Oriental Culture, Tokyo Institute, 1951

van Schaik, Sam. "Christianity in Early Tibet." earlytibet.com December 2, 2007.

Stewart, Columba. "Imageless Prayer and the Theological Vision of Evagrius Ponticus," *Journal of Early Christian Studies* 9, no. 2 (Summer 2001): 173–204.

Teodoreto. *Storia dei Monaci della Siria.* A cura di Salvatore di Meglio. Padova, It.: Edizioni Messaggero Padova, Abbazia di Praglia, 1986.

Thomas, P. *Christians and Christianity in India and Pakistan: A General Survey of the Progress of Christianity in India from Apostolic Times to the Present Day.* London: George Allen & Unwin, 1954.

Treece, Patricia. *The Mystical Body: An Investigation of Supernatural Phenomena* (formerly published as *The Sanctified Body*). New York: Crossroad Publishing Company, 1989, 2005.

Wilson. Ian. *The Blood and the Shroud: New Evidence That the World's Most Sacred Relic Is Real.* New York: Simon and Schuster, 1998.

Buddhist, Dzogchen, and Tibetan Studies

Abhayadatta. *Buddha's Lions: The Lives of the Eighty-Four Siddhas.* Translated by James B. Robinson. Berkeley, CA: Dharma Publishing, 1979.

Achard, Jean-Luc. "Le Corps d'Arc-en-ciel ('ja' lus) de Shardza Rinpoche Illustrant la perfection de la Voie rDzogs Chen." *Tibetan Studies in Honor of Samten Karmay,* no. 15 (2008): 503–532.

————. Les Corps d'Arc-en-ciel: Selon leur description par Düdjom Rinpoche. Khyung-mkhar online pdf, Courdimanche-su-Essonne, 2012.

Agnew, Nevile, e Fan Jinshi. "I tesori del buddismo cinese a Dunhuang." *Le Scienze,* no. 350, (ottobre 1997).

Anacker, Stefan. *Seven Works of Vasubandhu: The Buddhist Psychological Doctor.* Delhi: Motilal Banarsidass, 1984.

Aris, Michael. *Hidden Treasures and Secret Lives: A Study of Pemalingpa and the Sixth Dalai Lama*. Delhi: Motilal Banarsidass, 1988.

Asvaghosa. *Buddhacarita, or Acts of the Buddha*. Translated by E. H. Johnston. Delhi: Motilal Banarsidass, 1984.

Baker, Ian A. *The Dalai Lama's Secret Temple: Tantric Wall Paintings from Tibet*. Photographs by Thomas Laird. New York: Thames and Hudson, 2000.

Bentor, Yael. "Interiorized Fire Offerings of Breathing, Inner Heat, and the Subtle Body". In Helmut Krasser, et. al. International Association for Tibetan Studies, Graz, 1997.

Bru-sgom rGyal-ba g.yung-drung. The Stages of A-Khrid Meditation: Dzogchen Practice of the Bon Tradition. Library of Tibetan Works and Archives, 1996.

Cabezon, Jose Ignacio, and Robert R. Jackson, eds. *Tibetan Literature: Studies in Genre*. Ithaca: Snow Lion, 1996.

Chang, Garma C. C. *The Buddhist Teaching of Totality: The Philosophy of Hwa Yen Buddhism*. University Park, PA: Pennsylvania State University Press, 1977.

Ch'en, Kenneth K. S. *Buddhism in China: A Historical Survey*. Princeton NJ: Princeton University Press, 1964.

Clemente, Adriano. *The Sgra Bla, Gods of the Ancestors of Gshen-Rab Mi-Bo: According to the Sgra Bla Go Bsang from the Gzi Brjid*. Arcidosso, It.: Shang Shung Edizioni, 1995.

Cuppers, Christoph, ed. *The Relationship between Religion and State (chos srid zung 'brel) in Traditional Tibet*. Proceedings of a Seminar Held in Lumbini, Nepal, March 2000. Lumbini: Lumbini International Research Institute, 2004.

Dargyay, Eva M. *The Rise of Esoteric Buddhism in Tibet*. Delhi: Motilal Banarsidass, 1977

Dilgo Khyentse Rinpoche. *Zurchungpa's Testament: A Commentary on Zurchung Sherab Trakpa's Eighty Chapters of Personal Advice*. Translated by the Padmakara Translation Group. Ithaca, NY: Snow Lion Publications, 2006.

Dowman, Keith, trans. *Eye of the Storm: Vairotsana's Five Original Transmissions*. Commentary by Keith Dowman. Kathmandu: Vajra Publications, 2006.

Dowman, Keith, ed. and trans. *The Flight of the Garuda*. Boston: Wisdom Publications, 1994.

Dowman, Keith. *Masters of Mahamudra: Songs and Histories of the Eighty-Four Buddhist Siddhas.* Albany: State University of New York Press, 1985.

Dube, S.N. *Cross Currents in Early Buddhism.* New Delhi: Manohar, 1980.

Dudjom Lingpa. *Buddhahood without Meditation: A Visionary Account Known as Refining One's Perception (Nang-jang).* Translated by Chagdud Tulku Rinpoche, Lama Padma Drimed Norbu, Richard Barron and Susanne Fairclough. Junction City, CA: Padma Publishing, 2002.

Dudjom Rinpoche, Jikdrel Yeshe Dorje. *The Nyingma School of Tibetan Buddhism: Its Fundamentals and History,* 2 Vols. Translated and edited by Gyurme Dorje and Matthew Kapstein. Boston: Wisdom Publications, 1991.

_____. *Extraire la Quintessence de la Realisation.* Ogyan Kunsang Choekhorling: Ballimaran, Delhi, N.D.

Ehrhard, Franz-Karl. *Buddhism in Tibet & the Himalayas: Texts and Traditions.* Kathmandu: Vajra Publications, 2013.

Ermakov, Dmitry. *Bo and Bon: Ancient Shamanic Traditions of Siberia and Tibet in Their Relation to the Teachings of a Central Asian Buddha.* Kathmandu: Vajra Publications, 2008.

Esler, Dylan. "The Exposition of Atiyoga in gNubs-chen Sangs-rgyas ye-shes' bSamgtan mig-sgron. *Revue d'Etudes Tibétaines* 28, (Octobre 2012): 81–136.

Francke H. *A History of Western Tibet: One of the Unknown Empires.* Reprint of 1907 edition. Delhi: Motilal Banarsidass, 1998.

Guenther, Herbert. *Buddhist Philosophy in Theory and Practice.* Boulder: Shambhala, 1976.

Gyatrul Rinpoche. *Natural Liberation: Padmasambhava's Teachings on the Six Bardos.* Boston: Wisdom Publications, 1998.

———, commentary. *Ancient Wisdom: Nyingma Teachings on Dream Yoga, Meditation and Transformation.* Translated by B. Alan Wallace and Sangye Khandro. Ithaca NY: Snow Lion Publications, 1993.

Gyatso, Janet. *Apparitions of the Self: The Secret Autobiographies of a Tibetan Visionary.* Princeton, NJ: Princeton University Press, 1998.

Hookham, S.K. *The Buddha Within: Tathagatagarbha Doctrine According to the Shentong Interpretation of the Ratnagotravibhaga.* Albany: State University of New York Press, 1991.

Hopkins, Jeffrey. *Meditation on Emptiness.* London: Wisdom Publications, 1983.

Jackson, David. *Enlightenment by a Single Means.* Vienna: Verlag der Osterre- ichischen Akademie der Wissenschaften, 1994.

Kapstein, Matthew T. *The Tibetans.* Oxford: Blackwell Publishing, 2006.

Kapstein, Matthew T., ed. *Buddhism between Tibet & China.* Boston: Wisdom Pub- lications, 2009.

Karma Chagmé. *Naked Awareness: Practical Instructions on the Union of Mahamudra and Dzogchen.* Commentary by Gyatrul Rinpoche. Ithaca, NY: Snow Lion, 2000.

Karmay, Samten G. "A Discussion of the Doctrinal Position of rDzogs-chen from the Tenth to the Thirteenth centuries." *Journal Asiatique* 263, 147–55.

———. "The rdzogs-chen in Its Earliest Text: A Manuscript from Tun-Huang." In *Soundings in Tibetan Civilization.* Edited by Aziz and Kapstein. Delhi: Mano- har, 1985.

———. *The Little Luminous Boy: The Oral Tradition from the Land of Zhangzhung Depicted on Two Tibetan Paintings.* Bangkok: Orchid Press, 1998.

———, *Secret Visions of the Fifth Dalai Lama: The Gold Manuscript in the Fournier Collection, Musée Guimet, Paris.* London: Serindia Publications, 1988.

———, *The Great Perfection (rDzogs Chen).* Leiden: E.J. Brill, 1988.

Khamtul Rinpoche. *Dzog Chen Meditation.* Translated and edited by Gareth Spar- ham. Delhi: Sri Satguru Publications, 1994.

Khetsun Sangpo Rinpoche. *Tantric Practice in Nying-ma.* Translated and edited by Jeffrey Hopkins and Anne Klein. Ithaca NY: Gabriel/ Snow Lion Publica- tions, 1982.

Klein, Anne Carolyn. *Heart Essence of the Vast Expanse: A Story of Transmission.* Itha- ca, NY: Snow Lion Publications, 2009.

Geshe Konchok, Lama. *The Thousand Buddha Relic Stupa, Commemorating the Great Mahasiddha Geshe Lama Konchok.* Compiled by Tenzin Zopa. Edited by Robina Courtin. January 2003. Kopan Library, P O Box 817, Kathman- du, Nepal. kopan@ecomail.com.np.

Jamgon Kongtrul. *Creation and Completion: Essential Points of Tantric Meditation.* Translated by Sarah Harding. Boston: Wisdom Publications, 1996.

Kvaerne, Per. *An Anthology of Buddhist Tantric Songs: A Study of the Caryagiti.* Bangkok: White Orchid Press, 1986.

The Lalitavistara Sutra: The Voice of the Buddha, The Beauty of Compassion. Translated by Gwendolyn Bays. Berkeley: Dharma Publishing, 1983.

Lamotte, Etienne, trans. and commentary. *La Somme du Grand Vehicule d'Asanga (Mahayanasamgraha)*, Tome 2. Louvain-La-Neuve, Bel.: Institut Orientaliste, Université de Louvain, 1973.

Lhundrub Tso. *A Brief Biography of Adzam Drugpa.* Translated by Chogyal Namkhai Norbu, Adriano Clemente, and Nancy Simmons. Arcidosso, It.: Shang Shung Edizioni, 1993.

kLong-chen rab-'byams-pa. *Kindly Bent to Ease Us. The Trilogy of Finding Comfort and Ease.* 3 Vols. Translated and annotated by Herbert V. Guenther. Emeryville, CA: Dharma Publishing, 1975.

Longchen Rabjam. *The Practice of Dzogchen.* Introduced, translated, and annotated by Tulku Thondup. Edited by Harold Talbott. Ithaca: Snow Lion Publications, 1996.

———. *The Precious Treasury of the Way of Abiding and the Exposition of the Quintessential Meaning of the Three Categories.* Translated by Chagdud Tulku Rinpoche, Richard Barron, Susanne Fairclough, Jeff Miller, and Robert Racine. Junction City, CA: Padma Publishing, 1998.

———. *You Are the Eyes of the World.* Translated by Kennard Lipman and Merrill Peterson with Namkhai Norbu. Ithaca NY: Snow Lion Publications, 2000.

Lowenthal, Martin. *Dawning of Clear Light: A Western Approach to Tibetan Dark Retreat Meditation.* Hampton Roads, 2003.

Manjusrimitra. *Primordial Experience: An Introduction to rDzogs-chen Meditation.* Translated by Namkhai Norbu and Kennard Lipman. Boston: Shambhala Publications, 1986.

Martin, Dan. "The Early Education of Milarepa." *Journal of the Tibet Society* 2 (1982): 52–76.

Mayer, Robert. "Were the Gsar-ma-pa Polemicists Justified in Rejecting Some Rnyingma-pa Tantras?" Steinkellner, ed. *Proceedings of the 7th Seminar of the International Association for Tibetan Studies,* Graz, Austria, 1997, 618–31.

Minling Terchen Gyurmed Dorjee. *The Jewel Ladder: A Preliminary Nyingma Lam-rim.* Translated and Edited by Tsepak Rigzin. Dharamsala: Library of Tibetan Works and Archives, 1990.

Mullin, Glenn H. trans.and ed. *Tsongkhapa's Six Yogas of Naropa.* Ithaca NY: Snow Lion Publications, 1996.

———— *Readings on the Six Yogas of Naropa.* Ithaca: Snow Lion Publications, 1997.

Yongdzin Lopon Tenzin Namdak. *Heart Essence of the Khandro: Experiential Instructions on Bonpo Dzogchen.* Recorded by Drespa Namkha. Translated by Nagru Geshe Gelek Jinpa, Carol Ermakova and Dmitry Ermakov.

Lopon Tenzin Namdak. "The Dark Retreat According to Shardza Rinpoche." Transcribed and edited by John M. Reynolds, Typescript, 1991.

———— *Practices from the Zhang-Zhung Nyan Gyud.* Compiled and edited by John M. Reynolds. Freehold, NJ: Bonpo Translation Project, 1989.

———— "Oral Commentary on the Twenty One Nails." Jemez Springs, NM, typescript, 1995.

———— "Bonpo Dzogchen Teachings." Transcribed and edited by John M Reynolds. Freehold, NJ: Bonpo Translation Project. Typescript, 1992

———— "The Teaching of the Eight Chapters." Typescript, 1995.

———— *Masters of the Zhang Zhung Nyengyud: Pith Instructions from the Experiential Transmission of Bonpo Dzoghcen.* Edited by Carol Ermakova and Dmitry Ermakov. New Delhi, Heritage Publishers, 2010.

Namkhai Norbu. *The Crystal and the Way of Light: Sutra, Tantra and Dzogchen.* Oxford: Routledge and Kegan Paul, 1986.

———— *The Cycle of the Day and Night: An Essential Tibetan Text on the Practice of Dzogchen.* Translated and edited by John M. Reynolds. Barrytown, NY: Station Hill Press, 1987.

————. *Dream Yoga and the Practice of Natural Light.* Ithaca, NY: Snow Lion, 1992.

———— *Drung, Deu and Bon: Narrations, Symbolic Languages and the Bon Tradition in Ancient Tibet.* Translated by Andrew Lukianowicz. Dharamsala: Library of Tibetan Works and Archives, 1995.

————. *The Four Chogshag: The Practice of Tregchod*. Edited by Adriano Clemente. Translated by Alison Duguid. Arcidosso, It.: Shang Shung Edizioni, 1998.

————. *An Introduction to the General Principles of Yantra Yoga*. Arcidosso, It.: Shang Shung Edizioni, 1996.

————. *The Lamp That Enlightens Narrow Minds: The Life and Times of a Realized Tibetan Master, Khyentse Chokyi Wangchug*. Edited by Enrico Dell'Angelo. Translated by Nancy Simmons. Berkeley, CA: North Atlantic Books, 2012.

————. *Longde Teachings: Based on the Original Texts by Vairochana and Dzin Dharmabodhi*. Namgyalgar. Arcidosso, It.: Shang Shung Edizioni, 1997.

————. *The Practice of the Seven Samdzins*. Edited by Adriano Clemente. Translated by Maria Simmons. Arcidosso It.: Shang Shung Edizioni, 1993.

————. *Rainbow Body: The Life and Realization of a Tibetan Yogin, Togden Ugyen Tendzin*. Translated by Adriano Clemente. Berkeley, CA: North Atlantic Books, 2012.

————. *The Real Meaning of Integration in the Dzogchen Teachings*. Arcidosso, It.: Shang-Shung Edizioni, 1992.

————. *Rigbai Kujyug: The Six Vajra Verses*. With an oral commentary by Namkhai Norbu. Edited by Cheh-Ngee Goh. Singapore: Rinchen Editions, 1990.

————. *The Seventh Lojong: The Experiences of Pleasure, Clarity, and Void*. Arcidosso, It.: Shang Shung Edizioni, 1996.

————. *The Supreme Source: The Kunjed Gyalpo, The Fundamental Tantra of Dzogchen Semde*. Translation by Andrew Lukianowicz. Ithaca NY: Snow Lion Publications, 1999.

————. *Thos-Grol: La pratica dei venticinque thigle*. Traduzione: Mario Maglietti. Arcidosso, It.: Shang Shung Edizioni, 1996.

————. *Vairocana's Secret Instructions on the Four Signs*. Translated by Adriano Clemente and John Shane. Arcidosso, It.: Shang Shung Edizioni, 1993.

————. *Yantra Yoga*. Translated by Des Barry, Nina Robinson, and Liz Granger. Arcidosso, It.: Shang Shung Edizioni, 1991.

Nyagla Padma Dundul. *The Song of Energy*. Namkhai Norbu Rinpoche, Enrico Dell'Angelo and Andy Lukianowicz, translators. Arcidosso, It.: Shang Shung Publications, 1997.

Yudra Nyingpo, compiler. *The Great Image: The Life Story of Vairocana the Translator*. Ani Jinba Palmo, translator. Boston and London: Shambhala, 2004.

Khenpo Nyima Dondrup. *Guide to the Hidden Land of the Yolmo Snow Enclosure and Its History.* Kathmandu: Vajra Publications, 2010.

Nyoshul Khenpo Rinpoche and Lama Surya Das. *Natural Great Perfection: Dzogchen Teachings and Vajra Songs*. Ithaca, NY: Snow Lion Publications, 1995.

Padmasambhava. *Advice from the Lotus-Born*. Translated by Erik Pema Kunsang. Kathmandu: Rangjung Yeshe Publications, 1994.

——— *The Light of Wisdom,* Vol. I and II. With Commentary by Jamgon Kongtrul, Jamyang Drakpa, Jokyab Rinpoche, Kyabje Dilgo Khyentse, and Kyabje Tulku Urgyen Rinpoche. Translated by Erik Pema Kunsang. Kathmandu: Rangjung Yeshe Publications, 1999.

Prats, Ramon N. *The Pandita and the Siddha: Tibetan Studies in Honour of E. Gene Smith*. Dharamshala, India: Amnye Machen Institute, 2007.

Puri, B. N. *Buddhism in Central Asia*. Delhi: Motilal Banarsidass, 1993.

Reynolds, John Myrdhin. *The Golden Letters. The Three Statements of Garab Dorje, First Dzogchen Master*. Ithaca, NY: Snow Lion, 1996.

——— *Self-Liberation through Seeing with Naked Awareness*. Barrytown, NY, Station Hill Press, 1989.

Roerich, George N. translator and editor. *The Blue Annals* by 'Gos Lotsawa. Delhi: Motilal Banarsidass, 1979.

Shardza Tashi Gyaltsen. *Heart Drops of Dharmakaya: Dzogchen Practice of the Bon Tradition*. Ithaca, NY: Snow Lion 2002.

Smith, E. Gene. *Among Tibetan Texts: History and Literature of the Himalayan Plateau*. Edited by Kurtis R. Schaeffer. Boston: Wisdom Publications, 2001.

Surya Das, Lama. Dzogchen Foundation. www.dzogchen.org Dzogchen Foundation Prayer Book.

Sakya Pandita Kunga Gyaltshen. *A Clear Differentiation of the Three Codes*. Translated by Jared Douglas Rhoton, Edited by Victoria R. M. Scott. Albany: State University of New York Press, 2002.

Saha, Kshanika. *Buddhism and Buddhist Literature in Central Asia*. Calcutta: Firma K. L. Mukhopadhyay, 1970.

Schaeffer, Kurtis R. *Himalayan Hermitess: The Life of a Tibetan Buddhist Nun.* Oxford: Oxford University Press, 2004.

van Schaik, Sam. *Approaching the Great Perfection: Simultaneous and Gradual Methods of Dzogchen Practice in Jigme Lingpa's Longchen Nyingtig.* Boston: Wisdom Publications, 2004.

Schlingloff, Dieter. *Ein Buddhistisches Yogalehrbuch.* Berlin: Akademie-Verlag, 1964.

Shahidullah, Muhammad. Les chants mystiques de Kanha et de Saraha: Les Doha-Kosa e les Carya. Paris: Adrien-Maisonneuve, 1928.

Shardza Tashi Gyaltsen. Heart Drops of Dharmakaya: Dzogchen Practice of the Bon Tradition. Ithaca: Snow Lion Publications, 2002.

Stein, R. A., ed. Une chronique ancienne de bSam-yas: sBa-Bzed. Paris: Publications de L'Institut des Hautes Etudes Chinoises, 1961.

Jo Nang Taranatha. *The Seven Instruction Lineages.* Translated and edited by David Templeman. Dharamsala: Library of Tibetan Works and Archives, 1983.

Tenzin Wangyal Rinpoche. *Healing with Form, Energy and Light: The Five Elements in Tibetan Shamanism, Tantra, and Dzogchen.* Ithaca: Snow Lion Publications, 2002.

Tiso, Francis V. *Liberation in One Lifetime: Biographies and Teachings of Milarepa.* Berkeley CA: North Atlantic Books, 2014.

Tiso, Francis V. and Fabrizio Torricelli. "The Tibetan Text of Tilopa's Mahamudropadesa." East and West: IsMEO, Vol. 41 (December 1991):205–229.

Tsele Natsok Rangdrol. Empowerment and the Path of Liberation. Translated by Erik Pema Kunsang. Kathmandu: Rangjung Yeshe Publications, 1993.

———. Lamp of Mahamudra. Translated by Erik Pema Kunsang. Boston: Shambhala, 1989.

———. The Mirror of Mindfulness: The Cycle of the Four Bardos. Translated. By Erik Pema Kunsang. Kathmandu: Rangjung Yeshe Publications, 1987.

Tucci, Giuseppe. *Minor Buddhist Texts*, Prts. 1 and 2. Delhi: Motilal Banarsidass, 1978.

———. *Rin-chen-bzang-po and the Renaissance of Buddhism in Tibet Around the Millenium.* Translated by Nancy Kipp Smith and Thomas J. Pritzker. Edited by Lokesh Chandra. New Delhi: Aditya Prakashan, 1988.

————. *The Religions of Tibet.* Translated by Geoffrey Samuel. Berkeley: University of California Press, 1980.

Tulku Thondup. *Masters of Meditation and Miracles: The Longchen Nyingthig Lineage of Tibetan Buddhism.* Edited by Harold Talbott. Boston: Shambhala Publications, 1996.

————. *Hidden Teachings of Tibet: An Explanation of the Terma Tradition of Tibetan Buddhism.* Edited by Harold Talbott. Boston: Wisdom Publications, 1997.

Vairocana. *Secret Instructions on the Four Signs.* Translated by Adriano Clemente. Arcidosso, It.: Shang Shung Edizioni, 1993.

Vimalamitra. *The Stages of Meditation.* Edited and translated by Lozang Jamspal. Leh, Ladakh: Ladakhratnashridipika, 2000.

Walter, Michael. "Jabir, The Buddhist Yogi, Part I," *Journal of Indian Philosophy* 20 (1992): 425–438.

————. "Jabir, The Buddhist Yogi, Part II, Winds and Immortality," *Journal of Indian Philosophy* 24 (1996): 145–164.

————. "Jabir, The Buddhist Yogi, Part III: Considerations on an International Yoga of Transformation," *Lungta* 16 (2003): 21–36.

White, David Gordon, ed. *Tantra in Practice.* Princeton: Princeton University Press, 2000.

————. *Yoga in Practice.* Princeton: Princeton University Press, 2012.

Wright, Arthur F. *Buddhism in Chinese History.* London: Oxford University Press, 1971.

Yangthang Rinpoche. *Dzogchen and the Nine Yanas.* Translated by Sangye Khandro. Ashland, OR: Yeshe Melong Publications, 1993.

———— *Introduction to the Nature of the Mind.* Mt. Shasta, CA: Yeshe Melong Publications, 1994.

Yesce, Lama. La Beatitudine del Fuoco Interiore: Il Cuore della Pratica dei Sei yoga di Naropa. Edito da Robina Courtin e Ailasa Cameron. Traduzione di Lorenzo Vassallo. Pomaia, It: Chiara Luce Edizioni, 2003.

————. L'arte Buddhista di Saper Morire. Pomaia, It.: Chiara Luce Edizioni, 1992.

Yeshe Tsogyal. *The Lotus-Born: The Life Story of Padmasambhava.* Translated by Erik Pema Kunsang. Edited by Marcia Binder Schmidt. Boston: Shambhala, 1993.

Yudra Nyingpo, compiler. *The Great Image: The Life Story of Vairocana the Translator.* Translated by Ani Jinba Palmo. Boston & London: Shambhala, 2004

Young, Serinity. *Dreaming in the Lotus: Buddhist Dream Narrative, Imagery, and Practice.* Boston: Wisdom Publications, 1999.

Historical and Scientific Studies

Aziz, Barbara Nimri, and Matthew Kapstein. *Soundings in Tibetan Civilization.* Delhi: Manohar, 1985.

Baker, Ian A., and Thomas Laird. *The Dalai Lama's Secret Temple: Tantric Wall Paintings from Tibet.* New York: Thames & Hudson, 2000.

Beckwith, Christopher I. *Empires of the Silk Road: A History of Central Eurasia from the Bronze Age to the Present.* Princeton NJ: Princeton University Press, 2009.

_____. *The Tibetan Empire in Central Asia.* Princeton NJ: Princeton University Press, 1987.

Blezer, Henk. ed. *Religion and Secular Culture in Tibet.* Proceedings of the Ninth Seminar of the International Association for Tibetan Studies. Reprint of Brill Edition. Leiden. Kathmandu: Vajra Publications, 2010.

Bogin, Benjamin, and Andrew Quintman. *Himalayan Passages: Tibetan and Newar Studies in Honor of Hubert Decleer.* Boston: Wisdom Publications, 2014.

Boswoth, C. E., and M.S. Asimov, eds. *History of Civilizations of Central Asia,* Vol.4. Prt 2. Delhi: Motilal Banarsidass, 2000.

Diamond, Jared. *Guns, Germs, and Steel: The Fates of Human Societies.* New York: W.W. Norton & Company, 1999.

Duncan, Marion H. *Customs and Superstitions of Tibetans.* Reprint. Delhi: Book Faith India, 1998.

Ehrhard, Franz-Karl. *Buddhism in Tibet and the Himalayas: Texts and Translations.* Kathmandu: Vajra Publications, 2013.

Kapstein, Matthew. *The Tibetans.* Oxford: Blackwell Publishing 2006.

_____. *The Presence of Light: Divine Radiance and Religious Experience.* Chicago: University of Chicago Press, 2004.

Litvinsky, B. A., Zhang Guang-Da, R. Shabani Samghabadi, eds. *History of Civilizations of Central Asia,* Vol. 3. Delhi: Motilal Banarsidass, 1999.

Narain, A. K. *The Indo-Greeks.* Reprint. Delhi: Oxford University Press, 1980.

Obeyesekere, Gananath *Imagining Karma: Ethical Transformation in Amerindian, Buddhist and Greek Rebirth.* Berkeley: University of California Press, 2002.

——— *Medusa's Hair: An Essay on Personal Symbols and Religious Experience.* Chicago: T University of Chicago Press, 1981.

Ramble, Charles, and Martin Brauen, eds. *Anthropology of Tibet and the Himalaya.* Kathmandu: Vajra Publications, 2008.

Reinaud, M. "Relations politiques et commerciales de l'Empire Romain avec l'Asie Orientale (l'Hyrcanie, l'Inde, La Bactriane et la Chine) pendant les cinq premiers siècles de l'Ére Chrétienne d'après les témoignages Latins, Grecs, Arabes, Persans, Indiens et Chinois." *Journal Asiatique,* Tome I/1863. I: 93–234; II: 297–441.

Samuel, Geoffrey. *The Origins of Yoga and Tantra: Indic Religions to the Thirteenth Century.* Delhi: Cambridge University Press, 2008.

———. *Tantric Revisionings: New Understandings of Tibetan Buddhism and Indian Religion.* Aldershot, UK: Ashgate Publishing, 2005.

Schopen, Gregory. *Bones, Stones, and Buddhist Monks: Collected Papers on the Archeology, Epigraphy and Texts of Monastic Buddhism in India.* Honolulu: University of Hawaii Press, 1997.

Stein, R.A. *Une chronique ancienne de bSam-yas: sBa-bzed.* Paris: Publications de l'Institut des Hautes Études Chinoises, 1961.

Tipler, Frank J. *The Physics of Immortality: Modern Cosmology, God and the Resurrection of the Dead.* New York: Doubleday, 1994.

Vitali, Roberto. *A Short History of Mustang (Tenth–Fifteenth Century).* Dharamsala, India: Amnye Machen Institute, 2012.

Hindu, Manichaean, and Other Religious Traditions

BeDuhn, Jason David. *The Manichean Body: In Discipline and Ritual.* Baltimore: Johns Hopkins University Press, 2000.

Corbin, Henry. "Divine Epiphany and Spiritual Birth in Ismailian Gnosis," in *Man and Transformation: Papers from the Eranos Yearbooks.* Edited by Joseph Campbell. Bollingen Series XXX.5. Princeton NJ: Princeton University Press, 1980.

Klimkeit, Hans-Joachim. "Religion in a Pluralistic Society: The Case of Central Asia," In *The Notion of "Religion" in Comparative Research: Selected Proceedings of the XVIth Congress of the International Association for the History of Religions* (Rome, September, 1990) Edited by Ugo Bianchi. Rome: "L'Erma" di Bretschneider, 1994.

Paranjape, Makarand, and Sunthar Visuvalingam, eds. *Abhinavagupta: Reconsiderations.* Evam Forum on Indian Representations 4:1 & 2. New Delhi: Samvad India Foundation, 2006.

Ries, Julien. "Buddhism and Manichaeism: The Stages of an Enquiry." *Buddhist Studies Review* 3, No. 2 (1986): 108–124.

Singh, Jaideva. *Siva Sutras: The Yoga of Supreme Identity.* Delhi: Motilal Banarsidass, 2000.

Uray, G. "Tibet's Connections with Nestorianism and Manicheism in the Eighth–Tenth Centuries." Contributions on Tibetan Language, History and Culture. Proceedings of the Csoma De Koros Symposium held at Velm-Ienna, Austria, 13–19 September 1981. Edited by E. Steinkellner and H. Tauscher, Vienna, 1983, pp. 399–429.

Vijnanabhairava. *La Conoscenza del Tremendo.* Translation and commentary by Attilia Sironi. Milano, It.: Adelphi Edizioni, 1989.

ABOUT THE AUTHOR

CNS PHOTO/BOB ROLLER

FATHER FRANCIS V. TISO holds an A.B. in Medieval Studies from Cornell University, a Master of Divinity degree from Harvard University, and a doctorate from Columbia University and Union Theological Seminary where his specialization was Buddhist studies. He also has a degree in Oriental Languages and Cultures from the Istituto Universitario Orientale in Naples. He was Associate Director of the Secretariat for Ecumenical and Interreligious Affairs of the U.S. Conference of Catholic Bishops from 2004 to 2009, where he served as liaison to Islam, Hinduism, Buddhism, the Sikhs, and Traditional religions as well as the Reformed confessions. He is the author of *Liberation in One Lifetime* (North Atlantic Books, 2014), which includes his translations of several early biographies of the Tibetan yogi and poet, Milarepa.